Founding Psychoanalysis Phenomenologically

PHAENOMENOLOGICA
SERIES FOUNDED BY H.L. VAN BREDA AND PUBLISHED
UNDER THE AUSPICES OF THE HUSSERL-ARCHIVES

199

DIETER LOHMAR AND JAGNA BRUDZIŃSKA

FOUNDING PSYCHOANALYSIS PHENOMENOLOGICALLY

PHENOMENOLOGICAL THEORY OF SUBJECTIVITY AND THE PSYCHOANALYTIC EXPERIENCE

For further volumes:
http://www.springer.com/series/6409

Dieter Lohmar • Jagna Brudzińska
Editors

Founding Psychoanalysis Phenomenologically

Phenomenological Theory of Subjectivity and the Psychoanalytic Experience

Springer

Editors
Dieter Lohmar
Philosophy
Husserl-Archiv der
Universität zu Köln
Albertus Magnus Platz
50923 Cologne
Germany
dieter.lohmar@uni-koeln.de

Jagna Brudzińska
Philosophy
Polish Academy of Sciences/
Husserl-Archiv der
Universität zu Köln
Albertus Magnus Platz
50923 Cologne
Germany
jagna.brudzinska@uni-koeln.de

ISSN 0079-1350
ISBN 978-94-007-1847-0 e-ISBN 978-94-007-1848-7
DOI 10.1007/978-94-007-1848-7
Springer Dordrecht Heidelberg London New York

Library of Congress Control Number: 2011935037

Printed on acid-free paper

Springer is part of Springer Science+Business Media (www.springer.com)

Contents

Abbreviations

Works of Edmund Husserl

Hua	Husserliana: Edmund Husserl Gesammelte Werke, Nijhoff: Den Haag 1950 et seq.
C.W.	Edmund Husserl Collected Works, Kluwer: Dordrecht 1980 et seq.

Works of Sigmund Freud

GW	Gesammelte Werke, 18 vol., Imago: London 1940–1952.
S.E.	The Standard Edition of the Complete Psychological Works of Sigmund Freud, Ed. & Trans. By J. Strachey, Hogarth Press: London 1953–1966.
SA	Studienausgabe, 10 vol. Fischer: Frankfurt a/M 2000 (1989)

Introduction

The present anthology seeks to give an overview of current phenomenological research in its relation to psychoanalysis and psychoanalytic topics. It compiles different perspectives and approaches to psychoanalytic problems from the viewpoint of current phenomenology. At the same time, the editors hope that this selection encourages further systematic collaboration between the two disciplines.

Phenomenology today in many cases is discovering its interdisciplinary potential. Providing a profound and comprehensive theory of subjectivity, which at the same time serves as a critique of experience, phenomenology increasingly seeks to exchange ideas with those disciplines whose research employs concepts of the subject, consciousness or subjective experience – either by presupposing, adopting or newly developing them. In this regard, the connection to psychoanalysis could assume a particular significance.

Phenomenological interest in psychoanalysis has a long history. Already during the lifetime of the founders of the two disciplines, Edmund Husserl (1859–1938) and Sigmund Freud (1856–1939), phenomenological and phenomenologically oriented authors attended to psychoanalytic theses. On the one hand, there is the phenomenologically justified psychiatry and psychology of that time which, often rather critically, responds to Freud's theses. In 1912, Arthur Kronfeld publishes his extensive critique of psychoanalysis (*Über die psychologischen Theorien Freuds und verwandte Anschauungen*), and Karl Jaspers critically addresses Freud's viewpoint in his *General Psychopathology* (*Allgemeine Psychopathologie*) of 1913. Ludwig Binswanger, former assistant of C.G. Jung, founds his phenomenological anthropology, or later, *daseinsanalytic* psychiatry, on phenomenological ground and on an intensive examination of psychoanalysis.

Within the philosophical phenomenological school itself, Max Scheler was especially interested in Freud's theses. Primarily in his concept of anthropology, there are numerous traces of Freudian psychoanalysis. Thus, an indirect influence of psychoanalytical ideas on the reception of his work in first-generation phenomenological circles can be assumed.

At the same time, phenomenological motives can also be found in the work of Freud, who, 10 years before Husserl, studied under Franz Brentano for four semesters. His approving engagement with the works of Theodor Lipps and his phenomenological-psychological writings, for example, are rather well-known.

For both traditions, The Second World War presents a painful and devastating disruption of their development and history of reception, as well as for their mutual exchange. During the postwar period, especially French phenomenologists revisit psychoanalytic topics. In this second generation of phenomenology, firstly, Maurice Merleau-Ponty and Jean-Paul Sartre attend to psychoanalysis. Merleau-Ponty in particular values the humanization of sexuality in Freud's thinking and the focus on bodily experience as determined by sense. He emphasizes that Freud's approach helps to overcome the division between physiology and psychology which he views as inadequate for such matters. Sartre is especially interested in the unconscious and the accomplishments of imagination. Through the engagement with the work of Freud, he develops his existential psychoanalysis. Both authors are strongly influenced by George Polizer's interpretations.

The latter, in his partly politically motivated interpretations, stresses the linguistic foundation of the unconscious. The linguistic idea acts strongest in the work of the French psychiatrist and psychoanalyst Jacques Lacan. Beginning in the middle of the 1950s, he develops a reinterpretation of Freud's psychoanalysis which at first is influenced by linguistic and structuralist ideas and later by fundamental ontology. Through an intensive recourse to language, he tries to evade the controversial naturalism of Freud. His psychoanalysis has particularly influenced authors in postmodern and poststructuralist philosophy such as Michel Foucault, Jacques Derrida, Gilles Deleuze, Roland Barthes, Jean Baudrillard, Slavoj Žižek, Judith Butler, Hélène Cixous. Here, cultural-philosophical, anthropological, gender-theoretical, sociological and socio-political observations are made with reference to phenomenological, psychoanalytic and structuralist ideas. Emmanuel Levinas' philosophy of the Other and his phenomenologically oriented ethics present an example of a unique connection of poststructuralist and psychoanalytic thinking. Likewise, Paul Ricoeur advances a discrete attempt at a hermeneutic interpretation of psychoanalysis on phenomenological ground. His *De l'Interpretation: Essais sur Freud* (1965) provides an interpretation of psychoanalysis as a theory of subjectivity and thus as a theory of subjective experience. Therein, he regards psychoanalytic clinical methods as a differentiated instrument for the hermeneutic exploration of subjectivity and its mechanisms. He emphasizes, in line with a phenomenologically descriptive basic understanding, that the kind of subjective experience which psychoanalysis brings to light, is always an intentional and sense-achieving experience. Therefore, sense-relations become the subject-matter of psychoanalytic research. His interpretation is strongly influenced by the insight that psychoanalysis is an entanglement of energetics and hermeneutics. This means that, on the one hand, it aims to expose the sense of psychic phenomena and therefore proceeds hermeneutically or phenomenologically, respectively. Yet, on the other hand, it strives to explain these phenomena through recourse to the economics of psychic forces and their conflicts, following the ideal of the natural sciences. Thereby Ricoeur addresses the old problem of the understanding of psychoanalysis and its theoretic positioning as a science of human experience.

Although psychoanalysis by now has found a permanent place in clinical practice – on the open psychotherapeutic 'market' as well as in the institutional realm of psychosomatic medicine – its status as a scientifically based theory of human beings and human experience is still challenged. As doctrine of the unconscious it is often considered to be speculative, evading the sphere of scientific proof, and is even regarded as esoteric. This discussion has lasted for decades. Psychoanalysis is challenged to clarify its scientific character and to ensure its subject matter as well as its methods according to scientific and epistemological theory. In particular, positivistic and analytic epistemology frequently contests the epistemological and methodological foundation of psychoanalysis and criticizes the lack of a validation of its contents through experiments. In 1972, Karl Popper famously regarded psychoanalysis among the pseudosciences which are characterized by the impossibility to be falsified and are oriented towards a dogma. Consequential criticism, primarily from the logical-analytical standpoint, can be found, for example, in the works of S. Hook, H.-J. Möller or M. Perrez. These critiques, however, mostly assume a nomothetical understanding of science. Yet, such an understanding presupposes a certain concept of objective experience and requires its independence of the subject, objective measurability, reproducibility etc. Psychoanalytic experience can hardly do justice to these posits.

At that time, scientists oriented towards phenomenology, in line with their interpretation of descriptive phenomenology of consciousness as a science of mental experience, also have contributed to the critical stance towards psychoanalysis. We only have to think back to the already mentioned initial critiques of Arthur Kronfeld and Karl Jaspers. In his first phenomenologically based epistemological examination of psychoanalysis in 1912, Kronfeld expresses the conviction that psychoanalysis falls short of the criteria of a strict scientific methodology. Likewise, Jaspers repeatedly diagnoses substantial deficiencies regarding the scientific character of psychoanalysis. Paul Ricoeur's as well as Jürgen Habermas' subsequent phenomenological and hermeneutical works can do only little to counteract this stance towards psychoanalysis in terms of scientific theory. Adolf Grünbaum, from the standpoint of analytical epistemology, heavily criticizes their predominantly hermeneutical-idiographical attempts at a reconstruction of psychoanalysis. In 1984, in *The Foundations of Psychoanalysis*, Grünbaum particularly problematizes the claim to explain relations of sense and meaning through causal relations. His theses, however, succeed in re-opening psychoanalysis to scientific criticism. Even within the sphere of psychoanalytic research, they bring into being an initiative to meet the criteria of scientific research – objectivity, validity and reliability.

Today, psychoanalysts oriented towards scientific theory seem to agree that psychoanalytic treatment constitutes a distinct situation and assumes a specific concept of empiricism.

On the one hand, these convictions result in psychoanalytic research attempting to conform to today's theoretical and methodological understanding of empirical research. On the other hand, there is the tendency to extend this understanding and to further differentiate today's concept of psychological empiricism. In doing so, psychoanalysis as therapeutic method aims to position itself within the area of conflict between nomothetical and idiographic science. Supporters of this kind of research view themselves as 'nomothetics of the singular case'. Here, the challenge lies in the formalization and clinical investigation of the interpretational aspect of psychoanalytic work with respect to the psychoanalytic situation, i.e. the exchange between the analyst and the analysand. Particular psychodynamic processes have to be taken into account: transference and counter-transference, defense and resistance and so forth. In this regard, so-called process-oriented research is conducted. Here, the temporal progress of psychoanalytic processes is empirically investigated. Also, along these lines, result-oriented research has lately been developed and applied. Its objective is the empirical revision of the effectiveness of psychoanalytical therapy. These developments are concerned with the integration of psychoanalysis as therapy into the current scientific discourse of psychology, the adjustment of its positions and results to the obligatory standards of current empirical research in order to strengthen it institutionally, to methodologically secure its distinct mode of treatment and ultimately open it to dialogue. A discussion of these tendencies in research and an overview of the newest findings are provided, for example, by Helmut Thomä and Horst Kächele in their anthology on research on psychoanalytical therapy, which was reissued in 2006. Moreover, the latest attempts at an interdisciplinary collaboration between psychoanalysis and neurosciences also follow this line of research. Here, particularly the work of M. Leuzinger-Bohleber and her team ought to be mentioned.

At the same time, we are aware that within psychoanalysis there have always been genuine endeavours to comprehend the specificity of experience in the psychoanalytic situation and to base a psychoanalytic theory of human mental and psychic life upon it. This was Freud's pronounced aim. His former pupils C.G. Jung, Alfred Adler and Sandor Ferenczi, for example, follow this guideline. They build on Freud's fundamental discovery regarding the unconscious as a dynamic and constitutive structure of human subjectivity. Among other things, they extend the notion of association as the law of the unconscious (C.G. Jung), the social and intersubjective aspects of human individuation (Adler) and particular unconscious, subject-genetic activities, especially that of identification (Ferenczi). In the second generation, Sigmund Freud's daughter Anna Freud and Heinz Hartmann notably establish a psychoanalytic psychology of the ego. It is developed apart from the empirical and philosophical subject-discourse. Here, the focus lies on the unconscious subjective activities, the so-called defense mechanisms. These are regarded as unconscious activities that – through the dynamics of drive and adaptation – determine the inner-psychic genesis. Meanwhile, the school of Melanie Klein, a British analyst of Austrian origin, concentrates on infantile or pre-egologic unconscious dynamics. A psychoanalytical developmental psychology arises which becomes the foundation for the psychoanalytical object-relations theory. This, especially in neo-psychoanalysis, is further developed by researchers like D. W. Winnicott, and currently Wilfred R. Bion or André Green. Here, issues are addressed that could be of particular interest for genetic phenomenology: the emergence of thinking and the role played by emotions in this process, a theory of affects or the constitution of intersubjectivity. Several points of contact result in recent attachment theory (Peter Fonagy) as well as infant research (David Stern, for example).

The achievements of these researchers, which can only be mentioned as examples here, should be of paramount importance for a theory of subjective experience. Since they largely go beyond the scope of an analytical epistemology, they remain apart from current epistemological discussions and are hardly considered theoretically. An important contribution to the integration of these results into contemporary philosophy of subjectivity and culture has been made by the poststructuralist interpretations of authors such as M. Foucault, J. Derrida, G. Deleuze, J. Kristeva and others. Yet, they cannot help to develop a sustainable and adequate epistemological foundation for psychoanalysis either. They decidedly introduce it into philosophical discourse, but actually pursue other, non-epistemological aims. Therefore, an epistemologically-oriented reflection of basic psychoanalytic concepts and processes on a genuinely phenomenological base seems promising. At the same time, it can be understood as supplementary to the current endeavour to integrate psychoanalysis into the field of analytic and scientific understanding. Here, the reflection from the experienced inner perspective is associated with and helps to support verifiability through external observation; not, however, as a frequently frowned upon introspectivism but as an informed and capable method of phenomenological reflection.

Besides the application of intentional analysis in the sense of a hermeneutic interpretation as psychoanalytically ascertainable contents of meaning – as has been particularly pointed out by the tradition following Ricoeur, among others – concepts of the experience of the Other, of subjective and intersubjective genesis, of drive and affect as effective moments of this genesis, the experiencing of time, of phantasy and of non-linguistic thought, of the experiencing of the body and also of the subjective dynamics of conflict, of suppression, of transfer and especially of the unconscious as phenomenologically interpreted sphere of experience can be subjected to a phenomenological analysis. The abundant material of intuitions provided by psychoanalytical case studies ought to be of tremendous value to phenomenology. Furthermore, the connection to clinical and medical practice will remain of utmost importance. In the case of a successful collaboration and the promotion of further corporate projects, one might even hope for the development of phenomenological-psychoanalytical fundamental research. The editors of the present anthology hope for this publication to be a step towards this aim.

Some of the following essays stem from a conference, which, under the heading of *Phänomenologie und Psychoanalyse*, took place in May 2007 at the University of Cologne. Apart from the speakers, further phenomenologists, psychotherapists and psychoanalysts were invited to contribute to this publication.

In the following, the contributions will be briefly introduced.

Rudolf Bernet connects Husserl's doctrine of (pure) phantasy as an act of intuitive re-presentation and Freud's analysis of phantasizing and different kinds of phantasma. Husserl's description of the consciousness of the performance of phantasy-acts implies not only an ego-splitting but also the possibility of distancing oneself and thus also self-liberation, which opens up a chance for a new formation of one's own life. The reconstruction of the development of Freud's analyses of phantasy reveals the difference between transitory phantasizing (*Phantasieren*) and relatively rigid, visual and narrative phantasies (*Phantasien*). As already in Husserl an inquiry about the implications of the ego in its conscious and unconscious phantasms is thereby suggested. Beside the regressive flight from reality of the (day-) dream we find in Freud a creative phantasizing which is freed from the urge to repeat of fixed phantasma. This creative phantasizing makes understandable what was unimaginable and thus helps the unconsciousness to come up in discussion.

Jagna Brudzińska outlines a research program for the cooperation of phenomenology and psychoanalysis. She begins with a clarification of the relation of phenomenology and psychology in order to prepare the common ground for such a collaboration. She conceives of unconscious experience as a particular form of subjective life that cannot be immediately perceived, but that is originally re-presented in intentional and pre-intentional achievements. It finds its expression in emotively structured phenomena of phantasmatic eruptions into experiences, especially those involving involuntary ideas (*freie Einfälle*) in processes of free association, (day) dreams, so-called transfer-processes, kinaesthetic manifestations and others. Phenomenological-genetic analysis of these kinds of phenomena gives psychoanalysis an epistemological foundation. At the same time, phenomenology gains new insights which concern the deep subjective dynamics of processes of individuation as processes of personal and interpersonal genesis. As such phenomenology can be defined as *depth phenomenology* of the emotive dynamic.

Felix Duportail points out that the genetic conditions of vision are governed by a group of propositions he calls 'axioms of the flesh' following the descriptions of Merleau-Ponty in *The Visible and the Invisible*. Additionally, he suggests a reflection on the qualitative, topological space of position. This topological space is understood by Merleau-Ponty as "a model of being" in opposition to the Euclidean space that he associates with the classic ontology of an *ens realissimum*. The analysis of space becomes the common thread in the representation of the field of original Being. The aim is to find here an *indirect* ontology that involves a pre-objective description of the world. The world is now interpreted in the mode of "wild being", a mode which was repressed in the philosophical tradition for a long time. This concentrated reflection on the ontology of the flesh should serve as a foundation for the psychoanalysis of Freud and Lacan.

Thomas Fuchs' discussion of body memory starts with the general consideration that traditional psychoanalysis conceived the unconscious as a primary intra-psychic reality, somehow hidden in a realm 'below consciousness'. Therefore it is accessible to a 'depth psychology' based on metapsychological premises and concepts. This might be interpreted as a *vertical* conception of unconsciousness. In contrast to this concept Fuchs' paper presents a phenomenological approach to the unconscious conceived as a *horizontal* dimension of the lived body, lived space and intercorporeality. This approach is based on a phenomenology of body memory which is not to be identified with a form of explicit memory. Body memory is defined as the totality of implicit dispositions of perception and behaviour mediated by the body and sedimented in the course of earlier experiences. In this view unconscious fixations are considered as restrictions in the potentiality of a person. These restrictions are caused by a past, including traumatic experiences, which is still effective in the present. The traces of the past are thus not hidden in an interior psychic world but manifest themselves in the everyday behavior of a person, in behavior patterns to which one repeatedly returns, in actions that one avoids without being aware of it, etc.

The article of Patrizia Giampieri-Deutsch starts from the seemingly incompatible viewpoints of psychoanalysis, philosophy of mind, and phenomenology. In spite of this diversity, some current positions within these disciplines overlap and interface on the crucial topic of subjective experience. The article subsequently discusses Paul Ricœur's phenomenological approach to the psychoanalytic experience, some philosophical contributions to psychoanalysis from both philosophy of mind and phenomenology and in the end some contributions to psychoanalysis from cognitive science. The limits of Ricœur's hermeneutical understanding of psychoanalysis are revealed and Giampieri-Deutsch points out the value of his first approach in *Freud and Philosophy.* Here Ricœur focuses on the analytic experience as an excellent way to reach the phenomenon of subjective experience. Thus he regards phenomenology as a way to as well as an approximation to psychoanalysis. Unfortunately, in his later *The Question of Proof in Freud's Psychoanalytic Writings* he moves away from phenomenology and almost exclusively restricts the analytic experience to speech acts circumscribing the analytic experience as a narrative enterprise. The next section compares the psychoanalytic approaches to the subjective mind in relation to philosophy of mind and also to the phenomenology of subjective experience. Additionally, some convergent data from cognitive science are discussed that may support the striving of psychoanalysis to become a science of the general mechanisms of the subjective mind. These external challenges might help to overcome the inner fragmentation of psychoanalysis and offer an opportunity to reconstruct the knowledge base of psychoanalysis.

In his historical analysis Günter Gödde addresses the philosophical background of Freud's theory and its relations to phenomenology. It is argued that Freud from his youth on had a negative attitude to philosophy. However, close evaluation of his letters and other sources on the development of psychoanalysis gives a more ambivalent impression: As a young student Freud was strongly interested in philosophical questions and studied for four semesters with Franz Brentano before he went on to more biological research projects. In the first years of the development of psychoanalysis Freud's interest in philosophy revives and he concentrates on Theodor Lipps as a source for his psychology of unconsciousness. Only in the discussions of the psychoanalytical Wednesday Society does Freud change his attitude more and more towards a sharp and polemic critique of philosophy. In doing so he sets the course which has made exchange and understanding between psychoanalysis and philosophy difficult up to now. But already at this time there were skeptics concerning Freud's critique of philosophy, such as Ludwig Binswanger. After the First World War, Freud still demarcates his scientific conception of the world from philosophy, but his critique was never a general rejection of philosophy but rather a concentrated rejection of speculative metaphysics and system-thinkers. Gödde's contribution tries to shed some light on the little known relation of Freud to phenomenological thinking in Brentano, Lipps and Binswanger. All of them were descriptively, intentionally and phenomenologically oriented, and at times Freud had close personal or scientific relations to each of them.

Andrzej Leder examines Husserlian phenomenology and Lacanian psychoanalysis under the presumption that philosophical concepts and theories can be read as expressions of attitudes towards what is experienced and analyzed. Thus the differences could be restated in terms of the optimistic confidence of phenomenology in the possibilities of human thought, in contrast to the careful apprehension of psychoanalysis concerning its own limitations or inherent failures. Husserl trusted in our epistemic capacities attaining the realm of pure consciousness through *phenomenological reduction*, in which essential structures of pure consciousness could be studied adequately. Psychoanalysis turned consciousness into the great unknown. While Freud was interested – like Husserl – in preserving trust in our cognitive abilities, he introduced the unconscious as the 'given' source of meaning that permits us to decrypt the sense of experience. With Lacan we face a double *epoche*. Consciousness is not 'the given', nor is the unconscious, as the later must always be retroactively "reconstructed" from a given meaning, which is the product of a "catastrophe". Is this already a kind of skepticism? Andrzej Leder's proposal doesn't lead in the direction of sceptical doubt, but rather towards the realization that we face a *crisis* of the purely cognitive attitude towards experience. Epistemology appears here as a way of dealing with a depressive, post-traumatic position. The different epistemological attitudes of Husserl, Freud, Levinas and Lacan represent different ways of transcending this position.

Dieter Lohmar seeks to understand whether we can conceive of neurotic displacement in the forms of denying, inversion etc. as rational actions of the mind. From a philosophical point of view this makes sense; otherwise it seems as if psychoanalysis incorporates the alarming insight that our consciousness is opaque and asks for psychoanalytical hermeneutics to become partly lucid. The theoretical background of this attempt to understand neurotic displacement is a theory of thinking without language. It turns out that human non-linguistic thinking is centred on the mode of scenic phantasma we commonly identify with daydreams. The leading hypothesis is that daydreams are an old, non-linguistic form of thinking about the present world, our former experiences, our wishes and future plans. Daydreams are the medium in which to bind my former experiences with possible future actions and possible events. They are problem-solving activities even if they take the specific form of neurotic displacement. From the point of view of non-linguistic thinking, some enigmas of our wakeful daydreams can be solved and turn out to be quite rational processes.

In his contribution Aaron Mishara presents three approaches to the phenomenology of the unconscious: Conrad, Binswanger and Husserl. Conrad and Binswanger challenge the classical view that the delusional perception in schizophrenia is an abnormal symbolic meaning attached to an otherwise intact perception. For them it looks more like a perceptual aspect or expressive (physiognomic) quality, detached from its visual context, becoming salient and developing into the delusion.

Both believe that the delusional object involves a transformation of perceptual Gestalt-meaning at a "lower" unconscious phase of its development, but they apply different methods. While Conrad appeals to contemporary experimental work on microgenesis (*Aktualgenese*), Binswanger applies Husserl's genetic phenomenology. Conrad describes the delusional object as a pre-Gestalt (*Vorgestalt*), a physiognomic-expressive Gestalt-quality arrested at an earlier phase in the development of meaning which "normally" remains unconscious. For Binswanger, the delusional object is formed from a sensory profile-aspect (*Abschattung*) released during the loosening of the perceptual object's internal structure. The phenomenological unconscious in Husserl has two faces in the dimension of time-constitution: it is what underlies the lowermost background of any emergent Gestalt in the present, but it is also the past. (The topic of schizophrenia is also treated in this volume by Wiggins/Schwartz.)

Ian Rory Owen investigates a phenomenon of gender constitution-trans-sexualism. People who are 'primary' trans-sexuals help explain the nature of psychological meaning concerning roles, identity and culturally-constituted meanings. Owen presents a phenomenological analysis of the constitution of trans-sexual as well as intersexual identity in the context of Husserl's phenomenology of intentional and intersubjective experiences. The terminology employed distinguishes between 'gender' as referring to intersubjective (or psychosocial) aspects of culturally-defined identity and roles; 'sex' as referring to physical aspects of the body. The relation between physical sex and intersubjective gender is explored to show how people find and place themselves within pre-existing codes of cultural objects and their manifolds of meaning. The usual assumption is that gender follows a simple binary classification of two mutually exclusive sexes. But the assumptions concerning mutually-exclusive gender and sex are challenged by a full attention to the evidence. The focus is not on Husserl exegesis but on showing how being trans-sexual and intersexual is part of the way in which people create and express their identities. Specific comments on trans-sexuality have been derived from first-person accounts that are interpreted in a Husserlian way.

Sonja Rinofner-Kreidl analyzes the logical structure of self-deception in order to begin to delineate the difference between normal, that is interpersonal, deception and self-deception. Also, simple errors with regard to oneself have to be distinguished from proper cases of self-deception that obviously have a more complicated structure. Persons who fall prey to self-deception seem to harbour antagonistic tendencies. If one considers self-deception as some kind of cognitive deficiency one might try to interpret these tendencies in terms of simultaneously held incompatible beliefs. Contrary to this and following Alfred Mele's pioneering analyses Rinofner-Kreidl argues that a phenomenological description has the chance to result in a more balanced concept of self-deception. A phenomenological approach steers clear both of presuming unconscious processes (in terms of a Freudian theory of the unconscious) and of referring to contradicting beliefs. Phenomenologists neither overestimate the irrational aspects of human life (Freudian interpretation) nor do they defend a strongly rationalized account of human action (Cognitivist interpretation). Following this line, the author shows that in many cases self-deception is due to an emotionally motivated temporary suspension of our will to acquire knowledge or true belief. This special type of avoidance behaviour obviously has moral implications which, among others, touch on our notions of truthfulness, self-control and responsibility.

The investigation of Francesco Trincia is directed to the connection of the theme of the unconscious to the philosophies of the twentieth century and to phenomenological inquiries in particular. The issue of the unconscious enters philosophy as an effect of a sort of "reaction to the originary" that took place in the previous century. As a result of this reaction, it is difficult to find a philosophical sphere in which that theme is absent, overlooked or forgotten. Even in Husserl's profound investigations into the deepest level of constitution we can detect the unconscious. The author offers some far-reaching comparative reflections on the relationship between Husserl's inquiry on time-consciousness and Freud's thought in order to delineate the limits of the concepts of the "unconscious" and a "philosophy of the unconscious" in a clear and productive way.

The paper of Donn Welton and Wolfram Schüffel analyzes the case of a thirty-year-old woman suffering from tinnitus and aims at understanding the semantics of psychosomatic symptoms. On the assumption that her symptom has a *truth-bearing* function, they try to understand it as situated in her *world*, i.e. in terms of the phenomenological notion of world as a *horizon*. The horizon is interpreted as a nexus of significance in three different structures supporting human engagement: *setting*, *context*, and *background*. This way of world-analysis provides a salient contribution to the theory of psychosomatic symptoms. The paper then concentrates on the difficult notion of background and contrasts the origins and the *telos* of bodily symptoms. Making use of these categories in the case of Frau D offers the insight that the truth of her conflict-generated symptoms can be found not just in the history of her conflicts but also in four interlocking functions organized teleologically: delimiting, bordering, gate-keeping, and attaching.

The contribution of Daniel Widlöcher investigates the origin of the central Freudian concept of psychic reality. From a psychoanalytical point of view, 'unconscious proper' must be reserved for material that cannot gain any access to becoming conscious. The reality of the unconscious contents of mind, the structural 'Unconscious', creates in the mind *illusory* beliefs, i.e. the psychic reality. It derives from a hallucinatory activity issued from the person which imposes itself on the Ego as reality. The Ego *must* believe in the reality of his unconscious fantasy as he believes in the external world. The analyst's understanding of the psychic reality of a person results from the associative work that the analyst experiences with the patient. The term 'co-thinking' is suggested for linking patient and analyst through this emerging process. It turns out, that of all the fundamental concepts which we owe to Freud's genius, none is more clearly his discovery than the concept of psychic reality.

Osborne Wiggins and Michael Alan Schwartz analyze the more common forms of schizophrenia from the point of view of phenomenological-anthropological psychiatry. A short introduction to the phenomenological-anthropological perspective paints the background for the explication of basic phenomenological concepts following Husserl and Gurwitsch: intentionality, synthesis, constitution, automatic and active mental life, and the Ego. From this point of view the authors address schizophrenic mental life as a whole claiming that the transformation of experience that it entails affects even the most basic *ontological* constituents of the world, namely, space, time, causality, and the nature of objects. Usually this complete transformation of the lifeworld leads to suffering and disorientation. Only in rare cases, like that of the schizophrenic poet, playwright, and actor Antonin Artaud, individuals succeed in harnessing those aspects of their disease to serve an impressive creativity. Most people afflicted with schizophrenia remain incapable of such creative breakthroughs. This phenomenological discussion adapts a concept from philosophical anthropology and applies it to schizophrenia: namely, the concept of "world openness" and the need to reduce that openness. The authors also focus on one of the more puzzling aspects of schizophrenia, which psychiatrists call 'thought insertion'. In the end the difference between an early stage of schizophrenia and a later one is indicated.

***

In closing, we would like to express our gratitude to those who have – besides the contributors – engaged in the present project either in the formatting of the text or by making suggestions to improve the style. We would like to mention Frances Bottenberg, Jasmin Dücker, Dr. Dirk Fonfara, Dr. Saulius Geniusas, Monika Heidenreich, Jacob Rump, Klaus Sellge and Ina Marie Weber.

Cologne in August 2010, the editors

Phantasieren und Phantasma bei Husserl und Freud

Rudolf Bernet

Abstract In diesem Aufsatz werden Husserls Lehre von der (insbesondere „reinen“) Phantasie als dem Akt einer anschaulichen „Vergegenwärtigung“ mit Freuds Analyse vom Phantasieren und (verschiedenen Arten) von Phantasmen miteinander in Verbindung gebracht. Husserls Beschreibung des Vollzugsbewusstseins des Phantasieaktes impliziert nicht nur eine Ichspaltung, sondern auch eine Möglichkeit der Distanzierung und somit der Selbstbefreiung, die einer Neugestaltung des eigenen Lebens den Weg bereitet. Eine Rekonstruktion der Entwicklung von Freuds Beschäftigung mit der Phantasie zeigt, wie sich die Scheidung zwischen einem flüchtigen „Phantasieren“ und den relativ starren (visuellen und narrativen) „Phantasien“ (bzw. Phantasmen) schrittweise durchsetzt. Wie schon bei Husserl stellt sich dann auch bei Freud die Frage nach der Implikation des Ich in seinen (bewussten und unbewussten) Phantasmen. Neben der regressiven Realitätsflucht der (Tag-)Träume kommt auch bei Freud ein kreatives Phantasieren zur Geltung, das vom (Wiederholungs-)Zwang fixierter Phantasmen befreit, Unvorstellbares verständlich macht und dem Unbewussten zur Sprache verhilft. ‘-- End of Abstract’

R. Bernet (✉)
Husserl-Archief te Leuven, Katholieke Universiteit Leuven, Kardinaal Mercier Plein, 2, B 3000 Leuven, Belgium
e-mail: rudolf.bernet@hiw.kuleuven.be.ac

D. Lohmar and J. Brudzińska (eds.), *Founding Psychoanalysis Phenomenologically*,
Phaenomenologica 199, DOI 10.1007/978-94-007-1848-7_1,

1 Husserl. Reine Phantasie und Selbstentzweiung

1.1 Die Entwicklung von Husserls Phänomenologie des Phantasiebewusstseins

Husserls phänomenologisches Verständnis des Phantasiebewusstseins hat sich über verschiedene Phasen der Neuorientierung entwickelt.[1] Seine im Wesentlichen zwischen 1904 und 1912 entwickelten Auffassungen hat Husserl dann bis Mitte der zwanziger Jahre immer wieder revidiert. Die im Folgenden diskutierte husserlsche Lehre von der „reinen Phantasie" ist das Resultat von zwei großen Veränderungen. Diese betreffen eine Vertiefung und Bereicherung nicht nur des Verständnisses der spezifisch *phantasiemäßigen* Form der Anwesenheit eines abwesenden, unwirklichen Gegenstandes, sondern gleichermaßen auch des phänomenologischen Verständnisses sowohl der *wahrnehmungsmäßigen* Anwesenheit eines wirklichen Gegenstandes als auch der Abwesenheit eines nur *symbolisch*, d.h. unanschaulich angedeuteten Gegenstandes.

Ein erster markanter Einschnitt in Husserls Entwicklung bildete die Abkehr von der Bestimmung der Phantasie als einer „uneigentlichen" Vorstellung im Sinne Brentanos. Im Gegensatz zu Brentano wird die Phantasie von Husserl nun konsequent als ein zugleich *intuitives und sinnliches* intentionales Bewusstsein bestimmt. Das Imaginäre im Sinne des phänomenologischen Verständnisses der Phantasie hebt sich damit endgültig ab von einem mathematischen Begriff des Imaginären. Als eine Art anschaulichen Bewusstseins wird die Phantasie auch von den unanschaulichen bzw. unerfüllten oder leeren (in der Terminologie der *Logischen Untersuchungen*: „signitiven") Akten abgehoben, in denen eine abwesende intentionale Gegenständlichkeit bloß gedacht oder durch ein *Zeichen* repräsentiert wird. Diese Bestimmung der Phantasie als ein *anschauliches* Bewusstsein von einem abwesenden Gegenstand[2] hat dann wiederum zur Folge, dass diejenigen Momente oder Teile eines räumlichen Gegenstandes, welche in einer sinnlich-anschaulichen *Wahrnehmung* nur „uneigentlich" oder „leer" zur Erscheinung kommen, nicht mehr (wie noch in den *Logischen Untersuchungen*) vom Wesen einer *signitiven* Intention her verstanden werden können. Damit wird zwar keineswegs behauptet, dass ich die jeweils unsichtbare Rückseite eines Würfels in meiner Wahrnehmung von ihm einfach hinzuphantasiere (denn diese Rückseite ist Teil eines wirklichen und nicht eines fiktiven Gegenstandes), wohl aber, dass diese uneigentliche oder leere Wahrnehmung von etwas Unsichtbarem Moment eines selbst anschaulichen und nicht etwa eines symbolischen Bewusstseins ist.[3]

Die zweite Transformation der husserlschen Lehre von der Phantasie ergab sich aus der Entdeckung einer neuen Differenz, welche zwar ausschließlich das *vergegenwärtigende* Bewusstsein selbst betrifft, die aber wiederum nicht ohne Folgen für die Bestimmung derjenigen Akte war, die ihren intentionalen Gegenstand anschaulich gegenwärtigen. Husserls wachsendes Interesse für die so genannte „reine" Phantasie führte zur neuen Einsicht, dass ein solches Phantasiebewusstsein auch ohne die Vermittlung durch ein (äußeres oder inneres) Bild möglich ist.

Die neu entdeckte Differenz betrifft somit den Unterschied zwischen einem reinen Phantasiebewusstsein und einem *Bildbewusstsein*. Reine Phantasieakte haben dieser neuen Einsicht zufolge keine bildliche Darstellung ihres abwesenden und fiktiven Gegenstandes nötig, ihre Vergegenwärtigung des fiktiven Gegenstandes stützt sich vielmehr allein auf die reproduktive Verdoppelung des intentionalen Bewusstseins selbst. Diese neue und in der Folge konsequent festgehaltene Bestimmung des Phantasiebewusstseins als Akt einer neutralisierten (bzw. nicht setzenden), anschaulichen Vergegenwärtigung eines fiktiven Gegenstandes ist eng verbunden mit einem neuen Verständnis der Wiedererinnerung als einer setzenden anschaulichen Vergegenwärtigung eines abwesenden (nämlich vergangenen) Gegenstandes. Keine dieser beiden Arten von Vergegenwärtigung hat, Husserls neuer Ansicht zufolge, den Charakter eines Bildbewusstseins, aber bei beiden handelt es sich um einen intentionalen Akt, der einen anderen Akt modifiziert „reproduziert".

1.2 Reine Phantasien

Eine Phantasie ist nach Husserl dann „rein", wenn sie von jeder Kontaminierung durch die Wirklichkeit eines Gegenstandes oder eines (inneren oder äußeren) Bildes gereinigt bzw. befreit ist. Es handelt sich dabei um ein intuitives Bewusstsein, das sich seine fiktiven Objekte oder Phantasiewelten in größter Unabhängigkeit von der wirklichen Welt frei schafft bzw. erfindet. Eine phänomenologische Analyse der reinen Phantasie muss somit erklären, wie ein *anschauliches*, jedoch nicht perzeptives Bewusstsein eines *nicht für wirklich gehaltenen* Gegenstandes möglich ist. Es ist in der Tat die Abwesenheit des Glaubens an die Wirklichkeit des anschaulich gegebenen fiktiven Gegenstandes bzw. die „Neutralisierung" seiner Setzung als eines wirklichen Gegenstandes, welche die reine Phantasie von jeder Art Illusion unterscheidet. Offenbar weiß der Phantasierende um den fiktiven Charakter seiner phantasierten Gegenstände und Ereignisse, während derjenige, der einer Trugwahrnehmung verfallen ist, erst im Nachhinein seinen früheren Glauben an die Wirklichkeit des Gegenstandes als Trug erkennt. Sowohl in der reinen Phantasie als auch in der (überwundenen) Trugwahrnehmung ist zwar ein Bewusstsein vom Unterschied oder Kontrast zwischen Wirklichkeit und Unwirklichkeit auszumachen, aber dieses Bewusstsein ist in den beiden Fällen anders motiviert. Es gibt also offensichtlich verschiedene Arten des „Widerstreits" zwischen Wirklichkeit und Unwirklichkeit und somit auch verschiedene Arten von „Schein".

Eine Illusion oder Halluzination ist eine Trugwahrnehmung. Sie besteht einem bekannten Beispiel Husserls zufolge etwa darin, vermeintlich eine wirkliche Person wahrzunehmen, wo es sich in Wirklichkeit um eine Schaufensterpuppe handelt. Eine solche Trugwahrnehmung löst sich nicht von selbst auf, sie kann nur durch eine wahre Wahrnehmung aufgehoben werden. Einmal als Illusion entlarvt, verliert die Trugwahrnehmung ihren Wahrnehmungscharakter und ihren Glauben an die Wirklichkeit des Gegenstandes. Es ist also die neue Wahr-Nehmung des Gegenstandes als eine Puppe, die mich daran hindert, den Gegenstand weiterhin als eine wirkliche menschliche Person wahrzunehmen. Die Korrektur der neuen Wahrnehmung besteht also darin, die frühere Wahrnehmung zu „durchstreichen", d.h. sie als eine bloße Illusion bewusst zu machen. Trugwahrnehmungen werden also nie als solche wirklich erlebt oder „vollzogen", denn sie werden entweder als vermeintliche Wahrnehmungen wirklich vollzogen oder sie sperren sich als entlarvte Illusionen gegen ihre Auffassung als Wahrnehmungen. Es handelt sich hier also um einen Widerstreit zwischen zwei Wahrnehmungen, der bereits zugunsten der einen oder der anderen entschieden ist, und zwar aufgrund der anschaulich-„leibhaften" Gegebenheit des wirklichen Gegenstandes. Das Phänomen selbst hat entschieden, und die trügerische frühere Wahrnehmung bleibt mir nur noch als die Vorstellung von etwas Unwirklichem erhalten. Ich kann mich zwar noch daran erinnern, die Puppe als eine wirkliche Dame wahrgenommen zu haben; ich kann meistens auch noch verstehen, wie dies möglich war; aber jetzt ist es mir nicht mehr möglich, diese Puppe als eine wirkliche Person wahrzunehmen.

Ganz anders verhält es sich diesbezüglich bei der reinen Phantasie. Die Enthaltung vom Glauben an die Wirklichkeit des anschaulich gegebenen Gegenstandes, welche jede Art von Phantasie kennzeichnet, wird mir keineswegs *von außen* her durch das wahrnehmungsmäßige Erscheinen eines (anderen) *wirklichen* Gegenstandes aufgezwungen, dessen Existenz mit dem unwirklichen Charakter meines Phantasiegegenstandes streiten würde. Es ist nämlich prinzipiell ausgeschlossen, dass zwischen einem wirklichen Gegenstand und einem Phantasiegegenstand ein echter Konflikt oder Widerstreit entstehen kann. Ein als wirklich seiend vermeinter Gegenstand kann nämlich nur mit einem anderen als wirklich seiend vermeinten Gegenstand unvereinbar sein, und er kann deshalb keinem Gegenstand widersprechen, der von vornherein als nicht wirklich existierend vorgestellt wurde. Zwischen der wirklichen Welt und möglichen Phantasiewelten besteht zwar ein erheblicher Unterschied, aber kein eigentlicher Widerstreit. Man mag es zwar bereuen, dass die Welt, in der wir wirklich leben, keine Märchenwelt ist, aber die wirkliche Welt zwingt uns nie, auf unsere Freude an unwirklichen Märchenwelten zu verzichten. Damit ist auch gesagt, dass das Bewusstsein von der Unwirklichkeit der phantasierten Gegenstände, d.h. die doxische „Neutralitätsmodifikation", welche alles Phantasiebewusstsein nach Husserl charakterisiert, sich nicht aus einem von der Wirklichkeit ausgehenden Zwang ergeben kann. Es muss sich vielmehr um eine durch das phantasierende Subjekt *frei* gewählte Haltung handeln. Phantasierte Gegenstände gelten deshalb von vornherein als unwirklich, weil ich im Vollzug des Phantasierens immer schon davon weiß, dass ich phantasiere und nicht wirkliche Gegenstände wahrnehme.

Wie stellt es das Bewusstsein nun aber an, fiktive Gegenstände frei zu erschaffen, und wie weiß es davon, dass diese Gegenstände nicht der wirklichen Welt angehören? Was die erste Frage betrifft, so liegt die Schwierigkeit darin, dass Husserl die reine Phantasie als einen Akt anschaulicher Vergegenwärtigung bezeichnet, der weder mit der Modifikation einer gegenwärtigen wirklichen Wahrnehmung (wie im Falle der perzeptiven Phantasie) noch mit der Reproduktion einer früheren wirklichen Wahrnehmung (wie im Falle einer Wiedererinnerung) verbunden ist. Die Wahrnehmung, die in einer reinen Phantasie reproduziert wird, ist somit eine fiktive

Wahrnehmung, die in dieser vergegenwärtigenden Reproduktion frei erschaffen wird. *Die reine Phantasie muss somit als ein nicht-setzendes reproduktives Bewusstsein verstanden werden, das in kreativer Weise einen Gegenstand intuitiv vergegenwärtigt, dessen Unwirklichkeit den Charakter einer fiktiven Existenz hat.* Was motiviert Husserl nun aber, diese freie Schöpfung einer fiktiven Wahrnehmung noch als einen Akt der Reproduktion zu verstehen? Der Grund dafür scheint die Ähnlichkeit der reinen Phantasie mit einer Wiedererinnerung zu sein, die in der Tat ebenfalls einen Gegenstand intuitiv vergegenwärtigt, der sich wesentlich von den wirklichen gegenwärtigen Gegenständen unterscheidet, die man während des Phantasierens und Erinnerns weiterhin wahrnimmt. Husserl meint nun, dass ein (vergegenwärtigendes) Bewusstsein der anschaulichen Gegenwart eines Phantasiegegenstandes nur dadurch möglich ist, dass das Phantasieren die fiktive Wahrnehmung dieses Gegenstandes „intentional impliziert" – gerade so, wie auch die Erinnerung an einen vergangenen Gegenstand dessen frühere wirkliche Wahrnehmung intentional impliziert. Diese Analyse verdankt ihre Plausibilität vor allem dem Umstand, dass eine reine Phantasie ihren fiktiven Gegenstand zwar nicht für einen wirklichen Gegenstand hält, ihn aber dennoch so anschaulich vor Augen hat, dass er „quasi" wahrgenommen wird. Als eine solche „Quasi-Wahrnehmung" eines abwesenden Gegenstandes gleicht die reine Phantasie mehr einer Wiedererinnerung als etwa einem Bildbewusstsein, das ein abwesendes Objekt mittels der *wirklichen* Wahrnehmung eines *gegenwärtigen* Bildes vergegenwärtigt.

1.3 Das innere Bewusstsein vom Phantasieren

Der *Unterschied* zwischen der reinen Phantasie und der Wiedererinnerung ist jedoch mindestens ebenso wichtig wie die Ähnlichkeit zwischen diesen beiden Formen eines anschaulich vergegenwärtigenden Bewusstseins. Mit der Behandlung dieses Unterschieds sind wir auch schon bei der zweiten, oben erwähnten Frage angelangt. Der Unterschied zwischen einer reinen Phantasie als Akt der Reproduktion einer gegenwärtigen, aber bloß eingebildeten bzw. fiktiven Wahrnehmung einerseits und einer Wiedererinnerung als Akt der Reproduktion einer vergangenen, wirklichen Wahrnehmung andererseits manifestiert sich am deutlichsten in der Verschiedenheit ihres Vollzugsbewusstseins. Die fiktive Wahrnehmung, die in einer reinen Phantasie frei erschaffen wird, kann durch das „innere Bewusstsein" bloß „quasi" bzw. im Modus des „Als ob" (als ob ich wahrnehmen würde, dass ...) erlebt werden. Die eigentümliche Seinsweise dieses Quasi ergibt sich daraus, dass die imaginäre Wahrnehmung, in der der Phantasierende lebt, in Wahrheit keine wirkliche Wahrnehmung eines wirklichen Gegenstandes ist noch überhaupt je war. Die Quasi-Wahrnehmung eines fiktiven Objekts muss also als die Modifikation einer Wahrnehmung verstanden werden, die es unmodifiziert noch nie gegeben hat. Es handelt sich dabei also im Gegensatz zu einer Wiedererinnerung um die freie Produktion einer reproduzierten Quasi-Wahrnehmung, d.h. um eine Modifikation, die das durch sie Modifizierte überhaupt erst dadurch entstehen lässt, dass sie es modifiziert.

Den Schlüssel zum Verständnis dieser paradoxen oder zumindest rätselhaften Lehre von der reinen Phantasie muss man in Husserls Lehre vom „inneren Bewusstsein" des Vollzugs eines Phantasieaktes suchen.

Jeder wirkliche Vollzug eines intentionalen Aktes wird als solcher vom inneren Bewusstsein „impressional" erlebt. Dies gilt nach Husserl für alle wirklich vollzogenen Akte gleichermaßen, also etwa auch für den Akt einer erinnerungsmäßigen Vergegenwärtigung einer vergangenen Begebenheit. Ein Akt reiner Phantasie wird ebenfalls wirklich vollzogen und als solcher vom inneren Bewusstsein impressional erlebt – ungeachtet des Umstandes, dass dieser Akt aus der imaginären Reproduktion einer unwirklichen bzw. fiktiven Wahrnehmung besteht. Wenn ich mir eine Schlacht zwischen Zentauren und Amazonen vorstelle, so stelle ich mir *wirklich* etwas *Unwirkliches* vor; ebenso, wenn ich mir nur vorstelle, dass ich mir vorstellen könnte, dass … Ein deutlicher Beweis dafür, dass es sich bei diesen Akten des Phantasierens um wirklich vollzogene Akte handeln muss, ergibt sich aus der Tatsache, dass ich mich später an Ort, Zeit und Umstände meiner Phantasien, genauer: meiner Akte des Phantasierens erinnern kann. Was ich im Phantasieren wirklich, d.h. impressional erlebe, ist aber einzig der Akt des reinen Phantasierens während dessen aktuellem Vollzug, nicht aber das Phantasierte und auch nicht dessen Quasi-Wahrnehmung. Die sagenhafte Schlacht ist somit der intentionale Gegenstand einer von mir bloß eingebildeten Wahrnehmung, d.h. einer Wahrnehmung, die in meinem gegenwärtigen und wirklich vollzogenen Akt des Phantasierens im Modus einer produktiven Reproduktion intentional impliziert ist. Was ich im inneren Bewusstsein vom intentionalen Akt reinen Phantasierens erlebe, ist m.a.W. der wirkliche Vollzug eines intentionalen Aktes, der einen Akt imaginären Wahrnehmens reproduziert, in dem Gegenstände intentional vergegenwärtigt werden, die nicht der wirklichen Welt, sondern der einen oder anderen Phantasiewelt angehören.

Das innere Bewusstsein vom Vollzug eines Aktes reiner Phantasie ist somit das impressionale Bewusstsein vom wirklichen Vollzug eines vergegenwärtigenden intentionalen Bewusstseinsaktes, welcher den intentionalen Akt einer fiktiven Wahrnehmung produktiv reproduziert. *Das innere Bewusstsein vom Vollzug eines Aktes reiner Phantasie muss somit als das Erleben einer Verdoppelung des intentionalen Bewusstseins verstanden werden.* Anders als im Falle des Aktes einer erinnerungsmäßigen Vergegenwärtigung handelt es sich bei dieser phantasiemäßigen Verdoppelung des intentionalen Bewusstseins um eine eigentliche *Spaltung* des Bewusstseins, denn zwischen dem phantasierenden und dem phantasierten (bzw. dem reproduzierenden und dem reproduzierten) Bewusstsein besteht anders als beim wiedererinnernden und wiedererinnerten Bewusstsein ein wesentlicher Unterschied. In der reinen Phantasie lassen sich nämlich der wirklich vollzogene Akt des Phantasierens und der phantasierte Akt einer bloß fiktiven Wahrnehmung nie der Einheit ein und desselben wirklichen Bewusstseinsflusses einordnen. Man kann diesen Sachverhalt wohl am besten so beschreiben, dass die phantasierte Quasi-Wahrnehmung der Schlacht zwischen den Zentauren und den Amazonen vom inneren Bewusstsein gewissermaßen aus einem *Abstand* erlebt wird, nämlich als eine Quasi-Wahrnehmung, die im gegenwärtig wirklich vollzogenen Akt einer phantasiemäßigen Reproduktion intentional „impliziert" ist. Das innere Bewusstsein vom Vollzug einer reinen Phantasie muss somit genauer als das Bewusstsein sowohl von einer Differenz zwischen zwei verschiedenen Arten des intentionalen Bewusstseins als auch von ihrer Vereinigung in einem selben intentionalen Akt phantasiemäßiger Vergegenwärtigung bestimmt werden. Das innere Bewusstsein einer reinen Phantasie ist also das Bewusstsein der Unvereinbarkeit von zwei verschiedenen Formen des intentionalen Bewusstseins, die jedoch in *der* Art miteinander verbunden sind, dass es die eine (nämlich die phantasierte Wahrnehmung) nie ohne die andere (nämlich das wirkliche Phantasieren) geben kann.

Alle unsere bisherigen Beobachtungen zur subjektiven Vollzugsweise der Quasi-Wahrnehmungen in der reproduktiven Phantasie sowie zur Erscheinungsweise ihrer fiktiven Gegenstände bestätigen den Eindruck, dass eine reine Phantasie auch für das in ihr lebende Subjekt etwas Befremdliches bzw. Außerordentliches ist.[4] Damit soll aber nicht bestritten werden, dass die sich am Rande meines wirklichen Lebens abspielenden phantasierten Quasi-Leben sich ihrerseits zu Quasi-Lebenseinheiten zusammenschließen, denen die Einheit verschiedener, von mir inszenierter „Phantasiewelten" entspricht. Eine Phantasiewelt ist somit das intentionale Korrelat der ununterbrochenen, aber notwendigerweise beschränkten zeitlichen Dauer des Phantasielebens eines und desselben „Phantasie-Ichs".[5] Zu jeder Phantasiewelt gehört also die interne Kohärenz des Phantasielebens eines und desselben Phantasie-Ichs. Ein solches Phantasie-Ich hat in sich selbst normalerweise keinen guten Grund, an der Existenz seiner Phantasiewelt zu zweifeln. Phantasie-Ich und seine intentionale Phantasiewelt verbinden sich dergestalt zur Einheit eines Quasi-Lebens oder Parallellebens, das als Leben im Schein jedoch ein bloß scheinbares Leben ist, nämlich eine Art Widerschein oder Simulakrum des sich in der realen Welt abspielenden wirklichen Lebens eines „Real-Ichs". Im Gegensatz zum Real-Ich und dessen wirklicher Welt dauert ein solches phantasiertes Ich und dessen fiktive Welt nur gerade so lange, als eine Phantasie dauert, z.B. die in einem Märchen oder einer Sage inszenierte narrative Fiktion. Verschiedene Phantasiewelten mit ihren verschiedenen Phantasie-Ichs sind meistens auch inkompatibel, und sie sperren sich gegen jeden Versuch einer Vereinheitlichung. Die Welt, in der Zentauren ihr Unwesen treiben, und die Welt, in welcher der Kuss eines Prinzen Dornröschen aus ihrem hundertjährigen Schlaf erweckt, sind verschiedene Welten, die verschiedenen Geschichten zugehören, und nicht etwa verschiedene Episoden ein und desselben phantasierten Lebens. Jedes Phantasie-Ich lebt in seiner eigenen Welt, und es gibt somit gerade so viele Phantasieleben und Phantasiewelten als es Phantasie-Ichs gibt.

Der Kontrast mit dem Real-Ich und seinem wirklichen Leben in der realen Welt ist also unübersehbar, und es ist die Erfahrung dieses Kontrasts zwischen zwei verschiedenen Lebensformen durch das innere Bewusstsein, die dafür sorgt, dass die Gegenstände, welchen ein Phantasie-Ich seinen Glauben schenkt, durch das Real-Ich zu fiktiven Pseudo-Objekten „degradiert" werden (wie Sartre sich ausdrückt). Anders als die Phantasien mit ihren verschiedenen Phantasie-Ichs und Phantasiewelten gehören alle wirklichen Erfahrungen ein und desselben Real-Ichs in den Zusammenhang ein und desselben wirklichen Lebens in ein und derselben wirklichen Welt. Ich habe nur ein einziges wirkliches Leben, dafür aber unendlich viele mögliche Phantasieleben. Diese Phantasieleben müssen aber deswegen noch als *meine* Phantasieleben bezeichnet werden, weil sie von mir als Real-Ich phantasiert werden. Wenn nun aber ein und dasselbe Subjekt gleichzeitig in der wirklichen Welt und in der einen oder anderen Phantasiewelt leben kann, so bedeutet dies, dass es ein Doppelleben führen kann. In diesem Doppelleben überschneidet sich das von einem Real-Ich inszenierte fiktive Leben eines besonderen Phantasie-Ichs für eine beschränkte Zeit mit dem wirklichen Leben dieses Real-Ichs. Eine solche Überschneidung oder Verdoppelung ist deswegen möglich, weil die vielen Phantasieleben und deren Phantasie-Ichs von mir phantasiert werden und somit letztlich noch immer in meinem wirklichen Leben verankert sind.

2 Freud. Phantasieren und unbewusste Phantasmen

Im Gegensatz zu Husserl bewertet sein Zeitgenosse Freud das Phantasieren nicht als einen Akt der Freiheit und der Selbstbefreiung, sondern zumeist als einen Akt der Flucht aus der Wirklichkeit der äußeren Umstände und der psychischen Konflikte. Zur theoretischen Beobachtung einer Ichspaltung tritt bei Freud denn auch ein klinisches Interesse an der Motivation des Phantasierens sowie an dessen pathologischen Folgen. Das Phantasieren wird im weiteren Umfeld der Verdrängung bzw. der Ausbildung von neurotischen Symptomen verstanden, und damit eröffnet sich auch neu die Möglichkeit eines Phantasierens, von dem das Subjekt nichts weiß und auch nichts wissen will. Phantasien verändern (im guten und unguten Sinn) das wirkliche Leben einer Person, und in der Wahrnehmung sowie vor allem im subjektiven Umgang mit der Wirklichkeit und den Widerfahrnissen des eigenen Lebens spielt das Phantasieren eine wesentliche, vermittelnde Rolle. Bereits ein oberflächlicher Blick auf die Literatur lehrt allerdings, dass die Psychoanalyse dem „Phantasma" genannten Resultat des Phantasierens mehr Aufmerksamkeit schenkte als der Aktivität des Phantasierens selbst. Diesen Phantasmen wird ein entscheidender Einfluss auf die Bildung von (Tag-)Träumen und neurotischen Symptomen zugebilligt, obwohl sie als solche (mit der Ausnahme von perversen Verhaltensweisen) kaum bewusst in Erscheinung treten. Als meist unsichtbare und unaussprechbare Grundphantasie, die nur von ihren Folgen her greifbar ist, haftet an der psychoanalytischen Lehre vom Phantasma der Verdacht einer willkürlichen theoretischen Konstruktion. Einer Konstruktion allerdings, die für die Psychoanalyse unverzichtbar ist, wenn es darum geht, Phänomene des Übergangs verständlich zu machen: Übergang vom Trieb zum Begehren, von vorbewussten zu bewussten Vorstellungen, von phylogenetischen Mythen zur subjektiven Entwicklungsgeschichte.

Aus einem genaueren Studium der umfangreichen psychoanalytischen Literatur zur Problematik des Phantasma gewinnt man allerdings zugleich auch den Eindruck einer gewissen Ratlosigkeit. Dafür gibt es gute Gründe. So etwa, dass Freud den Begriff „Phantasma" in der heutigen Bedeutung nicht verwendet, und den Leser seiner Schriften oftmals darüber im Unklaren lässt, ob mit dem „Phantasieren" nun ein starres Phantasma oder die freie Beweglichkeit der Aktivität des Phantasierens gemeint ist. Als Erklärungsprinzip für strukturelle Übergänge ist das Phantasma zudem auch kein eigenständiges Phänomen mit einem topisch eindeutig bestimmten *locus naturalis*. Schließlich haben wir auch schon darauf aufmerksam gemacht, dass Phantasmen als solche kaum je in Erscheinung treten. Andererseits fällt aber doch auf, dass die psychoanalytischen Lehren vom Phantasma entscheidende und auch entscheidbare Fragen entweder vernachlässigt oder gar nicht gesehen haben.

So wird der Leser oftmals nicht darüber aufgeklärt, ob das Phantasma nun eigentlich etwas inhaltlich Bestimmtes (ein Gegenstand, ein Sachverhalt) ist, worauf das Begehren sich richtet oder das es zu verwirklichen versucht, – oder ob es sich um den bloßen Rahmen der Inszenierung des eigenen Begehrens und dessen Objekte handelt. Auch scheint man kaum darauf geachtet zu haben, dass es neben den genuin visuellen Phantasmen möglicherweise auch Phantasmen mit einer narrativen Struktur gibt. Daran anschließend stellt sich dann auch die Frage, welche Rolle (gehörten) sprachlichen Ausdrücken bzw. der Sprache im Allgemeinen bei der Bildung eines Phantasma zukommt. Sicher ist jedenfalls, dass das Subjekt in der Bildung seiner Phantasmen aus fremden Quellen, nämlich aus Gesehenem, Gehörtem und vielleicht auch unbewusst Überliefertem schöpft. Wenn es ein unbewusstes Phantasieren gibt, dann ist es auch nicht mehr selbstverständlich mit Husserl davon auszugehen, dass das Phantasieren ein bewusstes Subjekt bzw. „Real-Ich" voraussetzt. Es wäre dann nämlich durchaus denkbar, dass sich ein Subjekt des Begehrens erst aus Phantasmen ergeben könnte. Überhaupt müsste die ganze Beziehung zwischen dem Subjekt und seinen Phantasmen neu bedacht werden. Bietet das Phantasma dem Subjekt in allen Fällen einen narzisstischen Schutz oder kann das Subjekt nicht auch das Opfer seiner eigenen Phantasmen werden und sich darin verlieren und verirren? Schließlich herrscht in der Psychoanalyse auch Uneinigkeit über die Fragen, ob Phantasmen nun eigentlich als Hindernisse auf dem Weg zur Wahrheit des eigenen Begehrens verstanden werden müssen, ob sie verbalisierbar oder nur rekonstruierbar sind. Geht es in der psychoanalytischen Behandlung darum, sich seiner Phantasmen zu entledigen oder einem Phantasieren wieder auf die Sprünge zu helfen?

2.1 Die Entwicklung von Freuds Verständnis des Phantasierens

Überblickt man die verschiedenen Phasen von Freuds Beschäftigung mit dem Phantasieren, so lässt sich eine wachsende Tendenz zur Unterscheidung zwischen der freien Aktivität des Phantasierens einerseits und relativ starren schematischen Vorstellungen bzw. Szenarios andererseits beobachten. Insbesondere in Freuds frühen Texten erscheint das Phantasieren meist mit dem negativen Vorzeichen einer Realitätsflucht, einer regressiven Wunschbefriedigung oder einer narzisstischen Erhöhung der eigenen Allmacht. Neben dieser negativ bewerteten Aktivität des Phantasierens setzt sich dann aber immer mehr die Einsicht in eine formgebende und sinnstiftende Rolle der Phantasie durch. Als wesentliche Momente einer „psychischen Realität" vermitteln Phantasien den Bezug des Subjekts auf sein Begehren sowie den Bezug dieses Begehrens auf Objekte. Wie bei Vermittlern üblich, können sich diese Phantasien aber auch in den Vordergrund drängen und diese Bezüge verschatten oder gar verhindern. Allerdings kann weder der negative noch der positive Wert des Phantasierens an seiner Übereinstimmung mit der objektiven, äußeren Wirklichkeit gemessen werden. Psychische Gesundheit zeigt sich nicht in der Anpassung an eine möglicherweise feindliche Wirklichkeit, sondern in der Bewältigung von inneren und äußeren Konflikten. Mit dem Nachweis, dass eine Phantasie der Wirklichkeit nicht entspricht, ist somit über den Wert dieser Phantasie noch gar nichts entschieden.

Freuds frühe Texte sehen im Phantasieren, wie gesagt, vor allem den Versuch, einer schmerzhaften und frustrierenden Realität zu entfliehen. Tagträume, in denen man aus einer unangenehmen Situation flüchtet und sich seine eigenen Wünsche mit Halluzinationen selbst erfüllt, sind das bevorzugte Modell für ein solches Phantasieren. Nicht selten bringt Freud dieses Phantasieren auch in Beziehung zu autoerotischen Betätigungen und regressiven Befriedigungen, mit denen das Subjekt sich für sein Leben in einer enttäuschenden Wirklichkeit entschädigt. Wie Freud es einmal formuliert: Phantasien bilden in unserem Leben ein geheimes „Naturreservat", in dem der eigene Wunsch noch Befehl ist. Wie bei Kompensationsleistungen üblich, führen phantasierte Notlösungen allerdings meist zu neuen Nöten. Dies ist wohl auch die Erklärung für Freuds anfängliche Mühe, dem Phantasieren einen positiven Sinn abzugewinnen. Stellvertretend für diese negative Einschätzung der Rolle, welche die Phantasie in unserem Leben spielt, ist Freuds Behandlung der dichterischen Phantasie. Aus seinem Aufsatz *Der Dichter und das Phantasieren*[6] spricht eine Verkennung der schöpferischen Kraft des Phantasierens, wie man es sonst von Freud nicht gewohnt ist. Freud erweist sich hier als blind für die Einsicht, dass Künstler nicht nur egoistische Kinder sind, die mit der Wirklichkeit nicht zurechtkommen und ihrem grenzenlosen Narzissmus mit regressiven Phantasien frönen. Von der sublimierenden Kraft der Kunst und einer Phantasie, die neue Horizonte eröffnet und das eigene Schicksal in einen größeren Rahmen stellt und damit auch relativiert, ist in diesem Text nie die Rede. Nicht ein Künstler wie Leonardo da Vinci, sondern ein Schriftsteller wie Karl May scheint Freuds Gedanken zum dichterischen Phantasieren Pate gestanden zu haben.

Freuds Briefwechsel mit Wilhelm Fliess (1896–1897) ist auch für das Thema der Phantasie eine ergiebige Quelle. Das Phantasieren erscheint hier weniger in der Gestalt einer Realitätsflucht als vielmehr eines Versuchs, sich etwas Unvorstellbares vorzustellen. Dadurch kommt dem Phantasieren innerhalb der hier neu entdeckten „psychischen Realität" eine Schlüsselrolle zu. Wenn nämlich das als wirklich gilt, was psychisch wirksam ist, dann kann den Phantasien auch dann eine Realität nicht abgesprochen werden, wenn ihr Inhalt fiktiv ist, d.h. durch die Mitmenschen objektiv weder bestätigt noch falsifiziert werden kann. Die infantilen Phantasien, in denen das kleine Kind sich Unverständliches zurechtzulegen versucht, wirken auch im Leben des Erwachsenen nach. So schreibt Freud am 6. April 1897 an Fließ: „Ich meine die hysterischen Phantasien, die regelmäßig, wie ich sehe, auf die Dinge zurückgehen, welche die Kinder früh gehört und erst nachträglich verstanden haben."[7] Dieses Zitat macht deutlich, dass das Phantasieren nicht nur eigene frühere Erlebnisse bewahrt und verarbeitet, sondern seinen Ausgang auch von bloß

„Gehörtem" nehmen kann. Auch wenn das Phantasieren immer (mehr oder weniger) der Funktion einer Selbstdarstellung dient, so kann es sich dabei doch aus einer sprachlichen und zudem oft narrativ gegliederten Erbschaft nähren. Dies gilt insbesondere für diejenigen kindlichen Phantasien, denen Freud in seinem Aufsatz *Der Familienroman der Neurotiker* (1909) nachgegangen ist. Wir kommen auf diesen Text noch zurück. Halten wir vorläufig fest, dass nicht nur eigene, wirkliche Erfahrungen oder verdrängte eigene Wünsche Eingang finden in den Inhalt unserer Phantasien, sondern ebenso gehörte Sprachfetzen oder mythische Erzählungen und Sagen.

Es wird also fraglich, ob man alle Phantasien, deren man sich bedient, auch selbst erschaffen hat und ob man sich des eigenen Phantasierens immer bewusst ist. Mit seiner Hypothese von unbewussten Phantasien und einem unbewussten Phantasieren überschreitet Freud endgültig den Rahmen von Husserls eidetischer Analyse der Akte reinen Phantasierens. Kehrt er damit auch jeder phänomenologischen Bestimmung der Phantasie den Rücken? Nicht ohne Weiteres, denn auch unbewusste Phantasien machen sich (mehr oder weniger deutlich) im Inhalt von Bewusstseinsakten geltend. Es fällt denn auch auf, dass Freuds frühere Texte das Phantasieren vor allem als einen Bestandteil der Erinnerungs- und Traumarbeit untersuchen. Ein Textfragment aus dem Jahr 1914 fasst Freuds frühe Auffassung über den Zusammenhang von unbewussten Phantasien mit Deckerinnerungen und Träumen prägnant zusammen: Deckerinnerungen „repräsentieren die vergessenen Kinderjahre so zureichend wie der manifeste Trauminhalt die Traumgedanken."[8] Nicht nur Deckerinnerungen, sondern auch der Inhalt unserer normalen Erinnerungen wird zwangsläufig mehr oder weniger durch unsere unbewussten Wünsche und Phantasien beeinflusst. Nicht die in Husserls eidetischer Analyse künstlich herauspräparierten „reinen" Phantasien und „reinen" Erinnerungen sind der Normalfall, sondern vielmehr die Mischformen. Eine solche Kontamination unserer Erinnerungen durch unsere Phantasien erhellt nicht nur das Phänomen einer Erinnerungstäuschung, sondern sie erklärt auch, warum Erinnerungen zu neurotischen (nach Freud insbes. hysterischen) Symptomen und anderen pathologischen Folgen führen können. Allgemein gilt, dass unbewusste Phantasien durchaus zu einer bewussten Darstellung kommen können, die ihre Zugehörigkeit zum Unbewussten jedoch keineswegs aufhebt. So etwa in den Fällen, wo eine unbewusste Phantasie sich unter dem Deckmantel einer vermeintlichen Erinnerung (einer sogenannten „Deckerinnerung") oder einer falschen Erinnerung (eines „déjà vu") manifestiert. Ähnliches gilt nach obigem Zitat auch für den Traum. Das „Denken", in dem die Traumarbeit verdrängte Wünsche unter Einbeziehung von Tagesresten zu einem manifesten Trauminhalt verarbeitet, ist in Wirklichkeit weniger ein eigentliches Denken als ein kreatives Phantasieren.

Bedenkt man die Rolle, welche die Phantasien sowohl in den Deckerinnerungen als auch im Träumen spielen, so liegt es nahe, auch bei den Phantasien (gerade so wie bei den Träumen) zwischen einem latenten, unbewussten und einem manifesten, bewussten Inhalt zu unterscheiden. Wenn Freud den manifesten Trauminhalt als den „Königsweg" zum Unbewussten bezeichnet, so gilt das sicher auch für den manifesten Inhalt unseres bewussten Phantasierens. Wenn schon unsere Witze doppelbödig sind, so gilt das sicher in noch vermehrtem Maße für unsere bewussten Phantasien, zu denen wir uns mehr oder weniger freiwillig bekennen.

Unsere Betrachtung hat auch noch einen weiteren Fortschritt gemacht. Die Beobachtung, dass Phantasien meist mit Träumen und Erinnerungen verwoben sind, verdeutlicht nämlich auch den guten Sinn einer Unterscheidung zwischen dem Phantasieren als einer eigenständigen psychischen Tätigkeit und den Phantasmen oder Phantasiebildern als einem formgebenden und sinnstiftenden schematischen Element im Träumen und Erinnern – sowie auch im Wahrnehmen.

2.2 *Phantasieren und Phantasma*

Ein guter Grund zu einer terminologischen Unterscheidung zwischen dem Phantasieren und den Phantasien ergibt sich bei Freud schon allein daraus, dass er in der Aktivität eines freien Phantasierens wenig Positives und Kreatives zu sehen vermag. *Phantasieren* ist für Freud eine reaktive Tätigkeit, mit der das Subjekt sich vor gefährdenden Erfahrungen schützt und mit der es sich für eine wenig lustvolle Lebenswirklichkeit „entschädigt“. Phantasieren dient auch der Abwehr gegen zugleich unverständliche und triebreizende (visuelle und akustische) Wahrnehmungen und Erinnerungen. Freuds frühere Texte betonen vor allem die Rolle des Phantasierens in der kompensatorischen und symptomatischen Verarbeitung der Erinnerungen an frühkindliche traumatische Ereignisse. In den späteren Texten und nach der Entdeckung des Narzissmus erscheint das Phantasieren vermehrt als ein Mechanismus der Abwehr und Kompensation von narzisstischen Kränkungen. *Phantasien* bzw. *Phantasmen* drängen sich als Gegenstand einer eigenen theoretischen Betrachtung zuerst da auf, wo sie nicht mehr auf den mehr oder weniger willkürlichen Inhalt eines solchen kompensatorischen Phantasierens reduziert werden können. Es war vor allem Freuds Beschäftigung mit der Traumarbeit, mit den sogenannten „Urphantasien“ sowie mit dem „Familienroman“ der Neurotiker, die ihn zur Anerkennung einer vom bloßen Phantasieren unterschiedenen Funktion der Phantasmen genötigt haben. Entscheidend war dabei – in philosophischer Sprache ausgedrückt – die Einsicht in die Rolle der Einbildungskraft als dem Vermögen zu einer schematisch ausgebildeten Vermittlung. Einer solchen schematisch vermittelnden Vorstellung bedarf nicht nur der Trieb (oder die Libido) in seinem Verhältnis zu einem wirklichen, Lust spendenden Objekt, sondern auch das Subjekt in seinem Verhältnis zu seinem eigenen Begehren. Anders als etwa in Kants Schematismus verbindet sich diese transzendentale Funktion der Einbildungskraft bei Freud jedoch mit einem Schein, der trügt, und mit dem das Subjekt sich selbst betrügt. Phantasien täuschen. Sie täuschen uns hinweg über die Willkürlichkeiten unseres Begehrens, über die Fremdheit und Unzulänglichkeit aller wirklichen Objekte, über die Unstillbarkeit des menschlichen Verlangens.

Wenn nun aber Phantasmen gleichermaβen notwendig und täuschend sind, handelt es sich dann bei ihnen um notwendige Täuschungen? Oder gibt es wahre und täuschende bzw. mehr oder weniger täuschende Phantasien? Ist es denkbar, dass ein Subjekt sich – etwa am Ende einer psychoanalytischen Behandlung – all seiner Phantasmen entledigt hat und der Wahrheit seines eigenen Begehrens luzid und unerschrocken ins Auge blickt? Diese Fragen können nur dann eine sinnvolle Antwort finden, wenn man voraussetzt, dass man Phantasmen nicht einfach nur „hat" oder zu „verwirklichen" versucht, sondern dass man sich zu seinen eigenen Phantasien auch, und zwar in verschiedener Weise, verhalten kann. Wir werden im Zusammenhang mit unserer Besprechung von Freuds Text aus dem Jahre 1919 *Ein Kind wird geschlagen* noch auf diese Kernfragen zurückkommen.

Die drei Sachfragen, bei deren Behandlung sich eine Unterscheidung zwischen dem bloßen Phantasieren und den schematischen Phantasmen aufdrängt, sind, wie schon angedeutet, der Traum, die Urphantasien und der Familienroman. Jedem dieser Phänomene hat Freud in den Jahren 1900 bis 1909 einen eigenen Text gewidmet.

A. *Die Traumdeutung* (1900)[9] bezeichnet den Traum, die Deckerinnerung und das hysterische Symptom als „Darstellung einer Phantasie". Was so dargestellt wird, muss (entweder in sich selbst oder durch die Darstellung) eine relativ feste Gestalt haben, es kann sich also nicht um den flüchtigen Inhalt eines willkürlichen und kurzlebigen Phantasierens handeln. Ein und dieselbe Phantasie kann zudem offensichtlich auch in verschiedenen Darstellungen zum Ausdruck kommen. Es handelt sich dabei zumeist um eine unbewusste Phantasie, die aber dennoch nicht dasselbe ist wie ein verdrängter Wunsch. Auch muss man die Phantasie noch unterscheiden von ihrer Verwirklichung, etwa unter der Form einer traumhaften Halluzination. Das Phantasma vermittelt also in der Traumarbeit zwischen dem verdrängten Wunsch einerseits und seiner Erfüllung im halluzinierten Traumgeschehen andererseits. Der Wunsch ist der Vater der Phantasie, aber nicht die Phantasie selbst, sondern die Halluzination erfüllt den Wunsch. Die Phantasie gibt, mit anderen Worten, dem Wunsch eine Gestalt, aber der so gestaltete Wunsch bleibt ein Wunsch, der zu seiner Befriedigung des Traums (oder der Ersatzbefriedigung durch ein neurotisches Symptom) bedarf.

B. In seinem späteren Text *Hysterische Phantasien und ihre Beziehung zur Bisexualität* (1908) spricht Freud dann ausdrücklich von „unbewussten Phantasien", die „von jeher unbewusst gewesen, im Unbewussten gebildet worden" sind.[10] Solche Phantasien verdienen eben deswegen „Urphantasien" genannt zu werden, weil sie „von jeher unbewusst gewesen" sind. Es handelt sich also nicht um verdrängte Phantasien, sondern um Phantasmen, die sich dem Subjekt offenbar mit einer gewissen Notwendigkeit aufgedrängt haben. Mit den bewusst inszenierten, kompensatorischen Phantasien eines von der Wirklichkeit enttäuschten Subjekts haben sie somit wenig gemein. Die „im Unbewussten gebildeten" Urphantasmen müssen offenbar eher als ein imaginärer Kernbestand der psychischen Realität verstanden werden, auf den das Subjekt bei der Ausbildung seiner Träume, Deckerinnerungen und neurotischen Symptome spontan und immer wieder zurückgreift. Es handelt sich also auch deswegen um „Urphantasien", weil sie in der Bildung aller weiteren Phantasien eine wichtige

Rolle spielen. Mehr noch als auf alle anderen Phantasmen trifft auf sie die Bestimmung als ein imaginäres Schema zu. Bringt man die Regelmäßigkeit, mit der solche Urphantasien auftreten, mit der biologischen und psychologischen Entwicklung des Kindes in Verbindung, dann muss man auch davon ausgehen, dass diese Urphantasmen durch eine gewisse Allgemeinheit gekennzeichnet sind und somit eine sehr beschränkte individuelle Beliebigkeit aufweisen. Obwohl von Freud hier unerwähnt, ist die Vorstellung der „Urszene" des elterlichen Beischlafs sicher ein solches Urphantasma, das sich bei jedem Kind unbewusst bildet. Ähnliches gilt wohl auch für die Kastrationsphantasie. Der Oedipuskomplex selbst kann zwar nicht ohne Weiteres ein Urphantasma genannt werden, aber seine Verarbeitung ist sicher mit der Mobilisierung von Urphantasien und insbesondere der Urphantasie von der Urszene verbunden.

Die Not, aus der sich die Notwendigkeit der Urphantasien ergibt, ist somit die mit dem Reifungsprozess der kindlichen Libido verbundene psychische Not, sich etwas Unvorstellbares vorstellen zu müssen. Urphantasmen sind also, streng genommen, überhaupt keine subjektiven Vorstellungen, sondern als Darstellungen eines Unvorstellbaren und Undenkbaren eignet ihnen ein gewissermaßen objektiver oder zumindest anonymer Charakter. Als Ausdruck von unbewussten und vor-subjektiven Vorstellungen behalten die Urphantasmen für das Subjekt auch den Charakter von etwas Fremdem und Geheimnisvollem. Es scheint also wenig plausibel, dass das Kleinkind diese Leistung ganz aus dem eigenen, noch sehr beschränkten Vermögen erbringen kann. Es muss also so etwas wie einen angeborenen Schatz von virtuellen imaginären Vorstellungen geben, die Freud selbst mit der phylogenetischen Entwicklung des Menschengeschlechtes in Verbindung bringt. Mit dieser Lehre von phylogenetischen Urphantasien kommt Freud somit Jungs Begriff eines „kollektiven Unbewussten" näher, als er sich einzugestehen bereit war. Seine „Urphantasien" sind nicht nur ursprünglich unbewusst, nicht nur Matrizen für weitere Phantasmen, sondern auch Ausdruck der Verortung des Subjekts in einer geschichtlich tradierten symbolischen Ordnung, die eine Vielzahl von vielen individuellen Begehren miteinander vermittelt. Die imaginären Urphantasien machen uns darauf aufmerksam, dass die menschliche Einbildungskraft symbolischen Einflüssen nicht nur offensteht, sondern von Anfang an von überlieferten symbolischen Elementen zehrt. Die Urphantasmen eines individuellen Subjekts sind zugleich Mythen der Menschheit.

C. Freuds Text *Der Familienroman der Neurotiker* (1909)[11] verdeutlicht diesen Zusammenhang von Phantasie und symbolischer Überlieferung und er macht uns auch darauf aufmerksam, dass Phantasmen einen narrativen Charakter haben können. Wenn das Phantasma eines Familienromans der durch das eigene Begehren geleiteten Darstellung der eigenen Herkunft aus einem Geflecht von fremdem Begehren dient, so muss davon ausgegangen werden, dass dergleichen sich nicht nur beim „Neurotiker" findet. Offensichtlich konnte sich Freud bei seiner Behandlung des Familienromans nie ganz vom Vorurteil befreien, dass es sich dabei um eine bloß reaktive und kompensatorische Phantasiebildung handelt.

Das Phantasma des Familienromans hätte demzufolge seinen Ursprung in der narzisstischen Kränkung, nicht das einzige Kind seiner Eltern zu sein, aus kleinen Verhältnissen zu stammen usw. In Wirklichkeit stellen sich weder die klinische Erfahrung noch theoretische Erwägungen der Anerkennung des Familienromans als ein ‚normales' Urphantasma in den Weg. Zu den bereits genannten Bedeutungen einer „Urphantasie" gesellt sich nun also noch der Bezug des Subjekts auf seine eigene Herkunft. Mit einem sich auf den eigenen Ursprung beziehenden Urphantasma ist hier übrigens weniger die Verarbeitung des sogenannten Geburtstraumas gemeint als vielmehr der kindliche Versuch, seinen eigenen Platz im symbolischen Netzwerk der familiären Ordnung und der damit verbundenen Erwartungen und Wünsche zur Darstellung zu bringen. Im Familienroman beschäftigt sich das Kind mit einer Vergangenheit, die es selbst nicht erlebt hat, und es übt sich ein in die lebenslange Aufgabe, sein eigenes Begehren auf das Begehren der Anderen abzustimmen.

Die symbolisch strukturierende Funktion dieses Urphantasma, das der sozialen und symbolischen Einbettung des kindlichen Begehrens dient, bestätigt sich auch in der bereits bei Freud anzutreffenden Beobachtung, dass die Inhalte des Familienromans sich von Kind zu Kind erstaunlich wenig unterscheiden. Es gibt also offenbar eigentliche Standardversionen des Familienromans. Bringt man den Familienroman, wie alle anderen Urphantasien, zudem mit dem Reifungsprozess der kindlichen Libido in Beziehung, so bietet es sich an, die verschiedenen Typen des Familienromans mit den verschiedenen Typen von (oralen, analen und phallischen) infantilen Sexualtheorien in Verbindung zu setzen. Nicht nur entspräche dann jedem Entwicklungsstadium der kindlichen Sexualität ein eigener Familienroman, sondern diese Familienromane wären dann auch eine Vorlage für die verschiedenen infantilen Sexualtheorien, die sich ja ebenfalls mit der eigenen Herkunft beschäftigen. Eine solche Verankerung der infantilen Sexualtheorien in der symbolischen Struktur des Familienromans macht einmal mehr deutlich, dass die Register des Imaginären und des Symbolischen zumeist miteinander verflochten sind. M. Robert hat unter diesem Gesichtspunkt in ihrer bekannten Monographie zum Familienroman einen Versuch der Einteilung der verschiedenen Typen des Familienromans in zwei große Gruppen unternommen.[12] Als Kostprobe sei hier einzig die Verschränkung des Familienromans vom Typus des „Bastards" mit der ödipalen Problematik und demjenigen vom Typus „Findelkind" mit einer früheren, wesentlich narzisstischen Problematik erwähnt. Beide Typen des Familienromans sind somit in einem leicht erkennbaren Stadium der kindlichen Entwicklung verankert.

Als Darstellung der Struktur des eigenen Begehrens ist der Familienroman zweifellos kein Zufallsprodukt eines willkürlichen Phantasierens, sondern ein Phantasma, und als narrative Inszenierung der eigenen Herkunft ist er ebenso zweifellos ein Urphantasma. Auch handelt es sich dabei um ein Urphantasma, in dem der Diskurs der Anderen, Sagen und Mythen, kurzum: symbolische Überlieferungen, eine bedeutungsvolle Rolle spielen. Mit dem Familienroman verlässt das Phantasma die visuelle Szene und verstrickt sich in Geschichten.

2.3 Verschiedene Arten von Phantasmen

Die Lektüre von Freuds Texten bestätigt also keineswegs das Vorurteil, dass Phantasmen als das Resultat eines Phantasierens verstanden werden müssen, das sich ausschließlich oder auch nur vorzüglich in visuellen Bildern ergeht. Nicht nur gibt es offenbar verschiedene Formen und Modi der Sichtbarkeit von Phantasmen, sondern es gibt auch Phantasmen, in denen das Sehen keine oder eine bloß untergeordnete Rolle spielt. Wir haben auch festgestellt, dass Phantasmen nicht nur aus Bildern und imaginären Szenen bestehen, sondern dass sie sich auch aus der Quelle der Sprache („Gehörtes") und frei erfundener oder überlieferter (kleiner und großer) Erzählungen nähren. Freuds Ausführungen bestätigen somit, dass das Reich des Imaginären und des Symbolischen zwar verschieden strukturiert, dass diese beiden Register menschlicher Erfahrung aber trotzdem sehr eng miteinander verwoben sind. Man möchte die Phantasmen geradezu als eine imaginäre Verarbeitung von symbolischen Elementen oder als symbolhaltige Imaginationen bezeichnen. Sie können jedenfalls nicht schlechthin als eine Form der imaginären Befangenheit (Lacan spricht von „captivation"), als ein Rückzug des Subjekts in seine private Phantasiewelt und als Flucht in eine regressive (autoerotische oder perverse) Befriedigung des eigenen Begehrens bewertet werden. Damit ist auch deutlich, dass es nicht die Aufgabe des Analytikers sein kann, seinen Analysanden von allen Phantasmen zu befreien und ihn dergestalt der nackten Wahrheit seines Begehrens auszuliefern.

Hält man sich an die visuellen Phantasmen, so sind es die verschiedenen Formen der *Sichtbarkeit* und insbesondere der Platz, den das Subjekt in der phantasmatischen Szene einnimmt, welche besondere Aufmerksamkeit verdienen. Im Allgemeinen gebärdet das Subjekt sich als ein Zuschauer, aber es ist in Wirklichkeit am phantasmatischen Geschehen keineswegs so unbeteiligt, wie es (sich selbst) vorgibt. Die unentwegte Wiederholung einer beschränkten Anzahl von Phantasmen, zu denen das Subjekt immer wieder zurückkehrt, verrät vielmehr seine passionierte Anteilnahme und Implikation. Die vorgetäuschte eigene Neutralität und die anonyme Äußerlichkeit der phantasmatischen Szene sollen darüber hinwegtäuschen, dass das Subjekt in Wahrheit sowohl der verantwortliche Autor des Drehbuches als auch der geheime Hauptdarsteller ist. Wenn es sich schließlich zur Einsicht durchringt, dass „*Madame Bovary, c'est moi*", dann hat die Szene ihren phantasmatischen Charakter bereits eingebüßt. Das Subjekt hat dann sein Phantasma bereits abgelegt oder, wie Lacan es formuliert, „durchquert" (*traversé*).

Es verhält sich bei einem ausgestalteten Phantasma also gerade so wie beim Traum: Die als Inspirationsquelle dienende Phantasie wird bis zur Unerkenntlichkeit deformiert, und der bildhaft visuelle Charakter des phantasierten Geschehens verstärkt noch den Eindruck der Distanz. Dies gilt jedenfalls für all diejenigen Phantasmen, auf welche ein Phantasieren zurückgreift, das von verdrängten Wünschen gesteuert wird. Das doppelte Spiel, welches das Subjekt mit seinen Phantasmen spielt, kommt auch darin zum Ausdruck, dass es selbst seinen bewussten und gewissermaßen objektivierten Phantasmen nicht ohne Scheu begegnet und sie nur zurückhaltend ausspricht. Fällt diese Scheu weg und werden Phantasmen hemmungslos verwirklicht, so handelt es sich nicht mehr um neurotische Phantasien, sondern um Strategien der Perversion.

Das neurotische Subjekt bewegt sich somit immer am Rande oder in der Marge seiner bewussten und unbewussten Phantasmen. Es gibt vor, ein bloß externer Zuschauer seines eigenen Begehrens zu sein, das dann folglich auch einem Anderen zugeschrieben werden muss. Dieser zwiespältige Umgang mit seinem eigenen Verlangen kommt in Freuds wichtigstem Text zum Wesen des Phantasma besonders deutlich zum Ausdruck, nämlich in seinem Aufsatz *Ein Kind wird geschlagen* (1919).[13] Man kann das in diesem Text analysierte, komplexe Phantasma schematisch in drei verschiedene „Phasen" gliedern: (1) „Der Vater schlägt das Kind"; (2) „Ich werde vom Vater geschlagen"; (3) „Ein Kind wird geschlagen" oder „Knaben werden von einem Vatervertreter (Lehrer) geschlagen". Vergleicht man diese drei Formulierungen miteinander, so fällt unmittelbar auf, dass die Verbalform nur in der ersten Formulierung aktiv („schlägt"), in den beiden anderen hingegen passiv ist („wird geschlagen"). Darin liegt kein Widerspruch, denn man kann sich darüber freuen, dass der Vater den verhassten Bruder „schlägt" und dass möglicherweise alle anderen Knaben auch „geschlagen werden". Freud kommt nun aber aus verschiedenen Gründen zum Schluss, dass es sich bei dieser Jungmädchenphantasie nicht um ein sadistisches, sondern um ein masochistisches Phantasma handelt. Seine wahre Formulierung müsste also eigentlich lauten: „Ich werde vom Vater geschlagen". Das hat die Patientin von Freud zwar nie selbst so gesagt, aber Freud meint schon aus rein sprachlichen Gründen beweisen zu können, dass der Übergang von der ersten zur dritten Formulierung diese (im Gegensatz zu den beiden anderen) durch die Patientin verschwiegene zweite Formulierung logischerweise impliziert. Deswegen spricht Freud auch von den drei „Phasen" der Formulierung derselben Phantasie. Die deutlichste Formulierung ist nicht zufällig die verschwiegene, und die verschwiegene ist nicht zufällig die einzige, in der das Subjekt seinen Zuschauerplatz verlässt und sich selbst auf die Bühne begibt und dies unter Gebrauch der Ichform bekennt: „Ich werde vom Vater geschlagen". Was verschwiegen wird ist somit letztlich etwas, von dem das Mädchen gar nichts wissen will, nämlich sein verdrängter Wunsch, vom Vater geschlagen zu werden. Wenn ein Phantasma die Darstellung eines *unbewussten* Wunsches ist, dann kann das Subjekt sich zwangsläufig nur in der Form eines Zuschauers und nicht eines Hauptdarstellers manifestieren.

Es liegt nahe, diesem dreigliedrigen Phantasma die Struktur einer verdoppelten Ichspaltung zuzuschreiben. Bekanntlich impliziert jede Ichrede bereits eine Spaltung des Subjekts in den Sprechenden und in den mit dem Personalpronomen „ich" Bezeichneten oder Ausgesprochenen. Hätte das Mädchen wirklich gesagt: „Ich will vom Vater geschlagen werden", so hätte es sich in diesem Sagen zu seinem eigenen Begehren bekannt und sich zugleich dadurch davon distanziert, dass es den Ausdruck seines geheimen Wunsches dem äußerlichen Medium einer natürlichen Sprache und damit auch einer Sprachgemeinschaft anvertraut hätte. Stattdessen verschweigt es seinen eigenen Wunsch und gebärdet sich als unbeteiligte Zuschauerin oder objektive Reporterin eines es nicht weiter angehenden und somit anonymen Geschehens.

Im Stil der Bild-Zeitung wird von ihm kurz und betont sachlich festgestellt: „Der Vater schlägt das Kind“ oder noch griffiger: „Ein Kind wird geschlagen“. An die Stelle des doppelten Ich (sagend und ausgesagt) einer normalen Aussage in der ersten Person tritt hier der Gegensatz zwischen der Nennung eines anonymen geschlagenen Kindes männlichen Geschlechts und einem ungenannt bleibenden weiblichen Zuschauer.

Es ist nicht ganz leicht, diesem komplizierten Sachverhalt einigermaßen gerecht zu werden. Einerseits ist man versucht, die Zuschauerversion als einen listigen oder jedenfalls unaufrichtigen Ersatz für die mit dem Bekenntnis des eigenen Begehrens verbundene Ichspaltung zu verstehen. Andererseits darf man aber nicht vergessen, dass bereits die verschwiegene Aussage „Ich werde vom Vater geschlagen“ genauer besehen bei Freud nicht der bekennende Ausdruck eines expliziten Begehrens ist, sondern vielmehr einer „Phantasie“, in der ein *verdrängter* masochistischer Wunsch zur Darstellung kommt. „Ich werde vom Vater geschlagen“ heißt noch nicht: „Ich will vom Vater geschlagen werden“!

Es gibt also verschiedene Arten von Phantasmen, in denen ein verdrängtes Begehren zur Darstellung kommt. So haben wir in Anspielung auf die Positionierung des Subjekts als Zuschauer oder als Hauptdarsteller bereits auf verschiedene Formen der Sichtbarkeit hingewiesen. Lyotard plädiert in seinem Kommentar zu Freuds Text dafür, die Differenz zwischen den beiden ersten Phasen des Phantasma im Rahmen von Freuds Unterscheidung zwischen „Sachvorstellungen“ und „Wortvorstellungen“ zu verstehen.[14] Dieser Interpretation zufolge wäre das „Ich werde vom Vater geschlagen“ deswegen zugleich ursprünglicher und unaussprechbar, weil es als Sachvorstellung der Sache selbst zu nahe kommt. Diese zweite Phase des Phantasma müsste somit als das Ergebnis einer regressiven Bewegung von der Wortvorstellung „Der Vater schlägt das Kind“ zu einer primitiven Sachvorstellung verstanden werden. Freuds dreigliedriges Phantasma wäre demnach nicht nur eine Darstellung seiner Lehre vom Unbewussten *ad usum delphini*, sondern zugleich ein Beispiel dafür, wie sich verschiedene Elemente zu einer „Figur“ vereinigen können, ohne dabei ihre Differenz bzw. Inkommensurabilität einzubüßen.

Es gibt bei Freud somit nicht nur den Unterschied zwischen bewussten und unbewussten Phantasmen, sondern auch (wie im Traum) Verwandlungen eines Phantasma, die sich entweder im Medium der Wortvorstellungen oder der Sachvorstellungen abspielen. Damit ist auch gesagt, dass selbst visuelle Phantasmen der Sprache bzw. sprachlichen Signifikanten noch entscheidende Elemente verdanken können. Neben diesen visuellen Phantasien gibt es nun aber auch noch Phantasien, die wir „narrativ“ genannt haben. Solchen Phantasmen kommt eine „diskursiv“ zu nennende Struktur zu, sie bedienen sich sprachlicher Artikulationen und vorgegebener Geschichten und sie kennzeichnen sich durch einen zeitlich ausgebreiteten, sukzessiven Ablauf. Visuelle Phantasien sind meist bloße Schnappschüsse, narrative Phantasien hingegen Kurzgeschichten. Momentaufnahmen sieht man sich als unbeteiligter Zuschauer kurz an, während eine Kurzgeschichte den Leser in Bann schlägt und mitreißt. Geschichten sind weniger objektiv, aber auch weniger lebensfremd als bloße Bilder. Aber es gibt bekanntlich auch Bilderromane und *comic strips*. Üblicherweise finden sich in den Phantasien sowohl visuelle als auch narrative Elemente. Reichlicher ausgestaltete Phantasmen gleichen denn auch nicht zufällig Tagträumen, auf die man in bestimmten Situationen immer wieder zurückgreift. Bei beiden handelt es sich um die Darstellung eines Begehrens, das weniger die Erreichung eines festen Zieles anstrebt als vielmehr die unablässige Fortsetzung seiner eigenen Bewegung und Metamorphosen. Phantasmen mit einer starren Form legen das Begehren still oder verdammen es zu endlosen Wiederholungen. Die Beweglichkeit narrativer Phantasmen hingegen beflügelt das Begehren – auch wenn sie das Subjekt über seine eigenen Wünsche im Ungewissen lassen oder es darüber hinwegtäuschen. Wehe dem Analytiker, der mit seiner Interpretation den Analysanden auf eine Momentaufnahme seines Phantasma fixiert, und wehe auch dem Analytiker, der sich durch die Phantasien seines Analysanden mitreißen lässt und sie auf eigenes Konto weiter ausspinnt!

Unter den sogenannten „Urphantasmen" zeichnet sich einzig der „Familienroman" durch seinen gänzlichen Verzicht auf visuelle Bilder aus. Dies ist wohl auch der Grund, warum Freud sich so schwer getan hat, den Familienroman als ein Phantasma anzuerkennen. Die Bezeichnung als „Roman" betont zugleich seinen narrativen und sprachlichen Charakter. Im Familienroman spielen nicht sprechende Bilder eine Schlüsselrolle, sondern die geflüsterten suggestiven Reizworte, von denen Freud in seinem schon zitierten Brief an Fliess schrieb, dass „die Kinder [sie] früh gehört und erst nachträglich verstanden haben." Geheimnisvolle Worte wie „Findelkind" oder „Ehebruch" funktionieren für das Kind wie Signale für die Ausgestaltung seiner wunschgeleiteten Phantasien über die eigene Geburt. Unverstandene Wörter sind keine bloßen sprachlichen Signifikanten (im Sinne von Lacan), die mit anderen Signifikanten verwoben und durch noch andere Signifikanten ersetzt werden können. Sie sind im eigentlichen Sinne überhaupt keine Signifikanten, sondern eben Signale, die einen zum Phantasieren animieren. Die Sprache spricht (nicht immer die Wahrheit!), aber sie phantasiert nicht. Phantasieren im Medium der Sprache ist somit keineswegs ein sprachliches Phantasieren.

Damit ist auch gesagt, dass mit dem Aussprechen des Phantasma dessen phantasmatische Kraft keineswegs von selbst erlischt. Nur wenn es bloß eine einzige Art des Redens gäbe, nur wenn ein Phantasma sich je voll aussprechen ließe und nur wenn ein ausgesprochenes Phantasma *eo ipso* erledigt und abgelegt wäre, dann bedürfte es keines „Durcharbeitens" des Phantasma. Auch im Aussprechen seiner Phantasmen, in denen seine unbewussten Wünsche zur Darstellung kommen, spricht das Subjekt anfänglich noch eine Privatsprache, die sich zur Normalsprache wie ein Dialekt verhält. Dieser eigene Dialekt ist auch für das phantasierende Subjekt nur verständlich mittels einer Übersetzung, zu der es in seiner Verstricktheit in seine eigenen Phantasmen nicht aus eigener Kraft fähig ist. Allerdings eröffnet sich die Möglichkeit einer Übersetzung bzw. einer „Interpretation" erst da, wo sich eine Phantasie sprachlich kundgetan hat. Eine solche sprachliche Kundgabe von Phantasien ist zwar noch keine Befreiung, aber sie bedeutet eine Öffnung. Sie ist ein Angebot, das sich an einen Anderen richtet, und sie bewirkt eine Verlagerung des Schwerpunkts im Phantasma, eine Dezentrierung des phantasierenden Subjekts. Das sprechende Subjekt bewegt sich am Rande seiner bewussten und unbewussten Phantasmen, die ihrerseits schon aus eigenen und fremden, übernommenen und mit eigener Bedeutung aufgeladenen imaginären und symbolischen Elementen zusammengestellt sind. Die zumindest teilweise Entfremdung von den eigenen Phantasmen in der psychoanalytischen Behandlung ist denn auch immer verbunden mit der Einsicht in die unbemerkte Anwesenheit der Anderen in diesen Phantasien. Nicht der Widerspruch bzw. der Hinweis auf die Wirklichkeitsfremdheit seiner Phantasmen befreit das Subjekt aus dessen Schlingen. Zur Überwindung der Starrheit einer Phantasie und des damit verbundenen mechanischen Wiederholungszwangs bedarf es einer anderen, symbolischen Form der Wiederholung in der Übertragung und dem wiederholten Durchsprechen in immer wieder neuen Assoziationszusammenhängen.

Als Maßstab der Wahrheit des Phantasma kann also nicht die äußere Wirklichkeit, sondern letztlich nur das eigene Begehren dienen. Entscheidend für die Struktur des Phantasma ist somit nicht die Scheidung zwischen wirklicher Welt und Phantasiewelt, sondern die Spaltung des Subjekts. Die Selbstentzweiung des Subjekts in ein Subjekt des Begehrens und in ein phantasiertes Subjekt kann sowohl der Darstellung und Realisierung des eigenen Begehrens dienen wie auch der Verdrängung und Selbsttäuschung. Darüber entscheidet letztlich nur das Subjekt – nicht allein, aber selbst.

Aus unserer Lektüre sowohl von Husserl als auch von Freud ergibt sich also die Einsicht, dass wirkliches Leben und Phantasieleben ihrem Wesen nach zwar ganz anders strukturiert sind, dass aber ihr Vollzug durch ein und dasselbe Subjekt sie schon immer miteinander verwoben hat. Der folgenreichste Beitrag der reinen Phantasie zum menschlichen Leben ist denn auch nicht die Möglichkeit der Flucht in ein verantwortungsloses Doppelleben, in dem sich nichts mehr den eigenen narzisstischen Wünschen und Träumen widersetzt. Nicht die Flucht aus dem wirklichen Leben in die Phantasie verändert unser Leben, sondern, umgekehrt, die Rückkehr aus der Phantasie in das wirkliche Leben. Jede Veränderung des eigenen Lebens bedarf zwar der Mithilfe von Anderen, aber sie setzt letztlich doch das subjektive Vermögen voraus, sein wirkliches Leben im Modus eines „Als ob" oder eines „Quasi" zu betrachten. Erst dieser Umgang mit dem eigenen Leben als ein mögliches, erst die Fähigkeit, es so zu erleben, „als ob" es wirklich sei, befreit von der Last, leben zu *müssen*, und eröffnet die Möglichkeit einer (Neu-)Gestaltung dieses Lebens.

Notes

1. Edmund Husserl, *Phantasie, Bildbewusstsein, Erinnerung. Zur Phänomenologie der anschaulichen Vergegenwärtigungen. Texte aus dem Nachlass (1898–1925)*. Hua XXIII. Hrsg. von E. Marbach, Den Haag/Boston/London 1980; Edmund Husserl, *Die Bernauer Manuskripte über das Zeitbewusstsein (1917/18)*. Hua XXXIII. Hrsg. von R. Bernet und D. Lohmar. Dordrecht/Boston/London 2001.
2. Mit "Gegenstand" sind hier und im Folgenden selbstverständlich nicht nur Gegenständlichkeiten dinglicher Art gemeint, sondern auch Zustände, Ereignisse oder Geschichten.
3. Vgl. dazu sowie insbesondere zum Unterschied zwischen einer „Leermodifikation" und einer „Phantasiemodifikation"; Edmund Husserl, *Logische Untersuchungen. Ergänzungsband. Erster Teil. Entwürfe zur Umarbeitung der VI. Untersuchung und zur Vorrede für die*

Neuauflage der Logischen Untersuchungen (Sommer 1913), Hua XX/1. Hg. von U. Melle, Dordrecht/Boston/London 2002, 96 ff.

4. Vgl. Rudolf Bernet, Husserls Begriff des Phantasiebewusstseins als Fundierung von Freuds Begriff des Unbewussten, Hg. von Ch. Jamme, in *Grundlinien der Vernunftkritik*, (Frankfurt a.M.: Suhrkamp 1997), 277–306.
5. Dieses „Phantasie-Ich" (als ein Subjekt, das in der phantasiemäßigen Quasi-Wahrnehmung lebt) darf nicht mit dem Ich verwechselt werden, das wirklich phantasiert, d.h. mit dem Vollzugs-Ich des vergegenwärtigenden Phantasieaktes. Letzteres ist ein „phantasierendes Ich". Dieses phantasierende Ich ist im Gegensatz zum phantasierten Ich ein wirkliches Ich, d.h. ein „Real-Ich", das phantasiert (und gleichzeitig die wirkliche Welt wahrnimmt).
6. Sigmund Freud, *Der Dichter und das Phantasieren* (1908), GW VII, 213–223 (1908).
7. Sigmund Freud, *Aus den Anfängen der Psychoanalyse. Briefe an Wilhelm Fließ. Abhandlungen und Notizen aus den Jahren 1887–1902* (Frankfurt a.M. 1962), 166.
8. Sigmund Freud, *Erinnern, Wiederholen und Durcharbeiten*, GW X, 128.
9. GW II/III.
10. Sigmund Freud, *Hysterische Phantasien und ihre Beziehung zur Bisexualität*, GW VII, 193.
11. GW VII, 227–231.
12. Marthe Robert, *Roman des origines et origines du roman* (Paris: Grasset 1972).
13. Sigmund Freud, "*Ein Kind wird geschlagen*". *Beitrag zur Kenntnis der Entstehung sexueller Perversionen*, GW XII, 197–226.
14. Jean-François Lyotard, *Discours, figure* (Paris: Klincksiek 1971), 327–354.

Depth Phenomenology of the Emotive Dynamic and the Psychoanalytic Experience*

Jagna Brudzińska

Abstract Phenomenological epistemology presents itself as a theory of experience oriented towards the phenomena and achievements of intentional consciousness. At the same time, the phenomenological interrogation of experience signifies a return to the concreteness of human experience, a return to human individuality and specific *tangibility*. We can understand it as a basic and fundamental theory of subjective experience, as a deepened and complex philosophy of subjective genesis, profound and exceptionally differentiated. In genetic phenomenology we are confronted with a new understanding of transcendental subjectivity. From the phenomenological point of view, transcendental subjectivity is not interpreted as a pure ego, as a metaphysical or purely logical or epistemological principle. Rather, it is understood as an infinite stream of consciousness, as a constantly concrete field of experience that is realized passively and actively, in temporal, historical and bodily as well as instinctive-affective and phantasmatic ways. As such, phenomenology shows a particularly intimacy to the psychology as theory of a subjective experience. It especially concerns its relation to the psychoanalysis. Then, in my view, psychoanalysis gains the deepest and most fine-grained psychological insights into the dynamic of psychic-subjective genesis, and these could prove very useful for the phenomenological analysis of subjective genesis.

The Freudian theory of unconsciousness is here interpreted as an area of subjective genesis that is given as a consciousness of the imaginary, of original re-presentation, as a particular form of subjective experience that cannot be immediately perceived, but that can originally be re-presented phantasmatically in intentional and pre-intentional achievements. It appears as a particular kind of phenomenon (emotive, phantasmatic, kinaesthetic) and not as a mere lack of experience. As such it can be

*My sincere gratitude to Francis Bottenberg for the translation of this essay into English, and to Saulius Geniusas and to Jacob Rump for their further careful corrections for the final version.

J. Brudzińska (✉)
Polish Academy of Sciences/Husserl-Archive, University of Cologne, Cologne, Germany
e-mail: jagna.brudzinska@uni-koeln.de

D. Lohmar and J. Brudzińska (eds.), *Founding Psychoanalysis Phenomenologically*,
Phaenomenologica 199, DOI 10.1007/978-94-007-1848-7_2,

systematically observed in psychoanalytic contexts, in experiences of dreams, resistance, transference as well as counter-transference. Phenomenological analysis of this kind of experience makes it possible to give psychoanalysis as inner psychology an epistemological foundation within the framework of a genuine theory of subjectivity and its experience. At the same time phenomenology gains new insights, which concern deep subjective dynamics of processes of individuation as processes of personal and interpersonal genesis. As such it will be defined as depth phenomenology of the emotive dynamic. '-- End of Abstract'

1 Introduction

Subjectivity, its experiencing and its unfolding, are key topics for both phenomenology and psychoanalysis. Yet these two disciplines begin in different places, with different motivations, aims and methods. Phenomenology begins as theory of knowledge, psychoanalysis as clinical method for the treatment of psychic disturbances. Although both come to develop concepts of experiential subjectivity, phenomenology orients itself epistemologically, studying consciousness and its intentional accomplishments, while psychoanalysis orients itself epistemically, bringing into focus the so-called unconscious psychic processes as *psychical reality*. Phenomenology gradually becomes a transcendental philosophy, which strives to demarcate even the most elementary subjective accomplishments within the constitution of objectivity and objective cognition, with the aim of grasping the *a priori* within achieving subjectivity. Its *telos* becomes the grounding of logic by means of unearthing the latter's genesis. Psychoanalysis, on the other hand, aiming toward a general psychology or theory of the human being and of culture that does justice to the phenomena of its clinical praxis, develops into a comprehensive anthropology of human experience. It seems as if the stated aims of both disciplines could not differ more.

Nonetheless, I wish to show that there is a particular, still far too rarely researched, but certainly theoretically and practically promising affinity between the two fields. Specifically, in my view the fertility of genetic phenomenology for the epistemological grounding and further development of psychoanalysis as a science of psychical subjectivity has not yet been sufficiently realized. A phenomenological reading of psychoanalysis also promises crucial insights into the processes and dynamics of passive genesis and into the processes of subjectivity forming at the most elementary levels of passive synthesis, levels of affective-associative generation that will likely prove very helpful for understanding the constitution of our shared world.

To understand this world and its constitution is, according to Husserl, the great task of every science that seeks to pose questions concerning the objectivity of cognition. From the phenomenological perspective, a phenomenology of the *lifeworld* is the ultimate ground of all constitution and cognition. In order to clarify its structure and dynamic, Husserl asserts, it is necessary to reflect on the most original subjective achievements by virtue of which the lifeworld's meaningful content can emerge. This entails the analysis of transcendental subjectivity (always to be taken concretely) in its processes of individuation and communalization [*Vergemeinschaftung*], which must be pursued to the most elementary levels of passive constitution. The self-evidences of these original subjective experiences must be uncovered and made comprehensible. The purpose of this exercise is not least to clarify the, broadly speaking, "unconscious" workings of subjectivity: pre-predicative, pre-intentional, associative experiencing, the emergence and influence of subjective, always affectively structured (and phantasmatically given) tendencies and strivings that precede all active doing. Finally, questions must be considered that concern the very first affections, i.e. the originary stirrings of consciousness that accompany or even make possible the formation of initial pre-given elements within the constitution of objectivity. What is sought is hence the *a priori* of concrete transcendental subjectivity, explored from the genetic perspective. This *a priori* must be emergent, attached to a history of its development and meaning. This history is the history of experiential subjectivity.

This perspective gives genetic phenomenological research a special intimacy to psychology as science of subjectivity, which in turn paves the way for its cooperation with psychoanalysis. For although the latter in no way aspires to transcendental philosophical conclusions, it can still be considered a genetic theory of experiential subjectivity. As such it delivers, in my view, the deepest and most fine-grained psychological insights into the dynamic of psychic-subjective genesis.

Against this background a research program can be outlined for the above mentioned cooperation of phenomenology and psychoanalysis, a program whose several aspects I would like to treat, in a necessarily limited manner, in what follows. These considerations should be prefaced by a short clarification of the relation of phenomenology, including transcendental phenomenology, and psychology to prepare the common ground for the hoped-for collaboration. Then the question whether psychoanalysis can be grasped from a phenomenological perspective as a general psychology of inner experience or even as an intentional and ultimately genetic pure inner psychology can be considered. Building on this, I would like to position psychoanalytic results as an intuitive field for the phenomenology of the lifeworld in regards to the genesis of experiential, lifeworld-constituting subjectivity, while also displaying phenomenology as depth phenomenology of the emotive dynamic.

2 Phenomenology and Psychology

Husserlian phenomenology in its inception already possesses interdisciplinary traits. Phenomenology, as is well-known, begins as an inquiry into the correlation of the *a priori* and empirical sciences, or more precisely, as a reflection on the relation between logic and psychology. At the close of the nineteenth century, this relation was largely defined by the assumption that logic, the science of thought, could be undermined by psychology. In his critique of this view known as psychologism, Husserl shows already in the *Prolegomena to Pure Logic* (1900) that the founding of logical truths on (empirical) psychology is unacceptable, rests on false premises and ignores the essential insights of both disciplines into knowledge competencies. Phenomenology begins with the analysis of these competencies. The author of the *Logical Investigations* distances himself from his own earlier attempts to explain thought and cognitive processes psychologically or psychologistically, unmasking markedly unjustified usurpations of causal-empirical psychology in the areas of epistemology and logic, and postulating a strict distinction between psychological genesis and the result of a cognitive process.[1] Yet this treatment in no way amounts to a final adieu to psychology. Quite the contrary: it practically invites intense epistemological and scientific reflection on logic and also on psychology, and becomes a landmark for the phenomenological study of subjective experience. Pursuit of this study will invite a rapprochement of phenomenology and psychology, though under the umbrella of a pure or immanent study of the psyche.

Already in the first phase of the formation of phenomenological theory two traits of this rapprochement reveal themselves. On the one hand, the Husserlian idea of intentionality is taken up by the study of the psyche and psychopathology, which distance themselves from causal-empirical psychology. On the basis of the descriptive phenomenology of the *Logical Investigations* it becomes possible to study psychical phenomena as intentional experiences, with meaning and sense contexts that determine them, rather than merely interpreting them in terms of concomitant bodily events. Phenomenology, especially the phenomenological study of essences, plays a prominent role in respect to psychology: it helps prepare psychology to become a pure science. It analyzes and describes (specifically the phenomenology of thinking and cognizing) the imagining, judging, epistemic experiences that are to find their genetic explanation and whose empirical law-like connections are to be investigated in psychology. (E. Husserl (1900/01), 166.)[2] In concrete practice this means that descriptive eidetic phenomenology should handle the task of clarifying the basic concepts and phenomena of psychology as the science of experiencing.[3] Psychic phenomena are to be grasped in their immanent contents, free of all causal genetic conditions, and described in terms of their invariant structures. These structures, grasped over the course of phenomenological description, form the secure and adequate foundation for every further empirical psychological investigation: they form the *a priori* for the study of the psyche.

Husserl's research during his Göttingen years (1901–1916) is marked by an intense grappling with phenomenology's concept of experience and frequently returns to the question concerning psychology. The lectures on *The Basic Problems of Phenomenology* from the years 1910/11 play a key role in this development. These are lectures that, so it seems to me, still await exhaustive interpretation in terms of their systematic position and importance for the development of the (transcendental-) phenomenological theory of experience.[4] In them, a comprehensive phenomenological theory of experience is sketched out on transcendental ground for the first time. In these lectures, Husserl tests the program of an *experiential phenomenology,* redefines the concept of subjective experience, and stakes off the experiential terrain of transcendental empiricism, conceived in a novel way. Phenomenology – as he clearly formulates in a note attached to the lecture manuscript – "is here not from the outset regarded as a phenomenological theory concerned with *essences* but rather the attempt is made to consider whether an *experiential phenomenology* is possible, which is not a theory concerned with essence." (E. Husserl (1910/11), 1, n.1 [111], emphasis added.)

These lectures arise from the so-called non-egological position; in other words, the conception of a pure or transcendental I is not yet on the table. And yet Husserl undertakes a comprehensive description of the subjective experiential terrain, which is of central importance for the (especially later) understanding of concrete transcendental subjectivity and its accomplishments as well as its relational structure.

Within the transcendental turn, subjective reality shows itself to us as the temporal flow of lived experiencing, as the streaming present, which enfolds the past as well as the future, perceiving as well as phantasying, remembering as well as expecting. Further, it envelops the life of the self as well as the self of the other. Its accomplishments include actual presentations [*Gegenwärtigungen*] that underlie perceptual processes, as well as representations which bring past events to appearance in the present of experiencing [*Vergegenwärtigungen*], but beyond that also quasi- and co-presentations or empathic presentifications, which make it possible to experience future expectations, dreams, the realm of the not yet actual but possible, as well as the experience of others. We are thus presented with a radical extension of the phenomenological terrain of experience beyond the realm of the *actual impression* or the immediately perceivable.[5] The consciousness of the past, the future, as well as the consciousness of the other become *phenomenological experiential consciousness*. The flow of consciousness, the streaming of lived experience as it shows itself to us in inner experience, prior to any scientific interpretation and explanation, evaluation and assessment, prior to any reduction to physical-causal, naturalizing, or metaphysical-speculative assumptions, is laid out in all of its modes of givenness as an infinite field of subjective life and accomplishment to be experienced.[6]

Husserl designates association as the principle of connection within this infinite flow of consciousness, initially in terms of its formal temporal laws of coexistence and succession. But he also points to the related contents of the motivational complex, which is of great psychological as well as transcendental-genetic significance.[7] For, in that the motivational complex is linked with the contents of pure consciousness, a central notion for the transcendental-genetic study of subjectivity is touched on for the first time: the notion of the stream of consciousness as an encompassing complex of effective tendencies [*Wirkungszusammenhang*], in which the past affects the experience of the present as well as what is still expected, the expected affects the present, which in turn influences the view of the past, the view of the other in the personal, the personal in the experience of the other. And these effects also depend on personal, historical, biographical and bodily factors. Everything depends on everything else, and their interrelation follows particular temporal and motivational laws. Important to note is that the motivational series identified in phenomenological observation are not haphazard, but have their particular *syntax*, their *form* and *rule*.

(cf. E. Husserl (1910/11), 60, [166]) It is the task of the phenomenological science of experience to investigate this syntax, identify the general rules of the motivational experiential complex, as well as to pursue – with concrete and practical topics especially – these motivational relationships in terms of their content. It is also in this context that Husserl for the first time reflects on the meaning of a *transcendental psychology*.[8]

A certain rapprochement with psychology plays out on transcendental-egological ground in the mid 1920s. The results of phenomenological research spanning over 20 years – the theory of subjectivity and the reduction, interpretations of the intentional accomplishments of subjectivity, phenomenological genetics and most of all a new view of the relations between empirical and transcendental subjectivity as two aspects or sides of the *same* consciousness – permit phenomenology to innovatively engage with the results of psychological research. Husserl considers psychology to be a methodical middleman on the path to the transcendental realm of experience, and the way through psychology as the proper way to the reduction.[9] He dedicates a lecture to phenomenological psychology in 1925, in which he deals with its meaning and its possibilities as well as presenting against this backdrop the results of his extended work on the eidetic method. In the *Amsterdam lectures* among others he notes the propaedeutic function psychology bears in relation to pure transcendental phenomenology and emphasizes the parallelism between psychic and transcendental subjectivity.[10] And it is neither accidental nor of lesser importance that in the year 1929 in the *Formal and Transcendental Logic* on the ground of his genetic transcendental phenomenology, Husserl once again foregrounds the significance of psychological experience for the construction of a transcendental theory of the genesis of objectivity and its ideal form. It is precisely here that Husserl expressly defends the meaningfulness of a psychological theory of knowledge, while also emphasizing that a *pure psychology* does not have or perhaps cannot give any answers to transcendental-philosophical questions, though it does make possible the gaining of *structural views* [*Strukturansichten*] in respect to the constitution of achieving subjectivity. As descriptive psychology it marks out the fields of subjective experience, as a priori psychology it attains – or is capable of attaining – insights into the structural relations of intentional consciousness. Husserl here identifies the area of *structural views* as the common research area and the domain of cooperation for transcendental phenomenology and pure inner psychology. He maintains that the recognition of constitutive *structures* of subjectivity is possible both in the natural, psychological, and transcendental attitudes: as the idiosyncratic architectonic of empirical subjectivity, which underlies the constitution of the psyche with its empirical-real states and lived experiences, or as the constitution of transcendental subjectivity, which cannot presuppose any reality. For this reason, Husserl emphasizes, all achievements of cognitive psychology, understood in the above sense as the study of experience in reference to inner-psychic structural views, simultaneously represent, with an appropriate recast gaze, the results of transcendental phenomenology. Even if it should come to an initial mixing of empirical and transcendental knowledge, it is in principle possible to retrospectively resolve such a conflation and to correct it.[11] In the *Crisis*, the paradox of human subjectivity is after all exposed as a pseudo-paradox on empirical-psychological grounds on the one hand and on transcendental grounds on the other. (Cf. E. Husserl (1936), §53 et sqq.)[12]

Even though the new intimacy to psychology brings with it many problems and invites the danger of transcendental psychologism,[13] it does permit a radical deepening of transcendental methodology as well as the further unfolding and differentiation of the genetic train of thought. This especially pertains to late genetic phenomenology of the original constitution of the concrete transcendental I, hence the studies of the thirties having to do with the analyses of the constitution of the transcendental monad, the constitution of the lifeworld and the intersubjective community of monads. Husserl appreciates that psychological experience and its description can open the doors to the *concrete*. He is concerned with a genetic analysis of the sphere of original subjective experience, with a construal of the deep levels of subjective passivity, and the analysis of the laws and law-like tendencies that organize these realms. His attention is increasingly drawn to the processes of emotive-volitional nature, to the area of drive-syntheses in the processes of passive genesis, to pre-egoic instinctive intentionality, to pre-intentional kinaesthetic activity. He admits that the results of inner psychology that pursues genetic connections can deliver immeasurably valuable insights for phenomenological analysis. The question arises, however, *which* psychology can offer such insights and perspectives (as descriptively grasped structural views).

It is precisely at this point, so my thesis holds, that psychoanalysis as experience-bound theory of psychic-subjective life and its genesis is worth taking into account, i.e. as an 'inner psychology', as a psychology from the inner perspective in the sense of phenomenology.

3 Psychoanalysis as Inner Psychology

It is certainly not a matter of course to view psychoanalysis as a pure inner psychology. Its status as a psychological discipline is continually put into question. From its inception it has had to fight in particular the accusation of naturalism. This accusation is especially directed against the drive-theoretical aspect of the theory. Philosophical critiques of psychoanalysis at the start of the twentieth century already leveled this charge and located the problem of naturalism in Freud within his drive-theoretical premise, as for instance in his early analysis of Dasein, or in Karl Jaspers within his existential-philosophical psychopathology. This line of interpretation is countered by hermeneutically oriented works, found for instance in the studies of Paul Ricoeur or Jürgen Habermas. In 1965, Ricoeur offers a phenomenological-hermeneutical reading of psychoanalysis, which emphasizes that the task of psychoanalysis is to produce sense-connections and not causal connections. Its method is to understand meaning through meaning. Causal explanations that reach for drive-type energies (the topical-economical perspective) are to be avoided if one does not wish to end up with naturalism.[14] (How meaning comes from energy is a question that falls by the wayside, though.) Appealing to this, Jürgen Habermas considers the focus of psychoanalytic research to lie in semantic connections. In so doing he disputes Freud's own wishes to build psychoanalytic theory on the natural sciences and speaks in this context of the *scientistic self-misunderstanding* of Freudian meta-psychology.[15] He sums up psychoanalytical therapy as an interpretative and not an explanatory procedure, emphasizing that the analyst as "suitable interpreter" inherits the task of dissolving the communicative blockage of the patient. The fruit of therapy he sees as lying in the growth of meaning in the lived sphere of the patient.[16]

These hermeneutic attempts to reconstruct psychoanalysis – only the central positions were mentioned illustratively here – are exhaustively critiqued by Adolf Grünbaum. Grünbaum works intensively on the *scientistic self-misunderstanding* of psychoanalysis and problematizes its claim to be able to explain semantic connections through causal ones. From the standpoint of an analytical concept of experience, he declares the untenability of these hermeneutic efforts.[17]

Phenomenological-hermeneutical attempts that zero in on psychic productions of meaning, such as the attempt to capture the meaning of drive merely symbolically, does not seal off the possibility of a phenomenological interpretation of basic psychoanalytic assumptions. Moreover, the challenge of a transcendental-phenomenological analysis of psychoanalytic experience is indeed set thereby. From the phenomenological standpoint, the intuitive basis of psychoanalysis is the first question that must be clarified. In other words, the experiential consciousness of psychoanalysis and its intentional structure must be revealed.[18] This can be followed by further analyses into the function or genesis of unconscious effective moments expressed through drives, affect, libido, etc. This research program is phenomenologically more aligned with the area of noetic analysis – an analysis that concentrates on on subjective fulfilments and the differentiation of the structure of elementary subjective accomplishments. This, too, distinguishes it from the above mentioned phenomenological-hermeneutical approaches that concentrate primarily on noematic aspects that refer to objective sense and the semantic content of psychic experiences.

4 The Psychoanalytic Method of Treatment: Free Association and the Discovery of the Involuntary Idea

In 1923, Sigmund Freud defines his psychoanalysis in terms of three aspects: as investigative process, as clinical treatment method, and as culmination of psychological insights harvested from both tracks. He foresees these combined insights growing into a new scientific discipline.[19]

Historically viewed, psychoanalysis begins as a treatment method. Hysteria, compulsion, bodily and psychic suffering that seem without biological-physiological explanation are its first concerns. Charcot's experiments, which Freud familiarizes himself with while in Paris, show him that certain symptoms can be temporarily alleviated through the use of hypnotic suggestion. This points to a complex of *effective* psychic moments that are not accessible to conscious lived experience. In *Studies on Hysteria*, Freud recounts the use of a further procedure, developed by his friend and colleague Joseph Breuer. This is the *cathartic* method, also based on hypnosis, but to a large extent circumventing suggestion. Freud, inspired by Breuer, applies it to hysterical symptoms. The symptom is taken to be a stand-in for a repressed or "strangulated" [*eingeklammert*] affect that once accompanied a pathogenic psychical experience and that cannot easily be recalled. Only recollection from within hypnosis can lead to an adequate abreacting of the affect and thus to liberation from the symptom. It is assumed that in hypnosis, memories, feelings, impulses or thoughts, which originally were linked with the pathogenic situation, are beckoned through suggestion. They find expression, also verbally, and are thus taken back up into conscious experiencing. An *extension of consciousness* – as Freud calls it – takes place. This sequence, only represented schematically here, leads to the dissolution of the symptom.[20] From the theoretical perspective, it establishes the notion that there is a psychic realm that is kept separate from conscious experience – the realm of the unconscious. Its contents withdraw from conscious representation, yet their affective power does not fade, but rather continues to manifest itself in feelings, phantasy and even bodily symptoms. This observation sets the first goal of psychoanalytic therapy, namely the extension of consciousness achieved by reestablishing the original links between representation and affect, leading to recollective – reproductive – reliving and its concomitant neutralizing. Treatments using this method uncover initial insights into the realm of unconscious processes and the pathogenesis of neurotic disruptions. At the same time, they settle the core perspective of psychoanalytic research as the *inner perspective*. From the start, everything depends on the inner *reality* of the patient, on his remembering, reliving, feeling and finally also his understanding and imagining. The extension of consciousness is a genetic moment in the constitution of subjectivity in need of more precise phenomenological analysis. This analysis should be situated within the area of passive genesis; in this context the affective-associative syntheses underlying the process of becoming conscious would be most in need of consideration. Indeed, Freud discovers association there.

The psychoanalytical perspective refines itself with the very nearly revolutionary notion of *free association*. The resistance of some patients towards hypnosis and suggestion, their difficulties with voluntary recollecting, force Freud to distance himself from the cathartic method. He begins to pursue what his patients utter involuntarily. Every involuntary expression is considered a *free association*. The method of *free association* can not only root out isolated unconscious relations of dependency in psychic lived experience that are founded on neurotic symptoms, it can also bring to the light of day the psyche's complex unconscious dynamic and motivation structures. The exploratory field of psychoanalytical treatment is redefined, initially only implicitly. The inner perspective of the patient is foregrounded in a novel way. Freud discovers the free spontaneous idea, a discovery of fundamental importance for the treatment method of psychoanalysis and in effect its theory construction. That which comes spontaneously to mind shows itself to be an *involuntary idea* [*freier Einfall*] and not a coincidence, it is something meaningful, which in the psychoanalytical process can be integrated into the entire lived context, to be relived and understood from within this context. For therapy this means first and foremost that the *involuntary ideas* of the patient lead the clarificatory process, not the assumptions of the analyst, and also not the focus on presumed (pathogenic) experiences and representations. As Laplanche and Pontalis aptly remark, "this persistent search for the pathogenic factor gave way to an emphasis on the patient's spontaneous free self-expression."[21] The individual story of the patient henceforth becomes a topic for psychoanalysis in a novel way. This story presents itself in *involuntary ideas*, and understanding it becomes – to borrow an expression from Wilhelm Dilthey's *Critique of Historical Reason* - "creation along the line of events."[22] Not the reconstruction of the past in new recollections, dependent on reference to factual events, but present (re)living becomes the exploratory field of psychoanalysis. Phenomenologically, we can speak here with good right of the constitution of a quasi-present – of an *other* present which occurs parallel to the *actually* present. Phantasy plays a key role therein.[23] Of course, we are dealing with a multi-layered experiential context. With Husserl, as well as with Dilthey and James we can say that the entire stream of lived experience, with its horizons of the actual and the possible, the real and the phantasied, becomes the field of inquiry for psychoanalysis. The associative complex of reference and effect is laid bare. At the same time, important epistemological questions arise – questions concerning the experience of the *involuntary idea* in regards to its temporal integration, its basis in sensibility, its intentional intuitive structure. These questions can in my opinion be very fruitfully broached on the grounds of the Husserlian phenomenology of imaginary experience. But before I head into just such an analysis, a few more aspects of psychoanalytic experience call for elucidation.

In order to enable the patient to pursue his inner experiencing, his *involuntary ideas*, in as undisturbed a manner as possible, Freud keeps to special therapeutic arrangements: the patient lies on the couch, his body should be in a relaxed pose, demanding no effort from him, the room should be as free of external distractions as possible. The patient is bound to only one rule, the psychoanalytic *ground rule of free association,* as Freud puts it: he must report *everything* that comes to mind.[24] The analyst is also not in the visual field of the patient. These precautions might seem secondary, yet with keen observation we would likely realize that pursuing *involuntary ideas* is not an easy task. We live in the world, hold multiple intentional relations to it, are directed at things, topics, concerns of the day and of life as a whole, we sense others' expectations of us as well as our own. We strive for *rational* dealings with ourselves and our (common) world, we act: valuing, evaluating, preferring, choosing, deciding. The turning inwards, a turning toward one's own experiencing, demands a radical letting go, precisely from that which seems necessary for successful "functioning" in the world: looking past diverse inner, often conflicting impulses, ignoring involuntary ideas, suppressing inappropriate feelings, not losing sight of thematic threads, etc. The "distraction poverty" of the external environment should support this turning inwards, the recumbent pose should benefit the state of the *daydream*.[25] It thereby becomes evident that the turn to the inner, the turn to one's own lived experiencing, is not a merely mental, but also a thoroughly bodily supported phenomenon. This can be of great significance for a theory of subjectivity like the phenomenological one. The conception of and praxis in the psychoanalytic setting in my opinion enables the recuperation of insights concerning the psychosomatic basis of mental achievements, in the sense of the inner psychical, comprehending experience, not in the sense of an external causal genetic analysis of the bodily influences on psychic experience. Moreover, we gain intuitions for handling the question as to how the somatic state is an effective moment in intentional accomplishment.

Now the question arises whether all of the experiences evoked link to special, i.e. pathological forms of psychic activity or to general capacities of psychic subjectivity, its generally valid experiential structures. Psychoanalysis commences after all as the study of neuroses. Freud treats this question quite early on, and his answer is: no, they are general, i.e. normal psychological law-like tendencies. Psychoanalysis grows out of clinical experience, yet its insights are also derived from the realm of normal psychological research. The discovery of the dream marks a milestone in the founding of psychoanalysis as general psychology.

5 The Dream and Unconscious Phantasy as Fields of Subjective Experience

With the application of the method of *free association*, Freud succeeds in gaining ever-deeper insights into the structures of the psychic apparatus and its mode of operation. The analisis of dreams plays an essential role to this end. Aside from analyzing the dreams of his patients, Freud applies the procedure of *free association* to his own self-analyses, in order to crack the code of his own dreams. In the process he hits upon a fundamental discovery that holds many crucial theoretical implications; this is the recognition of dreaming as a normal psychological manifestation of the unconscious. Until then, dreams tended to be viewed as the meaningless remainders of waking psychic activity or as related to somatic processes such as digestion.[26] Freud now postulates in his *Interpretation of Dreams* of 1900 that they represent a meaningful psychic activity, and he promises to deliver evidence for the fact that

> there is a psychological technique which makes it possible to interpret dreams, and that, if that procedure is employed, every dream reveals itself as a psychical structure which has a meaning and which can be inserted at an assignable point in the mental activities of waking life. (S. Freud (1900): S.E. IV, 9)

Dreams and hence also the unconscious attract the attention for their meaning not only in the study of neuroses, but also in the general theory of the psychic. Because dreams, like phenomena treated later on, such as parapraxes [*Fehlleistungen*] and jokes, also appear regularly in normal psychic life, their study sheds light on general psychological law-like tendencies and is not only of relevance for the study of neuroses.

Dreaming is no longer waved aside as a meaningless melee of images or as a medium for expressing highly pathological unconscious contents. Instead, it is grasped as the prominent manifestation of the unconscious, i.e. as the complex of effective tendencies, strivings and wishes in every psyche that are especially linked with original drives. As latent dream-thoughts, they make up the deeper meaning of the dream, but they are transformed by unconscious processing (e.g., displacement, condensation) during sleep, influenced by inner-psychic censoring (as well as by representability constraints) and then appear in the manifest dream. The interpretation of dreams thus has the task of solving the meaning and sense of the latent dream-thoughts, unconscious wishes that are made experienceable and comprehensible through dream expression. Freud develops these findings, which can only be briefly addressed here, in the seventh chapter of his *Interpretation of Dreams* in particular, which is devoted to the *Psychology of dream processes*. It can be taken as the first sketch at a general psychology from the psychoanalytic standpoint.[27] In it, the dream is taken to be the "royal road to knowledge of the unconscious in psychic life," and the unconscious as the actual psychic reality. (Cf. S. Freud (1900): S.E. V, 608) This reality cannot be perceived in the same way the external world can. It nonetheless is noted as a special form of existence for unconscious wishes.[28] Freud shows that these wishes find their appropriate expression in dreams and phantasies, indeed, this is how they become accessible to study. The unconscious as *psychic reality* is grasped psycho-phenomenally as a collection of affective wish-representations, usually originating in drives, which come particularly to light in dreams, and can be thought of as a special form of thinking. As such, they should be of interest to any encompassing theory of subjectivity.

They can in particular serve phenomenology as genetic epistemology and theory of subjective experience. Dreaming as experiential consciousness is as significant to phenomenology as is the dream phenomenon, if not more so. The dream permits the study of dream consciousness as a different experiential mode from that of perceptual awareness. Freud describes not only the mechanisms of dream formation, but also the specific structure of dreaming as a form of thinking. This form of thinking is laid out in *Formulations on the Two Principles of Mental Functioning* of 1911 as *hallucinating* or *phantasying* and interpreted as a psychic activity within the *primary process*. Freud discerns therein a special and primordial form of human thought, from out of which perceptual thought or *secondary process* only later develops. In structural regard, primary thinking (*primary process*) is characterized by contradiction and polysemy, it makes use of the mechanisms of displacement and condensation, it follows no logico-temporal order, and it is image-based. In teleological terms, it seeks out hallucinatory experiences of pleasure and avoids displeasure.

This form of thought is almost wholly replaced by the so-called *secondary process* during the course of a child's development. Gradually, logical and discursive forms of thought, the capacity for abstraction, the linear ordering of time, and so on develop. In its essence, *secondary process* is characterized by the capacity to postpone the satisfaction of wants. In the teleological sense thinking within *secondary process* is subordinate to a pragmatic tendency, which adopts the conditions of (external) reality. Thinking within *primary process* by contrast is ruled by the dictate of the immediate satisfaction of wants and does not recognize the conditions of (objective) reality.[29] From the genetic perspective, Freud assumes that it is the frustration of wants that forces the child to slowly come to recognize the conditions of external reality and to develop pragmatically-oriented thinking. Initially, the *wished for* object is hallucinatorily "postulated," so that the hungry baby hallucinates the mother's breast, for instance. If satisfaction fails, i.e. the want is not satisfied despite *hallucinatory postulation*, then it becomes necessary (for survival) to consider the real relationships of the external world: to represent them and to attempt real changes. The key ability to these ends is delaying the satisfaction of wants. This ability relies on multiple psychological mechanisms,[30] most of all the sensing and representing of time, which develop alongside these processes. From this emerges the premise of the *reality principle* or so-called *reality-testing*, which ushers in the *secondary process*.[31] According to Freud, *primary process* thinking recedes over the course of the development of the *secondary process*. Yet it never vanishes wholly. Freud concludes that the original capacity for *primary process* thinking, which can be described as *wish-led hallucinating,* is never fully relinquished. He emphasizes that a special kind of thinking act, which leads back to the primary process, splits off with the introduction of the reality principle. It is severed from the reality test and remains subject to the pleasure principle: "This activity is *phantasying*, which begins already in children's play, and later, continued as *day-dreaming*, abandons dependence on real objects."(S. Freud (1911): S.E. XII, 222.) The capacity for phantasy, according to Freud, characterizes every mature psychic organization. It is lived out as *unconscious thinking* in dreams especially. (Cf. S. Freud (1911): S.E. XII, 219) In genetic-phenomenological regard we have here to do with essential moments in the constitution of reality or realities and their core experiential modes; we can also say: we have to do with the development of two structures of experiential consciousness. On the one hand there is the development of perceptual consciousness, which is directed towards external reality; on the other, there is phantasy consciousness, which is guided by wishes. The latter can be studied in the phenomena of the dream, child's play, the daydream, or even poetry. From the clinical perspective it takes effect in the symptom.

Freud's analyses of children's games and (hysterical and poetical) phantasies reveal the presence of a constituting consciousness that – phenomenologically speaking – postulates a kind of quasi-reality. He calls this *psychic reality.*

Freud describes how the playing child creates its own world with imaginary objects and relations or brings a new order to its existing world. Its playing is done in great earnestness and is accompanied by intense emotions. It creates for itself an alternative world to experience. Freud emphasizes that the contrast to play so understood is not earnestness, but (objective) reality.[32]

Hence, we are here concerned not with non-serious fun or harmless imitations of reality, but with the meaningful constitutive work of phantasy as experiential consciousness. This constitutive accomplishment is not guided by reality, but by wish, and it generates a parallel – also correcting – experiential present to the common (objective) present. Psychic reality finds expression as a counter-balance to external reality. Viewed from the phenomenological perspective, this entails the constitution of a quasi-present – a performance that takes place synchronically with the experience of the objective present. As supported by further developments in psychoanalysis, these are constitutive accomplishments of key importance for processes of self-realization and object relations.[33] Phantasy and phantasying therein reveal their independent productive capacity. And this capacity of phantasy extends far beyond mere imagistic experiencing. It is also constitutive of the construction of perceptions of external reality and of the life of the other.

Freud discovers this capacity for the first time in the clinical context, with his work on hysterical phantasies. He initially traces these phantasies to actual experiences of seduction. He notes the imitative or re-imaging function of phantasy as recollection and considers this remembering to have the capacity of deferred [*nachträglich*] repression of unbearable representations.[34] With time he recognizes, however, that hysterical phantasies need not be derived from real experiences. In 1897, he revises his earlier assumption to the effect that constitutively at work phantasy is freed from the requirement of a prior event. He concludes that such representations can also function and have effects as *merely* phantasied. He isolates their source in the structure of infantile sexuality and infantile sexual wishes – an assumption that, as is well-known, meets resistance in psychoanalytic circles. Yet, psychoanalytically speaking this discovery is of great significance. (Unconscious) phantasy is grasped in its creative, constitutive work. In 1915, Freud recognizes the "replacement of external reality through the psychical" one as an essential accomplishment of the unconscious, alongside the traits of non-contradiction, atemporality and primary process thinking.[35] If we think at this point about the phenomenon of transference, it can be interpreted as an achievement of unconscious phantasy that influences intersubjective experience. Freud determines that this achievement is in fact most significant for the formation of neuroses. But he also finds it confirmed in the normal psychological realm.

The study of the dreams and daydreams of adolescents and adults allows Freud to see that phantasies, as expressed in dreams, are in the majority of cases unconscious and can be traced back to original libidinous wants or unconscious wishes that were suppressed in the biographical context.[36] The affectivity of these wishes continues to take effect however. It also structures the experiential consciousness of phantasy in dreams.[37] And this structuring is mirrored in the inner temporal construction of phantasying. It is not the linear time of common (external) reality, but a circular time of the unconscious, as it is today frequently termed in psychoanalytic circles.[38] Freud draws attention to the fact that the relation of phantasy to time is very significant, that in phantasy the past, present and future link in and to one another, not in the order of the chronometer, but *on the thread of the wish that runs through them*.[39]

Essential traits of *psychic reality* are thus identified and can be understood in the phenomenological-epistemological sense as an affectively structured experiential and effective complex of constitutive phantasy.

Psychoanalysis teaches us to study and to comprehend this experiential realm. It develops techniques that enable us to gain insights into those spheres that are inaccessible to perceptual consciousness. Beside neurosis these include dream, child's play, and artistic expression. But phantasying as experiential mode also means a lot for the intersubjective context. Within psychoanalysis, the phenomena of transference and counter-transference play a role in clinical praxis, as well as in all social realities. Furthermore, the technique of *evenly suspended attention,* as the form of communication from unconscious to unconscious, can be traced back to the productive capacity of phantasy as experiential consciousness of the unconscious, in fact to its most elementary level. That this phenomenal realm is not subject to mere speculation, but to epistemologically justified experiential modes, can be shown with the aid of phenomenology qua theory of knowledge. With phenomenology, the intuitive bases and sources of the self-evidence of psychoanalytic work on the unconscious can be epistemologically and experientially revealed to be the experiential structure of the phantasmatical-imaginary. This means at the same time that this structure can enrich a phenomenological theory of experience.

6 The Dynamic of Psychoanalytic Experience

6.1 *Resistance and Transference*

With the use of the psychoanalytic procedure, association shows itself to possess a highly dynamic nature. What it reveals is not a harmonious flow of experiencing. Rather, imagistic and emotional breaks, eruptions, and contradictions determine the dynamic of experiencing. Conflict phenomena appear. Tendencies hit against counter-tendencies, representations against counter-representations, feelings against counter-feelings. Interruptions, selections, inhibitions, the prevention of involuntary ideas, and even sensations of inner emptiness result. Ideas are kept from spontaneous utterance or even from appearing altogether. This allows Freud to gain insight into the subjective moment of inner-psychic *resistance.* This moment is to become the special subject of psychoanalytic treatment. According to Freud, innerpsychic resistance expresses the subjective moment of inner-psychic conflict that defines a neurosis not only in genetic but also in structural terms.[40]

Transference is traced out as a singular and decisive method for the treatment of inner-psychic resistance. Freud discovers transference while still using the cathartic method. It is in general an unconscious process that actualizes earlier influential relationship patterns *(clichés)*, or libidinous, and thus unconscious, sexually driven felt attitudes towards desires and expectations, which in the psychoanalytic situation are attached to the analyst, but originally and in their original sense belonged to prior objects.[41] The psychoanalyst becomes, to a certain extent, a space of *projection.*

In his *Studies on Hysteria*, Freud considers transference as a form of resistance and an impediment to treatment. (Cf. S. Freud (1895): S.E. II, 302 et sqq.) In subsequent years he even acknowledges it to constitute the strongest resistance to treatment. (Cf. S. Freud (1912): S.E., 101) But with time he discovers that it also represents an invaluable opportunity for working out the patient's unconscious conflicts. Transference gains a central place in the domain of psychoanalytic treatment.[42] In transference, the unconscious dynamic seems to gain expression, if not in representational, so at least in a specifically apparent form. Here, too, the phenomenological question concerning the experiential awareness of this activity arises. We have here less to do with an impressionally-founded perceptual consciousness than with the constitutive accomplishments of phantasy consciousness. There are unconscious phantasies of libidinous origin, which co-determine the perception of otherness.

From the beginning, Freud assumes the drive forces of neurotic symptom formation to be of a sexual nature. He constructs his theory believing initially that it is sufficient or that it is possible to recall the earlier – pathogenic – experiences of sexual life that were repressed, in order to liberate their originally accompanying, so to speak *strangulated* affects. Every liberation should immediately release the patient from any neurosis-dictated effects of these affects. He then recognizes, though, that the experiences in play are not always real and hence cannot be reconstructed. Further, he notes that the recollection of earlier experience in the sense of reproducing representations is often not possible at all. In theoretical regard, his interest shifts from individual affects to the fate of the *libido* as the drive-oriented, sexual energy of the psychic.[43] But the goals of the libido are only partially known. The lived experiences and experiential contexts which determine the fate of the libido cannot easily be recollected in conscious representations. Freud does observe, though, that these unconscious goals find partial expression in (hallucinatory) wishes and most of all emerge in the phenomenon of *transference*, albeit alongside strong resistances. He presents his insights as early as 1914 in a short volume titled, *Remembering, Repeating, and Working-Through,* where he deals with a phenomenologically especially interesting – dynamic – structure of remembering, namely that of *acting out.* He states: "the patient does not *remember* anything of what he has forgotten and repressed, but *acts* it out. He reproduces it not as a memory but as an action; he *repeats* it, without, of course, knowing that he is repeating it." (S. Freud (1914), S.E. XII, 149) As examples of such *remembering as acting out* Freud mentions among other things the sulky and doubting behavior of the patient toward the authority of the doctor, which in earlier times characterized his behavior toward parental authority. Freud describes the patient's earlier experienced helplessness, his early feelings of shame and finally the failure of his infantile sexual exploration, which the analysand, in the therapeutic context, allows to emerge in the form of *a tangle of blurred dreams and associations*, expressing involuntary ideas, severe complaints about the failure of every intention and the incapacity to complete projects, and so on. (Cf. S. Freud (1914), S.E. XII, 149) Should the resistances to remembering and appropriation be overcome, so the patient comes to understand the connections emotionally. We have here a kind of emotional evidence, which seems to characterize processes of self-becoming. In a special sense, a *retrospective* appropriation occurs of the patient's own psychic life that had become other. The retrospectiveness receives a special phenomenological sense, for it realizes itself in a double present: the present and the past as quasi-present.

Freud speaks here of a reproducing in the present, as a "reproducing on psychical ground." (Cf. S. Freud (1914), S.E. XII, 153) But the presence of remembering as acting out also points to an intentional structure other than the one of the past's presentification in recollection. In the first case we are dealing with the simple consciousness of experience, which is not, however, perception and which shows a non-reflective structure. In the second, we have a consciousness of the past that is grounded in perception and shows a reflective structure. Two different kinds of accomplishment of phantasy consciousness are exhibited here: the imaginative and the imaginary. Imaginative (recreating) accomplishment is realized in the reproductive consciousness of memory being made present; the original imaginary accomplishment is realized in quasi-presenting. The latter turns out in epistemological respect to be the actual experiential structure of the unconscious from the phenomenological perspective. Freud speaks here of *repetition*, which he considers in its relation to transference and resistance, thereby gaining the insight that transference is "itself only a piece of repetition, and that the repetition is a transference of the forgotten past not only on to the doctor but also on to all the other aspects of the current situation." (S. Freud (1914): S.E., 150.) Furthermore, Freud notices that the greater the resistance to remembering, the more intensely remembering is expressed through acting out, i.e. repeating. This lets him conclude that illness should not be treated "as an event of the past, but as a present-day force." (S. Freud (1914): S.E., 151) Working on this power, working on remembering in acting out defines the dynamic of the psychoanalytical situation. Theoretically speaking, this work permits the discovery of unconscious mechanisms, which unconsciously co-determine the formation of subjective and intersubjective psychic reality, the so-called *defense mechanisms*: projection, identification, disavowal, splitting, idealization, displacement, negation, undoing (what has been done), intellectualization, repression, rationalization, sublimation, etc.[44] In the frame of a transcendental analysis of the genesis of subjectivity, such mechanisms can be seen as noetic (subjective) accomplishments in the constitution of reality. They are then to be interpreted as content-determined, affectively structured accomplishments within passive genesis. The consideration of such mechanisms, as they appear in the processes of transference in psychoanalytic treatment, could prove particularly fruitful for the phenomenological analysis of the constitution of subjective as well as intersubjective reality.

6.2 The Phenomenon of Resonance and Communication from Unconscious to Unconscious

Regarding transference, a further phenomenon needs to be mentioned, a phenomenon which may be of great importance both for the classifying of psychoanalysis as inner psychology as well as for the phenomenology of intersubjectivity: countertransference. Generally speaking, it consists of the psychoanalyst's equally unconscious reactions to the transference of the patient, or in an extended sense to his person. The reactions of the analyst can vary widely – emotive movements, mental processes, bodily sensations that could easily be overlooked or misinterpreted by the unschooled. In his clinical practice, Freud distills the possibility that these are *resonances* of the other psyche, a kind of *echo* of the other unconscious. At one place he remarks that "everyone possesses in his own unconscious an instrument with which he can interpret the utterances of the unconscious in other people"[45] and treats counter-transference as a particular mode of communication between the unconscious of the analyst and that of the analysand.

> Just as the patient must relate everything that his self-observation can detect, and keep back all the logical and affective objections that seek to induce him to make a selection from among them, so the doctor must put himself in a position to make use of everything he is told for the purposes of interpretation and of recognizing the concealed unconscious material without substituting a censorship of his own for the selection that the patient has forgone. To put it in a formula: he must turn his own unconscious like a receptive organ towards the transmitting unconscious of the patient. He must adjust himself to the patient as a telephone receiver is adjusted to the transmitting microphone. Just as the receiver converts back into sound waves the electric oscillations in the telephone line which were set up by sound waves, so the doctor's unconscious is able, from the derivatives of the unconscious which are communicated to him, to reconstruct that unconscious, which has determined the patient's free associations.[46]

The metaphor of the telephone receiver chiefly illustrates the concept of an inner resonance space that the psychoanalyst presents to the analysand as a resonance space of his own unconscious against the other unconscious.[47] In this context Freud describes the phenomenon of *evenly suspended attention* [*gleichschwebende Aufmerksamkeit*], which he takes to be the counter-part to the basic rule of *free association*. Here, too, Freud decides on certain framing conditions. He demands the relinquishing of all tools, such as note-taking or committing particular details to memory. Everything that emerges from the side of the analysand is to be given just the same *evenly suspended attention*. And this entails a special *letting go*. The personal motivations of the analyst must remain latent, his presuppositions must not shape his perception of the other psyche. This in effect amounts to not making any effort to analyze, but simply listening and allowing the patient's utterances to take their effect. It is certainly no easy task. Freud hopes that the training of the candidate analyst enables him to discern his own equally unconscious motivations and expectations, and so become immune to their seduction in later treatment sessions. Freud considers this special abstention a condition for bringing the novel and previously unknown into the open.[48]

Phenomenologically speaking, this notion introduces a highly interesting experiential structure, a structure that could be of particular interest to the phenomenology of perceiving the experience of another. It consists of a certain unintending attention, a dreamlike state even.[49] Freud here offers a challenging concept of the understanding that does not begin with the interpretation of a grasped noematic content, but instead reaches much deeper and, crucially, takes into account noetic achievements. It begins with the passivity of understanding and concerns the inner perception of one's own and another's noetic processes and noematic contents, the latter of which find an echo in one's own unconscious. These are associative-affective awakenings of subjective or intersubjective tendencies that are sensed, strivings and counter-strivings, disjointed phantasies and seemingly unmotivated involuntary ideas noticed in their transformations, developments and effects.

And this noticing seems to be completely different from logico-discursive processes and activities.

From a phenomenological point of view, we have here to do with a highly complicated phenomenon in need of elucidation. On the one hand, the unconscious as a *giving* [*gebend*] consciousness should be analyzed in its intentional structure. On the other, the phenomenon of resonance (the unconscious as *receiving organ*) is in need of phenomenological epistemological clarification, along with *evenly suspended attention* as an emotionally structured, medial and pre-intentional thinking embedded in the temporal structure of the quasi-present.

7 Phenomenology of Phantasy and the Emotive Dynamic of Unconscious Genesis

Phenomenology as a theory of experience and knowledge is bound from the beginning to a demand for the intuitability [*Anschaulichkeit*] of its finds. Of course, the concept of simple sensuous intuition is profoundly reinterpreted and becomes more differentiated over the course of the development of phenomenological epistemology. The special significance of phantasy is grasped in the process. Alongside simple sense-perceptual intuition, such as is achieved in straight-forward perception, Husserl uncovers simple (imaginary) intuition of pure phantasy-consciousness in its primordial and immediately accomplishing intentional structure, namely as phantasmatic consciousness, which performs not only re-imaging (image consciousness), but also originarily re-presentational functions. Phantasy is rehabilitated as *primordial achieving consciousness,* or as *originarily giving consciousness.* In my view, every attempt is also made to place pure phantasy-experience, phantasmatic-imaginary experience, on par as an experiential mode with percept-based perception. One can legitimately speak of the *bivalent relation* between the two experiential and effective orders of subjective life: that of the phantasmatic-imaginary and that of the impressional-perceptual.[50]

Phantasmatic sensibility inherits incredible significance in the process. In 1905, Husserl concludes that phantasms, in contrast to impressions or sensations, fulfill the function of representing something *other*, something not given impressionally. The phantasm – so Husserl suggests – "[primarily] has the function of being taken as something else". (E. Husserl (1904/05), 87) In other words, it counts for everything that presently or principally cannot be transmitted via the senses and yet still occurs in experience.[51] On the one hand, these include imaginative contents that fill the gaps in the building of perceptions and memories. On the other, these are principally imperceptible contents, especially of inner sensibility, which are derived from drives and instinctive tendencies, sensuous feelings, kinaesthetic sensations and somatic experience. Alternatively, as is shown in later genetic phenomenology especially, these are manifestations of psychic otherness within one's own experiencing. Phantasms seem to serve primordial representational and medializing functions in such cases. As long as we remain in the realm of analysis of perceptual awareness, we do not indeed notice much of the primordiality of phantasmatic accomplishment. To be sure, every perceptual representation is built on phantasmatic-imaginative *mediations*, as the phenomenological analysis of intentionality demonstrates. In every perceiving we anticipate aspects of objects that are not sensuously perceivable, we "see" for instance the whole house, not only its sides as evidenced by sense-impressional means, we hence "see" whole objects. The phantasmatic material required for this operation serves in the building of intentions of expectation in regards to the constitution of so-called objective reality and obeys the demand for the uniformity of its experience. But we also all have experiences that hinder this uniformity, that shatter it even. We experience contradiction and uncertainty, for example. Doubt, inhibition, ambivalence suddenly arise. Seemingly unmotivated breaks in mood can influence the course of experience. Sometimes there are images that cannot be spontaneously understood, or *inappropriate* feelings. Even simple bodily manifestations such as tensions or releases take over these functions. All are best viewed as phantasmatic *eruptions* into experience. As such they can make us aware of elements as yet unnoticed, but nonetheless operative. As experiences of fear, for instance, they can protect us from dangers not recognized in time, they can signal the wants and needs of our bodies and minds. Most of all, what psychoanalysis in particular brings to light, originary phantasmatic activity takes effect in dreaming and in hallucinating.[52] Here we can also observe that such phantasmatic eruption follows its own logic: a logic that differs from that of perception. It is guided not by the uniformity constraint of the objective world, but rather by individual, indeed even private goals and interests. Following Freud, we can speak here of the *logic of the wish* - with its specific structure of time, its needs motivated associations and emotive founded intuitions.

Husserl, too, concedes that phantasy consciousness differs essentially from intuiting perceptually, which is oriented by the identity of the object that is to be perceived, being led on, so to speak, by its uniformity and coherence. That which is experienced in phantasy, Husserl assesses, cannot necessarily be measured according to the rules of classical logic. Original affective tendencies and phenomena, emotively determined and phantasmatically realized processes are often particularly characterized by a sort of inner contradictoriness. Husserl speaks in this context of a particular trait of phantasy consciousness, of its *protean* transformative character, which is contrasted with the synthetic unity of perceptual appearances and appearances of perceptually-based image-consciousness.[53]

Phenomenology uncovers particular traits of phantasy experience; its transformative flexibility is not beholden to the identity of the object, does not have to orient itself to real spatio-temporal order, follows its own, often initially hidden goals. In late genetic phenomenology, this take becomes more sophisticated. Specifically, Husserl locates drive as well as instinct to be at work in the passive structure of intentionality. He finds anticipatory intentions that are determined drive-affectively and as such continually intervene in perception. Moreover, he finds phantasmatic representations that can be traced back to these intentions, which constantly operate on elements of our experience, inscribing, overwriting, pushing away, or transforming them. The transformative flexibility of phantasy inherits a teleological vein.

In the context of his later investigation into passive synthesis, Husserl observes the moment of auto-affective subjective awakenings, which we for instance can observe in our daydreams. Suddenly our attention is redirected, images are formed that have nothing to do with the actual situation. We certainly know it from our everyday experience: When we are hungry or tired, images of eating or of relaxing situations verily crowd in on us; when we miss someone that person comes, as it were, unbidden to our representations. Sometimes these representations are stirred by something in our perceptual field, Husserl says, and from this so-termed *pregivenness* pleasant wish-representations or unpleasant fear-representations form and are further transformed. With Freud we can say that phantasy, with its protean transformative range, associatively follows the impulses of the body or deeper-lying psychosomatic wants and wishes striving for fulfillment. For the sake of these wants associative analogies are formed, representations are transformed. From the economical psychoanalytic standpoint, one could speak here of a gratification compulsion. In structural respect, we are dealing with primary processes that Freudian description would call phantasying or hallucinating and that follow the logic of the wish. In this case, the associative capacity places itself in the service of the wish. The ultimate source of the wish is, according to Freud, libidinous, in effect drive-based. But Husserl, too, cites this drive-based, instinctual, associatively realized trait of intentionality. In his studies on passive genesis, he tracks the elementary, pre-intentional accomplishments of inner sensibility, which follow the primordial tendencies of the body. In 1932, he even addresses a direct relation to Freud:

> [The] entire remaining unfulfilled of a drive as absolute inhibition [persists] in subjectivity, in every living present of propelling actuality, [which] incessantly screams, as it were, for completion. Naturally this anticipates Freudian psychoanalysis with its strangulated affects, its 'repressions,' and so on. Obviously, the radical element for the clarification of that which is really subjective fact in these psychoanalytic matters is to be found here. (Husserl, Ms. B II 3, 16a)[54]

Here Husserl adresses the deep emotive moments of passive intentionality, about the originary tendencies of the body, its instincts and drives, which in a certain sense remain blind volitions, indefinite and yet still affective wants at work that cannot be grasped as pregiven elements of an impressional-perceptual nature.

Already at the start of his genetic investigation into the affective function in associative process, Husserl remarks upon the fact that association realizes itself as an *awakening transfer of affection* that is constructed according to a lawfulness based on essential needs.[55] This thesis permits him to interpret the objective organization of the impressional sphere as an affectively dynamic one. From the genetic perspective, the affective liveliness of the primal impressional sphere achieves special importance as a *material* or *hyletic*, hence sensuously founded, and *affectively* structured complex of effective tendencies, which creates the first *formations* of the impressional sphere: initial separations and overlappings, risings and fallings, differentiations amongst and against elements in the field of the living present. Here Husserl again draws on the very plastic metaphor of the *affective relief* – the relief of *noticeability, noticing,* and *effectiveness* –, which he assesses to be the *concrete* basis for and subject matter of the structurally dynamic (awakening) relations of the primordial constitutive sphere.[56]

The *relief* structure, seen to a certain extent 'from the outside' as a finished product, lets itself on the one hand be conceived as the context for the *objective* capacity to affect, as the terrain on which the first pregiven sense-affective elements are noticed and acted upon by the I.

On the other hand, this striking metaphor evokes the *subjective* side of primordial constitution, namely the *subjective preparedness* or *tendency* to permit one's being affected. For, as Husserl says: "In terms of the hyletic data the I is being affected, in terms of the I there is a tending, striving towards" (Ms. B III 9, 70a). For this *subjective* preparedness or tendency is not a mere formal answer to pregiven external, impressional elements. It always bears the stamp of its origins as soma, body, drive, as biographical or situational context, or even as the other's significance to me. It thus functions as transcendental expression of the influence of biological, anthropological and cultural determinations, as well as of the concrete history of the *I*. For this reason, it continually surfaces in the concept of *interest* in Husserl's genetic phenomenology, as an interest that plays a role in all perceptual processes.

The phenomenology of the affective relief sheds light on the awakening processes at work in the method of free association, with consideration for the constitutive role of inner sensibility in the formation of the primal associative sphere. It can, as a consequence, provide an epistemological clarification of the psychoanalytic thesis concerning libidinous accomplishment in the constitution of perceptions and phantasies. A systematic analysis of these relations – only a basic outline could be provided here – holds the promise of a more sophisticated and more probing account of passive genesis. Chiefly, it can help with the further formulation of the teleological character of passive genesis. Defense mechanisms, so termed and studied by psychoanalysis, could then be interpreted as formative mechanisms and figures in the passive sphere, constructing associative but most of all dissociative processes (repression, displacement, splitting etc.). These processes would have to be considered in the analyses of perception, self-realization, and most of all the intersubjective processes that underlie the constitution of our shared world.

Regarding the structure of inner time consciousness, this last analysis would treat the co-presentations mentioned earlier – the co-experiencing that is part of the synchronic, phantasmatic medialization of the other. This structure differs markedly from that of reproductive analogizing, which foregoes all synchronicity. This latter consists of passive processes of the quasi-sensing of the other. In the context of these experiences, the subject does not show herself as only passive and pathetic. She shows herself as capable of primal *sym-pathetic* experiencing, capable of an originary emotive experiencing of the other. Husserl himself acknowledges the phenomenon of the sym-pathetic in one of his later commentaries on the *Fifth Cartesian Meditation*, namely in discussing the phenomena of communalization. He speaks of the primal *commerce* in sym-pathy. He emphasizes that the other is already there for me, prior to any intentional act of comprehension, she *speaks to* me, whether I decide to attend further to her or not – she moves me and effects something:

> We can say address (*Angang*) in place of contact (*Umgang*); psyches are not there only for themselves, rather they concern one another. (...) It (the other I) already concerns me prior to any contact with it, I (...) not only experience, but also live with, perceive with, believe with, judge with, agree with, disagree with, doubt, feel joy with, fear with etc. its life *eo ipso*. All the modi of this With are modi of primal communalization in which I, living in my (primordial, original) life, at the same time *live with* the other life, which for me is empathetically felt as co-existing, a unity of life [is] thus established along with an I-You-harmony of the ego-poles through the medium of empathy. (Hua XXXVIII, 342)

This description lets us go back to the psychoanalytic study of phenomena like transference and conter-transference, in which the originally intersubjective, pre-predicative experience of resonance appears. As such, these phenomena mark a field for analysis of subjective sympathetical genesis and have for this reason a great significance for the phenomenological study of intersubjective constitution. We can learn here, in which way the other *reasons* in me, and does so prior to any activity of reflection. The original feeling-with, sensing-with or experiencing-with is expressed in primary phantasmatic manifestations prior to any act of comprehension. This permanent involvement in the other works itself out in mutual influencings, but also in emotively realized dependencies, conflicts, and ambivalences. In everyday life, this takes effect in simple phenomena such as the influencing of one another's moods or spontaneously feeling the pain or the joy of the other, for instance. All this also has somatic effect: whether it is 'contagious' laughing, or blushing for another's shame in social contexts.

We can think at this juncture of the psychoanalytic technique of *evenly suspended attention* as the analytical access to the other's psyche, which may open up for phenomenology a highly interesting cognitive structure of sym-pathetic experience.

8 Conclusion

To sum up we can resolve that psychoanalysis as treatment method as well as general psychology can in every respect be considered a psychology of inner experience. Further, it can be considered the most radical inner psychology, for it not only introspectively schematizes conscious representations, it also develops complex methods and concepts, especially for the investigation of unconscious motivations and subjective processes. The discovery of the free involuntary idea and of the dream as meaningful psychic phenomena and experiential terrain of the unconscious is of fundamental significance. Investigation into dream and dreaming or phantasying as normal psychological subjective processes in particular lends psychoanalysis the status of a general psychology of inner experience. The unconscious is no longer conceived as a residuum of repressed pathogenic affects that must be eliminated. Rather, it is understood as the productive complex in every psychic life of effective tendencies, strivings and forces, which come to light psychically and become accessible to study in the form of affective wish representations. Phantasy is thereby acknowledged as an experiential consciousness that is co-constitutive in the building of our lifeworld. The lifeworld will always remain the world of our goals, needs and wishes, our fears and anxieties, hopes and disappointments, in the end also the world of our bodies, our drives and instincts as well as our bonds and intersubjective relations. From the genetic standpoint, this is the world of our continuing individuation as personal subjects, as well as our – pre-intentional – communalization.

The constitution of the lifeworld always takes place between the poles of individuation and communalization. Psychoanalytic experience especially uncovers the unconscious dynamics of this constitution, thanks to the specific techniques described above. These techniques permit systematic observation of this domain of experience. Psychoanalysis thus offers lifeworld phenomenology an incredibly valuable intuitive scope in matters concerning the apriori of the lifeworld, as the apriori of concrete subjectivity and its genesis.

The phenomenology of the lifeworld can hence be viewed as the systematic site for the integration of psychoanalytic results into a philosophical theory of subjectivity and of subjective experience.

Notes

1. The status of psychology in Husserl's work is dealt with in a systematic way in H. Drüe (1963), *Edmund Husserls System der Phänomenologischen Psychologie* (Berlin: Walter de Gruyter, 1963).
2. E. Husserl (1900/01), *Logical Investigations,* vol. 1, trans. J. N. Findlay (London: Routledge and Kegan Paul, 1970), 166. Husserl's texts will be cited directly in the text in abbreviated format (author, year of origin, page).
3. Worth mentioning here is the work of T. Lipps, M. Geiger, A. Pfänder, Max Scheler but also of L. Binswanger or K. Jaspers.
4. These lectures were printed as text no. 6 in Hua XIII, the first volume of the *Phenomenology of Intersubjectivity*. (English translation: E. Husserl (1910/11), *The Basic Problems of Phenomenology. From the Lectures, Winter Semester, 1910–1911*, trans. I. Farin and J. G. Hart (Dordrecht: Springer, 2006).) Their systematic significance for phenomenology, which extends far beyond the specific topic of intersubjectivity, was frequently invoked by Husserl himself, who repeatedly spoke of develop them into an introduction to phenomenology. Cf. I. Kern: *Einleitung* zur *Phänomenologie der Intersubjektivität* (1905–1920), in: Hua XIII, VI ff. Husserl's texts found in *Husserliana* editions will be cited: Hua, volume (numeral), page.
5. "The phenomenological (not eidetic) reduction thereby yields the possibility, within the subjective (transcendental-subjective) sphere, to go beyond what is actually impressional." (E. Husserl (1910/11), 1, n.1[177]).
6. The entire stream of consciousness thus becomes "an experiential field of its own, a region of theoretical discovery." (E. Husserl (1910/11), 73 [177]); "Whereas phenomenological perception, with a suitable qualification, can claim absolute indubitability, this does not hold [...] for these new forms of the phenomenological experience. Yet experience is experience; as such it has its value. [...] If we suppose that a similar sketch can be made of expectation, then it becomes really evident that phenomenological experience does not depend on isolated cogitationes that are presences (*Gegenwärtigkeiten*) noticed now, but, rather, [...] phenomenological experience extends over the whole stream of consciousness, as a unique temporal context

which, however, in its total breadth and length does not fall under the light of intuition." (E. Husserl (1910/11), 72 [176].)

7. "And it is a discovery of enormous importance *that each natural experience, taken as immanent being, motivates a manifold of other natural experiences and a manifold of real possibilities of natural experiences, and that we can explicate these motivational contexts, which are contexts of pure consciousness, and direct our gaze at them.*" (E. Husserl (1910/11), 75 [180].)
8. "Therefore, nothing at all stands in the way of attempting [...] a transcendental psychology, [...] a science [...] of the lived experiences in the phenomenological reduction." (cf. E. Husserl (1910/11), 62, [169].)
9. This methodical turn is presented for the first time in the second part of the *First Philosophy* lecture, which is dedicated to the phenomenological reduction (cf. E. Husserl (1923/4): *Erste Philosophie (1923/4).* Zweiter Teil: Theorie der phänomenologischen Reduktion. [First philosophy (1923/24). Second part: The theory of phenomenological reduction.] Ed. by Rudolf Boehm. The Hague 1959, (Hua VIII), 162 ff.).
10. E. Husserl (1928), "The Amsterdam Lectures <on> Phenomenological Psychology," in *Psychological and Transcendental Phenomenology and the Confrontation with Heidegger (1927–1931),* trans. and ed. T. Sheehan and R. E. Palmer (Dordrecht: Kluwer Academic Press, 1997), 213–253.
11. "And yet it can be said that, if this psychology of cognition had ever gone to work with a consciousness of its aim and had consequently been successful, its results would also have been work accomplished directly for the philosophical theory of cognition. All insights into structure that had been acquired for the psychology of cognition would also have benefited transcendental phenomenology. Even if the latter had remained involved in a confounding of results attained in the psychological attitude (a confounding hardly avoidable at the outset), this fault could have been remedied later by revaluation, without changing the essential core of the insights already gained. The interpretation that is decisive here, and that necessarily remains hidden at first, is the very thing that causes such great difficulty – and defines the transcendental problem of psychologism. (E. Husserl (1929), *Formal and Transcendental Logic,* trans. D. Cairns (The Hague: Martinus Nijhoff, 1977), 254.)
12. E. Husserl (1936), *The Crisis of European Sciences and Transcendental Phenomenology,* trans. D. Carr (Evanston: Northwestern University Press, 1970).
13. Rinofner-Kreidl among others points us to this: S. Rinofner-Kreidl (1997), "Das Psychologismusproblem und die Idee einer phänomenologischen Wissenschaft," in *Phänomenologische Forschungen, NF 2* (Freiburg/München 1997), 3–34.
14. "Within a topographic-economic explanation," Ricoeur remarks, "the status of interpretation, or *Deutung*, presents itself at first as an aporia. If we emphasize the deliberately antiphenomenological bent of the topography, we appear to remove any basis for a reading of psychoanalysis as hermeneutics; the substitution of the economic notions of cathexis – i.e. placement and displacement of energy – for the notions of intentional consciousness and intended object apparently calls for a naturalistic explanation and excludes an understanding of meaning through meaning." P. Ricoeur (1965), *Freud and Philosophy: An Essay on Interpretation,* trans. D. Savage (New Haven: Yale University Press, 1977), 65–66.
15. Cf. J. Habermas (1968), *Knowledge and Human Interests,* trans. J. J. Shapiro (Boston: Beacon Press, 1971), chap. 11.
16. Cf. A. Stephan, *Sinn als Bedeutung. Bedeutungstheoretische Untersuchungen zur Psychoanalyse Sigmund Freuds* (Berlin/New York:Walter de Gruyter, 1989), S. 112 et sqq.
17. Cf. A. Grünbaum, *The Foundations of Psychoanalysis. A Philosophical Critique* (Berkely/Los Angeles/London: University of California Press, 1984), 1–95.
18. As a central enquiry from the phenomenological point of view Rudolf Bernet has already mentioned the question of the unconscious as an appearance in consciousness. R. Bernet (1997), "Husserls Begriff des Phantasiebewußtseins als Fundierung von Freuds Begriff des Unbewußten," in Jamme, Christoph (Hg.): *Grundlinien der Vernunftkritik* (Frankfurt a. M.: Suhrkamp, 1997), 279.

19. "Psycho-analysis is the name (1) of a procedure for the investigation of mental processes which are almost inaccessible in any other way, (2) of a method (based upon that investigation) for the treatment of neurotic disorders and (3) of a collection of psychological information obtained along those lines, which is gradually being accumulated into a new scientific discipline." (S. Freud (1923): *Two Encyclopaedia Articles*, in: The Standard Edition of the Complete Psychological Works of Sigmund Freud, Trans. J. Strachey, London 1950, S.E. XVIII, 235.) In the following, Freud's texts from the Standard Edition will be cited in terms of: author, year of origin, S.E., volume (numeral), page.
20. Cf. S. Freud (1893). *On the Psychical Mechanism of Hysterical Phenomena: Preliminary Communication* (Breuer and Freud), S.E. II, pp. 7, 11.
21. J. Laplanche and J.-B. Pontalis (1973): *The Language of Psycho-Analysis*, trans. D. Nicholson-Smith (London: W W Norton, 1974), 169.
22. W. Dilthey (1910): *The Formation of the Historical World in the Human Sciences*, vol. 3 *Selected Works*, eds. R.A. Makkreel and F. Rodi, 235 (Princeton: Princeton University Press, 2002).
23. From the phenomenological standpoint, a quasi-present exhibits the same (simple) intentional structure as that of the perceptual present. In contrast to recollection, future anticipation or image consciousness, it possesses, as Husserl states, a *single stream* [einstrahlig] of intentional experiencing in the mode of the *as-if* actually. Husserl mainly mentions the phenomena of vision and dream in this context: "The phantasy formations no longer hover before the inner eye as images. Empirical perception, the reality in which the visionary as a bodily organism lives, is suspended; and simultaneously with the suspension the opposition between this reality and the phantasy imagery, the imaging function of the phantasy images, escapes. The visionary is then in a trance state; the world of phantasy is then his real world. He himself takes it to be real; that is to say, his intuitions are perceptions, even endowed with the characteristic of belief. We will assume the same thing in the case of dreams, and not only in the dreaming that occurs in sleep but also in daydreaming. Sometimes we give ourselves up to the attractions of phantasy to such an extent that we begin to react to the phantasy appearances in actions just as if perceptions were at stake: our fist clenches, we hold audible dialogues with the imagined persons, and so on." (E. Husserl (1904/05): *Phantasy, Image Consciousness, and Memory (1898–1925)*, trans. J. Brough (Dordrecht: Springer, 2005), 45.)
24. "Instead of urging the patient to say something upon some particular subject, I now asked him to abandon himself to a process of free association – that is, to say whatever came into his head, while ceasing to give any conscious direction to his thoughts. It was essential, however, that he should bind himself to report literally everything that occurred to his self-perception and not to give way to critical objections which sought to put certain associations on one side on the ground that they were not sufficiently important or that they were irrelevant or that they were altogether meaningless." (S. Freud (1925): *An Autobiographical Study*, S.E. XX, 40.)
25. The recumbent pose and the external poverty of distractions are also meant to support so-called *regressive* experiences, i.e. experiences that are characteristic of earlier stages of development. This aspect gains importance with the continued development of psychoanalytic method and its theory. The phenomenon of regression as mechanism is studied by Michael Balint in particular. He focuses especially on the pre-Oedipal, infant stage of development as well as the early mother-child relationship, shedding light not only on the inner psychic but also the intersubjective aspects of regression. Cf. e.g., M. Balint (1968): *The Basic Fault: Therapeutic Aspects of Regression* (London: Tavistock, 1968).
26. Freud presents an exhaustive discussion of the scientific, psychological, and philosophical positions on the problem of dreaming, from antiquity to the contemporary research of his time, as chapter 1 of his *Interpretation of Dreams*. Cf. S. Freud (1900): S.E. IV, pp. 9–81.
27. Baßler also develops this thesis in systematic fashion. Cf. W. Baßler (1993), "Der Traum als Phänomen der ‚Allgemeinen Psychologie'. Skizze einer Interpretation des VII. Kapitel der Traumdeutung Sigmund Freuds," in: *Entschieden psychologisch. Festschrift für Wilhelm Salber* (Bonn: Bouvier, 1993), 113–123.

28. "Whether we are to attribute *reality* to unconscious wishes, I cannot say. It must be denied, of course, to any transitional or intermediate thoughts. If we look at unconscious wishes reduced to their most fundamental and truest shape, we shall have to conclude, no doubt, that psychical reality is a particular form of existence not to be confused with *material* reality" (S. Freud (1900): S.E. V, 620).
29. In this context Freud also distinguishes between the pleasure-ego and reality-ego: "Just as the pleasure-ego can do nothing but wish, work for a yield of pleasure, and avoid unpleasure, so the reality-ego need do nothing but strive for what is *useful* and guard itself against damage." (S. Freud (1911): *Formulations on the Two Principles of Mental Functioning*, S.E. XII, 73.
30. Freud discusses in this context multiple adaptive processes of the psychic apparatus: the development of perceptual consciousness, of attention, or memory, or judgment etc. Cf. S. Freud (1911): S.E. XII, 220 et sqq.
31. The complexity of this development is treated by, e.g., R. Spitz. He also shows that and in what ways it can fail. Spitz demonstrates that there are not just physiological, but also equally psychological and psychosomatic needs (for closeness, bodily contact, attention or affective input), whose failure motivates the reality check. On the other hand he shows that babies cannot automatically perform the reality check, there must be failure of certain kind. Otherwise they experience developmental problems that hinder the reality check or even make it impossible and that can lead to death, even if the concern is "only" with affective needs. Cf. e.g., R. Spitz, *The First Year of Life* (New York: International Universities Press, 1965), chapter 14–15.
32. Cf. S. Freud (1908a): *Creative Writers and Day-Dreaming*, S.E. IX, 144.
33. In particular the British pediatrician and psychoanalyst D. Winnicott inquired systematically into the meaning of play and phantasying in the development of the child. In the process he investigated the constitutive function of phantasy experience in self-realization and the formation of the relation between inner and outer reality. It is within this context that he coined the concept of the *transitional object*. Winnicott showed how such transitional objects such as teddy bears, blankies, and so on, regulate the transition from waking to sleeping and serve as necessary intermediaries between the two experiential orders of subject life in its developing stages. They support in an essential way the formation of internal representations in the inner world of external objects. They hence play an important role in the constitution of object relations in general. At this juncture, further detail concerning Winnicott's results will not be presented. I refer the reader to D.W. Winnicott, "Transitional Objects and Transitional Phenomena," *International Journal of Psychoanalysis* 34 (1953): 89–97 and D.W. Winnicott. *Playing and Reality* (London: Tavistock, 1971).
34. "Here, indeed, we have the one possibility of a memory subsequently producing a more powerful release than that produced in the first instance by the corresponding experience itself." S. Freud: *The origins of psycho-analysis letters to Wilhelm Fliess, drafts and notes, 1887–1902*. Ed. by Marie Bonaparte, Anna Freud [and] Ernst Kris; authorized translation by Eric Mosbacher and James Strachey. Introd. by Ernst Kris. [1st ed.]. New York 1954, 147.
35. S. Freud (1915): *The Unconscious*, S.E. XIV, 187.
36. Cf. e.g., S. Freud (1908b): *Hysterical phantasies and their relation to bisexuality*, S.E. IX, 161.
37. Freud speaks in this context of phantasy equipped with (high) affective value. Cf. e.g., S. Freud (1908a), S.E. IX, 144.
38. A highly illuminating discussion of the understanding of time in psychoanalysis from Freud to the present is offered by e.g., F. Wellendorf, "Die Zeit der Psychoanalyse und die Psychoanalyse der Zeit," *Forum der Psychoanalyse* 16, no. 3 (2000): 189–203. The temporal modalizations of the unconscious in the context of neonatal traumata are the topic in G. Schmithüsen, "Psychoanalytische Einzelfallstudie zu frühem Trauma und Zeiterleben," *Psyche – Z Psychoanal* 58, no. 4 (2004): 293–320. Time as central category of psychoanalysis is discussed by O. Seidl, "Zeit und Zeitlosigkeit der Psychoanalyse," *Forum der Psychoanalyse* 25, no. 2 (2009): 101–117.
39. The relation of a phantasy to time is in general very important. We may say that it hovers, as it were, between three times – the three moments of time which our ideation involves. Mental

work is linked to some current impression, some provoking occasion in the present which has been able to arouse one of the subject's major wishes. From there it harks back to a memory of an earlier experience (usually an infantile one) in which this wish was fulfilled; and it now creates a situation relating to the future which represents a fulfilment of the wish. What it thus creates is a day-dream or phantasy, which carries about it traces of its origin from the occasion which provoked it and from the memory. Thus past, present and future are strung together, as it were, on the thread of the wish that runs through them. (S. Freud (1908a): S.E. IX, 147.)

40. Freud discovers resistance while working with the cathartic procedure. With the introduction of the method of free association, it is integrated into his theory in systematic fashion. Originally, Freud assumes that resistance is an expression of something repressed, which "fights" its unconcealment. In the second theory of psychic personality, in which the structural model of the psyche is developed and the three subjective instances of the ego, id, and super-ego are detailed, resistance becomes an important unconscious egoic or super-egoic achievement. In 1937 Freud writes: "The crux of the matter is that the defensive mechanisms directed against fromer danger recur in the treatment as resistances against recovery. It follows from this that the ego treats recovery itself as new danger." (S. Freud (1937): *Analysis Terminable And Interminable*, in: S.E. XXIII, 238. Cf. also E. Freud (1920): *Beyond the Pleasure Principle*, S.E. XVIII, 19. A revealing treatment of the phenomenon of resistance and its place in psycho-analysis is to be found in E. Glover, *The Technique of Psycho-Analysis* (New York: International Universities Press, 1955).
41. Cf. S. Freud (1912): *The Dynamics of Transference*. S.E. XII, 99 et sqq.
42. In 1923, Freud points out that "in the course of analytic treatment a special emotional relation is regularly formed between the patient and the physician. This goes far beyond rational limits. It varies between the most affectionate devotion and the most obstinate enmity and derives all of its characteristics from earlier erotic attitudes of the patient's which have become unconscious. This transference alike in its positive and in its negative form is used as a weapon by the resistance; but in the hands of the physician it becomes the most powerful therapeutic instrument and it plays a part scarcely to be over-estimated in the dynamics of the process of cure." (S. Freud (1923): S.E., 246 et sqq.)
43. *Libido* is the dynamic expression of the sexual drive in psychic life. Freud assumes that the sexual drive is patched together from partial drives that over the course of psychic development unify into a particular organization. It can however under certain circumstances collapse into partial drives or these can attain special significance (*fixations*). A short and concise presentation of his theory of the libido is found in e.g., Freud (1923): S.E., 244 et sqq.
44. Defense mechanisms as unconscious accomplishments of the ego were analyzed and described by Freud's daughter, Anna Freud, in particular. Cf. e.g., A. Freud (1937), *The Ego and the Mechanisms of Defence* (London: Karnac Books, 1966).
45. S. Freud (1913): *The Disposition to Obsessional Neurosis, a Contribution to the Problem of the Choice of Neurosis*, S.E. XII, 319.
46. S. Freud (1912a): *Recommendations to Physicians Practising Psycho-Analysis*, S.E. XII, 116.
47. Laplanche and Pontalis remark that "[this] approach is based on the tenet that resonance 'from unconscious to unconscious' constitutes the only authentically psycho-analytic form of communication." J. Laplanche/J.-B. Pontalis (1974), 93.
48. "In this way we spare ourselves a strain on our attention [...] and we avoid a danger which is inseparable from the exercise of deliberate attention. For as soon as anyone deliberately concentrates his attention to a certain degree, he begins to select from the material before him; one point will be fixed in his mind with particular clearness and some other will be correspondingly disregarded, and in making this selection he will be following his expectations or inclinations. This, however, is precisely what must not be done. In making the selection, if he follows his expectations he is in danger of never finding anything but what he already knows; and if he follows his inclinations he will certainly falsify what he may perceive. It must not be forgotten that the things one hears are for the most part things whose meaning is only recognized later on." (S. Freud (1912a), S.E. XII, 112.)

49. W.R. Bion in particular emphasizes the *dream-like* aspect of psychoanalytic work following the work of Melanie Klein and D.W. Winnicott. In his neo-psychoanalytic interpretation, he speaks of *dream-like prescience* (rêverie) and compares this capability with the mother's capability to arrange a kind of resonance space (container) for the primal sensing of the infant. Bion describes this capability as rêverie and gives it a central place in regards to the success of psychic development, especially the development of thinking and the sense of reality. (Cf. W.R. Bion, *Learning from Experience* (New York: Basic Books Pub. Co., 1962), 230.) Klaus Grabska, among others, is undertaking a comparison of the concepts of Freud and Bion. He demonstrates that Bion's reverie refers to deeper, more minimalistic and fragmented dimensions of transference than the evenly suspended attention of Freud. (K. Grabska, "Gleichschwebende Aufmerksamkeit und träumerisches Ahnungsvermögen (Rêverie)," *Forum der Psychoanalyse* 16, no. 3 (2000): 247–260.)
50. I systematically unpack the thesis of the bivalence of the experiential orders of in J. Brudzińska, "Assoziation, Imaginäres, Trieb. Phänomenologische Untersuchungen zur Subjektivitätsgenesis bei Husserl und Freud" (Köln, Dissertation, 2005), Kap. 4. A condensed version is found in Ibid., "Die phänomenologische Erfahrung und die Frage nach dem Unbewussten. Überlegungen im Anschluss an Husserl und Freud," in *Interdisziplinäre Perspektiven der Phänomenologie. Neue Felder der Kooperation: Cognitive Science, Neurowissenschaften, Psychologie, Soziologie, Politikwissenschaft und Religionswissenschaft* (Dordrecht: Springer, 2006), 54–71.
51. "The perceptual apprehension essentially belongs to sensations. First of all, sensations are apprehended as present themselves [...]. Imaginational apprehensions, however, belong to phantasms. These imaginational apprehensions are not founded in direct apprehensions of a perceptual sort that first posit the sensuous content as something present and then take it as the image of something else. On the contrary, by virtue of their more or less remote resemblance they immediately found an immanent re-presentational consciousness, a modified consciousness of seeing what is meant in what is experienced, without, however, first taking what is sensuously experienced as something existing independently, more precisely, as something present." (E. Husserl (1904/05), 85.)
52. Worth pointing out here is that Husserl also arrives on the track of *pure phantasy* in reflecting on the phenomena of hallucination and dream. (Cf. E. Husserl (1904/05), §20)
53. "In the unity of a perception, the only alterations in the basis of the appearance are those that change the homogeneous into the homogeneous. The synthetic unity of the perceptual nexus, or of the nexus in the apprehensional basis, is firmly ordered. [...] The same is true of the unity of the representational image in physical image presentation. [...] Standing in contrast to this is the protean character of the phantasy appearance: inherent in this character is that the unity of the representational image does not remain preserved in the unity of the phantasy presentation." (E. Husserl (1904/05), 66.)
54. Husserl's unpublished manuscripts. I thank the Director of the Husserl Archive in Leuven, Prof. Ullrich Melle, for granting me access to quote from Husserl's unpublished manuscripts.
55. In this context – with regard to the time structure of the primordial experience and its dynamic Husserl also considers phenomenology of the *so-called unconscious*: "Accordingly, the question arises: In their regulated dependency of those essential conditions of the formation of unity, but also codetermined by novel essential laws, do affection and association not first make possible the constitution of objects that exist for themselves? Are there not regulated inhibiting, weakening counter potencies which, by not letting affection arise any longer, also make the emergence of self-subsistent unities impossible, unities in other words that would not emerge at all without affection? These questions are difficult to answer; and they are especially difficult if we wish to make our way from the sphere of the living present into the sphere of forgetfulness and to comprehend reproductive awakening, as will be necessary to do later. I do not need to say that the entirety o f these observations that we are undertaking can also be given the famed title of the ·unconscious." Thus, our considerations concern a phenomenology of the so-called unconscious." E. Husserl (1918–26), *Analyses Concerning Passive and Active Synthesis: Lectures on Transcendental Logic*, trans. A.J. Steinbock (Dordrecht: Kluwer Academic Publishers, 2001), 201.

56. "In every living present that is looked upon universally, there is naturally a certain relief of salience, a relief of noticeability, and a relief that can get my attention [...]. In this case, we accordingly distinguish between background and foreground. The foreground is what is thematic in the broadest sense. The nil of salience is found in a potentially considerable vivacity of a conscious having that does not, however, arouse any special responsive tendency in the ego, does not make it to the ego-pole. [...] I have already employed the quite suitable expression, affective relief. (...) On the one hand, this alludes to a unity, on the other hand, to a difference of "peaks" for the different particular moments, finally, too, the possibility of entire augmentations or entire diminutions insofar as the affective relief can arch out more prominently or become more flattened depending upon the alterations of the living present. I am alluding here to the differences of freshness in which all present objects, possibly through a sudden transition, but altogether, gain (or in the opposing case, lose) something of the vivacity of consciousness, of affective force. But at the same time within every present there are relative differences of vivacity, differences of more or less affectively efficacious data. Hence the discourse of affective relief." E. Husserl (1918–26), 215 et sqq.)

Axiomatics of the Flesh

Guy Félix Duportail

Abstract I am advancing here a group of propositions, based on the descriptions compiled in Merleau-Ponty's *The Visible and the Invisible*, which can be denominated as axioms of the flesh. The purpose of this work is to reflect upon an ontology of the flesh that can serve as a foundation for the psychoanalysis of Freud and Lacan. '-- End of Abstract'

In the following lines, I would like to show that the genetic conditions of vision are governed by a group of propositions that I will denominate as axioms of the flesh. This axiomatics essentially owes its beginnings to the descriptions of perception compiled in *The Visible and the Invisible* by Merleau-Ponty, as well as to a reflection on the qualitative space of position – notably that of *topology*.[1] Indeed, this is the topological space that Merleau-Ponty suggests as "a model of being"[2]; in opposition to the Euclidean space that he associates with the classic ontology of *Ens realissimum*. Therefore, the analysis of space now becomes the common thread in the representation of the field of original Being. It is this line of *indirect* ontology that I intend to pursue. The epistemic issue at hand involves finding a form of a pre-objective description of the world, the world of "wild being", whose repressed situation in philosophical tradition sheds new light on the discoveries of Freud and Lacan.

1

In *Eye and Mind,* Merleau-Ponty writes: "Vision is not a certain mode of thought or presence to self; it is the means given me for being absent from myself, for being present at the fission of Being from the inside [...]".[3]

G.F. Duportail (✉)
Université de Paris I, Pantheon-Sorbonne, 70 rue Barrault, Paris 75013, France
e-mail: dupsf@aol.com

D. Lohmar and J. Brudzińska (eds.), *Founding Psychoanalysis Phenomenologically*, Phaenomenologica 199, DOI 10.1007/978-94-007-1848-7_3,

Vision, liberated from intellectualism, would therefore come to term in the non-coincidence of the seer with himself, the scission of the perceived being – while it is perceiving and perceptible –, following the two famous branches of the chiasm. Accordingly, consciousness no longer appears as if it were unifying, unified and separated from the body, but as if it were simultaneously an incarnate and fragmentary presence. Yet, how is it that *vision from within being* appears as a thing outside the constituted subject? How is such vision possible? How does one conceive *immanence from out of transcendence*? One of the essential conditions of this vision, effectuated within being, is the identification of sight's limitation to that which can be touched. The seeing body cannot be visible and yet incorporated in the entirety of the visible, or otherwise be so much a part of it so as to feel its own dehiscence from the interior; unless it, too, is submitted to a state of quasi-tactile reflexivity. Consequently, in order for the seer to carry out his vision from *within being*, from inside the world splitting open to be seen, the eye must touch things *from a distance*, in the way that a hand would touch them. The gaze must, as Merleau-Ponty states, "envelop, palpitate, [and] espouse visible things." Furthermore, it must recognise the general law of the reversibility of the sensible. This world sees the seer who sees it, just like the touched becomes the touching. Similarly, a painter may feel his motif watching him, as Paul Cézanne felt Mont Sainte-Victoire watching him. The extension of the characteristic reversibility of the flesh into all of the senses is the essential condition that allows a being to have an internal tele-vision; in which the Self, flipped inside out, sees in on itself from the outside. At this point, we are at the heart of a contradictory field of being, where the opening of a being is correlated to a "fundamental narcissism" –, since the seeing is implicated in that which it sees.

What does it mean however *to generalise the reversibility* of the inside and outside? Does it not amount to hylozoism, for which Merleau-Ponty is sometimes reproached? It means, in my opinion – and this is my hermeneutic responsibility – to recognise the founding role of elementary topological relations in the organisation of the field of perception.[4]

The notion that could at first glance satisfy this hypothesis might be what psychologies have called the "body scheme." This, as we know, combines internal sensations and space in its representation of the body proper.[5] Having read *The Image and Appearance of the Human Body* by Paul Schilder,[6] Merleau-Ponty does indeed see a body scheme and a system of equivalences between the inside and the outside:

> Schilder: the *topology* of the body scheme is its "equivalences". [...] Reciprocity-overcrowding (*promiscuité*) of the "inside" and the "outside" around the body scheme as an axis: condensation and displacement [...] in the body scheme by virtue of its dynamic structure: equivalence of "orifices" and of "prominences" [...] Notions of incorporations (introjection) and of ejection (projection). The inside and the outside. Inevitable condensation and displacement in the body as a topological being – in the general sense.[7]

Moreover, this system of reversibility of inside and outside is dynamic. It is animated by the desire to "search for the inside in the outside and for the outside in the inside".[8] Therefore, in addition to Piaget's contribution to the primary role of topological relations in the child's mental development of spatial representation, he also established the body scheme as a relational axis to the world. This allowed

Merleau-Ponty to generalise spatial structuring and to apply it to the perceptive field as a primordial field of Being. And thus we move from the ontological domain into the realm of psychology. In fact, we have crossed the border as soon as we grasp that desire must not be understood here as an anthropological category, but instead as a form of opening onto Being.

Nonetheless, it is difficult to take topology for a "model" of Being without some mathematical references. The mathematical sciences first gave a distinct form to this primordial space by naming it topology in the mid-nineteenth century, when Listing revisited Leibniz's *Analysis Situs* (1847, in his *Vorstudien zur Topologie*).[9] A century later in 1948, Bourbaki reformed the mathematical discoveries pursuant to the notion of structure, enumerating three groups: the structures of order, the structures of groups, and topological structures. It is these structures, steeped in a long history and numerous transformations, which Merleau-Ponty considers pertinent for the articulation of being through the flesh.

The question now hanging undetermined before us – between Piaget, Schilder and Bourbaki – is the following: What is the precise philosophical meaning of this ontologisation of topology? One wonders, despite everything up to this point, if the ideality of the flesh – though not Cartesian – might not be expressible in mathematic terms.[10]

This is an important question, after all, for one of the possible scientific destinies of phenomenological description and, therefore, the possibility or impossibility of conceiving a new path toward a phenomenological reduction is at stake here. Let us not forget that according to Husserl, "The descriptive concepts of all pure description, i.e. of description adapted to intuition immediately and with truth and so of all phenomenological description, differ in principle from those which dominate objective science".[11] This thesis, contained in the *Third Research on Logic*, would be reiterated on several occasions, notably in the first book of *Ideas* where Husserl states: "Transcendental phenomenology as descriptive science of Essential Beings belongs in fact to *a* main class of eidetic science wholly other than that to which the mathematical sciences belong (§75)".[12]

Yet apparently, *at* the shared line between mathematical concepts, which correlate ideal essences, and descriptive concepts, which correlate morphological essences; there is, according to Merleau-Ponty, an overlap between: (a), topological analysis, revealing the invisible spatial order of the flesh, and (b), the body's participating empathy at the crossroads of the sentient being. Merleau-Ponty is an innovative phenomenologist, who leads us to a new way of articulating the field of the original being precisely because of his identification of this overlap – the subjective and the objective, correlating the coincidence of the two conceptual systems. Contemporary science, *via* mathematics and its non-objectivist and non-Cartesian methods – as Merleau-Ponty articulates it in his course on nature in 1960[13] – thus reveals as much as Cézanne's paintings, *another ontology*. What a different image this gives us of Merleau-Ponty than the one we usually have of the philosopher!

Be that as it may, we are still missing an intermediary notion in order to clearly understand the bridge that Merleau-Ponty constructs between mathematics and the being of flesh. Surely we need another paradigm than that offered by Galileanism in order to circumscribe what is scientific. Merleau-Ponty reflected upon this question after reading Husserl*'s Krisis.* It is imperative to find a path that crosses between, on the one hand, the simple metaphorical or literary usage of concepts, which would considerably diminish the importance of *The Visible and the Invisible*; and, on the other hand, the idea of a literal reading of these same concepts, which would imply, in itself, the impossible possibility of a geometry *stricto sensu* of experience. Yet, if we exclude these last two alternatives, the only path remaining for us would be *a spatial metaphor of the crude Being's structure.* The topological metaphor used to express the flesh is not in this case "literary", because the flesh stands in for a spatial axiom (the flesh is subjugated to other axioms, pursuant to the logic of a space, in which the body is immerged and provides the space's truth such as in the works of Fichte or Maine de Biran). The flesh simultaneously authorises hypotheses and deductions in relation to the aesthetic structure of the being of flesh. This topological axiom is metaphorical, by the same relationship, insofar as it carries out a non-original *making-present* (in the sense of a *Vergegenwärtigung*) of the primordial ontological field. At this point, we are very close to what Bernard Waldenfels designated as an "indirect description".[14] The topological *making-present* of the flesh appears at this point as a way of showing the invisible inside the visible, which can accordingly only be shown in an indirect fashion. It is consistent with the idea of a representation of *Nichturpräsentierbar,* which stays a *hidden,* yet *simultaneously exposed* dimension.

This hypothesis strikes me, in any event, as a necessary step on the way to conferring a philosophical status to Merleau-Ponty's working notes on topology. This hypothesis does not originate from Merleau-Ponty himself. It is mine, but it is a prerequisite for conferring the proper status to that which has remained all too undetermined in his works (the idea of topology as a "model" for being). To reiterate, without this hypothesis, we are reduced to interpreting Merleau-Ponty's references to topology, either as literary fragments, or as mathematical outlines. In either case, we loose the autonomy of his philosophy. Of course, this interpretative hypothesis, which has already proven fruitful in elucidating questions concerning Merleau-Ponty's method, calls upon ulterior developments. Merleau-Ponty opened the path of *the reduction of the pre-objective world, to the brute being.* We understand it as an *archaeological reduction evoking an indirect making-present of the flesh.*

This is the very path that remains faithful to experience.[15] We will discover a topology of experience if we do not cut the umbilical cord with the experience of the brute being. We *feel* the whirlwind of the flesh – these lived experiences beyond presence – which are also the invisible of the visible and that are governed by a topological logic: introjection, projection, separation, alienation, the reversal of instincts, *et cetera.* It is therefore not surprising that this psychoanalysis of being intersects, and neatly ties in with Freudian psychoanalysis. Merleau-Ponty writes:

> Therefore Freud's philosophy is not one of the body, but rather of the flesh – the Id, the unconscious – and the Ego (correlative) to be understood on the basis of the flesh [.][16]

This can be shown in a precise and rigorous manner with the aid of the topological schematisations. I therefore posit that the dehiscence and the indivision, which Merleau-Ponty considers as general characteristics of the flesh, can also, in and of themselves, be made-present according to topological concepts or relations. I will subsequently draw my conclusions regarding the relationship between archaeological phenomenology and psychoanalysis.

1.1 The Axiom of the Indivision of Being

In *The Visible and the Invisible*, the starting point for the phenomenology of the flesh is the pre-given of the Being of flesh's vertical perception of the body.[17] The beginning thus consists in describing the world in a corporeal way. Being is "standing before the world" and the world is "standing" before the self, in an "embracing" or contact relationship.[18] For Merleau-Ponty, this way of seeing entails a fundamental structure of imaginary specularness where the reflections resemble the reflected, and things of the world look like seen and memorised things. By virtue of *ressemblance,* the pre-given of Being is therefore familiar with a fundamental structure of passive unification. In addition, this structure is *presupposed* by relinquishing all difference, starting with corporeal difference, which by excellence is the body's torsion left/right:

> Consider the right, the left: these are not simply contents within a relational spatiality (i.e. *positive*): they are not *parts of space* (Kant's reasoning is valid here: the whole is primary), they are total parts, cuts in an encompassing, topological space – Consider the *two*, the *pair*, this is not *two* acts, *two syntheses*, it is a fragmentation of being, it is a possibility for separation (two eyes, two ears: the possibility for *discrimination,* for the use of the diacritical), it is the advent of difference (on the ground of *resemblance* therefore, on the ground of the *ομου ην παντα*).[19]

The initial "whole" of being, not yet carved into parts, each one foreign to the other ("*partes extra partes*"), is therefore a "fabric" in which the intentional threads (of being and not of the consciousness) are intertwined and appear simultaneously. They constitute the material of the world and of the body. Hence, Merleau-Ponty describes that:

> When I perceive the child, he is given precisely in a certain divergence (*écart*) [...] and the same for my perceptual lived experience for myself, and the same for my alter ego, and the same for the pre-analytic thing. Here is the common fabric of which we are all made. The wild Being.[20]

The first principle of vertical intelligibility – the type of thought that reveals the roots of the world on this side of its representation – must therefore be the expression of an archaic space which, like the daubs of colour in Paul Klee's paintings, is the image of being "older than everything" and "born today". It constitutes the enveloping *milieu* in which general being and its immanent differences are woven, the whole of the neighbourhood's topological relations, at the foundation of the universal ressemblance between things. It is here that we find the original place of truth where the "overcrowding (*promiscuité*)[21] of Being" reigns supreme. This overcrowding is, for example, the proximity between my body and another body or all bodies, the reciprocal encroachment of my flesh on the flesh of the world, in the sense that overcrowding also connotes the idea of an intolerable proximity that one must push away or forget similar to a sexual thought or the *Unheimlich*. The field of the being of the flesh is a primordial unconscious. The intersection with the Freudian notion of the unconscious is therefore inevitable for Merleau-Ponty, as it corresponds to structural "convergence" between phenomenology and psychoanalysis. Yet, the object of this convergence is none other than the corner stone of the two disciplines, of which neither is at first aware. It is their common *arche*, which unifies them – the pre-objective universe already there as it has always been –, and which reveals itself to either discipline only indirectly and at a later time, through interpretation in psychoanalysis and through reduction in philosophy. Accordingly, the notions of flesh and the unconscious refer to the same field with different names, anterior to the subject-object scission –, an inaccessible domain for classical representative rationality.

On the ontological plane, it is important to note that the topological character of the original field supposes a fundamental *ressemblance* between being (*Sein*) and entities (*Seindes*) in the form of the flesh. The fabric and its folds are here images of the continuous spatial structure of being and the primary ontological axiom[22] – being in indivision – is the philosophical expression of this general pre-eminence of interweaving over the separation of neighbourhood over segregation. On the epistemic plane, this signifies that ambiguity and entanglements clarify, whereas analysis divides, and as a result, obscures.

On the philosophical plane, this supposes that the new starting point for philosophy is no longer the *cogito* and its transparency to the self, but *the original institution of an opaque and unconscious field of being where everything is close and intertwined,* where one does not make oneself think anymore than one makes one's heart beat, as Merleau-Ponty writes in *The Visible and the Invisible*. It is the *topological being that I am and that I do not know.* Accordingly, in philosophical debate, Merleau-Ponty inverses Sartre's starting point:

> I take my starting point where Sartre ends, in the Being taken up by the for-itself – It is for him the finishing point because he starts with being and negentity and *constructs* their union. For me it is structure or transcendence that explains, and being and nothingness (in Sartre's sense) are its two abstract properties. For an ontology from within, transcendence does not have to be constructed, from the first it is, as Being [lined *(doublé)*] with nothingness, and what is to be explained is its [splitting *(dédoublement)*] (which, moreover is never finished)[...][23]

Once the first axiom of ontological indivisibility is laid down, the problem then becomes, contrary to Sartre's approach, one of the splitting (*dédoublement*) of being. It's the transition from one into two, the division in and of itself, which creates the question. Hence the following axiom:

1.2 The Axiom of the Division of Being

How does the splitting of the perceived being occur? The answer: by relying on a prerequisite fault line that reigns at the heart of the visible. According to Merleau-Ponty, the perceived being is, in fact, lined with nothingness. A seen thing is never identical to another, the thing is always "behind", beyond, far-off.[24] On the basis of this transcendence or the profound inadequacy of perceived things, we come back to the fission which transforms the expanse of the unitary sensible with its negentity, and which makes it open from within like a fruit that splits and bursts its pulp onto itself. Merleau-Ponty designates this continual splitting (which is never completed) as the "dehiscence of the seeing into the visible and of the visible into the seeing".[25]

The system of splitting seeing-visible by the process of dehiscence is more precisely a *double metamorphosis* of the seeing into the visible and the visible into the seeing. As the term dehiscence implies, one passes outside of the self by opening and wrapping around the self, although the transition from one to the other is *never a finished action.* The dehiscence of the flesh is a continuous and crossed process of metamorphosis which problematises all substantial identities. We should therefore understand that the division of the flesh of being is only a *quasi*-splitting and that the division is more an unfinished unity in a continuous splitting process or in a state of perpetual metamorphosis. In other words, it is *the same being* that is seeing and visible, visible and seeing; and, at the same time, it is not the same, for it is always altering and transforming. The solution to the problem posed by the subtle "splitting of Being" will be of a spatial nature, since the solution consists in a knot which links the different *dimensions* of the world together, and which thus constitutes a "real point", in the middle of the *singular* but *multidimensional* world:

> Philosophy as interrogation [...] can consist only in showing how the world is articulated starting from a zero of being which is not nothingness, that is, in installing itself on the edge of being, nor in the in Itself, at the joints, where the multiple *entries* of the world cross.[26]

The zero of being at the joints of a multi-entry world conflicts here with the dialectic of the one dividing into two. Not only is the zero of being not exterior to being, it is a *hinge of absence within being,* a button tuft that generally sews the differences together, the intertwining of fleshes in the *not one* of the totality, and the *not two* of the separation of independent parts. Still, it is a verbal *Wesen,* which joins as it separates. The dimensional differences of the world thus graft onto each another, such that the same is "other than the other", or such that identity is "difference of difference".[27]

The axiom of division is therefore to be understood as a principle of differentiation that takes place within the unity of the visible. This axiom presides over the differential (diacritic) segregation of entities (*Seindes*) according to the structure of transcendence of being (*Sein*)[28] by virtue of their common fabric.

1.3 The Axiom of Mediation Between Division and Indivision or the Principle of Reversibility

As we have already stated, the essential characteristic of this axiomatics is to be *spatially* accurate in the logos of its connections. Merleau-Ponty writes:

> What do I bring to the problem of the same and the other? This: that the same be the other than the other, and the identity difference of difference – this 1) does not realize a surpassing, a dialectic in the Hegelian sense; 2) is realized on the spot, by encroachment, thickness, *spatiality* –.[29]

Accordingly, for the two first axioms to be *consistent*, a *spatial connexion* between them is required. In this respect, what I will call the "cleverness" of topological reason is to ensure that *transformation* and alteration stay, form a certain point of view, a form of equivalency. As the old joke goes, a topologist cannot tell the difference between a doughnut and a coffee cup, as long as one can pass from the former to the latter by continuous deformation. From a topological point of view, a square ring is no different from a round ring; and a pretzel looks like a sphere with two handles. In the latter case, the alteration works for structural identity of a spatial order, which has its own non-metric criteria. Of course, in our context, it is the figure of the chiasm[30] that describes the structural relationship of transformation between the seeing and the visible and assures a continuous correlation between them:

> The chiasm is not only a me other exchange [...] it is also an exchange between me and the world, between the phenomenal body and the "objective" body, between the perceiving and the perceived: what begins as a thing ends as consciousness of the thing, what begins as a "state of consciousness" ends as a thing.[31]

The chiasm thus assures a certain form of identity through reversibility (without forgetting that resulting identity remains a difference of difference or identity by principle): "reversibility is not an actual *identity* of the touching and the touched. It is their identity by principle (always abortive) – ".[32]

The chiasm therefore does not give us a positive or substantial identity, but rather a difference of difference, equivalent to a structural identity. Hence, it perfectly schematizes transcendence as identity within difference. Reversibility accordingly imposes itself as a third axiom. It is in fact the necessary mediation between the one and the multiple, that which permits the chiasm to conserve a coherency, despite a missing conceptual unity (not one) *and* to preserve simultaneously a dimensional multiplicity, despite the perpetual incompleteness of the division (not two). As such, reversibility is the tertiary response to "neither one nor two", to the crossing double incompletion of the one and of the two, inherent in the nature of the chiasm. It constitutes an unending passage back and forth and into each other, based on the interweaving of the dimensions of being.

One can nonetheless improve the schematic representation of reversibility with the aid of topology. In fact, in order to actualize a continuous passage into each other, the chiasm must follow a *closed* line that intersects itself. Indeed, it is surprising that no one has yet emphasised the chiasm's self-intersection. Manifestly, the metamorphosis of the seeing in the visible and the visible in the seeing *closes on itself in a loop*. We can now explicitly represent this property of the loop – beyond the letter, but still in the spirit of Merleau-Ponty's ontology – through a topological schematisation by making use of the Möbius strip. This allows us to visually depict the characteristics of reversibility: its twisting and coiling over itself. Flattened out, the singular boundary of the Möbius strip can be depicted by a single line cutting over and under itself in order to create a quadripartite figure schematizing an "interior eight."

The Möbian aspect of the space of the flesh (*espace charnel*)[33] is present in Merleau-Ponty's descriptions when he says, for example, that the world is the extension of my body, that the rays of the world are the extension of motivity, that the other and myself are from the same side, *et cetera*. Far from seeing a triumph of the self over alterity, one should rather see the underpinnings of a spatial logic – a Möbian logic – that joins the same and the other along the edge of the division that represents the movement animating the flesh. With regard to the latter, which is situated at the origin of the loop, it can be none other than the movement of vision – that is, the "seeing force" immanent in the visible being. The movement is that of general visibility ("It is this Visibility, this generality of the Sensible in itself, this anonymity innate to Myself..."[34]), driven by an instinctual trajectory, in a closed circuit, that one can determine as being the circular libidinal movement that Merleau-Ponty precisely designates as *fundamental narcissism* of the visible.

> If we can show that the flesh is an ultimate notion, that it is not the union or compound of two substances, but thinkable by itself, if there is a relation of the visible with itself that traverses me and constitutes me as a seer, this circle which I do not form, which forms me, this coiling over of the visible upon the visible, can traverse, animate other bodies as well as my own. [...] If it lets itself be captivated by one of its fragments, the principle of captivation is established, the field open for other Narcissus, for an "intercorporeity."[35]

Moreover, as Merleau-Ponty points out, "the present does not stop at the limits of the visible"[36] with the *overlap* of the parts, which means that intentional transgression is inscribed in this primitive mereology. Correlatively, *a parte subjecti*, *discrepancies* stick out in subjective ways in the appearance of the world. There is as much movement as there is progressive distancing between perception and signification, as much separation between the glorious body of logical signification and the thick body, seen and perceiving. The "circular" movement thus assures the speculative, and never-ending "synthesis" of being in division and in indivision.

Accordingly, the twisted strip eventually knots together several distinct modalities, where all of the phenomenal nuances from the auto-representation of the thing to its symbolic absence are laid bare. One could depict the *modalisation* of appearances by the multiplication of twists in the Möbius strip to schematise fundamental narcissism. More precisely, two half-twists generate the intertwining between two rings, and correspond to the moment of fission between the perceptive unity of man and the world – that is, to the moment of the imaginary modalisation of perception by decentring in quasi-perception. Three half-twists generate a knot, specifically, a trefoil knot, which corresponds to the moment when vision is sublimated into ideal signification. The succession of half-twists produced by the dynamism of Visibility then passes from the Möbius strip to Borromean rings, or moreover from the topology of surfaces to that of knots, all the while conserving the aspect of the division, since the drawing of a knot is also the representation of the edge of a division.

That said, whatever the didactic virtues may be of the topological drawings that allow one to visualize the transformations that algebraic calculations cannot anticipate – even if they can describe them[37] –, we must nonetheless be wary of the danger posed by the possibility of a geometric objectification of being. When we put this method of zigzags into practice, we must not lose something like the *lived topology* that provides the basis for all of these schemas from sight.

An initial potential path in the direction of this "lived topology" consists in considering the addition and subtraction inherent to vision. *A parte subjecti*, the division of the visible and the invisible does correlate to (de)grasping of additions and subtractions of visibility that accompany the perception of entities (*Seindes*). The remarkable aspect of this situation resides in the fact that, that which in intuition is unperceived *counts* nonetheless as a phenomenon for the perceiving. The invisible does not sink into oblivion; on the contrary, it takes up its place on the two sides of the chiasm, in the perceived landscape and for the perceiving subject. In other words, we have already sketched it out in a philosophical mindset, which is no different here from that of the common conscience, the original division of the visible and the invisible presents itself to the consciousness as the unperceived coinciding with the perceived, as a sort of lining or false bottom. Therefore, the perceivable given of the negative, the thing named zero of being, as an incompleteness of the appearance, is not a nothing as distinguished from a something. It is, on the contrary, a "dimensional something", a ray of the world, *incorporated* in the visible, like depth or thickness, that the subject takes into account as a supplement or excess of the perceptible *in* the perceptible. Let us note in passing that the passivity of perception also therefore conceals an activity within passivity, namely that activity of the unconscious counting of dimensions taken away from the original polymorphic grandeur.[38] Be that as it may, the invisible within the visible is a supplement of texture that allows one to see the idealness of the flesh in and through the flesh. As Merleau-Ponty states, the imperception that lies within perception shows that *one sees more than one fails to see*. Hence the exemplary nature of the vocation of the painter who "gives a visible existence to that which profane vision believes to be invisible [...]. This voracious vision, reaching beyond 'the visual givens', opens upon a texture of Being [...]".[39]

Without going further into this subjective explanation of topology, we can see that the division of the One, as a division of the unity of the visible, *in the form of the "additional" and the "lacking one", co-present in coincidence, as the wrong and the right side of the same fabric* (to borrow sewing terms), replaces neither the One nor the Two of the first pair of axioms. One observation becomes apparent: the overlap of imperception and perception, of the invisible and visible, *is* the real-life experience of the Möbian division in action.

Yet, we really must consider the epistemic stakes of this observation and of its description *via* the topology of division. It henceforth makes the epistemic chiasm between psychoanalysis and phenomenology possible, in exchange for a new phenomenological description of the status of the former and an emphasis on the topological – of the spatiality of Being – in the latter. It is the object of the unconscious desire, the very same that Lacanian psychoanalysis identifies as being shared by the Möbian division, that gives fabric and flesh to the invisible of the visible. The invisible is the object of desire that causes a schism in vision.[40] Perception, insofar as it is inevitably lined (*doublée*) with imperception, forever remains an unconscious act of desire, and as such, a desire repressed by the conscious. The first corollary of this provisional conclusion is to assert that the Freudian unconscious is inscribed *de facto* in the structure of the seen.[41] Thus, Merleau-Ponty's topology *can* and *must* be combined with Lacan's. At least, this is my hypothesis. The second *sine qua non* needed to condition the bridge between these topologies is the understanding that the topological revelation being considered here always produces a concomitant concealment. As it is a non-original making-present (*Vergegenwärtigung*) of Being, it is not exact; it remains a metaphor.

1.4 The Axiom of Supplementary Texture

Let us now pursue further down this path. As we have seen, the topological explanation of the chiasm gives the chiasm the status of a Möbian division that generates Borromean rings. Yet, a new difficulty arises, namely, – one pointed out by Jacques Lacan – the difficulty of undifferentiation of all of the substances of the Borromean rings, which are actually cut from three different cloths. If the individual rings of the knot are not coloured and oriented, they remain completely interchangeable. One can indefinitely pass from one ring to another in any order desired. Moreover, when represented in this manner, the topological form is no longer faithful to the genetic logic of modal development of Visibility, which unfurls itself on an axis extending from the perceived world to the separated signification of perception and imagination. The completed and depicted Borromean rings therefore do not represent the chain of operations that generated the modal differences and the stability of these differences. The trefoil knot schematizes nonetheless the *confusion* between the dimensions; it places them into a state of continuity through the medium of a single substance. Lacan criticized this continuity as being one of the signs of paranoid psychosis[42] and used Joyce as a paradigmatic illustration of the dysfunction. In Seminar XXIII, Lancan states:

> After all, Joyce would not have been crazy, would he? Insofar as it's not a privilege, if it is true that in most people the symbolic, the imaginary and the real are confused to the point that they continue into each other, such that it bars any attempt to distinguish them in the chain of Borromean rings [...].[43]

Lacan is clearly using the trefoil knot to schematise the confusion of the three substances by their continuous flow into each other.[44]

We are now encountering what one could denominate as the problematics of knot avatars. From the perspective of lived topology, we are referring to the affections of the corporeal schema as a pre-reflective knowledge of the *situation of the body in the world*. This helps us, as was the case in the life of Joyce, when he had the feeling that his body dropped like a peel, during a physical altercation with his fellow students. Thanks to Lacan's analysis of Joyce, we know that the fall is the result of the dislocation of his body's topological dimensionality due to the autonomisation of the three unravelled dimensions. For physical equilibrium, the absolute discontinuity of the dimensions is no more important that their continuity.

That said, on the plane of the schematism of the structure, Lacan decides to add a fourth ring to the knot in order to differentiate the substances while simultaneously connecting them. This solution,[45] which Lacan – qua Joyce's analyst – opts for is, *in fine,* the solution found by Joyce's own unconscious. The fourth ring, which Lacan denominates as the sinthome,[46] simultaneously differentiates while unifying the dimensions, and becomes the "Additional one", "Joyce's ego corrector", such that the unravelled knot in Joyce – as much as by the absolutisation of the continuity as by the absolutisation of the discontinuity between the dimensions – may once again be linked.[47]

The utterly remarkable characteristic of the *Additional one* remarked by Lacan is the ability to transfer its substance as a hole to the whole of the other knotted rings. It thus becomes the ring that explains the Borromean properties of the knot, since it is only necessary to cut one ring to free each remaining element of the knot. The unity of the One in question is therefore not that of the final unity of a whole that connects all of the parts in either an internal or external fashion; but rather that – which is less common in philosophical reflection – of a hole which, closing around an emptiness, allows the knotting of three other Ones, "rings of string", or tori in topological terms. The structure of links is therefore supported by an emptiness that connects as it separates. The problem with the schematisation of the equilibrium of the continuity and discontinuity between the dimensions seems to find its solution here.

Yet, as for our concern with recognising the need for a fourth substance,[48] I must also advance a fourth axiom, namely that of the *supplementarity which creates distinction and connection*. The *additional one* is necessary here, because thanks to the supplementary One, the dimensions of being are simultaneously joined and differentiated. What shall its phenomenal contents be? On the side of Merleau-Ponty's descriptions – to which we must now return –, it is manifestly the essence described as a "frame" or "texture" of the sentient world, that which is not above but underneath the surface of the visible, which creates a relationship of belonging to the whole of the same dimensional generality and simultaneously conflicts with the other essentialities. Moreover, the essence – or pregnant form – is always signified by an expression that converts the invisible into the effable. It is simultaneously nominal and concrete. Accordingly, it lies on the hinge of the visible and the invisible, at the interface between the perceptible and meaning. We can therefore state that there are eminent pregnant forms – or "instituting significations" – equivalent to the *sinthome*, in that "their division" terminates their relationship with the world. They therefore negatively condition the substance of the being's nodal structure to the world.

One can already test the hypothesis by applying it to the problem of *Weltthesis.* The experience recorded by Merleau-Ponty as "Cezanne's doubt" reveals the nodal stakes stemming from the difficulty encountered when we try to express our world. *Any attempt to articulate the texture of the world* virtually confronts us with the *failure* of all languages to put the world and its fabric into words. Cezanne's anxiety, in this regard, was rather eloquent, so much so that it motivated Zola to write a novel. The world surpasses our capacities of representation and language. The possibility of failure is intrinsic in the articulation of the world, and it appears here as the Real that haunts the speaking being of the artist. For the phenomenologist, the risk that the knot may fail appears inside the mental experience of the world's *néantisation*. This is the case for Jacques Derrida among others, for whom, as we know, it assumes the shape of the loss of the friend in position of the "additional one" of the torus. He writes:

> The death of the other, not only but especially when one loves him, does not bring news of an absence, a disappearance, the end of *such-and-such* life, i.e. the possibility for a world (always unique) to appear *as* living. Death declares each and every time *the end of the totality of the world,* the end of all possible worlds, and each time the end of the world as a unique totality, therefore irreplaceable and therefore infinite.[49]

In conclusion, the famous transformation across the chiasm of the seeing into the visible (and reciprocally) must be, in my opinion, re-examined and explained in the light of a spatiality that recognises a logos proper – literally a topology. If I have reasoned correctly, the four axioms whereof I have spoken – the indivision of being, the division of being, the mediation-reversibility between the prior two, and the supplement of texture which knots the preceding three together, like the Lacanian sinthome –, will provide us with an axiomatic metaphor of the infrastructure of the unconscious of being, that is, a linked structure, founded on the ex-sistence of a hole. This opaque and real hole is not only forgotten, but indeed repressed by traditional representative thought. It is the other name of the flesh in harmony with the unconscious. This repression of the original being is what makes Freudian psychoanalysis and archaeological phenomenology structurally interdependent. Herein lies, no doubt, the mystery of the flesh and of human sexuality which Freud, Lacan and Merleau-Ponty reveal to us in a style reminiscent of Rembrandt or Caravaggio.

Notes

1. Jean-Claude Pont quotes a section of a letter written by J. B. Listing in April 1836 (which is conserved at the University Library of Göttingen): "One definition of topology might be: the study of qualitative laws governing relations in space." (Our translation). See: Jean-Claude Pont , La topologie algébrique. PUF, Paris, 42, 1974.
2. M. Merleau-Ponty, *The Visible and the Invisible,* trans. A. Lingis (Evanston: Northwestern University Press, 1968), 210.
3. M. Merleau-Ponty, *Eye and mind,* trans. Carleton Dallery. In: *The Primacy of Perception, and Other Essays on Phenomenological Psychology, the Philosophy of Art, History and Politics,* ed. James M. Edie (Evanston: Northwestern University Press, 1964), 186.
4. Jean Petitot also agrees that the characteristic segmentability of the visual field is intimately related to a spatial order. Husserl does not say anything different with the material synthesis of colour and extension.
5. Notably Paul Schilder's research. Merleau-Ponty wrote, in 1953, in the course summary of *The Sensible World and the World of Expression*: "The contemporary research on the body scheme [...] renews our idea of space". See: Merleau-Ponty: *The Sensible World and the World of Expression,* trans. John O'Neill. In *Themes from the Letters at the Collège de France 1952–1960,* (Evanston: Northwestern University Press, 1970), 7.
6. E. De Saint Aubert: *Sources et sens de la topologie chez Merleau-Ponty*. In: Alter, 9 (2001).
7. M. Merleau-Ponty: *Notes sur le corps* (1956–1957), Bibliothèque Nationale de France, box 7, envelope 3 (Our translation).
8. M. Merleau-Ponty: Préparation du cours de 1960 sur Nature et Logos: Le corps humain (Bibliothèque nationale de France), box 7, envelope 5 (Our translation).

9. J. B. Listing writes: "One definition of topology might be: the study of qualitative laws governing relations in space. This science is labile, I have a strong conviction in a method of exact research" (Our translation). See footnote 1.
10. If flesh is the other name for the unconscious, there is no doubt that Lacan would have responded in the affirmative to this question.
11. Edmund Husserl, *Logical Investigations,* vol. 2. trans. J. N. Findlay (Humanities Press, 1970), 451.
12. Edmund Husserl, *Ideas: General Introduction to Pure Phenomenology,* trans. W. R. Boyce Gibson (New York: Macmillan, 1952), 211.
13. "The Cartesian conception of nature will outlive this ontology, [...] until the quite un-Cartesian developments in contemporary science open them up for a different ontology." See: Merleau-Ponty, *The Concept of Nature, I,* trans. John O'Neill. *Themes from the Letters at the Collège de France 1952–1960* (Evanston: Northwestern University Press, 1970), 69.
14. Unpublished lecture delivered on March 22, 2007 at the Sorbonne in Paris, France (Our translation). Soon to be published in the journal of *Métaphysique et de Morale.*
15. M. Merleau-Ponty, *The Visible and the Invisible,* trans. A. Lingis (Evanston: Northwestern University Press, 1968), 157–158.
16. Ibid., 270.
17. Ibid., 204.
18. Ibid., 271.
19. Ibid., 216–217.
20. Ibid., 203.
21. In French, *promiscuité* refers to: a disparate gathering of things; a crowding together of individuals in tight quarters felt as particularly uncomfortable or contrary to morals; or sexual relations between individuals in violation of moral or legal codes.
22. M. Merleau-Ponty, *The Visible and the Invisible,* Ibid., 208.
23. Translation with modifications in brackets (followed by the French term): M. Merleau-Ponty: *The Visible and the Invisible,* Ibid., 237. Note the polysemy of the word *doublé,* which means: increased by two; covered on the inside surface with a layer of material; and "that which is also at the time." In addition, *dédoublement* can mean: to make two things appear where there was only one thing at first; the fact of being divided in two; the act of distinguishing two elements or aspects of a whole; and the act of removing a lining from an article of clothing.
24. M. Merleau-Ponty, *The Visible and the Invisible,* Ibid., 246.
25. Ibid., 153.
26. Ibid., 260.
27. Ibid., 264.
28. "We have to pass from the thing (spatial or temporal) as difference, i.e. as transcendence, i.e. as always 'behind', beyond, far-off..." See: M. Merleau-Ponty: *The Visible and the Invisible,* Ibid., 195.
29. Ibid., 264.
30. The chiasm designates first and foremost a rhetorical figure comprised of four terms whose interlacing provokes the opposite of what their symmetry would lead one to expect. The chiasm neither expresses identity, nor difference, but rather identity within the difference of traditionally opposed terms.
31. M. Merleau-Ponty, *The Visible and the Invisible,* Ibid., 215.
32. Ibid., 272.
33. Although *charnel* is a synonym for physical, the adjective echoes Merleau-Ponty's notion of the flesh, *chair.*
34. M. Merleau-Ponty, *The Visible and the Invisible,* Ibid., 139.
35. Ibid., 140–141.
36. Ibid., 218.
37. Using Pierre Soury's mathematical courses as a starting point, Erik Porge explains the Lacanian choice in favour of a topological presentation of knots, a choice which serves for our inspiration, as follows: "In the current state of mathematics, the algebrisation of the thrust does not suffice to characterise all of the knots and chains at the same time. Thus the calculations of

Milnor (which are among the most modern calculations regarding chains) (for more information, see: *Link groups,* in: Annals of mathematics 54 (1954); *Isotopy of links*, in *Algebraic Geometry and Topology* (Princeton: Princeton University Press, 1957 GFD)), ignore the difference between the two chains which Lacan opposed, that of fantasy and that which one had the ability to qualify as 'a sexual relation' (...). One can also affirm that the results of operations on a chain (linking, splitting, establishing continuity, changes in representation) could not be systematically predicted by algebraic writings, even if these writings can follow the steps of transformations. One needs the aid of a representation in order to follow such transformations." See: *Abords topologiques.* In: Littoral, *5* (1982), 50.

38. The psychoanalyst Erik Porge sees here the markings of all manifestations of the unconscious. (See: *Se compter trios* : *Le temps logique de Lacan.* Toulouse: Erès, 1982).
39. M. Merleau-Ponty, *The Merleau-Ponty Aesthetics Reader: Philosophy and Painting*, ed. Galen A. Johnson, trans. Michael B. Smith (Evanston: Northwestern University Press, 1993), 127.
40. Jacques Lacan, *The four fundamental concepts of psycho-analysis*, ed. Jacques-Alain Miller, trans. Alan Sheridan (New York: Norton, 1978).
41. In addition, Renaud Barbaras also notices this in his book: *Vie et Intentionnalité.* (Paris: Vrin, 2003), 22.
42. Le sinthome, in Ornicar ?, 12, July 1976, 7.
43. Jacques Lacan: *Séminaire 23, Le Sinthome.* February 17, 1976, 87.
44. Let us note in passing that Lacan is thinking of Hegel, his long-time collaborator, when talking about insanity. The confusion of essentialities is exactly what characterises the delirium of the good soul, since, as Hegel writes, "In this way self-consciousness is related to a twofold antithetic essence; it is in its own self a contradiction, and is distraught in its inmost being." Hegel: *Phenomenology of Spirit,* trans. A. V. Miller (Oxford: Clarendon Press, 1977) 225.
45. Jacques Lacan, *Séminaire 23, Le Sinthome* (Paris: Seuil, 2005) 54–55.
46. From a doctrinal point of view, on Lacan's side, the additional hole of the torus is referred to the One of the signifier of the Name-of-the-Father, which at the same time founds and makes the symbolic incomplete, or, more precisely, founds it in a paradoxical form of incompleteness. Only the nomination by the father was in fact the guaranty of making a hole for Lacan. In the lecture of February 11, 1975, he indeed stated: "I will, if I can so put it, ask this year the question to discover the import of the interlacing of the imaginary with the symbolic and the real, if this additional function in total of a supplementary torus is necessary, a torus whose substance would refer to the function accorded to the father." See the following diagram: Figure n° 5. As Lacan details: "in that they are tied together, everything depends on one, on one in its role as a hole, it transfers its substance to all of the others," RSI, class of April 15, 1975, unpublished (Our translations).
47. "Here is exactly what happens, and where I embody the ego as corrector of a missing connection, is what, in the case of Joyce, does not tie the Imaginary to that which makes a chain with the real and the unconscious" (Our translation). Jacques Lacan: *Séminaire 23, Le Sinthome, ibid.*, 152.
48. We are now meeting up with Lacan's analyses in his course on the *Sinthome*, Seuil, 2005.
49. Jacques Derrida: *Chaque fois unique, la fin du monde*, (Paris: Galilée, 2003), 9 (Our translation).

Body Memory and the Unconscious

Thomas Fuchs

> *...Il n'y pas d'homme intérieur, l'homme est au monde et c'est dans le monde qu'il se connaît.*
>
> Maurice Merleau-Ponty[1]

Abstract In traditional psychoanalysis the unconscious was conceived as a primary intra-psychic reality, hidden 'below consciousness' and only accessible to a 'depth psychology' based on metapsychological premises and concepts. In contrast to this *vertical* conception, the present paper presents a phenomenological approach to the unconscious as a *horizontal* dimension of the lived body, lived space and intercorporeality. This approach is based on a phenomenology of body memory which is defined as the totality of implicit dispositions of perception and behavior mediated by the body and sedimented in the course of earlier experiences.
What belongs to body memory, therefore, is what perseveres, not in the form of an explicit memory, but as a "style of existence" (Merleau-Ponty). This corporeal and intercorporeal unconscious "... is not to be sought in our innermost [psyche] behind the back of our 'consciousness', but before us, as the structure of our field" (Merleau-Ponty). Unconscious fixations are like restrictions in the spatial potentiality of a person, caused by a past which is implicit in the present and resists the progress of life; this includes traumatic experiences in particular. Their traces are not hidden in an interior psychic world, but manifest themselves – as in a figure-background relationship – in the form of "blind spots" or "empty spaces" in day-to-day living.

T. Fuchs (✉)
Psychiatrische Universitätsklinik, Universität Heidelberg,
Voßstr. 4, D-69115 Heidelberg, Germany
e-mail: thomas.fuchs@med.uni-heidelberg.de

D. Lohmar and J. Brudzińska (eds.), *Founding Psychoanalysis Phenomenologically*, Phaenomenologica 199, DOI 10.1007/978-94-007-1848-7_4,

They manifest themselves in behavior patterns into which a person repeatedly blunders, in actions that she avoids without being aware of it or in the opportunities offered by life which she does not dare to take or even to see. The unconscious of body memory is thus characterized by the absence of forgotten or repressed experiences, and at the same time by their corporeal and intercorporeal presence in the lived space and in the day-to-day life of a person. '-- End of Abstract'

1 Introduction: Psychoanalysis and Phenomenology

Psychoanalysis and phenomenology, two theories that arose at more or less the same time,[2] both considering themselves basic sciences of subjectivity, have nevertheless remained foreign to one another. The grounds for this are probably to be found primarily in their conflicting views of the role played by consciousness. To psychoanalysis, consciousness appeared only as a shimmering varnish concealing psychological forces and processes in unfathomable depths which are what is actually effective. For phenomenology, on the other hand, consciousness rather was the medium or the light through which all phenomena come to be seen in the first place, and appear as such. Consciousness as the sphere of mere *semblance (Schein)* or of *manifestation (Erscheinung)* – is a pointed distinction that could be made between the two. Accordingly, they held contrasting views also of the unconscious: either it was considered the actual source of the psyche's life, the hidden meaningful structure and driving force which made its way by various but coded means even in opposition to the conscious intentions of the subject. Or the unconscious had to be viewed as restricted to an implicit awareness that remained potentially accessible to consciousness or reflection, and, in any case, could not basically be foreign to the subject. In Husserl's words:

> What I do not 'know', what in my experience, my imagining, thinking, doing, is not present to me as perceived, remembered, thought, etc., will not 'influence' my mind. And what is not in my experience, be it ignored or implicitly-intentionally decided, does not motivate me even unconsciously (Husserl 1952, 231).

These two views seem hardly reconcilable. Antagonistic as they may seem, however, on closer analysis, psychoanalysis and phenomenology, do in fact have a common starting point: it is in the Cartesian view of consciousness as "clear and distinct perception", the assumption that consciousness is transparent to itself insofar as its own contents are concerned. For Husserl, the "cogito" is the present evidence, the necessary "appresentation" of all contents in the observing consciousness, without which it would melt or escape into the unreality of past or future. All memories, all ideas, all the possibilities of consciousness, must cling, as it were, to this evident present so as not to disintegrate. But Freud's view of consciousness is not much different: conscious is only "… the idea that is present in our consciousness and which we perceive" in each case (Freud 1943, 29). Consciousness, therefore, as in classical thought, is considered the space for current ideas or representations. The unconscious is then the space which is conceived as containing all the other ideas which are not present at a particular moment. Freud rejects an ambiguous knowing-unknowing consciousness for "… a consciousness of which one knows nothing seems to me many times more absurd than a psychic unconscious" (Freud 1940b, 243). Consciousness must be transparent to itself or it is not consciousness at all.

Psychoanalysis thus rebelled against the classical philosophy of consciousness, and not only failed to overcome it but, without being aware of it, even adopted its premises. The situation is similar to that in today's conflict between neurobiology and classical philosophy: The sovereign, autonomous conscious subject that neurobiology believes it must dethrone is itself merely a dualistic construct. Separated from its body and its life, restricted to present "mental states", the bodiless, and to this extent powerless, "ego" becomes easy prey to neurobiological reductionism, and the role of the unconscious as the actually powerful substrate is now taken over by the material brain. With this, of course, there is the threat of naturalizing subjectivity in a way that could have a much more reifying effect than Freud's interpretation of man as *"homo natura"*, criticized by Binswanger (1957).

Now, the dimension of *corporeality of the subject* which was increasingly brought to the fore by phenomenology as time went on, could just as easily have become the core of psychoanalysis. Freud, as is well known, did not only see the origin of the Ego in the body.[3] The body also played a decisive role in psychoanalytical drive theory, since this theory it assumed a step-by-step development of partial drives which are dominated by certain regions of the body, and whose "destinies" permanently affect the development of the individual. Nevertheless, despite this concept, the dualism of body and mind made an impact on psychoanalytic theory. For Freud, in the final analysis, drives are not phenomena of the lived body, but objective-somatic quantities; and their representations do not belong to a libidinous body of the subject but are already part of the psyche as an inner, hidden apparatus where drive derivatives and drive energies are converted into one another and distributed to various levels of the psyche – an apparatus which can only be decoded on the basis of external signs such as body-language or by way of speech. In the end, the body thus remained interesting only as the seat of symbolic or imagined meanings, as a primary projection field for the psyche, so to speak, which always had to be scrutinized for hidden meanings. That mental phenomena could at the same time be bodily as well was not imaginable in the dualistic paradigm.

With the idea of the "psychic apparatus" which doubtlessly goes back to Freud's own early brain theory, an entity had also been created that served as a sort of inner container for pictures and memories of external reality. Introjected as "object-representations", "imagos" etc., they populated the various compartments of the psyche and there developed a life of their own with the help of the drive energies. In this way, the Ego remained separated from important parts of these compartments through radical ignorance: the topologically structured, dynamic unconscious, according to Freud, is basically different from the pre-conscious as the latent and implicitly "previously known" (Freud 1940c, 77 f.). Between the pre-conscious and the unconscious stands the economical mechanism of repression, and both what is repressed and the repressing mechanism – i.e. the motivation for repression – elude consciousness.

As evidence for this concept, Freud could point to physical symptoms or *Freudian slips*, which appeared alien or meaningless to the Ego, furthermore to the difference between manifest and latent *dream content* which is attributable to an unconscious censor, and, last but not least, to the *resistance* shown by the patient during analysis to becoming aware of what has been repressed.

This radical separation of the unconscious, however, took place at the cost of its having to take a problematic ambiguous position between subjective experiencing and objective processes (Waldenfels 2002, 294). In fact, in the final analysis, it had to be assigned to the objectivity of the psychological apparatus. Freud solves the paradox he discovered, namely that one "knows something that one simultaneously does not know" and that "one is struck with blindness while the eyes see" (Freud 1957, 175 note) by the splitting of the psyche into two parts. As a consequence, the unconscious turns into an "internal foreign country", (Freud 1940c, 62), in other words to something external within oneself, whose meaning and effect are alien to the subject. – At this point, however, one should not only bear in mind Husserl's objection to a motivation which is entirely alien to the subject. How, over and above this, should the subject be in the position to re-appropriate such an alien meaning unless, both in origin and in its latency, it was always *his own* meaning? Psychoanalytical therapy could then do no more than convey rational insights into the mechanisms of one's own inner life, and could not contribute to a genuine integration of the personality. The aim of therapy: "where id was, ego shall be", would then remain a matter of explicit knowledge, not of actual self-appropriation.

The phenomenological critique of this concept now moved along various paths:

- Sartre saw the unconscious not as a circumstance imposing restrictions on the subject from outside, but as a basic modality of the subject's constitutive relationship to himself, namely, that of bad faith, *"mauvaise foi"* (Sartre 1962, 91 ff.). The subject assumes an ambivalent relationship to himself, he allows himself, so to speak, to slide into an "intentional inattention": one doesn't know something *and* doesn't want to know it; one doesn't see something *and* doesn't want to see it, and in this way becomes the deceived and the deceiver in one.
- A comparable form of double consciousness may be found, as Bernet (1997) has undertaken to show, in Husserl's analyses of the perception of images, of the reproductive consciousness, of memory, and above all, of *imagination*: these forms of consciousness in each case entail a duplicity of presence and absence so that the Ego lives in two worlds at the same time. In this way, they can also serve as paradigms for the relationship between conscious and unconscious.
- Another way of overcoming the dualism of conscious and unconscious consists of expanding the space of subjectivity *vertically* so to speak, so that it can include the phenomena of drive and urge as a basic stratum. This method of reinterpretation of Freud's metapsychological terms into an elementary activity of life which always precedes the conscious experience of oneself, was an approach partly adopted by Max Scheler (1983), and then, primarily, by Michel Henry (1992).
- Finally, there is the possibility of taking the ambiguity of the body, as understood by Merleau-Ponty, as the starting point, to extend subjectivity in the *horizontal*

dimension and to encounter the unconscious in physical *behavior*, in *day-to-day living* and in the structures of the person's *lived space*. Body memory plays a special part here, insofar as it changes a person's corporeal and intercorporeal experiences into implicitly effective predispositions, which provide the mostly unconscious basis for day-to-day living.

This is the course which I will take in what follows (without rejecting the other possibilities mentioned). So the question will be: Can the unconscious be localized in the lived relationships and conduct of a person – in other words in the *horizontal* dimension of the lived body and intercorporeality? How far can such a concept reflect elements of Freud's unconscious? – In what follows, I first want to develop the concept of body memory and the relational field that it constitutes, and then ask about the structures of this field where the unconscious can take up its abode as it were.

2 Body Memory

If, following Merleau-Ponty, we view the body not as the visible, touchable and sentient physical body but first and foremost as our *capacity* to see, touch, sense, then body memory designates the totality of these bodily predispositions as they have developed in the course of our development – in other words, in their historical dimension. In body memory, the situations and actions experienced in the past are, as it were, all fused together without any of them standing out individually. Through the repetition and superimposition of experiences, a habit structure has been formed: well-practiced motion sequences, repeatedly perceived *gestalten*, forms of actions and interactions have become an implicit bodily knowledge and skill. Body memory does not take one back to the past, but conveys an implicit effectiveness of the past in the present. This approach converges with the results of recent memory research on the central significance of *implicit* memory which is just as much at the basis of our customary behavior as of our unconscious *avoidance* of actions (Schacter 1999; Fuchs 2000c).

The body is thus the ensemble of organically developed predispositions and capacities to perceive, to act but also to desire and to communicate. Its experiences, anchored in body memory, blanket the environment like an invisible network which relates us to things and to people. It is, as Merleau-Ponty writes, "our permanent means of 'taking up attitudes' and thus constructing virtual presents", in other words to actualize our past and, with this, to make ourselves feel at home in situations (Merleau-Ponty 1962, 181). Even more: in the bodily experience structures, the other is always already included, he is understood in expression and intended in desire. Before I can reflect on what I am communicating through my gestures or speech, my body always already creates the feeling of being-with; it expresses itself through attitude and gestures, and at the same time reacts to the impressions of others. This "Intercorporeality" (Merleau-Ponty 2003, 256) forms an overriding, intersubjective system in which, from childhood on, forms of bodily interaction are established and constantly updated anew. It comprises the self and the others, the conscious and the unconscious: "I do not need to look for the others elsewhere, I find them within my experience, they dwell in the niches which contain what is hidden from me but visible to them" (Merleau-Ponty 1974, 166).

3 Body Memory and Life Space

Body memory – like the body schema – thus forms not only an interior system restricted to the physical body. Rather, it constitutes a sensomotoric, emotional and interactive field in which we, as embodied beings, constantly move and conduct ourselves. The terminology of Kurt Lewin's field psychology (1969) offers itself here, particularly the concept of *life space*. In order to link it with the structures of body memory, I want to give a brief outline of this in what follows.

The life space is centered around the person and the person's body. According to Lewin, it is characterized by experienced characteristics such as closeness or distance, narrowness or breadth, connectedness or separateness, attainability or elusiveness, and it is structured by physical or symbolic *boundaries* which offer resistance to movement. This produces more or less clearly bounded *sectors* such as the peripersonal space around one's own body, claimed territories (property, home), the sphere of influence which emanates from someone, but also prohibited or taboo zones. The lived space is further permeated by tangible *"field forces"* or *"vectors"*, in the first place those which attract and repel. Competing attracting or repelling forces in the life space lead to typical conflicts such as attraction *versus* aversion, attraction *versus* attraction etc. They can be considered as conflicting directions of movement or possibilities which are offered to a person in a given situation.

A good example of conflicting field forces is offered by the situation of a small child who is torn back and forth between his bond to his mother and curiosity (cf. Stern 1991, 101). The mother is first of all the "safe haven", the centre of gravity, so to speak, which curves the child's experienced space in such a way that he remains in her vicinity. The space thus acquires a gradient: the further the child moves away from his mother, the more empty, more lonely the space becomes. While it condenses again around other, i.e. strange, people, the child rather makes a detour around them: the space curvature near them is "negative". Little by little, the child's exploratory drive and the attractive charms of the environment loosen the child's tie to his mother, so that it becomes possible to increase the distance against the gradient – only until the bond is stretched too much, and the child runs back to his mother in the end. – This example is also a good illustration of the fact that the respective field structures are based on body memory, in this case, the history of the experiences the child has had in closeness and ties to his mother. Another proverbial example lies in the saying, "Once bitten, twice shy", which illustrates the aversive effect of body memory. A third example, finally, is given by the zones of prohibition which restrict the directions in which a child can move so that its spontaneous impulses interfere with parental imperatives, namely, inasmuch these have left a negative mark on its very life space.

Consequently, the life space – depending on the respective experiences, capabilities and motives of a person – can bear varying significances, relevances or valences. In analogy to a physical field, "gravitational effects", invisible "curvatures" of space, or barriers can appear which restrict or prevent spontaneous movements. Particularly in psychopathology, we encounter various deformations of the lived space, as, for instance, the taboo zones of obsessives and the avoidance zones of phobias, which are based on certain past experiences laid down in body memory.

4 On the Phenomenology of the Unconscious

With this, I have made a brief sketch of an approach and a terminology which permit the question of the unconscious to be put and answered in a different way.

If we reject a topologically structured unconscious beyond consciousness – an independent intra-psychic process which impacts on the experiencing subject from outside, so to speak – then we may ask whether the unconscious might not be considered another mode of experiencing that manifests itself in the *horizontal* dimension of the lived body and the lived space. The paradigm for this would be the ambiguity of the body itself which, while seeing, always remains unseen, and of whose dispositions I often remain unaware, which in fact come to meet me from outside, namely in the form of the attractive or repelling objects, the inviting characters and field structures of my environment. Such an unconscious would then, as Merleau-Ponty writes, "... be found not in our innermost sphere behind the back of 'consciousness', but before us as the structure of our field" (Merleau-Ponty 1986, 233). It would be the unrecognized reverse side of our experience and conduct, or its other, hidden meaning.

As our starting point, let us first consider the field structure of a repressed wish. In his short story "*Der Branntweinsäufer und die Berliner Glocken*" (The brandy drinker and Berlin's bells), Heinrich von Kleist recounts the story of an alcoholic soldier who, after insistent preaching and punishment, has resolved to become abstinent but was found drunk after only 3 days. Asked how this relapse could have happened after all his good resolutions, the soldier justified himself by saying that the devil must have had his hand in it because while walking through the town he suddenly heard the names of various brandies in the tolling of the bells – for example *"Kümmel! Kümmel!"*, in the ringing of the town hall bell, "*Pomm*eranzen, *Pomm*eranzen" in the ringing cathedral bell and so on. In the end, he could not help being defeated by these insidious sounds.[4] – While this humorous example relates only to a wish that was not repressed but merely suppressed by an act of will, it gives a fine illustration of the indirect way in which contrary bodily impulses or drives can get their way, namely from outside. The experiential field is, so to speak, interspersed with suppressed desire which becomes crystallized finally around certain perceptions – namely those which are sufficiently vague while offering a certain similarity for the purpose: in this case the various chimes. The uncertain or ambiguous is the place where a latent or hidden significance can take shape. The drive or the wish that was not satisfied breaks through circuitously and from outside so that, in principle, we can already recognize the mechanism of *displacement*. What is actually desired is fulfilled through something similar.

A comparable interference of expressed thematic and non-thematic directions of meaning is also found in the various types of *"Freudian slips"*. Freud himself says that "…slips are the result of two different intentions which interfere with one another, of which one can be called the disturbed and the other the disturbing intention" (Freud 1940a, 56). Mishearing is most like the example of Kleist's soldier: a latently desired meaning is "interpreted" from a similar sequence of sounds. With mistakes in speaking, writing and in (mis)placing things another intention interferes with the explicitly intended action, so that "the right hand – literally – does not know what the left hand is doing". Finally, with *forgetting*, an originally made but unpleasant intention is blanked out and replaced by others, for example, routine processes. Thus, in spontaneous bodily perceptions or actions which take place "of their own accord", the relevant latent intention breaks through – in a reversal or *chiasm* which is linguistically expressed by the prefix "mis-".

The producer of the slip can now either immediately or after some brief thought recognise its significance and ascribe it to himself, or he finds it "senseless", in other words, alien to himself. For example, Freud writes the following concerning "misspeaking":

> If later we present it [the intention on which the misspeaking was based] to the speaker, he may either acknowledge it as something familiar, so that it was only temporarily unconscious, or he may deny it as alien to himself, which means that it was permanently unconscious (Freud 1940c, 77).

It is on this difference, amongst other things, that Freud bases his categorical distinction between the pre-conscious and the true dynamic unconscious which is excluded or repressed from consciousness "by living forces" (Freud 1943, 436). The defence mechanism and the corresponding resistance to the latent meaning, obviously have as their prerequisite that the inhibitive trends and their motives are themselves excluded from consciousness. However, the question is whether this justifies establishing a special intrapsychic space for the dynamic unconscious. Against this, there is the merely gradual difference between a temporary and a permanent unconscious in the Freud quotation cited above. In both cases, after all, we are dealing mainly with a duplicity of intentions, to which only an additional repressive tendency is added in the second case. But if we do not assign the "living forces" of repression of which Freud speaks, to an intrapsychic mechanism beyond consciousness, but see them rather as field forces, we will easily find models for them in the bodily or life space.

The first thing that comes to mind would be the *relieving posture* adopted after sustaining an injury: spontaneously one avoids putting the injured limb at risk from dangerous objects and holds it back without having actually to think of the event. Avoidance behavior is thus incorporated into the implicit body memory. Moreover,

I have already mentioned the *zones of prohibition* which face the child and operate against its approach through negative field forces as long as the child respects them "of its own accord". We come one step closer to the dynamic unconscious with zones or objects which are *taboo*. For, unlike prohibition, the taboo has a special structure and effect in that it is not expressly formulated but is generated by the avoidance behavior of others, like a negative curvature of the shared life space around what is prohibited. Taboos are most effective when the members of the community are not aware of them. The infringement of taboos is not necessarily punished with open penalties, but automatically generates feelings of shame, guilt or abhorrence in the offender, reinforced by the contempt and the ostracizing silence of the others.

In all these cases, experience and conduct are determined by negative – i.e. "repulsive" – field forces exercising their effect unconsciously since the subject, like the "bitten" person, has gradually extricated herself from the possible conflict. Avoidance has become an implicit, bodily pattern of behavior so that what is potentially threatening in the environment is no longer consciously experienced. Nevertheless, repelling forces do not appear to consciousness as coming from outside but, in Hegel's terms, as its own otherness. They remain co-extensive with the experience field but as its negative. The manifest feelings of fear, guilt or shame which arise on stepping beyond the barriers in the life space were already latently present before, endowing these barriers with their affective loading.

In the same way as in the case of a "slip", the dynamic unconscious puts up resistance to its becoming conscious. This resistance is itself not conscious, nor is it pre-conscious, but on this account it is not altogether outside consciousness. It is rather an *ambiguity or duplicity of consciousness itself*; in such a way that the subject, if she hits on the manifestation of the hidden meaning, at least has an inkling that it is asking her a *question*, namely about her own otherness. The unconscious, writes Merleau-Ponty, "... cannot be a process 'in the third person', since it itself selects what will be admitted to official existence, since it detours around thoughts and situations which we resist, and is thus not a *non-knowing* but rather an unacknowledged, unformulated knowledge that we do not wish to tolerate. In a still imprecise language, Freud is here in the process of discovering what others more correctly have called an *ambiguous perception*" (Merleau-Ponty 2003, 79).

We can understand this ambiguity of consciousness with the example of another defence mechanism, namely *projection*. Here the beam in one's own eye becomes the splinter in another's eye, in other words, one perceives in others the impulses and motives against which one has built defences in oneself. Naturally, this perception is also ambiguous, since the excessive zeal with which the impulses in others are disapproved derives its energy precisely from the efforts one has to make to neutralize one's own impulses. The blind spot in self-awareness – and here Freud is doubtlessly right – does not result from a mere "overlooking", but from active and emotionally charged repression. Nevertheless, this repression remains the work and the effort of the subject herself, not of a mechanism outside her.

5 Trauma and Reiteration

Let us now turn to another phenomenon, namely, the unconscious effect of an emotional trauma which Merleau-Ponty set out to interpret in his "Phenomenology of Perception". What is repressed, he writes, is like a phantom limb for an amputee inasmuch as a bodily capacity continues in the latter which is no longer congruent with the present. Habitual and current body come into conflict with one another. Similarly, repression also creates an empty space in current subjectivity (Merleau-Ponty 1962, 87), as if the negative left by an experience which has not been dealt with interposes itself unnoticed before every new situation and thus imprisons the traumatized person in a past which is still present. "...(T)his fixation does not merge into memory; it even excludes memory in so far as the latter spreads out in front of us, like a picture, a former experience, whereas this past which remains our true present [the trauma, T.F.] does not leave us but remains constantly hidden behind our gaze instead being displayed before it. The traumatic experience does not survive as a representation in the mode of objective consciousness and as a 'dated' moment; it is of its essence to survive only as a manner of being and with a certain degree of generality" (ibid., 83).

This description assigns the repressed trauma to body memory: for this holds what is hidden "from sight" and goes on living in a general "style" of existence, not as an explicit memory. The injury has penetrated the body of the subject and has left behind a permanent responsiveness, a readiness to defend itself. The traumatized person becomes hypersensitive to threatening, shaming situations similar to the trauma in some manner, even if this similarity is not consciously known, and tries to circumvent them. "The resistance is directed to a certain area of experience, a certain category, a certain type of memory" (ibid., 194). All the same, at every step, the victim may encounter something that reawakens the trauma in her. Often it happens that a permanent predisposition develops to react with fear and nervousness, to become alarmed every time the doorbell rings, a feeling of being followed or observed by unknown people.

An impressive description is to be found in the memoirs of the Jewish writer Aharon Appelfeld, who from his seventh to his 13 year of age experienced the second world war hiding in the woods of the Ukraine:

> "More than fifty years have passed since the end of the second world war. I have forgotten a great deal, especially places, dates and people's names, but nevertheless I feel that time in my entire body. Whenever it rains, when it is cold or stormy, I go back to the ghetto, to the camp or into the woods where I spent such a long time. Memory apparently has deep roots in the body." – "Everything that happened at that time has left its mark in the cells of my body. Not in my memory. The body's cells seem to remember better than the memory which is intended for this. For years after the war, I did not walk in the middle of the pavement or path, but always close to the wall, always in the shade, always in a hurry like someone fleeing. (...) Sometimes it is enough to smell food, to feel dampness in my shoes or hear a sudden noise to bring me back to the war (...) The war sits in all my bones." – "(...) Hands, feet, back and knees know more than my memory. If I could dip into them, the pictures would just flood me" (Appelfeld 2005, 57, 95 f., 8 f.).

Here it is not a particular episode, but an entire segment of his life that has left its mark on the body, more deeply and permanently, of course, than the autobiographic memory could have done: Proprioception, touch, smell, hearing, even certain kinds of weather can suddenly allow the past to come to life again, and even bodily patterns of movement, such as the hunted walk close to the wall still imitates the behavior of the fugitive.

The effect of the trauma on the person can thus be viewed, first as a specific deformation of her lived space corresponding to an unconscious avoidance behavior which she adopts towards the anxiety-provoking or *"repelling zones"*. The lived space around these zones is to a certain extent negatively curved and prevents the free development of the life movement. Second, the life space is permeated with similarities in which the trauma approaches the traumatized person from outside, so that it is impossible to avoid it. For in one's attitude, one's stance, and in one's perceptive predispositions, one carries the trauma into one's world over and over again.

It is to this that the psychoanalytic concept of *repetition compulsion* relates. This is based on the clinical experience that patients continue to be drawn into the same, mostly damaging behavior or relationship patterns even if they try to prevent this at the conscious level. Their lived space is so to speak "positively curved" around these regions – in other words, these exercise an unnoticed *attraction*. If, for example, a person's early experiences were characterized by abusive and violent relationships, this issue will determine also that person's later relationship patterns. The types of abuse may vary, but the implicit behavior patterns deposited in body memory will have the effect of fulfilling her expectations and bring about the familiar type of relationship. These unconscious enactments, as they are called today, were, of course, seen by Freud as a form of transference. As he writes, we must

> ... say in analysis that the analysand *remembers* nothing at all of what has been forgotten and repressed, but he *acts it out*. He does not reproduce it as a memory but as action, he *repeats* it, naturally without realizing that he is repeating it. For example, the analysand does not say that he remembers being defiant and incredulous towards the authority of his parents, but he behaves in this manner towards the doctor (Freud 1946, 129).

The unconscious pre-history of intersubjective relations is re-enacted through the intercorporeal memory. However, this means that the unconscious is not a hidden chamber of the psyche any more, but is interwoven in the life style, in the bodily conduct of a person, as a sub-structure which remains hidden from her personally, but becomes visible to others because, in the final analysis, it is always implicitly directed to those others themselves. The "blind spot" in the centre of consciousness can also be viewed as the other side of the intersubjective relationship, in which our own being-with-others must necessarily remain hidden from us, so that this dark side of ourselves can only be illuminated in our communication with others. For in my world they dwell in "... the niches which contain what is hidden from me but visible to them" (Merleau-Ponty 1974, 166).

6 Summary

From the point of view of a phenomenology of the lived body, the unconscious is not an intrapsychic reality residing in the depths "below consciousness". Rather, it surrounds and permeates conscious life, just as in picture puzzles the figure hidden in the background surrounds the foreground, and just as the lived body conceals itself while functioning. It is an unconscious which is not located in the *vertical* dimension of the psyche but rather in the *horizontal* dimension of lived space, most of all lodging in the intercorporeality of dealings with others, as the hidden reverse side of day-to-day living. It is an unconscious which is not to be found inside the individual but in his relationships to others.[5]

Unconscious fixations are like certain restrictions in a person's space of potentialities produced by an implicit but ever-present past which declines to take part in the continuing progress of life. Their traces, however, are not hidden in an inner psychic world but manifest themselves rather as "blind spots", "empty spaces" or curvatures in the lived space: in the "slips" in speech and action; in the relationship patterns into which a person repeatedly blunders, in the actions which are avoided without being aware of it; in the spaces which are not entered, the opportunities offered by life which one does not take, and even does not dare to see. Such traces may be recognized as "negatives" so to speak, in the form of inhibitions or omissions which are characteristic of a person. They can also become symbolically or physically present in neurotic or psychosomatic symptoms. The symptom is to this extent neither meaningless nor a defective habit – as learning theory assumed[6] – nor is its meaning to be found outside itself, in the unconscious interior. Rather, it lies in the intercorporeal expression – in other words, it results from the meanings of the symptom in the interactive field, even if these meanings are not evident, but must be understood and interpreted.

The unconscious is thus absence in presence, the unperceived in the perceived (Merleau-Ponty 1986, 308 f.). Like a figure blanks out the background from which it stands out, consciousness, perception and language conceal the reverse side of the unconscious, of the unperceived and of silence which are always bound up with them. This reverse side, however, does not remain fully concealed but expresses itself in reversals, chiasmatic entanglements, in an ambiguity of consciousness: One does not know something *and* does not want to know it; one does not see something *and* does not want to see it – in other words, one looks past it intentionally-unintentionally. Consciousness is not fully transparent to itself because it hides itself from itself.

This duplicity of consciousness corresponds to the ambiguity of the body whose modes of appearing fluctuate between the thematic and the unthematic, between the physical (*Körper*) and the lived body (*Leib*). But it also corresponds to the ambivalent, conflict-prone nature of our existence itself where we as natural, embodied beings can always confront our own instinctive and natural side as well. This is what constitutes the contradictoriness or, to speak with Plessner (1975), the "eccentricity" of the way we relate to ourselves, the constant conflict between spontaneity and reflectivity, body and soul, nature and nurture, conscious and unconscious. One could then accuse Freud that even he, for all his skepticism, meant much too well with mankind in that he tried to relieve man's consciousness of this inherent conflict, and placed his opposing will in a separate space belonging to the unconscious – thus withdrawing this will from the subject's responsibility.

Notes

1. *Phénoménologie de la perception*, Paris 1945, S. V. – "… there is no inner man, man is in the world, and only in the world does he know himself. " (Merleau-Ponty 1962, S. xi).
2. As is well known, both Husserl's "*Logische Untersuchungen*" and Freud's "*Traumdeutung*" appeared in 1900.
3. Cf. Freud 1940b, 253.
4. Kleist 1984. – The story is also cited by Graumann (1960, 151) as an illustration of the motivational basis of perspectivity.
5. "(…) the latency of psychoanalysis is an unconscious that is *beneath* conscious life and *within* the individual, an *intrapsychic* reality that leads to a psychology of depth in the *vertical* dimension. (…) the latency of phenomenology is an unconscious which *surrounds* conscious life, an unconsciousness in the world, *between us*, an *ontological* theme that leads to a psychology of depth in the *lateral* dimension" (Romanyshyn 1977).
6. "Learning theory assumes no 'unconscious' causes whatsoever but views neurotic symptoms simply as learned habits. There is no neurosis at the bottom of the symptom, only the symptom itself" (Eysenck u. Rachmann 1972, 20).

References

Appelfeld, A. 2005. *Geschichte eines Lebens*. Berlin: Rowohlt.

Bernet, R. 1997. Husserls Begriff des Phantasiebewusstseins als Fundierung von Freuds Begriff des Unbewussten. In *Grundlinien der Vernunftkritik*, ed. C. Jamme, 277–306. Frankfurt: Suhrkamp.

Binswanger, L. 1957. Freuds Auffassung des Menschen im Lichte der Anthropologie. In Ders., *Der Mensch in der Psychiatrie*. Pfullingen: Neske.

Charbonneau, G. 1999. De quoi's'agit' l'inconscient phénoménologique? L'art du Comprendre: herméneutique générale. Anthropologie philosophique. Anthropologie phénoménologique. *Daseinsanalyse* 8: 132–146.

Eysenck, H.J., and S. Rachmann. 1972. *Neurosen – Ursachen und Heilmethoden*. Berlin: Deutscher Verlag der Wissenschaften.

Freud, S. 1940a. *Vorlesungen zur Einführung in die Psychoanalyse*. GW Bd. 11. Frankfurt: Fischer.

Freud, S. 1940b. *Das Ich und das* Es. GW Bd. 13, S. 235–289. Frankfurt: Fischer.

Freud, S. 1940c. *Neue Folge der Vorlesungen zur Einführung in die Psychoanalyse*. GW Bd. 15. Frankfurt: Fischer.

Freud, S. 1943. *Einige Bemerkungen über den Begriff des Unbewussten in der Psychoanalyse*. GW Bd. 8, S. 429–439. Frankfurt: Fischer.

Freud, S. 1946. *Erinnern, Wiederholen, Durcharbeiten*. GW Bd. 10, S. 126–136. Frankfurt: Fischer 1946.

Freud, S. 1957. *Studien über Hysterie (mit J. Breuer)*. GW Bd. 1, S. 77–312. Frankfurt: Fischer 1952.

Fuchs, T. 2000a. *Leib, Raum. Person. Entwurf einer phänomenologischen Anthropologie*. Stuttgart: Klett-Cotta.

Fuchs, T. 2000b. *Psychopathologie von Leib und Raum. Phänomenologisch-empirische Untersuchungen zu depressiven u nd paranoiden Erkrankungen*. Darmstadt: Steinkopff.

Fuchs, T. 2000c. Das Gedächtnis des Leibes. *Phänomenologische Forschungen* 5: 71–89.

Fuchs, T. 2006a. Psychotherapie des "gelebten Raums". Eine phänomenologisch-ökologische Konzeption. Psycho-Logik. Jahrbuch für Psychotherapie. *Philosophie und Kultur* 1: 286–303.

Fuchs, T. 2006b. *Gibt eine leibliche Persönlichkeitsstruktur? Ein phänomenologisch-psychodynamischer Ansatz. Psychodynamische Psychotherapie* (im Druck).
Graumann, C.F. 1960. *Grundlagen einer Phänomenologie und Psychologie der Perspektivität.* Berlin: De Gruyter.
Henry, M. 1992. Radikale Lebensphänomenologie. In *Ausgewählte Studien zur Phänomenologie*, ed. R. Kühn. Freiburg/München: Alber.
Husserl, E. 1952. *Ideen zu einer reinen Phänomenologie und phänomenologischen Philosophie. II. Phänomenologische Untersuchungen zur Konstitution.* Den Haag: Nijhoff.
Kleist, H.v. 1984. *Sämtliche Erzählungen und andere Prosa.* Stuttgart: Reclam.
Lewin, K. 1969. *Grundzüge der topologischen Psychologie.* Bern: Huber.
Merleau-Ponty, M. 1962. *Phenomenology of perception.* Trans. Colin Smith. London: Routledge and Kegan Paul.
Merleau-Ponty, M. 1974. *Die Abenteuer der Dialektik.* Frankfurt/M: Suhrkamp.
Merleau-Ponty, M. 1986. *Das Sichtbare und das Unsichtbare.* München: Fink.
Merleau-Ponty, M. 2003. *Das Auge und der Geist. Philosophische Essays.* Hamburg: Meiner.
Plessner, H. 1975. *Die Stufen des Organischen und der Mensch.* Berlin: De Gruyter.
Romanyshyn, R.D. 1977. Phenomenology and psychoanalysis. *Psychoanalytic Review* 64: 211–223.
Sartre, J.-P. 1962. *Das Sein und das Nichts.* Reinbek/Hamburg: Rowohlt.
Schacter, D.L. 1999. *Wir sind Erinnerung. Gedächtnis und Persönlichkeit.* Reinbek/Hamburg: Rowohlt.
Scheler, M. 1983. *Die Stellung des Menschen im Kosmos*, 10th ed. Bern/München: Francke.
Stern, D.N. 1991. *Tagebuch eines Babys. Was ein Kind sieht, spürt, fühlt und denkt.* München: Piper.
Stern, D.N. 1998. *Die Lebenserfahrungen des Säuglings*, 6th ed. Stuttgart: Klett-Cotta.
Waldenfels, B. 2002. *Bruchlinien der Erfahrung: Phänomenologie - Psychoanalyse - Phänomenotechnik.* Frankfurt: Suhrkamp.

Psychoanalysis: Philosophy and/or Science of Subjectivity? Prospects for a Dialogue Between Phenomenology, Philosophy of Mind, and Psychoanalysis

Patrizia Giampieri-Deutsch

Abstract In spite of current plurality in psychoanalysis, in philosophy of mind, and in phenomenology some current positions within these disciplines of the mind overlap and interface on the crucial topic of subjective experience.
This article includes three sections devoted to:
First, Paul Ricœur's phenomenological approach to the psychoanalytic experience;
Second, philosophical contributions to psychoanalysis from both philosophy of mind and phenomenology;
Third, scientific contributions to psychoanalysis from the cognitive field.
Commenting on Ricœur's position on psychoanalysis, this article shows some limits of his hermeneutical understanding of psychoanalysis and points out the value of his first approach in the chapter *Epistemology: Between Psychology and Phenomenology* from his *Freud and Philosophy. An Essay on Interpretation.* Here Ricœur focuses on the analytic experience as a *via regia* for reaching the phenomenon of subjective experience, and further chooses phenomenology for an approximation to psychoanalysis. But unfortunately in his later *The Question of Proof in Freud's Psychoanalytic Writings*, Ricœur moves away from phenomenology and almost exclusively restricts the analytic experience to speech acts circumscribing the analytic experience to a narrative enterprise.
The second and third sections of this article compare the psychoanalytic approach to the subjective mind within the analytic relation to both:
First, current philosophical investigations from philosophy of mind and phenomenology on subjective experience, because psychoanalysis can be also understood as a philosophy of the singular and irreducible aspects of the subjective mind;

P. Giampieri-Deutsch (✉)
University of Vienna, Universitaetsstraße 7 room C0215, A - 1010 Vienna, Austria
e-mail: Patrizia.Giampieri-Deutsch@univie.ac.at

D. Lohmar and J. Brudzińska (eds.), *Founding Psychoanalysis Phenomenologically*, Phaenomenologica 199, DOI 10.1007/978-94-007-1848-7_5,

Second, convergent scientific data from the cognitive field, because psychoanalysis strives also to become a science of the general mechanisms of the subjective mind. If a major flaw of current psychoanalysis is the inner fragmentation within its basic assumptions, facing the external challenges from the cognitive field offers the opportunity to reconstruct the knowledge base of psychoanalysis on a more adequate foundation. '-- End of Abstract'

Current plurality in psychoanalysis (but also in philosophy of mind and in phenomenology) may be either perceived as confusion or celebrated. Regarding the situation of psychoanalysis, what I am addressing here are not general epistemological issues like unity of science versus plurality of sciences, as discussed in Jerry Fodor's response[1] to Paul Oppenheim and Hilary Putnam,[2] but rather and more concretely current tendency toward entropy within the knowledge base of psychoanalysis. Though some psychoanalysts seem to welcome what they call "diversification", others, such as Peter Fonagy, find the proliferation of competing accounts through the dissolution of a common ground far more sobering: "This fragmentation and confusing absence of shared assumptions is what spells, to me, the inevitable demise of psychoanalysis – more than any of the external challenges that we face."[3] Is any reintegration thinkable at all? Is there already change in the air? However, some current positions within these disciplines of the mind, psychoanalysis, phenomenology, and philosophy of mind overlap and interface on the crucial topic of subjective experience, therefore being worth a more in-depth look.

1 Paul Ricœur's Phenomenological Approach to the Psychoanalytic Experience

A classical, ever-memorable comparison between the phenomenological approach to subjectivity and the psychoanalytic experience was endeavoured by Paul Ricoeur as early as 1965 in his *Freud and Philosophy. An Essay on Interpretation.*

At the core of his philosophical interpretation of Freud, Ricœur attempts to reformulate psychoanalysis both in terms of scientific psychology such as behaviourisms as well as in terms of phenomenology.[4] For the purpose of this article I would like to focus on Ricœur's tentative approach to the analytic experience through the phenomenological, an "experience that is deliberately philosophical and reflective."[5]

Here Ricœur's seminal intuition is to consider and to focus on the analytic experience as a *via regia* for reaching the phenomenon of subjective experience, and further to choose phenomenology for approximating to psychoanalysis. Ricœur seems to be aware that psychoanalytic clinical method is not only a unique source of information on the mind and its mechanisms, but also provides a systematic exploration of subjective experience.

Ricœur's approximation of phenomenology to psychoanalysis is developed along four steps, addressing the following issues:

1. The method of reduction or suspension of the immediate consciousness as origin and place of meaning is the starting point of the phenomenological investigation.

Its own natural attitude makes a self-deception of the immediate consciousness possible. Phenomenology reveals an "unconsciousness" or unawareness which has to do with the implicit or "co-intended".

2. The theme of intentionality shows that consciousness is not self-presence or self-possession, but first of all intentional vision of the other. Because thematic intentionality is sustained by intentionality in act, which precedes and founds it, it generates another form of unawareness, the unreflected, and this brings about some relevant consequences:

   (a) The mind is definable by meaning, before and without appealing to self-consciousness;
   (b) The lived relation can be dissociated from its conscious representation in consciousness;
   (c) The meaning in act is more primary than the expressed or represented meaning: the passive genesis of meaning introduces the concept of meaning in act without me;
   (d) The mode of being of this meaning, which exists without being conscious, is the mode of being of the body.

   Finally, as the two last steps, Ricœur suggests to take the following into consideration:

3. The attention of phenomenology given to the dialectic aspects of language.
4. The theme of intersubjectivity as constitutive of all our relations with the world.

Let me elaborate on Ricœur's steps of approximation of phenomenology to psychoanalysis, as well as on his frank admission of their failure to produce the equivalent of psychoanalytic experience.

1. Edmund Husserl calls reduction that *attitude* of phenomenology which suspends the natural attitude of "self-evidence" [*Selbstverständichkeit*] of the appearance of things. This methodological displacement reveals the self-misunderstanding of the immediate consciousness. Phenomenology presupposes a nucleus of experience named "the ego's living self-presence" [*lebendige Selbstgegenwart*], but beyond this lies an implicit horizon of the "properly nonexperienced" [*eigentlich nicht erfahren*] and the "necessarily co-intended" [*notwendig mitgemeint*]. The phenomenological unconscious is in fact unawareness about the implicit, co-intended or "co-implicit".

   Despite this approximation concerning the method of reduction, Ricœur must admit that the Freudian unconscious is rendered accessible through the psychoanalytic technique, which has no parallel in phenomenology: "Hence the suspicion analysis professes about the illusions of consciousness is different from the suspension of the natural attitude. [...] By starting from the very level of this bondage, that is, by unreservedly delivering oneself over the domineering flux of underlying motivation, the true situation of consciousness is discovered. The fiction of absence of motivation, on which consciousness based its illusion of self-determination, is recognised as fiction. The fullness of motivation is revealed in place of the emptiness and arbitrariness of consciousness."[6] As a major result of the psychoanalytic working through Ricœur finds a genuinely novel comprehension of freedom, which can no longer be related to the arbitrary but should be linked to understood determination.

2. For Ricœur intentionality is the *theme* of phenomenology which seems to mark another step toward the unconscious: "[C]onsciousness is first of all an intending of the other, and not self-presence or self-possession."[7] Ricœur evokes the "invincible unawareness of the self that characterizes intentionality in act"[8] because for the Husserl of *Krisis*, intentionality in act is broader than thematic intentionality, therefore leading to the "primacy of the unreflected over the reflected, of the operative over the uttered, of the actual over the thematic" (see note 8). The co-implicit and co-intended cannot become transparent to consciousness.

In the end, Ricœur must object to his second tentative approximation: "[O]ne moves from phenomenology to psychoanalysis when one understands that the main barrier separates the unconscious and the preconscious, and not the preconscious and the conscious: to replace the formula *Cs./Pcs., Ucs.* by the formula *Cs., Pcs./Ucs.* is to move from the phenomenological point of view to the topographic point of view. The unconscious of phenomenology is the preconscious of psychoanalysis, that is to say, an unconscious that is descriptive and not topographic. The meaning of the barrier is that the unconscious is inaccessible unless an appropriate technique is used."[9]

Ricœur also considers four corollaries to intentionality, his second step of approximation:

(a) He defines the mind as the intending of something and not as self-consciousness and refers to Antoine Vergote: "[T]he psychical is defined as meaning, and this meaning is dynamic and historical."[10] Ricœur explicates that the division of meaning in psychoanalysis is only one aspect of the laws of the systems of the mind, which have their own legality such as the laws of the system unconscious including primary process, absence of negation, absence of contradiction, timelessness, etc. He maintains that this "legality cannot be reconstructed phenomenologically but only through the familiarity provided by analytic technique."[11]

(b) Phenomenology shows that the lived relation is dissociable from its representation. By becoming representation, the relation to the world becomes self-knowing. In a philosophy of immediate consciousness, the subject is a knowing subject; on the contrary, in phenomenology the subject is primarily a desiring subject. If phenomenology shows that the lived meaning of a behaviour extends beyond its representation in consciousness, an investigation other then phenomenology is required. Psychoanalytic technique is indispensable for understanding the division at the basis of the distortion which is making the text of consciousness unrecognizable.

(c) According to Ricœur, in phenomenology the meaning in act is more primary than the expressed or represented meaning: the passive genesis of meaning introduces the concept of meaning in act without me. How are different experiences possible in the same ego? They are "compossible" through the genesis which links together past, present and future in the unity of a history. Also concerning the passive genesis, Ricœur remarks its unmistakable difference to Freud's dynamic of drives and conflicts, which are again decipherable only by means of the psychoanalytic technique.

(d) While asking how it is possible for a meaning to exist without being conscious, Ricœur answers that its mode of being is that of the body: "The phenomenologist is not saying that the Freudian unconscious is the body; he is simply saying that the mode of being of the body, neither representation in me nor thing outside of me, is the ontic model for any conceivable unconscious."[12]

3. For Ricœur an important implication of intentionality concerns the dialectical aspects of language, especially the interplay of the presence and absence characteristics of signs. Freud's *Beyond the Pleasure Principle*[13] describes the child's mastery over privation by playing the game of *fort-da*: "By alternately voicing the two words, the child interrelates absence and presence in a meaningful contrast; at the same time, he no longer undergoes absence as a fit of panic massively substituted for a close and saturating presence. Dominated thus by language, privation – and consequently presence as well – is signified and transformed into intentionality; being deprived of the mother becomes an intending of the mother."[14]

   Ricœur finds that the linguistic interpretation of psychoanalysis, as carried out by Lacan and his followers, does not constitute an alternative to the Freudian "economic" explanation, e. g. in terms of drives and intrapsychic conflict: "We are in presence of phenomena structured like a language; but the problem is to assign an appropriate meaning to the word 'like'."[15] In Freud's *Interpretation of Dreams*,[16] the dream mechanisms of condensation and displacement appear to be similar to figures of rhetoric like metaphor and metonymy. Ricœur is nonetheless aware that only Freud's economic explanation in terms of drives takes account of the barrier between the systems of the mind and therefore of their separation.

4. According to Ricœur, another relevant implication of intentionality involves the theory of intersubjectivity, which assumes its whole meaning in the semantic of desire, where the meaning is more lived than represented and where the human desire is intentional vision, that is, a desire of other desires.

But it is exactly on the theme of intersubjectivity that psychoanalytic experience diverges most distinctly from phenomenology: "[P]sychoanalysis is an arduous technique, learned by diligent exercise and practice. One cannot underestimate the amazing audacity of this discovery, namely of treating the intersubjective relationship as *technique*."[17] Undertaking an accurate investigation of the technical writings of Freud, Ricœur acknowledges that in the experience of psychoanalytic treatment, the crucial question is less about replacing the ignorance of the patient with knowledge, than overcoming her/his resistances.

Addressing that special kind of resistance called transference-love, Ricœur outlines the technique for its management during the psychoanalytic treatment as described by Freud in "Observation on Transference-Love",[18] consisting in the technique of exploiting it without satisfying it. Indeed the psychoanalytic treatment should be carried through in a state of abstinence: "For the phenomenologist, this technique of frustration is the most surprising aspect of the analytic method; he can no doubt understand the rule of veracity, but not the principle of frustration: the latter can only *be practiced*" (see note 17). There seems to be no relation which is so artificial and constructed as the psychoanalytic relation, as Freud points out: "The course the analyst must pursue is [...] one for which there is no model in real life."[19] Ricœur describes the conditions of possibility for an entirely technical relationship to be conducted as an intersubjective relation: "[T]he fact that the analytic dialogue, within a special context of disengagement, of isolation, of derealisation, brings to light the demands in which desire ultimately consists; but only the technique of transference, as a technique of frustration, could reveal the fact that desire is at bottom an unanswered demand..." (see note 17).

In the previously considered chapter *Epistemology: Between Psychology and Phenomenology* from *Freud and Philosophy. An Essay on Interpretation*, Ricoeur's tentative understanding of analytic experience through phenomenology seems promising. Due to the richness of his evocative style, Ricoeur's definition of analytic experience remains ambiguous but open. It is true that Ricœur has already described the analytic experience also as "a work of speech with the patient",[20] but for understanding the mode of being of the unconscious he suggests links to Maurice Merleau-Ponty's notions of one's own body. Further he explicitly criticizes Lacan's linguistic turn regarding the understanding of the unconscious: "The linguistic interpretation does not constitute an alternative to the economic explanation."[21] Even more, Ricœur seems to be attempting to grasp the rich variety of emotions occurring in the dynamic of transference and countertransference.

In his later *The Question of Proof in Freud's Psychoanalytic Writings*,[22] Ricœur holds – even more definitely and explicitly – psychoanalytic theory to be coextensive with what takes place in the analytic relationship, where the *analytic experience* happens. But unfortunately, Ricœur moves away from phenomenology and almost exclusively restricts the analytic experience to speech acts.

The philosopher of science Adolf Grünbaum in his *The Foundations of Psychoanalysis* argues that Ricœur "immures its [the psychoanalytic clinical theory] substantive purview within the *verbal* productions of the clinical transaction between the analyst and the patient. [...] the analysand's *non*verbal are excluded from its scope."[23] And he adds: "True enough, psychoanalysts generally regard their many observations of the patient's verbal and non verbal interactions with them in the treatment sessions as the source of findings that are simply peerless as evidence, not only heuristically but also probatively."[24]

Thus Ricœur's controversial epistemological understanding of psychoanalysis as hermeneutics receives a dismissive critique by Adolf Grünbaum who maintains "that the generic disavowal of causal attributions advocated by the radical hermeneuticians is a nihilistic, if not frivolous, trivialisation of Freud's entire clinical theory. Far from serving as a new citadel for psychoanalytic apologetics, the embrace of such hermeneuticians is, I submit, the kiss of death for the legacy that was to be saved."[25] Although Grünbaum criticizes both of Ricœur's works, especially because of the weakness of his epistemological approach, the plentiful suggestions of Ricœur's tentative phenomenological approach should not be devaluated.

Back to his later, through and through hermeneutical *The Question of Proof in Freud's Psychoanalytic Writings*, Ricœur first claims that "the equivalent of what the epistemology of logical empiricism calls 'observables' is to be sought first in the analytic situation, in the analytic relationship."[26] Ricœur's tentative answer to the widespread critique that psychoanalysis does not satisfy the required criteria of scientificity leads him to deny the scientific status of Freud's clinical theory. Ricœur argues that psychoanalysis should not be judged using the criteria of an empirical observational science, because facts in psychoanalysis are in no way facts of observable behaviour. Therefore he suggests changing the criteria for 'facts' in psychoanalysis.

It is worth mentioning that, even as early as 1983, before Grünbaum's *The Foundations of Psychoanalysis*, the psychoanalyst and philosopher Charles Hanly warned psychoanalysts and all "friends" of psychoanalysis of the trap of making "psychoanalysis more defensible as a science by weakening the epistemological criteria for scientific knowledge in general." [27]

The crucial limitation in Ricœur's approach is constituted by his four criteria of selection among the facts which can be taken into account using the narrowed frame of a psychoanalytic clinical theory so understood. According to this impoverishment of the domain of facts, only the following issues enter into the fields of investigation and treatment as the objects of psychoanalytic knowledge:

1. That part of experience which is capable of *being said*;
2. Even more, the analytic situation selects not only what is sayable, but what is said to *another person*;
3. Further, the analytic experience "requires that we add the reference to fantasies to the two preceding criteria; for what has been said (the first criterion) and what is demanded of the other person (the second criterion) bear the mark of the particular imaginary formations which Freud brings together under the term *phantasieren*."[28] Therefore Ricœur introduces a third criterion concerning "the coherence and the resistance of certain manifestations of the unconscious which led Freud to speak of 'psychic reality' in contrast to material reality."[29]
4. As the fourth criterion, the analytic situation singles out what is capable of entering into a story or narrative from a subject's experience, because to remember is "to be able to constitute one's own existence in the form of a story where a memory as such is only a fragment of the story."[30]

His conclusion about the verification of the assumptions of psychoanalysis is the following:

> [I]f the ultimate truth claim resides in the case histories, the means of proofs reside in the articulation of the entire network: theory, hermeneutics, therapeutic, and narration.[31]

Far from substantiating the psychoanalytic experience through linking it to results of the phenomenology of perception or to phenomenological inquiries on subjective experience, the later Ricœur increasingly circumscribes the analytic experience to a narrative enterprise.

Currently, the psychoanalytic approach to the subjective mind within the analytic relation could be compared with and perhaps substantiated through both:

First, philosophical investigations from philosophy of mind and phenomenology on "conscious" or better subjective experience (psychoanalysis is also a philosophy of the singular and irreducible aspects of the subjective mind);

Second, convergent scientific data from the cognitive field (psychoanalysis is also a science of the general mechanisms of the subjective mind).

2 Philosophical Investigations from Philosophy of Mind and Phenomenology Contribute to Psychoanalysis as a Philosophy of the Singular and Irreducible Aspects of the Subjective Mind

Speaking broadly, these three disciplines of the mind, phenomenology, philosophy of mind, and psychoanalysis, currently overlap on the topic of subjective experience. However it is important that the definition of experience from a first-person perspective remains substantial. It should be not confined to sensory experience, because in so doing it risks being considered merely epiphenomenal, as sometimes occurs in current philosophy of mind.

Galen Strawson complained of exactly this issue. As a phenomenologist he has a quite comprehensive understanding of experience. As such, Strawson indissolubly binds experience to the mind, as the very mark of the mental. He maintains that the only thing that is distinctively and essentially mental is experience: "Many think that developments in Artificial Intelligence oblige us to admit that the realm of the mental, and of mental being, is larger than we used to think, but the opposite view is at least as plausible: what developments in AI show is that the realm of the distinctively mental is actually smaller than we used to think, since so many of the abilities or properties that we used to take to be distinctively mental can now be seen to be possessed by things that are experienceless, and are not mental beings at all."[32]

Strawson overtly criticizes that a number of philosophers of mind reduce their understanding of experience to the far narrower notion of sensory experience as merely a 'sensation-mood-emotion-image-feeling experience': "When analytic philosophers talk generally about what I call 'EQ (= experiential qualitative) content – when they talk generally of the 'subjective character' of experience, or 'what-it's-likeness', or 'qualitative character', or 'phenomenology' in the current deviant use of the term – they standardly have only *sensory* EQ content, in mind, and the mistake has already been made. For this terminological habit simply forbids expression of the idea that there may be non-sensory or *cognitive* EQ content." [33]

Unfortunately, equating the mental with the "experiential qualitative" leads Strawson to embrace the opinion of the philosopher of mind John Searle that non-experiential phenomena are not genuinely intentional or mentally contentful. Consequently he also follows Searle's view that: "[T]he ontology of mental states, at the time they are unconscious, consists entirely in the existence of purely neurophysiological phenomena."[34]

The assumption that unconscious processes are merely physiological processes is understandable from the perspective of nineteenth century psychology, when it was proposed by Franz Brentano[35] or William James.[36] Nowadays, simply ignoring the graduality between mental processes conscious, preconscious and unconscious is outdated. The topic "subjective experience" is what current reductionism in philosophy does not entail. In fact, in the time of "consciousness explained", it is no longer astonishing that prospective "allies" overcome differences and move up: meaning, all who maintain that the subjective mind can be understood not only by describing general mechanisms but also by grasping its singular and irreducible aspects.

Actually, there are enough philosophers of mind who maintain that to refer the phenomenal aspect of the mind exclusively to sensory properties is a misunderstanding. Robert van Gulick states: "Phenomenal experience is not merely a succession of qualitatively distinguished sensory ideas, but rather the organized cognitive experience of a world of objects and of ourselves as subjects within that world."[37]

In the same vein, the philosophers of mind Terence Horgan, John Tienson, and George Graham discuss forms of non-sensory phenomenal experience "that are more subtle, less starkly vivid, and thus more easily overlooked than is sensory phenomenology."[38] They explicitly and appreciatively refer to Galen Strawson's notion of 'understanding experience',[39] a form of non-sensory, inherently intentional phenomenology. Strawson claims that "understanding and other related kind of occurrent mental states and processes are very commonly, if not always, laden with distinctive phenomenal character that is non-sensory and inherently involves the intentional content of what is understood"(see note 38). For example, he is concerned with distinguishing hearing speech in a language that one does not understand from hearing speech in a language that one does understand. It makes a phenomenological difference if two people are hearing the same spoken sequence, with one of them understanding the language and the other not: "At a certain relatively raw sensory level, their auditory experience is phenomenologically the same: the sounds are the same, and in some cases may be experienced in much the same way *qua sounds*. Yet it is obvious introspectively that there is something phenomenologically very different about what it is like for each of them: one person is having understanding experience with the distinctive phenomenology of understanding the sentence to mean just what it does, and the other is not."[40]

If it is true that the philosophers of mind Horgan, Tienson and Graham converge with the phenomenologist Galen Strawson on his notion of experience, it was another philosopher of mind, namely Frank Jackson, who in his widely discussed thought experiment defined even more distinctly the first-person experience as knowledge, through Mary, the dramatis persona of his thought experiment. The scientist Mary is confined to a black-and-white room and has complete physical knowledge of red. But because she does not know what it is like to see red, she does not have complete knowledge of red, since a complete knowledge of red should also include phenomenal knowledge of red. Therefore Jackson named his controversial argument the "knowledge argument", asserting that complete physical knowledge of the world is not complete knowledge of the world.[41]

Investigating the relationship between the physical sciences and psychology as his starting point, Jackson complains that any purely physical account of what our world is like has a big gap in it. In describing what goes on within us and how we relate to our environment, this physical account leaves out phenomenal consciousness.

Regarding the experience of Mary after her release and the following philosophical discussion, I have wondered if the what-is-like experience was to be thought of as merely a mental experience or whether it could be also understood as a psychophysical one. Further, I also posed the question whether what-is-like experiences generally can only be thought to be conscious experiences, or also preconscious or even unconscious experiences.[42]

It is also well known that Frank Jackson changed his mind, rejected his own argument and claimed that qualia can be given a complete physical explanation (and in so doing let down his followers).[43]

But for me it is crucial that in the following debate, the philosopher of mind David Chalmers, as recent as 2004 (9 years after Jackson retracted his argument), assumed the point of view of phenomenal realism, according to which Mary's phenomenal knowledge of red is a new factual knowledge.[44]

David Chalmers divides the problems of consciousness into "hard" and "easy" problems. The easy problems are cognitive abilities and functions, which can be explained specifying a mechanism able to perform the function. Among the easy problems of consciousness, which can be explained in term of computational or neural mechanisms by the standard methods of the disciplines of the cognitive field, Chalmers specifies and enlists the following phenomena:

> [O]ne sometime says that a mental state is conscious when it is verbally reportable, or when it is internally accessible. Sometimes a system is said to be conscious of some information when it has the ability to react on the basis of that information, or, more strongly, when it attends to that information, or when it can integrate that information and exploit it in the sophisticated control of behavior. We sometimes say that an action is conscious precisely when it is deliberate. Often, we say that an organism is conscious as another way of saying that it is awake.[45]

"Consciousness" could here be understood – *pars pro toto* – as "mind". From a psychoanalytic point of view the question arises whether the functions or abilities mentioned by Chalmers are performed consciously, preconsciously or unconsciously.

However, Chalmers maintains that if these phenomena were the only questions of consciousness, then consciousness would be not a problem, because in the long run, an explanation can be provided by the standard methods of cognitive science and neuroscience.

According to Chalmers, the hard problem are the questions why the performance of all these functions and abilities is accompanied by experience and why all this information-processing does not go on "in the dark": "How can we explain why there is something it's like to entertain a mental image, or to experience an emotion? It is widely agreed that experience arises from a physical basis, but we have no good explanation of why and how it so arises. Why should physical processing give rise to a rich inner life at all?"[46] He proposes to reserve the term consciousness for the conscious experience and in so doing takes a similar position to the phenomenologist Strawson's previously mentioned point of view.

Chalmers refers also to Joseph Levine's[47] term "explanatory gap", meaning between the answer in terms of mechanisms and the question about experience: "[W]e have no idea how we could really explain – in the sense of making intelligible to ourselves – how it is that certain physical or functional configurations have conscious mental features."[48]

The phenomenologist Shaun Gallagher also emphasizes that the experience should not be narrowed to a merely sensory experience, comparing the point of view of current phenomenology with the position of philosophers of mind on phenomenal consciousness: "Phenomenologists are in agreement with philosophers like Nagel (1974)[49] and Searle (1992),[50] that to have an experience necessarily means that there is *something it's like* for the subject to have that experience. Indeed, this applies not only to the obvious cases of pain, pleasure, emotion, and other bodily sensations, it extends to all kinds of experiences, including perception, desire, and thought. What it's like to taste a lemon is different from what it's like to remember tasting a lemon, or from what it's like to see a lemon, or to count the lemons on the table, or to think about photographing a lemon. These experiential qualitative differences are not anonymous; they are given in a first-person perspective."[51]

Further Gallagher points out that according to phenomenology consciousness is embodied as well as situated in the world: "The first-person point of view on the world is always defined by the situation of the perceiver's body, which concerns not simply location and posture, but action in pragmatic contexts and interaction with other people."[52]

He maintains that "it is this juncture of embodiment and consciousness which holds promise for bridging phenomenology and natural scientific approaches to consciousness [...] What natural science has to say about the body is necessarily correlated with the first-person accounts of phenomenology since the lived body [*Leib*] and the scientifically studied, biological body are one and the same body."[53]

Among phenomenologists there is some agreement, such as the interface on the unquestionable importance of subjective experience as well as the appreciation of the reflections of a number of philosophers of mind from Thomas Nagel, to Joseph Levine, to David Chalmers. There are overlapping positions on both these point.

But some important divergences can be noticed concerning the role of representations in perception. Current psychoanalytic theory includes as a building block the theory of self and object representations ("object" meaning another subject.[54]) During psychoanalytic treatment changes in self and object representations happen, predicting an improvement of the patient. What is changing is fare more then merely her/his verbal self-descriptions or her/his verbal accounts of others. The play of her/his features her/his facial expressions dramatically develop as well as the posture of the patient, who for example is not in hiding anymore, but at ease. But this occurs not only regarding what in the cognitive field is called "social cognition" and "social perception". Change occurs also in perception of inanimate objects and inanimate environment. Therefore, the psychoanalytic assumption of self and object representations seems to me to be questioning any theory of direct perception.

Some phenomenologists develop a nonrepresentationalist approach. Alva Noë's enactive approach to vision strictly refuses the assumption of mental representations.[55]

Concerning social cognition and social perception, James Jerome Gibson in his ecological theory of perception[56] assumes that the perception system resonates to the invariant structure of the environment, in his *How the Body Shapes the Mind*, Shaun Gallagher also assumes a direct perception[57] and using these positions as a starting point Thomas Fuchs[58] also pleads for a nonrepresentationalist approach to perception.

From the point of view of cognitive neurobiology but also integrating psychoanalytic knowledge, Eric Kandel convincingly pleads for a representationalist account.[59]

This divergence seems to me to be an open question to be clarified in the future.[60]

Indeed, going back to Shaun Gallagher the link to the cognitive field that he addresses is crucial. If philosophy is afraid of being relegated to a position of irrelevance in the face of the astonishing success of the naturalistic approach to humans (from cognitive psychology to cognitive neurobiology), it should develop a more sophisticated account of human subjects, including amongst other issues, current findings from the disciplines of the mind and the sciences of the brain. Much that has been learned in cognitive psychology and cognitive neurobiology is applicable to philosophy and should be integrated with it.

If philosophy fails at this task of integration, then the theoretical account of subjectivity will be overtaken by the disciplines traditionally named natural sciences.

A look at current cognitive neurobiology reveals that at least since the "Decade of the Brain" in the 1990s – and even earlier – "mind" and "consciousness" have been become its central darling topics.

A positive example of the suggested enterprise is the integrative initiative of classical analytical philosophy, which – through systematic study of methods and findings in cognitive science and cognitive neurobiology – transformed itself from armchair philosophy to philosophy of mind.

On the other side, the added value of the contributions of psychoanalysis, philosophy of mind, and phenomenology to the cognitive field is the subjective experiential account in first-person as well as a number of first-person methodologies.[61] Contributions from psychoanalysis are rich and imaginative: There is no question but that the psychoanalytic relation during the treatment provides a unique point of view on subjective experience.

3 Convergent Scientific Data from the Cognitive Field Contribute to Psychoanalysis as a Science of the General Mechanisms of the Subjective Mind

Current neurobiological and cognitive investigations are a timely example of how "consciousness studies" have become part of third-person science. Although "consciousness studies" is the term generally used, "consciousness" should here be understood – *pars pro toto* – as "mind", because the just mentioned investigations are actually about conscious, preconscious, and unconscious mind.

Even though such investigations are now acknowledged as third-person science, they nevertheless rely on subjects being able to report on what they currently experience. Without such reports it is impossible to know how observed activity in the brain relates to what subjects experience: "Although for much of twentieth century, psychology ostensibly tried to rid itself of the problem associated with such a first-person science, it never did so consistently. For example, in studies of perception, cognition, emotion, etc., researchers commonly relied to some extent on subjective reports of experience, whether in the form of verbal reports, or some other overt response, for example, pressing one button if subjects could see a difference between two stimuli and another button if not, placing a mark on a rating scale, filling out a questionnaire (about their feeling, thoughts, and behaviour), and so on. Once consciousness itself becomes the topic of study, such methods become particularly important."[62]

Studying the respective roles within the relationship during a "standard" experiment of experimental sciences, Max Velmans[63] argues, that the subject is asked to focus on all her/his own experiences, which she/he should report on or which she/he should respond to. The experimenter is required to concentrate on the subject's experience and how it depends on the offered stimulus or on brain states she/he can observe. Her/his observation is considered public and objective.

The difference in the intersubjective relationship between experiment and psychoanalytic situation consists of a further element. This additional and puzzling element in the psychoanalytic relationship is that the psychoanalyst is supplementarily required to focus her/his attention on two foci: not only on the patient's whole expression (meaning cognitive and emotional, conscious and unconscious, verbal and pre-, para- and nonverbal, etc.) of her/his own experiences, but at the same time on her/his own entire (meaning cognitive and emotional, conscious and unconscious, verbal and pre-, para- and nonverbal, etc.) reaction, or countertransference, to the former. Her/his countertransference is assumed to be the best way to reach the subjective experience of the patient.

The concept of evenly hovering, or free-floating, attention defines the analytic mode of listening, which, according to Joseph Sandler, is the "capacity to allow all sorts of thoughts, daydreams and associations to enter the analyst's consciousness while he is at the same time listening to and observing the patient."[64]

Concerning countertransference, long before Heinrich Racker[65] in Buenos Aires and Paula Heimann[66] in London recognised it to be not simply an interference but an important tool of the treatment Sándor Ferenczi led the way in this direction.[67] In the same vein, Sandler outlines the free-floating responsiveness in countertransference: "The analyst is, of course, not a machine in absolute self-control, only experiencing on the one hand, and delivering interpretations on the other [...] Among many other things he talks, he greets the patient, he makes arrangements about practical matters, he may joke and, to some degree, allow his responses to depart from the classical psychoanalytic norm. My contention is that the analyst's overt reactions to the patient as well as in his thoughts and feelings what can be called his 'role responsiveness' shows itself, not only in his feelings but also in his attitudes and behaviour, as a crucial element in his 'useful' countertransference."[68]

The analyst has the unique opportunity to take part in the subjective experience of her/his patient. This experience offered by the patient in the analytic session is often the instantiation *in vivo* of her/his very early preverbal past experience. A great clinical "object relation" tradition in psychoanalysis, starting with Sándor Ferenczi and carried on to the "Independent" group inside of the British Psycho-Analytical Society has always recognized the importance of all these pre-, para-, or simply non verbal expressions.[69] Another less well-known line was developed by the pioneers Paul Federn and Edoardo Weiss,[70] who devoted themselves to the treatment of severe disturbances and even psychoses, focusing firstly on the pure phenomenology of the analytic session. Nevertheless, they worked towards making psychoanalysis a science in the long run and they never dismissed this position.[71]

If in a clinical situation the analyst gains knowledge from the first-person perspective by evenly hovering attention and through the phenomena of countertransference and projective identification, this does not mean that she/he is not also able to know from the third-person perspective on two different levels: on the first level in clinical work in the session (interpretation) as well as by participating in supervision, intervision, or in case history seminars, and in clinical research by writing case histories.[72] Furthermore, the psychoanalytic extraclinical empirical research additionally provides a second level of third-person perspective, which claims an even more compelling objectivity.[73]

Concerning the scientific study of the relationship in the analytic situation, convergent extraclinical data from current neurobiology and cognitive science can also be considered. Pre-, para-, and non verbal communication in the dynamic of transference and countertransference as well as empathy are neither ineffable nor occult phenomena. On the contrary, much that has been learned in the cognitive field is applicable to psychoanalysis and should be integrated with it. Clinical interactions in psychoanalysis can additionally be understood drawing on convergent data collected from Simon Baron-Cohen's cognitive research on mindreading,[74] from the neurobiological investigations on mirror neurons of Giacomo Rizzolatti and Vittorio Gallese as well as from Colwyn Trevarthen's neurobiological developmental accounts on early infant-mother intersubjectivity.[75]

On the other hand, stemming from the clinical investigation of the dynamic of transference and countertransference, the emphasis on the psychoanalytic relation has unfortunately been turned into a sort of "epistemological interactionism" by a number of psychoanalysts (like Roy Shafer[76] and Owen Renik[77]) and psychotherapists (like Stephen A. Mitchell), which psychoanalyst and philosopher Charles Hanly argues against: "[I]nteractionism must be differentiated from the psychoanalytic study of the interactions occurring between patient and analyst. The study initiated by Freud has been carried forward by many psychoanalysts on the basis of critical realist epistemology. I criticize interactionism as a theory of knowledge for psychoanalysis not because it insists on taking account of the presence of the analyst in the clinical situation, but because it implies, by virtue of its subjectivism, that this cannot be done. The interactionist epistemology does not allow sufficient cognitive autonomy."[78]

In his paper Hanly is well aware that many clinicians who embrace interactionism "do not press their ideas through to their logical conclusion",[79] for example the denial of the differentiation between subject and object. In his effort to disentangle some unreflected positions within current psychoanalysis and psychotherapy, Hanly introduces the distinction between "contingent" and "necessary" interactionism: "Contingent interactionism is the idea that the analyst's subjectivity contributes in specific ways to the analytic process [...] first, the analyst's subjectivity may facilitate, interfere with, or distort the analytic process; second, however difficult the task, the analyst can at least at times identify and correct subjective influences that distort the analytic process. [...] This correction does not require, for example, that the analyst strangle affects in order to maintain neutrality or evenly suspended attention."[80]

I return to some epistemological reflections of Max Velmans on the topic. A science cannot be entirely "objective" in the sense of being completely observer-free, as the later Karl Popper claims: "Knowledge in the objective sense is knowledge without a knower; it is knowledge without a knowing subject."[81] A science can be "objective" in the sense of "inter-subjective" (meaning shared terminology, shared cognitive structure, a shared scientific paradigm, shared expertise, etc.). Further, the descriptions of observations or experiences can be truthful and accurate. Finally, scientific method can be "objective" following specified, repeatable procedure and using standard measuring instruments.[82]

With "necessary interactionism" Hanly means an *a priori* interactionism which assumes that "the influence of analyst and patient on one another insinuates its way into the associations of the patient, in such a way as to disallow any correction that could issue in intersubjective objectivity. [...] a solipsistic interactionism is implicit in the way some analysts use the idea that the facts of observation in psychoanalysis are creations of the analyst-analysand interaction. Spence's[83] notion (1982) of psychoanalysis as a created narrative the validation of which is limited to considerations of coherence implies necessary interactionism [...]"[84] According to Donald Spence's narrative view, quite similar to Ricœur's late proposal, psychoanalysis can at best become an account of the life history of a subject, and in doing so it abandons the terrain of the sciences.

I propose an understanding of Freud's psychoanalysis within the context of Austrian philosophical tradition.[85] Austrian philosophers such as Brentano, Mach, and Husserl either reject or ignore the Diltheyean division of sciences into humanities [*Geisteswissenschaften*] and natural sciences [*Naturwissenschaften*][86] and the subsequent distinction between their respective methodologies. In 1874 Brentano acknowledged two sciences, psychology and the natural sciences, which, however, utilize the same methodology, namely the traditionally named natural scientific methodology.[87] Brentano also confronts Dilthey and rejects his conception of a dichotomy of sciences. Arguing against the Diltheyean notion that a transfer of methodological know-how between the two branches must be opposed, Brentano pleads for a methodology in the humanities that incorporates the inner and outer experience as the standard and not the a priori foundation of knowledge. Incidentally, Brentano complains against a Diltheyean lack of respect towards rules of logic and scientific methodology.[88]

For Mach, there are only the natural sciences and there is only one valid scientific methodology, namely that of the natural sciences. Mach simply ignores the Diltheyean division.

Husserl proposes that phenomenological methodology can offer the only valid alternative to the natural scientific methodology.[89]

I plead for a suspension of the Diltheyean dichotomization at least at the level of thought experiments, because this separation leads to a continuous classification, e.g. bringing about Carlo Strenger's definition[90] of psychoanalysis as a hybrid, not-only-but-also, or an in-between-discipline (meaning between humanities [*Geisteswissenschaften*] and natural sciences [*Naturwissenschaften*]). My approach leads to the question whether the dualistic attitude, in the final analysis, rests upon the dualistic approach to the mind-brain/body problem.

There is no doubt that a discipline can investigate scientifically even though the epistemic model of the acquired knowledge is not derived from physics. Freud did not attempt to reduce the psychoanalytic model to that of physics, because he did not subscribe to theoretical reductionism. As a result of the misconception that a science must be construed after the hard model of physics, the conviction often emerges – for example in Paul Ricœur – that psychoanalysis may not be a science but rather a hermeneutic discipline.

The discussion of the methodology of psychoanalysis must proceed from the assumption that there are special sciences. Therefore, I am referring once more to Jerry Fodor's taxonomy as formulated in *The Language of Thought*.[91] According to Fodor, there are autonomous forms of knowledge which enjoy scientific status, such as psychology, sociology, economy, linguistics, or anthropology. Moreover, the common foundation of all sciences consists in the attempt to discover regularities in the relationship between phenomena, to investigate the causal relationship thereof, to generalize from the regularities in the relationship of the phenomena (or "laws") and put forth explanations.

First, a science isolates relevant aspects of a phenomenon relating to the respective science and it utilizes the corresponding concepts in order to describe the regularities of a specific field of investigation. Second, it formulates law-like generalizations to explain the regularities, and thirdly, it provides a series of arguments to justify its explanatory generalizations. Initially, the need for presentation of argumentation arises from empirical and inter-subjective evidence. In spite of the procedure outlined above, the knowledge remains preliminary and subject to examination and assessment.

What Fodor has outlined so far does not present an obstacle to the autonomy of special sciences. Different sciences investigate different fields and they pose different types of questions: "[T]here are special sciences not because of the nature of our epistemic relation to the world, but because of the way the world is put together: not all the kinds (not all the classes of things and events about which there are important, counterfactual supporting generalization to make) are, or correspond to, physical kinds."[92]

Some time ago, the psychoanalyst and researcher Peter Fonagy has once more expressed his concern that at the moment psychoanalysis is not yet a science. He tried to formulate some suggestions such as strengthening its evidence basis, moving from global to specific constructs, considering alternative accounts, integrating social influence and collaborating with neighbouring disciplines.[93] Especially his last proposal has been realised in the last years.[94]

All current cooperation notwithstanding, entering into an interdisciplinary exchange is challenging and risky. The psychoanalyst and researcher Drew Westen shows that just at a time when psychoanalysis seems to be largely ignored (or devaluated) by its neighbouring disciplines a considerable amount of experimental research, conducted mostly by cognitive researchers with little interest in psychoanalysis, definitively substantiated a number of Freud's assumptions, unfortunately without relating them to psychoanalysis: "A substantial body of evidence now suggests that Freud was right in a series of propositions that are central to *contemporary* psychoanalytic theory: (1) that enduring aspects of personality begin to coalesce in childhood, and that childhood experiences play an important role in personality development, shaping in particular the ways people form later social relationships; (2) that mental representations of self, others, and relationships guide people's interactions with others and play a substantial part in many forms of psychopathology; (3) that mental processes, including affective and motivational processes, operate simultaneously and in parallel, so that individuals can have conflicting feelings toward the same person or situation and can craft compromises outside of awareness; (4) that personality development involves not only learning to regulate sexual and aggressive feelings and wishes, but also moving from an immature dependent state to a mature interdependent one; and (5) that much of mental life is unconscious."[95] Furthermore, Drew Westen states that many psychoanalytic findings have already found a place within the cognitive field. The problem Westen has been addressing for more than 10 years is that many theoretical and clinical findings of psychoanalysis have simply migrated and been incorporated into fields adjacent to psychoanalysis without acknowledging their psychoanalytic origins. This is why, aside from cooperative efforts with the neighbouring disciplines, psychoanalysis will be facing competition.

Returning to Fonagy's statement at the beginning of this article that the core menace comes less from outside, but rather from the inner fragmentation of psychoanalysis, I would like to conclude by answering that facing external challenges could finally give us the opportunity to reconstruct the knowledge base of psychoanalysis on a more adequate foundation.

Notes

1. Jerry Fodor, "Special Sciences, or the Disunity of Science as a Working Hypothesis," in *The Language of Thought* (New York: Crowell, 1975), 9–25.
2. Paul Oppenheim and Hilary Putnam, "Unity of Science as a Working Hypothesis," in *Minnesota Studies in the Philosophy of Science,* eds. H. Feigl, M. Scriven and G. Maxwell, vol. 2, 3–36 (Minneapolis: University of Minnesota Press 1958).
3. Peter Fonagy, *An Open Door Review of Outcome Studies in Psychoanalysis* (London 2002), 12. And he adds: Ibidem, 16: "What is disappointing is that psychoanalysts have tended to accept the argument that complexity precludes unequivocal definition as an adequate reason to accept the argument for rarely attempting operationalisation and frequently embracing ambiguity."

4. Paul Ricœur, "Epistemology: Between Psychology and Phenomenology," in *Freud and Philosophy. An Essay on Interpretation* (New Haven/London: Yale University Press, 1970) (1965), 344–408.
5. Paul Ricœur, *Freud and Philosophy. An Essay on Interpretation* (New Haven/London: Yale University Press, 1970) (1965), 376.
6. Ibid., 390–391.
7. Ibid., 378.
8. Ibid., 379.
9. Ibid., 392.
10. Antoine Vergote, "L'intérêt philosophique de la psychanalyse freudienne," *Archives de Philosophie* 21 (Jan.–Feb. 1958): 38.
11. Paul Ricœur, *Freud and Philosophy. An Essay on Interpretation* (New Haven/London: Yale University Press, 1970) (1965), 393.
12. Ibid., 382.
13. Sigmund Freud, *Beyond the Pleasure Principle* (1920 g). In: *SE* 18, 7–64. [References to the works of Sigmund Freud are quoted from: *The Standard Edition of the Complete Psychological Works of Sigmund Freud*, vols. 1–24. (London: 1953–74) (further quoted as *SE*). The chronological order of Freud's writings is based upon the volume *Freud-Bibliographie mit Werkkonkordanz* [Freud-Bibliography and Concordance of His Publications]. ed. I. Meyer-Palmedo and G. Fichtner (Frankfurt am Main 1989), 15–90].
14. Paul Ricœur, *Freud and Philosophy. An Essay on Interpretation,* (New Haven/London: Yale University Press, 1970) (1965), 385 and see also Alphonse de Waelhens, *Réflexions sur une problématique husserlienne de l'inconscient: Husserl et Hegel*, in *Edmund Husserl, 1859–1959* (The Hague 1959), 232.
15. Paul Ricœur, *Freud and Philosophy. An Essay on Interpretation* (New Haven/London: Yale University Press, 1970) (1965), 400.
16. Sigmund Freud, *The Interpretation of Dreams* (1900 a). In: *SE* 4–5.
17. Paul Ricœur, *Freud and Philosophy. An Essay on Interpretation* (New Haven/London: Yale University Press, 1970) (1965), 417.
18. Sigmund Freud, *Observation on Transference-Love* (1914). In: *SE* 12, 159–171.
19. Ibid., 166.
20. Ibid., 369.
21. Ibid., 396.
22. Paul Ricœur, "The Question of Proof in Freud's Psychoanalytic Writings," in *Hermeneutics and the Human Sciences* (New York: Cambridge University Press, 1981), 247–305.
23. Adolf Grünbaum, *The Foundations of Psychoanalysis. A Philosophical Critique* (Berkeley/Los Angeles/London: University of California Press, 1984), 43.
24. Ibid., 44.
25. Ibid., 58.
26. Paul Ricœur "The Question of Proof in Freud's Psychoanalytic Writings," in *Hermeneutics and the Human Sciences* (New York: Cambridge University Press, 1981), 248.
27. Charles Hanly, "A Problem of Theory Testing," *The International Review of Psycho-Analysis* 10 (1983), 394.
28. Paul Ricœur "The Question of Proof in Freud's Psychoanalytic Writings," in *Hermeneutics and the Human Sciences* (New York: Cambridge University Press, 1981), 253.
29. Ibid., 250.
30. Ibid., 253.
31. Ibid., 268.
32. Galen Strawson, "Intentionality and Experience: Terminological Preliminaries," in *Phenomenology and Philosophy of Mind*, eds. D.W. Smith and A.L. Thomasson, 47 (Oxford: Oxford University Press, 2005).
33. Ibid., 48–49.
34. John Searle, *The Rediscovery of the Mind* (Cambridge: MIT Press, 1992), 159.
35. Franz Brentano, *Psychology from an Empirical Standpoint* (1874), vol. 1 (New Jersey: Princeton University Press, 1973).

36. William James, *The Principles of Psychology*, vol. 1 (New York: Henry Holt, 1890).
37. Robert Van Gulick, "Understanding the Phenomenal Mind: Are We All Just Armadillos?," in *Consciousness: Psychological and Philosophical Essays*, eds. M. Davies and G. Humphreys (Oxford: Blackwell, 1993), 137.
38. Terence Horgan, John Tienson and George Graham, "Phenomenal Intentionality and the Brain in a Vat," in *The Externalist Challenge* ed. R. Schanz (Berlin/New York 2004), 301.
39. Galen Strawson, *Mental Reality* (Cambridge: MIT Press, 1994).
40. Ibid., 302.
41. Frank Jackson, "Epiphenomenal Qualia." in *American Philosophical Quarterly* 32 (1982), 127–136 and Frank Jackson, "What Mary Didn't Know," *Journal of Philosophy* 83 (1986): 291–295.
42. Patrizia Giampieri-Deutsch, "Die psychoanalytische Theorie des Mentalen und die analytische Philosophie des Geistes," in *Psychoanalyse im Dialog der Wissenschaften. Europäische Perspektiven,* ed. P. Giampieri-Deutsch, vol. 1, (Stuttgart 2002), 71.
43. Frank Jackson, "Postscript," in *Contemporary Materialism* eds. P. K. Moser and J. D. Trout (New York: Routledge, 1995), 184–189; Postscript on Qualia, in *Mind, Method, and Conditionals* (London: Routledge, 1998), 76–79 and *From Metaphysics to Ethics* (Oxford: Clarendon Press, 1998).
44. David Chalmers, "Phenomenal Concepts and the Knowledge Arguments," in *There's Something About Mary. Essays on Phenomenal Consciousness and Frank Jackson's Knowledge Argument* eds. P. Ludlow, Y. Nagasawa and D. Stoljar (Cambridge: MIT Press, 2004), 269–298.
45. David Chalmers, "The Hard Problem of Consciousness," in *The Blackwell Companion to Consciousness* eds. M. Velmans and S. Schneider (Malden/Oxford 2007), 225.
46. Ibid., 226.
47. Joseph Levine, "Materialism and Qualia: the Explanatory Gap." *Pacific Philosophical Quarterly* 64, (1983) 354–361.
48. Joseph Levine, "Anti-materialist Arguments and Influential Replies," in *The Blackwell Companion to Consciousness* eds. M. Velmans and S. Schneider (Malden/Oxford 2007), 376.
49. Thomas Nagel, "What is it like to be a bat?," Philosophical Review 83 (1974): 435–450, reprinted in eds. N. Block, O. Flanagan and G. Güzeldere, *The Nature of Consciousness. Philosophical Debates* (Cambridge 1997), 519–527.
50. John Searle, *The Rediscovery of the Mind* (Cambridge: MIT Press, 1992).
51. Shaun Gallagher, "Phenomenological Approaches to Consciousness," in *The Blackwell Companion to Consciousness* eds. M. Velmans and S. Schneider (Malden/Oxford 2007), 693.
52. Ibid., 694.
53. Ibid., 695.
54. Patrizia Giampieri-Deutsch, Zum „Objekt" in der psychoanalytischen Theorie des Mentalen und in der klinischen Theorie. *Wiener Jahrbuch für Philosophie* 2000 32 (2001), 157–175.
55. Alva Noë, *Action in Perception* (Cambridge: MIT Press 2004).
56. James Jerome Gibson, *The Ecological Approach to Visual Perception* (Boston: Houghton Mifflin, 1979).
57. Shaun Gallagher, *How the Body Shapes the Mind* (Oxford: Clarendon Press, 2005).
58. Thomas Fuchs, *Das Gehirn – ein Beziehungsorgan. Eine phänomenologische-ökologische Konzeption* (Stuttgart: Kohlhammer, 2008).
59. Eric Kandel, "From Metapsychology to Molecular Biology: Exploration into the Nature of Anxiety." *American Journal of Psychiatry* 140 (1983): 1277–1293, reprinted in *Psychiatry, Psychoanalysis and the New Biology of Mind* (Arlington: American Psychiatric Publishing, 2005). See as commentary also: Patrizia Giampieri-Deutsch, Geist, Gehirn, Verhalten, "Sigmund Freuds wissenschaftliche Weltauffassung in der Gegenwart," ed. P. Giampieri-Deutsch, *Geist, Gehirn, Verhalten: Sigmund Freud und die modernen Wissenschaften* (Würzburg: Königshausen & Neumann, 2009), 115–126.
60. Friedrich Barth, Patrizia Giampieri-Deutsch and Hans-Dieter Klein, eds., *Sensory Perception. Mind and Matter* (Heidelberg/New York 2011) (forthcoming).
61. Max Velmans, ed., *Investigating Phenomenal Consciousness. New Methodologies and Maps* (Amsterdam/Philadelphia: John Benjamins, 2000).

62. Susan Schneider and Max Velmans, "Introduction," in *The Blackwell Companion to Consciousness* eds. M. Velmans and S. Schneider (Malden/Oxford: Blackwell, 2007), 4–5.
63. See especially chapter 8 in: Max Velmans, *Understanding Consciousness* (London: Routledge/ Psychology Press, 2000).
64. Joseph Sandler, "Countertransference and Role-Responsivness," *The International Review of Psycho-Analysis* 3 (1976): 44.
65. Heinrich Racker, "The Countertransference Neurosis (1948)", in *Transference and Countertransference* (London 1968), 105–126.
66. Paula Heimann, "On Countertransference". *The International Journal of Psycho-Analysis* 31 (1950): 81–84.
67. Sándor Ferenczi, On the Technique of Psycho–Analysis (1919), in *Further Contributions to the Theory and Technique of Psycho–Analysis* (New York 1950); see also Patrizia Giampieri-Deutsch, "The Influence of Ferenczi's Ideas on Contemporary Standard Technique," eds. P. Rudnytsky, A. Bókay e P. Giampieri-Deutsch, *Ferenczi´s Turn in Psychoanalysis* (New York/ London 1996), 224–247.
68. Ibid., 44–45.
69. Patrizia Giampieri-Deutsch, "Ferenczis Beitrag zur Theorie des psychoanalytischen Prozesses," *Zeitschrift für psychoanalytischen Theorie und Praxis* 10 (1995): 259–291 and "The Influence of Ferenczi´s Ideas on Contemporary Standard Technique," *Ferenczi's Turn in Psychoanalysis*, eds. P. Rudnytsky, A. Bókay e P. Giampieri-Deutsc (New York/London 1996), 224–247.
70. Edoardo Weiss, "Federn's Phenomenological Ego-psychology." *Journal of the History of the Behavioral Sciences* 7 (1972): 41–44.
71. Patrizia Giampieri-Deutsch, "Psicoanalisi," in *Storia d'Italia. Le regioni. Il Friuli Venezia Giulia*, eds. R. Finzi, C. Magris and G. Miccoli (Torino 2002).
72. For a more detailed account see Patrizia Giampieri-Deutsch, "Die psychoanalytische Theorie des Mentalen und die analytische Philosophie des Geistes," *Psychoanalyse im Dialog der Wissenschaften. Europäische Perspektiven*, ed. P. Giampieri-Deutsch, vol. 1, (Stuttgart: Kohlhammer, 2002), 71–72 and "Approaching Contemporary Psychoanalytic Research," *Psychoanalysis as an Empirical, Interdisciplinary Science. Collected Papers on Contemporary Psychoanalytic Research*, ed. P. Giampieri-Deutsch (Wien 2005), 31–37.
73. See also Patrizia Giampieri-Deutsch, "Auswirkungen der Kooperation zwischen der analytischen Philosophie des Geistes und der Psychoanalyse auf die empirische psychoanalytische Forschung," *Psychoanalyse im Dialog der Wissenschaften. Anglo-amerikanische Perspektiven* ed. P. Giampieri-Deutsch, vol. 2 (Stuttgart 2004), 80–91.
74. Patrizia Giampieri-Deutsch, "Approaching Contemporary Psychoanalytic Research," in *Psychoanalysis as an Empirical, Interdisciplinary Science. Collected Papers on Contemporary Psychoanalytic Research*, ed. P. Giampieri-Deutsch (Wien 2005), 34–37 and 41.
75. Patrizia Giampieri-Deutsch, "Psychanalyse: la science de la subjectivité," *En quête du sujet*, eds. Socratis Delivoyatzis, Sophia Panteliadou and Christos Sidiropoulos (Thessaloniki 2011), S. 9–23 (forthcoming).
76. Roy Shafer, "Narration in Psychoanalytic Dialogue," *On Narrative* (Chicago 1981), 25–49 and *Retelling a Life: Narration and Dialogue in Psychoanalysis*, ed. W. J. T. Mitchell (New York 1992).
77. Owen Renik, "Analytic Interaction: Conceptualizing Technique in Light of the Analyst's Irreducible Subjectivity," *Psychoanalytic Quarterly* 62, 553–571.
78. Charles Hanly, "On Subjectivity and Objectivity in Psychoanalysis," *Journal of the American Psychoanalytic Association* 47 (1999), 430.
79. Ibid., 439.
80. Ibid., 438.
81. Karl Popper, *Objective Knowledge: An Evolutionary Approach* (Oxford: Clarendon Press, 1971), 109.
82. See Chapter 8 in: Max Velmans, *Understanding Consciousness* (London: Routledge/ Psychology Press, 2000) and Max Velmans, "An Epistemology for the Study of Consciousness,"

eds. M. Velmans and S. Schneider, *The Blackwell Companion to Consciousness* (Malden/ Oxford: Blackwell, 2007), 711–725.
83. Donald Spence, *Narrative Truth and Historical Truth. Meaning and Interpretation in Psychoanalysis* (New York: W.W. Norton 1982).
84. Charles Hanly, "On Subjectivity and Objectivity in Psychoanalysis," *Journal of the American Psychoanalytic Association* 47 (1999): 438–439.
85. Patrizia Giampieri-Deutsch, "Freud: ein österreichischer Philosoph?," *Austriaca* 14/28 (1989): 69–86; Patrizia Giampieri-Deutsch, "Freud und die österreichische Philosophie," *Philosophie und Psychoanalyse*, eds. L. Nagl, H. Vetter, and H. Leupold-Löwenthal (Frankfurt am Main: Nexus Verlag, 1990), 41–54; "Mach und Freud: Ein Vergleich," *Zeitgeschichte* 17 (1990): 291–310; "Die Psychoanalyse als Wissenschaft und andere Aspekte des Briefwechsels zwischen Sigmund Freud und Sándor Ferenczi." *Jenseits von Kunst*, ed. P. Weibel (Wien 1997), 621–626; "Die psychoanalytische Theorie des Mentalen und die analytische Philosophie des Geistes," *Psychoanalyse im Dialog der Wissenschaften. Europäische Perspektiven*, ed. P. Giampieri-Deutsch, vol. 1, (Stuttgart 2002), 58–75; "Auswirkungen der Kooperation zwischen der analytischen Philosophie des Geistes und der Psychoanalyse auf die empirische psychoanalytische Forschung," *Psychoanalyse im Dialog der Wissenschaften. Anglo-amerikanische Perspektiven*, ed. P. Giampieri-Deutsch, vol. 2, (Stuttgart 2004), 80–91.
86. Wilhelm Dilthey, "Einleitung in die Geisteswissenschaften. Versuch einer Grundlegung für das Studium der Gesellschaft und der Geschichte (1883)," in *Gesammelte Schriften*, vol. 1, (Leipzig und Berlin 1927); *Studien zur Grundlegung der Geisteswissenschaften* (1905–1910), in *Gesammelte Schriften*, vol. 7, (Leipzig, Berlin 1914–1936), 3–75; *Der Aufbau der geschichtlichen Welt in den Geisteswissenschaften* (1910), in *Gesammelte Schriften*, vol. 7. (Leipzig, Berlin 1914–1936), 79–188.
87. Franz Brentano *Psychology from an Empirical Standpoint* (1874), vol. 1, (New Jersey 1973).
88. Franz Brentano, "Über die Zukunft der Philosophie (1893)." in *Über die Zukunft der Philosophie* (Hamburg 1929), 9; on Brentano's critique of Dilthey see Patrizia Giampieri-Deutsch, "Freud: ein österreichischer Philosoph?," *Austriaca* 14/28 (1989): 72.
89. Patrizia Giampieri-Deutsch, "Freud und die österreichische Philosophie,"in *Philosophie und Psychoanalyse* eds. L. Nagl, H. Vetter, and H. Leupold-Löwenthal (Frankfurt am Main 1990), 48.
90. Carlo Strenger, *Between Hermeneutics and Science. An Essay on the Epistemology of Psychoanalysis* (New York 1991).
91. Jerry Fodor, "Special Sciences, or the Disunity of Science as a Working Hypothesis," in *The Language of Thought.* (New York 1975), 9–25; reprinted in N. Block, ed., *Readings in Philosophy of Psychology*, vol. 1 (Cambridge 1980), 120–133.
92. Ibid., 131.
93. Peter Fonagy, *An Open Door Review of Outcome Studies in Psychoanalysis* (London: International Psychoanalytical Association, 2002), 23–29.
94. Patrizia Giampieri-Deutsch, ed., *Psychoanalyse im Dialog der Wissenschaften. Europäische Perspektiven,* vol. 1 (Stuttgart: Kohlhammer, 2002); *Psychoanalyse im Dialog der Wissenschaften. Anglo-amerikanische Perspektiven,* vol. 2, (Stuttgart: Kohlhammer, 2004); *Psychoanalysis as an Empirical, Interdisciplinary Science. Collected Papers on Contemporary Psychoanalytic Research* (Wien 2005); *Geist, Gehirn, Verhalten: Sigmund Freud und die modernen Wissenschaften* (Würzburg 2009); Friedrich Barth, Patrizia Giampieri-Deutsch and Hans-Dieter Klein, ed., *Sensory Perception. Mind and Matter* (Heidelberg & New York 2011) (forthcoming).
95. Drew Westen, "The Scientific Status of Unconscious Processes," *Journal of the American Psychoanalytic Association* 47 (1999), 1062–1063.

Berührungspunkte zwischen der „Philosophie“ Freuds und der Phänomenologie

Günter Gödde

Abstract Entgegen der vielfach vertretenen Auffassung, Freud hätte von den Jugendjahren an eine gleichbleibend negative Einstellung zur Philosophie gehabt, ergibt die Auswertung seiner Briefe und anderer psychoanalyse-interner Quellen ein differenzierteres Bild: Als junger Student interessierte er sich stark für philosophische Fragestellungen und studierte vier Semester lang bei dem Philosophen *Franz Brentano*, um sich dann im weiteren Studium vorrangig biologischen Forschungsprojekten zu widmen. In der Pionierzeit der Psychoanalyse keimte Freuds Interesse an der Philosophie wieder auf, wobei er sich besonders an *Theodor Lipps* als einem Kronzeugen für seine Psychologie des Unbewussten orientierte. Erst in den Diskussionen der psychoanalytischen Mittwoch-Gesellschaft vollzog Freud eine Wende zu einer zunehmend an Schärfe und Polemik gewinnenden Philosophiekritik und stellte damit die Weichen, die den Austausch und die Verständigung zwischen Psychoanalyse und Philosophie bis heute sehr erschwert haben. Schon damals gab es aber eine Reihe von Psychoanalytikern wie z.B. *Ludwig Binswanger*, die Freuds Philosophiekritik mit großer Skepsis begegneten. Nach dem Ersten Weltkrieg grenzte Freud die "wissenschaftliche Weltauffassung“ zwar weiterhin programmatisch von der Philosophie ab. Seine Philosophiekritik sollte aber nicht als generalisierende Ablehnung, sondern besser als Kritik an bestimmten Schulen der Philosophie, vor allem an der spekulativen Metaphysik und an den Systemdenkern verstanden werden.
Geht man der Frage nach, wie Freud mit dem phänomenologischen Denken in Berührung gekommen sein kann, dann liegt es nahe, in erster Linie an Franz Brentano, Theodor Lipps und Ludwig Binswanger zu denken, da sie der Phänomenologie nahe stehen und Freud mit ihnen – persönlich oder über deren Werk – zeitweise eng verbunden war. Aus psychoanalysehistorischer Sicht erscheinen die Verbindungen Freuds zu den deskriptiv, intentional und phänomenologisch orientierten Psychologien

G. Gödde (✉)
Kuno-Fischer-Straße 20, 14057 Berlin, Germany
e-mail: g.goedde@t-online.de

D. Lohmar and J. Brudzińska (eds.), *Founding Psychoanalysis Phenomenologically*, Phaenomenologica 199, DOI 10.1007/978-94-007-1848-7_6,

Brentanos, Lipps' und Binswangers noch keineswegs hinreichend erforscht. Der vorliegende Beitrag sucht dieses Dunkelfeld etwas zu erhellen. '-- End of Abstract'

Wie lässt sich Freuds Verhältnis zur phänomenologisch orientierten Philosophie und Psychologie einordnen? War ihm die Phänomenologie ganz fremd, war er ein Gegner der Phänomenologie oder gibt es schon in seinem Werk Anknüpfungspunkte, die für eine Annäherung und einen Ausbau der Kooperationsbeziehungen zwischen Psychoanalyse und Phänomenologie sprechen?

Um zur Klärung dieser Fragen beizutragen, erscheint es sinnvoll, zunächst auf Freuds Verhältnis zur Philosophie im allgemeinen einzugehen. Immer wieder werden Äußerungen seiner Philosophiekritik zitiert, die ihn als „Anti-Metaphysiker", ja als „Anti-Philosophen" erscheinen lassen.[1] Was hat es mit dieser Einschätzung auf sich? Was bedeutet es, dass Freud die Psychoanalyse als Naturwissenschaft konzipierte und daraus eine „Psychologie ohne Philosophie" machen wollte? Birgt Freuds Psychoanalyse nicht notwendig eine „implizite Philosophie" in sich,[2] so dass von da aus „implizite Konzepte"[3] in die klinische Theorie und Praxis hineinwirken? Und was bedeutet das im Hinblick auf den Wissenschaftsstatus der Psychoanalyse, der sich im Spannungsfeld von „Psychobiologie" (Sulloway) bzw. „Energetik" (Ricoeur) und „Tiefenhermeneutik" bzw. „Hermeneutik des Leibes" (Lorenzer) bewegt?[4]

Um sich ein Bild von Freuds impliziter Philosophie machen zu können, werden zunächst einige seiner Äußerungen über Philosophie und Philosophiekritik im Rahmen eines Phasenmodells seines Denkens miteinander verglichen. Im weiteren geht es um die Frage, über welche Vermittler Freud mit dem phänomenologischen Denken in Berührung gekommen ist und welche Spuren diese Begegnungen in seinem Werk hinterlassen haben.

1 Freuds Verhältnis zur Philosophie – ein Phasenmodell

Freuds Äußerungen zur Philosophie zeugen von einer tiefgehenden Ambivalenz. In Briefen an Wilhelm Fließ äußerte er, dass die Philosophie sein „Anfangsziel" gewesen sei, denn „das wollte ich ursprünglich, als mir noch gar nicht klar war, wozu ich auf der Welt bin"; und dass er „als junger Mensch keine andere Sehnsucht gekannt [habe] als die nach philosophischer Erkenntnis."[5] Demgegenüber verstand er sich schon in seinen Jugendbriefen als „Naturforscher"[6] und „Empiriker"[7], der alles ablehnte, was mit Metaphysik zu tun hat, und noch im Spätwerk postulierte er eine Kluft zwischen Philosophie und Wissenschaft, weil die Philosophie an der Illusion eines zusammenhängenden Denksystems festhalte, die logischen Operationen überschätze und nicht ausschließlich empirische Methoden verwende.[8] Im Spätwerk erklärte er aber auch erneut, er habe „nach großem Umweg die anfängliche Richtung wieder gefunden" und begründete dies mit dem in den Jugendjahren übermächtigen Bedürfnis, „etwas von den Rätseln dieser Welt zu verstehen."[9] Der Ausdruck „Rätsel der Welt" erinnert an Ernst Haeckels berühmtes Werk „Die Welträtsel" (1899) und zugleich an die erwähnte Formulierung von Freuds „philosophischer Sehnsucht" in den Jugendjahren.[10]

In Freuds Einstellung zur Philosophie lassen sich vier Entwicklungsphasen unterscheiden:

- die Phase wissenschaftlicher und philosophischer Sozialisation in den Jugendjahren,
- die Konstitutionsphase und
- die Institutionalisierungsphase der Psychoanalyse sowie
- die Phase des Spätwerks.

Die Jugendbriefe an Eduard Silberstein (1871–81) zeigen, dass Freud als junger Student weitläufigen Bildungsinteressen nachging. Vor Beginn des ersten Semesters kündigt der 17-Jährige an, dass er das erste Universitätsjahr „ganz und gar auf rein humanistische Studien verwenden werde, die mit meinem Fach noch nichts zu tun haben, mir aber gar nicht unnützlich sein sollen."[11] Im dritten Semester nimmt er seine Studien bei dem 1874 nach Wien übergesiedelten Philosophieprofessor Franz Brentano auf: „Leid täte es mir z. B., wenn Du, der Jurist, die Philosophie gänzlich vernachlässigen würdest, während ich gottloser Mediziner und Empiriker 2 philosophische Kollegien höre und in Gemeinschaft mit Paneth den Feuerbach lese. Eines davon handelt – höre und staune! – über das Dasein Gottes, und Prof. Brentano, der es liest, ist ein prächtiger Mensch, Gelehrter und Philosoph, obwohl er es für nötig hält, dieses luftige Dasein Gottes mit seinen Gründen zu stützen."[12] Gegen Ende des Semesters formulieren Freud und sein Freund Josef Paneth brieflich ihre Einwände gegen Brentanos Theismus. Daraufhin, schreibt Freud, „lud er uns in seine Wohnung, widerlegte uns, schien ein Interesse an uns zu finden [...] und hat uns jetzt, nachdem wir ihm einen zweiten Brief mit Einwänden überreicht, von neuem zu sich beschieden". Im selben Brief vertraut der knapp 19-Jährige seinem Jugendfreund den Plan an, das Doktorat der Philosophie auf Grund von Philosophie und Zoologie zu erwerben; "weitere Verhandlungen sind im Zuge, um entweder vom nächsten Semester oder vom nächsten Jahr an meinen Eintritt in die philosophische Fakultät zu bewerkstelligen."[13] Diesem Vorhaben stand aber entgegen, dass man nicht gleichzeitig an der zoologischen und philosophischen Fakultät studieren durfte.[14] Aber viel hat nicht gefehlt, und Brentano hätte den Medizinstudenten Freud für die Philosophie gewonnen.

Auch im „Leseverein der deutschen Studenten Wiens", dem er von 1873 bis 1878 angehörte, kam Freud mit der Philosophie und insbesondere mit dem Denken Schopenhauers, Richard Wagners und Nietzsches in Berührung.[15] Sein Eintritt in das physiologische Labor Ernst Brückes im Jahre 1876 bildete den Keim zu einer Abkehr von der Philosophie in den weiteren Studienjahren, denn Brücke gehörte mit Helmholtz, Du Bois-Reymond und Carl Ludwig zu jener berühmten Physiologengruppe, die jeglichen Vitalismus und Finalismus in den Naturwissenschaften bekämpfte und damit maßgeblich zur Entthronung der romantischen Naturphilosophie und spekulativen Physiologie beitrug. Das Selbstverständnis dieser Forscher entsprach der damals unter Naturwissenschaftlern verbreiteten Auffassung, die Philosophen hätten „eine von der unsrigen total verschiedene Denkweise". Es seien eben getrennte Gebiete und sie müssten getrennt bleiben.[16]

Mit einem viermonatigen Studienaufenthalt bei dem Neurologen Charcot an der Salpêtrière im Winter 1885/1886 begann Freuds Wende von einem Organmediziner zu einem Psychotherapeuten und Erforscher des Unbewussten. In seiner neurologischen Privatpraxis, die er 1886 eröffnete, sah er sich täglich vor die Aufgabe gestellt, nervöse Erkrankungen zu therapieren. Im ersten Jahrzehnt seiner Praxis kam es zu einer engen Zusammenarbeit mit seinem Freund und Mentor Josef Breuer, mit dem er 1895 die „Studien über Hysterie" veröffentlichte, doch bald danach endete die langjährige Arbeitsbeziehung der beiden. Der Berliner Freund Wilhelm Fließ trat an Breuers Stelle und war dann der wesentliche Austauschpartner Freuds.[17]

Anhand der Briefe an Fließ (1887–1904) kann man die Herausbildung des psychoanalytischen Paradigmas in statu nascendi mitverfolgen. In den beiden zu Anfang erwähnten Briefen[18] wird die ‚Philosophie' nicht als feindliche Macht betrachtet, sondern mit offenen Gefühlen wie Hoffnung und Sehnsucht begrüßt. Wenn Freud nunmehr einen Übergang von der Medizin zur ‚Psychologie' anvisierte, dann verband er mit dem praktischen Anliegen der Neurosentherapie das theoretisch anspruchsvolle Projekt einer wissenschaftlichen Fundierung. Zunächst wollte er eine Brücke zwischen Physiologie und Psychologie schlagen.[19] Von seinem 1895 niedergeschriebenen „Entwurf einer Psychologie"[20] nahm er aber drei Jahre später endgültig Abstand: „Ich bin [...] gar nicht geneigt, das Psychologische ohne organische Grundlage schwebend zu erhalten. Ich weiß nur von der Überzeugung aus nicht weiter, weder theoretisch noch therapeutisch, und muß also mich so benehmen, als läge mir nur das Psychologische vor."[21]

Im selben Jahr konfrontiert er Fließ mit der Frage, ob er für seine „hinter das Bewusstsein führende Psychologie den Namen Metapsychologie gebrauchen" dürfe.[22] Wie einige Briefe an Wilhelm Fließ aus der zweiten Hälfte der 1890er Jahre zeigen, hat er sich damals schon seit mehreren Jahren an Denkern orientiert, welche die Tragweite des Unbewussten erkannt hatten. Nach Wilhelm Jerusalem und Hippolyte Taine hebt er Gustav Theodor Fechner hervor,[23] und besonders gelegen kommt es ihm, dass er in Theodor Lipps, der damals neben Franz Brentano und Wilhelm Wundt zu den führenden Vertretern der Akademischen Psychologie in Deutschland gehörte, einen Kronzeugen für seine Psychologie des Unbewussten findet. In einem Brief an Fließ aus dem Jahre 1898 schreibt er: „Ich habe mir die Aufgabe gestellt, zwischen meiner keimenden Metapsychologie und der in den Büchern enthaltenen die Brücke herzustellen und mich darum in das Studium von Lipps versenkt [...]." Wenige Tage später fügt er hinzu: „Bei Lipps habe ich die Grundzüge meiner Einsicht ganz klar wiedergefunden, vielleicht etwas mehr, als mir recht ist. ‚Der Sucher fand oft mehr, als er zu finden wünschte!' Das Bewusstsein nur Sinnesorgan, aller psychische Inhalt nur Vorstellung, die seelischen Vorgänge sämtlich unbewusst."[24] Zusammenfassend kann man sagen, dass die Fließ-Briefe ebenso wenig wie die Silberstein-Briefe eine *anti*-philosophische Haltung erkennen lassen.

Die Gründung der Psychologischen ‚Mittwoch-Gesellschaft' im Jahre 1902 kann man als Beginn der Institutionalisierungsphase der Psychoanalyse betrachten. Anhand der von Otto Rank geführten Protokolle (1906–1918) lässt sich en detail nachvollziehen, dass Freuds Philosophiekritik seit etwa 1907 zunehmend an Schärfe gewann. Damals wurden die Weichen gestellt, die den Austausch und die Verständigung zwischen Psychoanalyse und Philosophie sehr erschwert haben.[25]

In der Sitzung vom 20. März 1907 zieht Freud eine Analogie zwischen den „Delirien" als „kombinierten Leistungen, denen das Systematische anhafte" und „den großen (philosophischen) Systemen".[26] Wird die Philosophie in Analogie zu psychischen Krankheiten gesehen, dann ist es nur folgerichtig, dass auch die Philosophen selbst zum Objekt der Psychoanalyse gemacht werden. In den Diskussionen des Wiener Freud-Kreises hat die ‚Pathographie' von Philosophen wie Schopenhauer und Nietzsche eine wichtige Rolle gespielt. Nietzsches ungewöhnliche psychologische Introspektionsfähigkeit wird zwar gewürdigt, aber darauf zurückgeführt, dass er sich aufgrund seiner Paralyse vollständig von der Außenwelt zurückgezogen und sich seinem Ich als einzigem Forschungsobjekt zugewandt habe: „Er macht eine Reihe glänzender Entdeckungen an seiner Person. Aber nun kommt die Krankheit. Er begnügt sich nicht damit, diese Zusammenhänge richtig zu erraten, sondern er projiziert die Erkenntnis, die er an sich gemacht hat, als Lebensanforderung nach außen."[27] Einen weiteren Aspekt der Philosophiekritik entnimmt Freud der positivistischen Geschichtsphilosophie, wonach die Philosophie als überholtes Stadium in der Fortschrittsgeschichte des menschlichen Geistes eingeordnet wird.[28]

Auf dieser Kritiklinie fortfahrend äußert er sich 1913 über „das philosophische Interesse" an der Psychoanalyse. Einerseits hätten die Philosophen umzudenken, weil das Unbewusste für sie „etwas Mystisches, nicht Greifbares und nicht Aufzeigbares" geblieben sei, das sie beurteilt hätten, ohne die Phänomene der unbewussten Seelentätigkeit hinreichend erforscht zu haben. Andererseits könne sich die Philosophie mit Hilfe der Psychoanalyse nunmehr selbst zum Objekt machen. Erst der Psychoanalyse sei es möglich, „die subjektive und individuelle Motivierung von philosophischen Lehren, welche vorgeblich unparteiischer Logik entsprungen sind", zu erkennen. und „der Kritik selbst die schwachen Punkte des Systems" anzuzeigen. Diese Kritik durchzuführen, sei aber nicht Sache der Psychoanalyse, „denn, wie begreiflich, schließt die psychologische Determinierung einer Lehre ihre wissenschaftliche Korrektheit keineswegs aus."[29] Obwohl hier eine klare Trennungslinie zwischen der Genesis und der Geltung philosophischer Lehren gezogen wird, schätzten die Psychoanalytiker ihre Kompetenz in der Anwendung auf die Philosophie recht unterschiedlich ein. Neben den Wienern Otto Rank und Hanns Sachs[30] waren es vor allem James J. Putnam[31] und Ludwig Binswanger[32], die Freuds Philosophiekritik skeptisch gegenüber standen.[33]

Bereits zu Ende des 19. Jahrhunderts ließen sich innerhalb des Empirismus und der Evolutionstheorie Tendenzen erkennen, den starren Gegensatz zwischen ‚beobachtender' Wissenschaft und ‚spekulativer' Philosophie abzubauen.[34] Nach dem Ersten Weltkrieg zeigt sich auch in Freuds Stellungnahmen zum Verhältnis von Empirie und Spekulation eine deutliche Akzentverschiebung. So bekennt er, in den drei metapsychologischen Schriften „Jenseits des Lustprinzips" (1920), „Massenpsychologie und Ich-Analyse" (1921) und „Das Ich und das Es" (1923) „der lange niedergehaltenen Neigung zur Spekulation freien Lauf gelassen" zu haben.[35] Nunmehr bewegt sich Freud verstärkt in den philosophischen Bahnen Schopenhauers und Nietzsches.[36] In der letzten seiner „Vorlesungen zur Einführung in die Psychoanalyse" hält er ein Plädoyer für die ‚wissenschaftliche Weltauffassung' und grenzt sie programmatisch von der Philosophie ab: „Die

Philosophie ist der Wissenschaft nicht gegensätzlich, sie gebärdet sich selbst wie eine Wissenschaft, arbeitet zum Teil mit den gleichen Methoden, entfernt sich aber von ihr, indem sie an der Illusion festhält, ein lückenloses und zusammenhängendes Weltbild liefern zu können, das doch bei jedem neuen Fortschritt unseres Wissens zusammenbrechen muß."[37]

Demnach erweist sich der lange Zeit vorherrschende Eindruck, Freud hätte von den Jugendjahren an eine gleichbleibend negative Einstellung zur Philosophie gehabt, als nicht zutreffend. Erst in der Institutionalisierungsphase der Psychoanalyse bekommt seine Philosophiekritik eine zunehmend schärfere Note. Wenn er dennoch bis zuletzt an der strikten Abgrenzung der Psychoanalyse von der Philosophie festgehalten hat, so lag dies wohl in erster Linie an seiner Befürchtung, eine philosophisch-hermeneutische Lesart der Psychoanalyse könnte einem „Subjektivismus" den Weg ebnen, „der nicht nur den von ihm stets betonten wissenschaftlichen Charakter seiner Schöpfung bedroht, sondern diese auch selbst ganz aushöhlt, indem sie dem subjektiven Belieben anheimgestellt wird."[38]

Mit seiner Kritik an der ‚Metaphysik' stand Freud zu seiner Zeit unter den in Österreich einflussreichen Denkern keineswegs allein. Auch für Franz Brentano, Edmund Husserl, Ernst Mach, Ludwig Wittgenstein und den ‚Wiener Kreis' erschien die Überwindung der Metaphysik durch Wissenschaftlichkeit wie eine Erlösungsformel. Man kann daher von einer „gemeinsamen Grundeinstellung" dieser Denker sprechen.[39]

Die Gefahr von Klischeebildungen in Freuds Philosophiekritik ist zwar nicht zu verkennen: Erkenntnistheoretisch gesehen wird die Philosophie mit negativen Konnotationen wie Intuition, Spekulation, Systembildung und Weltanschauung versehen; aus pathologischer Perspektive wird sie gar mit Krankheitsattributen wie narzisstischer Selbstbezogenheit, Grübelsucht und paranoider Projektion ausgestattet. Die weitergehende Charakterisierung Freuds als ‚Anti-Philosoph' erscheint aber als ‚Mythos'.[40] Seine Philosophiekritik sollte nicht als generalisierende Ablehnung, sondern besser als Kritik an bestimmten Schulen der Philosophie, vor allem an der spekulativen Metaphysik und an den Systemdenkern verstanden werden. Man kann daher von einer „impliziten" Philosophie Freuds sprechen, die einen wesentlichen Teil seiner Metapsychologie ausmacht.

Bei allen berechtigten Einwänden gegen Freuds Einstellung zur Philosophie dürfen seine Verdienste, die er sich mit seiner Philosophiekritik erworben hat, nicht gering geschätzt werden. „Die psychoanalytische Destruktion einer mächtigen philosophischen Tradition" bedeutete zugleich eine „indirekte Freilegung der Bedingungen eines neuen Philosophierens. [...] Durch den Verzicht auf die logische Konstruktion von Einheitssystemen scheint eine neue Offenheit für Erfahrung erreichbar."[41]

Hat sich Freud lange Zeit mit schriftlichen Äußerungen über Philosophie zurückgehalten, so gilt dies erst recht im Hinblick auf Stellungnahmen zur Phänomenologie. Im Gesamtregister findet man keinen einzigen Hinweis auf Husserl, Scheler oder Heidegger.

Ein einziges Mal spricht Freud explizit von Phänomenologie, aber nicht mit Bezug auf die phänomenologische Philosophie und Psychologie: „Vielen innerhalb wie außerhalb der Wissenschaft genügt es anzunehmen, das Bewusstsein sei allein das Psychische und dann bleibt in der Psychologie nichts anderes zu tun, als innerhalb der *psychischen Phänomenologie* (Hervorhebung, G.G.) Wahrnehmungen, Gefühle, Denkvorgänge und Willensakte zu unterscheiden." Und weiter heißt es: „Während man in der *Bewussteins-Psychologie* (Hervorhebung, G.G.) nie über jene lückenhaften, offenbar von anderswo abhängigen Reihen hinauskam, hat die andere Auffassung, das Psychische sei an sich unbewusst, gestattet, die Psychologie zu einer Naturwissenschaft wie jede andere auszugestalten."[42] An einer anderen Stelle wird der ‚Bewusstseinspsychologie' entgegen gehalten, dass sie insbesondere die Probleme des Traumes und der Hypnose nicht lösen könne.[43] In diesem Kontext geht Freud auf eine aktuelle Debatte zur Kritik des Unbewussten ein: „Manche Forscher, die sich der Anerkennung der psychoanalytischen Tatsachen nicht verschließen, das Unbewusste aber nicht annehmen wollen, schaffen sich eine Auskunft mit Hilfe der unbestrittenen Tatsache, dass auch das Bewusstsein – als Phänomen – eine große Reihe von Abstufungen der Intensität oder Deutlichkeit erkennen lässt. So wie es Vorgänge gibt, die sehr lebhaft, grell, greifbar bewusst sind, so erleben wir auch andere, die nur schwach, kaum eben merklich bewusst sind, und die am schwächsten bewussten seien eben die, für welche die Psychoanalyse das unpassende Wort unbewusst gebrauchen wolle. Sie seien aber doch auch bewusst oder ‘im Bewusstsein' und lassen sich voll und stark bewusst machen, wenn man ihnen genug Aufmerksamkeit schenkte."[44] Da Freud diese Kritik des Unbewussten ausdrücklich als „eine neuerliche Wendung" bezeichnet, bezieht er sich wahrscheinlich auf die Feldtheorie Wilhelm Wundts und auf phänomenologisch orientierte Konzepte in der Tradition Franz Brentanos.

Auf der Suche nach Spuren der Phänomenologie in Freuds Denkentwicklung möchte ich nunmehr auf drei bereits im ersten Teil erwähnte Autoren eingehen, die mehr oder weniger der Phänomenologie nahe stehen und mit denen Freud – persönlich oder über deren Werk – zeitweise in enger Verbindung stand:

- Freuds Philosophielehrer *Franz Brentano*, ohne den nach Stegmüllers Einschätzung „die ganze phänomenologische Philosophie undenkbar wäre"[45];
- *Theodor Lipps*, dem Freud das historische Verdienst zusprach, den Begriff des Unbewussten in die Psychologie eingeführt zu haben; und
- *Ludwig Binswanger*, der Freud über Jahrzehnte hinweg persönlich verbunden war, dann aber von der Psychoanalyse zur Phänomenologie Husserls und Heideggers überging und die Daseinsanalyse begründete.

2 Die Annahme der Intentionalität der psychischen Phänomene – Franz Brentanos Einfluss auf Freud und Husserl

Bei Franz Brentano (1838–1917) haben sowohl Freud als auch Husserl jeweils vier Semester studiert – Freud vom WS 1874/75 bis zum SS 1876 und Husserl genau zehn Jahre später vom WS 1884/85 bis zum SS 1886. Beide haben ihre Hauptwerke im

Jahre 1900 veröffentlicht: Freud die „Traumdeutung“ und Husserl die „Logischen Untersuchungen“. Bemerkenswert ist auch, dass die Gründungsphase der Psychoanalyse und die der Phänomenologie etwa in dieselbe Zeit fällt. Freuds Mustertraum von Irmas Injektion[46] stammt aus dem Jahre 1895; von der Methode der ‚Psychoanalyse'[47] sprach er erstmals 1896; die erste Fassung seiner „neuen Psychologie“ des Unbewussten, die er in der „Traumdeutung“ vorstellte, kann als Gründungsakt der Psychoanalyse betrachtet werden. Husserl begann 1897 mit der Ausarbeitung der „Logischen Untersuchungen“, die den Beginn der Phänomenologie markiert.

Freud war zu Beginn seines Studiums bei Franz Brentano erst 18 Jahre alt. Demgegenüber hatte der drei Jahre jüngere Edmund Husserl mit 25 Jahren bereits ein Studium der Mathematik und Philosophie abgeschlossen und mit einer mathematischen Arbeit promoviert. In der Philosophie sah er sich jedoch noch als „Anfänger“ und schwankte, ob er bei der Mathematik als Lebensaufgabe bleiben oder sich ganz der Philosophie widmen sollte. Brentanos Vorlesungen gaben den Ausschlag für die Philosophie.[48] Husserl gehörte dem engeren Schülerkreis Brentanos an und hat ihn stets als seinen Lehrer bezeichnet. Es hätte ihm aber nicht gelegen, „Mitglied seiner Schule zu bleiben“, da er sich innerlich gedrängt sah, „eigene, obschon von den seinen auslaufende Wege“ zu gehen. Dennoch habe er „die Kraft und den Wert der von ihm empfangenen Impulse immer höher einzuschätzen“ gelernt.[49]

Brentanos Antrittsvorlesung an der Wiener Universität vom 23. April 1874 bezog sich auf die „Gründe der Entmutigung auf philosophischem Gebiete“.[50] Vergleicht man Brentanos Text mit Freuds 1933 publizierter Vorlesung „Über eine wissenschaftliche Weltanschauung“, so ist darin ein erstaunlicher Grundkonsens zu erkennen. Brentano forderte schon damals mit programmatischem Anspruch, dass jene Art des Philosophierens, die, auf „Intuition“ und „a priorische Konstruktion“ gestützt, ein „Gebäude spekulativen Wissens“ und das „Ganze einer vollkommeneren Weltanschauung“ anstrebe, überwunden werden müsse. An ihre Stelle solle eine der „Naturforschung“ ähnliche Vorgehensweise treten, bei der man nur Schritt für Schritt durch „Beobachtung und Erfahrung“ zur Wahrheit vordringen könne.[51] Von einem starken Misstrauen gegen die traditionelle Philosophie erfüllt, ging er jedoch nicht so weit, deren Existenzberechtigung anzuzweifeln. Er wollte gerade umgekehrt die Entmutigung in der Philosophie durch Wissenschaftlichkeit überwinden.

In einem 1875 mit dem jungen Freud und dessen Freund Paneth geführten Gespräch wandte sich Brentano entschieden gegen Herbarts „aprioristische Konstruktionen in der Psychologie, hielt es für unverzeihlich, dass es ihm nie eingefallen sei, die Erfahrung oder das Experiment zu Rate zu ziehn und [...] erzählte uns einige merkwürdige psychologische Beobachtungen, die die Haltlosigkeit der Herbart'schen Spekulationen zeigen. Es tue mehr not, über einzelne Fragen gründliche Untersuchungen anzustellen, um zu einzelnen sicheren Resultaten zu gelangen, als das Ganze der Philosophie umfassen zu wollen, weil die Philosophie und Psychologie eine noch ganz junge Wissenschaft sei und besonders von der Physiologie keinerlei Unterstützung erwarten könne.“[52] In einer Gegenstellung zum vorherrschenden Herbartianismus initiierte Brentano in den folgenden Jahrzehnten eine zweite große Psychologierichtung in Österreich. Drei Momente an Brentanos Projekt einer wissenschaftlichen Philosophie (und Psychologie), die als Charakteristika der österreichischen Philosophie von 1874 bis 1936 gelten können, dürften den jungen Freud besonders angesprochen haben: der Empirismus, die Einteilung der menschlichen Denkentwicklung nach dem Comteschen Dreistadiengesetz und die Systemfeindlichkeit.[53]

In seinem Hauptwerk „Psychologie vom empirischen Standpunkt", das Brentano im Mai 1874, kurz nach dem Beginn seiner Wiener Professur veröffentlichte, ging es ihm um die Grundlegung einer empirisch orientierten „Wissenschaft von den psychischen Phänomenen". Dazu bedurfte es einer sorgfältigen Abgrenzung des Gegenstandes der Psychologie von der Physiologie und anderen Disziplinen:

Psychische Phänomene seien die ‚Vorstellungen', sei es durch Empfindung oder durch Phantasie, sowie „alle jene Erscheinungen, für welche Vorstellungen die Grundlage bilden", vor allem das Urteilen und das Begehren: „Nichts kann beurteilt, nichts kann aber auch begehrt, nichts kann gehofft oder gefürchtet werden, wenn es nicht vorgestellt wird."[54]

Im Anschluss an die aristotelisch-scholastische Tradition betrachtet Brentano die *‚Intentionalität'* als wesentliches Merkmal des Bewusstseins: „Jedes seelische Phänomen enthält etwas als Objekt in sich, obwohl nicht jedes in gleicher Weise. In der Vorstellung ist etwas vorgestellt, in dem Urteil ist etwas erkannt oder verworfen, in der Liebe geliebt, in dem Hasse gehasst, in dem Begehren begehrt usw." Daher gehörten zum Psychischen im Unterschied vom Physischen alle Phänomene, welche „intentional einen Gegenstand in sich enthalten".[55]

Die intentionale Gerichtetheit unseres Bewusstseins auf Gegenstände wird als psychischer ‚Akt' bezeichnet. In Brentanos Aktpsychologie sind drei Grundklassen zu unterscheiden: In den Vorstellungen sei der anschauliche Inhalt das Intendierte; in den Urteilen anerkenne oder verwerfe die Seele etwas; in den Gemütsbewegungen wie im Lieben oder Hassen sei das Vorziehen oder Ablehnen das Hervorstechende.

Eine weitere Gemeinsamkeit der psychischen Phänomene sei, dass sie „nur im inneren Bewusstsein wahrgenommen werden, während bei den physischen nur äußere Wahrnehmung möglich ist."[56] Dies lässt sich darauf zurückführen, dass mit jedem psychischen Akt „ein doppeltes inneres Bewusstsein" verbunden sei: „eine darauf bezügliche Vorstellung und ein darauf bezügliches Urteil, die sogenannte innere Wahrnehmung, welche eine unmittelbare, evidente Erkenntnis des Aktes ist".[57]

Neben dem auf das primäre Objekt bezogenen Bewusstsein sei in jedem psychischen Akt noch ein sekundäres, auf das Selbst bezogenes Bewusstsein mitgegeben. Das Selbst kann seinerseits vorgestellt, beurteilt und mit einem Gefühl begleitet werden. Daher lassen sich eine Vorstellung seiner selbst (Selbstbild), eine Einschätzung seiner selbst (Selbsterkenntnis) und ein Gefühl seiner selbst (Selbstgefühl) unterscheiden.[58]

Einen wesentlichen Bestandteil des sekundären Bewusstseins bildeten die Urteile der ‚inneren Wahrnehmung', deren sich der Urteilende nur deshalb sicher sein könne, weil er zu seinem Gegenstand im Verhältnis „realer Identität" stehe: Die innere Wahrnehmung sei „nichts anderes als die Konstatierung eines eigenen gegenwärtigen psychischen Phänomens, wir erleben sie fortwährend an uns selbst".

Solche Evidenzerlebnisse müssten allerdings von vermeintlich evidenten Urteilen unterschieden werden, die nur einem „blinden Drang zu glauben“ entspringen.[59]

Den psychischen Phänomenen komme „außer der intentionalen auch eine wirkliche Existenz“ zu.[60] Sie würden dem, der sie wahrnimmt, „trotz aller Mannigfaltigkeit immer als Einheit erscheinen“.[61]

Die weitere Frage, ob es neben den bewussten auch „*unbewusste psychische Akte*“ geben könne, verneinte Brentano mit großer Entschiedenheit.[62] Unbewusste Vorgänge könnten nur physiologische, nicht aber psychologische sein. Wenn man von einer im Bewusstsein gegebenen Tatsache auf die Wirkung unbewusster psychischer Phänomene schließen wolle, so müsse als erstes die Tatsache selbst hinreichend gesichert sein.[63] Zudem sei es nötig, „die Gesetze jener angeblichen unbewussten Phänomene darzulegen und durch die einheitliche Erklärung einer Fülle von Erfahrungstatsachen, die sonst unerklärt blieben, und durch die Voraussagung anderer, die sonst niemand erwarten würde, zu bewähren“.[64] Beide Voraussetzungen sah Brentano als nicht erfüllt an.

Liest man das VII. (metapsychologische) Kapitel der „Traumdeutung”, so sieht man sich mit einem Kontrastprogramm zu Brentano konfrontiert. Es geht Freud ja gerade darum, in Abgrenzung von der Bewusstseinspsychologie eine erste systematische Darstellung seiner neuen Psychologie des Unbewussten zu geben. Das Unbewusste sei „das eigentlich reale Psychische“, dem Bewusstsein komme hingegen nur die Rolle „eines Sinnesorgans zur Wahrnehmung psychischer Qualitäten“ zu. Auch „nur eine einzige verständnisvolle Beobachtung des Seelenlebens eines Neurotikers, eine einzige Traumanalyse“, müsse dem Arzt „die unerschütterliche Überzeugung aufdrängen, dass die kompliziertesten und korrektesten Denkvorgänge, denen man doch den Namen psychischer Vorgänge nicht versagen wird, vorfallen können, ohne das Bewusstsein der Person zu erregen.“ Zudem könne der „Bewusstseinseffekt [...] einen von dem unbewussten Vorgang ganz abweichenden psychischen Charakter zeigen, so dass die innere Wahrnehmung unmöglich den einen als den Ersatz des anderen erkennen kann.“[65] Freuds Kritik an der angeblichen ‚Evidenz’ der inneren Wahrnehmung als Garant wissenschaftlicher Erkenntnis geht auch aus seiner Zustimmung zu Wilhelms Jerusalems Buch „Die Urteilsfunktion“ hervor,[66] das ausdrücklich gegen Brentanos Auffassung von der ‚Evidenz’ der inneren Wahrnehmung gerichtet war.[67] Hier zeigt sich auch ein markanter Unterschied in anthropologischer Hinsicht. Während Brentano noch an dem seit der Aufklärung vorherrschenden Bild des rationalen Menschen festhielt, tendierte Freud zu „jenem reicheren, aber auch gefährlicheren und schwankenden Geschöpf, dem homo psychologicus“[68] und brachte sein Menschenbild später auf die berühmte Formel, dass „*das Ich nicht Herr sei in seinem eigenen Haus*“.[69]

Trotz dieser Divergenzen ist von verschiedenen Autoren darauf hingewiesen worden, dass Brentanos Philosophie und Psychologie deutliche Spuren in Freuds Werk hinterlassen hat.[70] Im folgenden möchte ich den zentralen Aspekt von Brentanos ‚deskriptiver Psychologie’, nämlich die Lehre von der *Intentionalität* der psychischen Akte, und ihren möglichen Einfluss auf Freuds Werk näher untersuchen. Mit diesem Schlüsselbegriff wandte er sich gegen die auf Descartes zurückgehende Annahme der binnenhaften Abgeschlossenheit des Bewusstseins und die Abbildtheorie der Erkenntnis sowie gegen die Mechanik des sensuellen Elementarismus und den auf die ‚objektiven' Tatsachen eingeschränkten Positivismus. Damit gab er die einseitige Orientierung an den Naturwissenschaften auf und ließ „nach Gegenstand (Sinn und Wesen) und Methode (eidetisch-deskriptiv) den geisteswissenschaftlichen Aspekt der Psychologie zu seinem Recht kommen."[71]

Ganz im Gegensatz zu Husserl, der in der fünften seiner „Logischen Untersuchungen" (1900) ausführlich "Über intentionale Erlebnisse und ihre 'Inhalte'" schrieb,[72] hat sich Freud an keiner Stelle explizit auf Brentano und dessen Begriff der Intentionalität bezogen. Wie lässt sich dennoch die Auffassung begründen, dass Freud seit der „Traumdeutung" auf intentionale Kategorien wie Wunsch, Motiv, Absicht und Sinn zurückgriff, die der Psychologie Brentanos und der aristotelischen Denktradition nahe stehen?[73]

Bereits in der „Traumdeutung" lassen sich Übereinstimmungen mit Brentanos Denken erkennen. So war die neue Konzeption des Unbewussten nur auf das Psychische bezogen, während das Somatische ausgeklammert blieb.[74] Mit dieser strikten Trennung näherte sich Freud den Bemühungen Brentanos, die Psychologie als eigenständige Wissenschaft sowohl von der Physiologie und physiologischen Psychologie als auch von den metaphysischen Voraussetzungen der Philosophie zu emanzipieren.

Schon auf der ersten Seite seines Hauptwerks führt Freud ein *Sinnkriterium* ein, das aufhorchen lässt.[75] Mit Hilfe der psychoanalytischen Methode lasse sich jeder Traum als „ein sinnvolles Gebilde" erfassen, das „an angebbarer Stelle in das seelische Treiben des Wachens einzureihen" sei. Die Deutungsarbeit diene dazu, „die Vorgänge klarzulegen, von denen die Fremdartigkeit und Unkenntlichkeit des Traumes herrührt, und aus ihnen einen Rückschluss auf die Natur der psychischen Kräfte zu ziehen, aus deren Zusammen- oder Gegeneinanderwirken der Traum hervorgeht".[76] Auf dieses Sinnkriterium und die sich daraus ergebenden Deutungsmöglichkeiten greift Freud an späteren Stellen wieder zurück. Einen Traum deuten heißt für ihn, seinen „Sinn" angeben – im Kontrast zu jenen Traumtheorien, für die der Traum „überhaupt kein seelischer Akt, sondern ein somatischer Vorgang" sei.[77] Wenn man seine Methode der Traumdeutung adäquat anwende, erkenne man, dass „der Traum wirklich einen Sinn hat und keineswegs der Ausdruck einer zerbröckelten Hirntätigkeit ist".[78] Sein „geheimer Sinn" bestehe stets in einer Wunscherfüllung,[79] die allerdings häufig nicht offen zutage liege, weil eine Tendenz zur Abwehr gegen diesen Wunsch vorhanden sei. Aufgrund dieses Konflikts zwischen Wunsch und Abwehr erscheint der Traum als „die (verkleidete) Erfüllung eines (unterdrückten, verdrängten) Wunsches".[80]

In der „Psychopathologie des Alltagslebens" (1901) und in „Der Witz und seine Beziehung zum Unbewussten" (1905) sind weitere Beispiele für die in der „Traumdeutung" angebahnte intentionale Denkweise zu finden.[81] Eine noch reichere Beute an intentionalen psychischen Vorgängen und ihr zugehöriger Begrifflichkeit kann man machen, wenn man sich Freuds „Vorlesungen zur Einführung in die

Psychoanalyse" zuwendet. Das Sinnkriterium, das er nunmehr für alle psychischen Phänomene postuliert, wird in systematisierender Form auf die Fehlleistungen, die Träume und die Symptome bezogen:

- Die Fehlleistungen seien „psychische Akte" und Ergebnisse „der Interferenz von zwei verschiedenen Intentionen", wobei „die eine dieser Intentionen eine gewisse Zurückdrängung von der Ausführung erfahren haben muss, um sich durch die Störung der anderen äußern zu können".[82] Im weiteren spricht Freud auch von der „Redeintention" und „einer die Redeabsicht störenden Intention".[83]
- Im Hinblick auf die Träume sucht Freud nochmals seine These zu untermauern, „welche neuen Beweise sich für die Existenz *unbewusster seelischer Akte* (Hervorhebung, G.G.) – das sind ja die latenten Traumgedanken – ergeben haben, und wie uns die Traumdeutung einen ungeahnt breiten Zugang zur Kenntnis des unbewussten Seelenlebens verspricht".[84]
- Dem „Sinn der Symptome" widmet Freud eine ganze Vorlesung (XVII), wobei er an Beispielen einer Symptomhandlung, einer Wahnidee und von Zwangssymptomen nachzuweisen sucht, dass sie sinnvoll, gut motiviert und in den Zusammenhang eines affektvollen Erlebnisses des Patienten gehören.[85] Im Unterschied zu den Symptomen der Psychoneurosen hätten die der Aktualneurosen keinen „Sinn", keine psychische Bedeutung, da es sich um körperliche Vorgänge handle, bei deren Entstehung „alle die komplizierten seelischen Mechanismen, die wir kennen gelernt haben, entfallen".[86]

Meinem Eindruck nach sind Freuds „Vorlesungen zur Einführung in die Psychoanalyse" der Text, in dem er sich am stärksten der Phänomenologie nähert. Man kann fast den ganzen Text als implizite Auseinandersetzung mit Brentanos Intentionalitätslehre betrachten[87] und daher annehmen, dass Freud sich in den vier Semestern seiner Philosophiestudien zumindest „indirekt mit den Fragen der Besonderheit des Psychisch-Geistigen und ihrer spezifisch Brentanoschen Grundlegung in der Intentionalität der Akte, sowie der Frage der Vereinbarkeit mit dem Physischen"[88] beschäftigt hat. In der Konstitutionsphase der Psychoanalyse könnte Josef Breuer eine wichtige Vermittlerrolle inne gehabt haben, da er nicht nur der Hausarzt Franz Brentanos war, bis dieser 1895 nach Florenz übersiedelte, sondern auch in einem philosophischen Austausch mit ihm stand.[89]

Bei dieser Lesart darf allerdings eine Formulierung nicht übersehen werden, die als Abgrenzung von der Intentionalitätslehre Brentanos verstanden werden kann: „Wir wollen die Erscheinungen nicht bloß beschreiben und klassifizieren, sondern sie als Anzeichen eines Kräftespiels in der Seele begreifen, als Äußerung von *zielstrebigen Tendenzen* (Hervorhebung, G.G.), die zusammen oder gegeneinander arbeiten. Wir bemühen uns um eine *dynamische Auffassung* der seelischen Erscheinungen. Die wahrgenommenen Phänomene müssen in unserer Auffassung gegen die nur angenommenen Strebungen zurücktreten."[90]

Zudem steht Freuds Sinndeutung der psychischen Phänomene von Traum, Fehlleistung und Symptom nicht in einem Ergänzungsverhältnis, sondern in einem antithetischen Verhältnis zur deskriptiven Psychologie Brentanos (und Husserls). Bei dem zugrunde gelegten Sinnkriterium handelt es sich ja gerade um einen gegenüber dem normalen Sinn verborgenen und entstellten Sinn. Die Intentionalität wurde, so Schöpf, „auf die Anforderungen einer Psychologie des Unbewussten hin abgewandelt". Dies sei dadurch möglich gewesen, dass den aus dem normalen, vorbewusst-bewussten Sinnverständnis ausgeschlossenen Phänomenen „ein alternativer, anderer Sinn" zugesprochen wurde. In der Annahme dieses anderen, verstehbaren und deutbaren Sinns kann man geradezu eine wissenschaftskonstituierende Voraussetzung der Psychoanalyse sehen und die Psychoanalyse dementsprechend als *„Psychologie des anderen Sinns"* bezeichnen.[91]

Gerd Kimmerle betont in diesem Zusammenhang, „wie sehr Freuds Begriff des Unbewussten von Franz Brentanos Konzeption des intentionalen Bewusstseins und der ihm zugeordneten Urteilslogik beeinflusst ist. Freuds Abhängigkeit von Brentano ist ja leider noch viel zu wenig erforscht. Würde man sie aufklären, könnte man die eigentümliche Verschmelzung von aristotelischen und cartesianischen Zügen in Freuds Lehre vom verdrängt Unbewussten besser verstehen"[92].

In der Nachfolge Freuds sei kurz auf wichtige psychoanalytische Konzeptionen eingegangen, die dem Thema der Intentionalität besondere Bedeutung beigemessen haben:[93] Heinz Hartmann erkannte, dass es in Freuds Werk eine auf Brentano zurückgehende Konzeption der Intentionalität gebe.[94] Insbesondere habe Freud die 'Wunscherfüllung' mit den Kategorien von Tendenz, Intention und Sinn in Verbindung gebracht. Diese seien jedoch letztlich nur als subjektive Inhalte zu betrachten, mit denen man im Rahmen einer naturwissenschaftlichen Theorie von Energien, Funktionen, Dynamismen und Systemen keinen Anspruch auf Objektivität erheben könne.[95] Während Hartmann dem naturwissenschaftlichen Denk- und Sprachmodell verhaftet blieb, äußerte Roy Schafer, es sei schon „sonderbar, um noch das Mindeste zu sagen, dass die Praktiker einer Disziplin, die sich so speziell der menschlichen Subjektivität und dem menschlichen Handeln zuwendet, beharrlich der unpersönlichen Rhetorik der Naturwissenschaften verhaftet geblieben sein sollten".[96] Daher hat Schafer den Versuch unternommen, die Psychoanalyse von Begriffen wie Ursache, Bedingung, Determinante und Kraft zu befreien, da sie der mechanistischen Denktradition zuzurechnen seien. Demgegenüber seien intentionale Begriffe wie Bedeutung, Handeln, Grund und Situation und eine darauf aufbauende, Handlungssprache' wesentlich besser geeignet, das erlebnismäßig Phänomenale und das aktiv Intentionale im menschlichen Seelenleben zu erfassen. Paul Ricoeur strebte seinerseits eine Art Mittelposition, eine Verbindung von Hermeneutik und Energetik in der Psychoanalyse an. Wegen ihrer Nähe zur Hermeneutik sei die Psychoanalyse nicht den Beobachtungswissenschaften, wegen ihres Naturalismus nicht der Phänomenologie zuzuordnen.[97] Auch Alfred Lorenzer wandte sich gegen die Auffassung, die Psychoanalyse sei nur eine „Naturwissenschaft vom Seelischen". Um zu Erkenntnissen über unbewusste Sinn- und Motivationszusammenhänge zu gelangen, bedürfe es notwendig auch eines verstehend-hermeneutischen Zugangs. Ähnlich wie Ricoeur postulierte aber auch Lorenzer eine Dialektik von Natur und Sinn, Leiblichkeit und Sozialität. „Indem Freud an der naturwissenschaftlichen Ausrichtung unnachsichtig festhielt, hob er auf eine lautlose, aber folgenreiche Weise die Grenze zwischen Naturwissenschaften und Kulturwissenschaften auf, stiftete er das neue Paradigma einer Wissenschaft, die man mit dem Titel einer, Hermeneutik des Leibes' versehen kann."[98] Begreift man Psychoanalyse als eine Naturwissenschaft und zugleich Analyse von Sinnstrukturen, so lassen sich Verbindungen zur Phänomenologie und insbesondere zu Merleau-Ponty herstellen.[99]

Zusammenfassend kann man sagen, dass sich vom Begriff des „psychischen Sinns" bei Freud eine Brücke zum Konzept der Intentionalität bei Brentano schlagen lässt.[100] Auch wenn sich die Intentionalitätskonzepte der Psychoanalytiker von denen Husserls[101] und der Phänomenologen unterscheiden, hätten sich die beiden Richtungen nicht so fremd bleiben müssen. Dies lag wohl in erster Linie an ihren starren antithetischen Auffassungen sowohl von der Rolle des Bewusstseins als auch der des Unbewussten, die heute nicht mehr aufrecht zu erhalten sind.[102] Auch wenn sich Husserls Versuche, in bisher unentdeckte „Tiefen" des Bewusstseins vorzudringen, auf die Rekonstruktion formaler Strukturen beschränkten, stehen sie Freuds Versuchen, die unbewussten Prozesse zu analysieren, durchaus nicht so fern, wie es oft angenommen wird.[103]

3 Auf der Suche nach einer neuen Wissensform des Unbewussten – Freuds und Husserls Anknüpfungen an Theodor Lipps

Theodor Lipps (1851–1914) gehört zu den wenigen Philosophen, auf die sich Freud häufig und stets mit großer Wertschätzung bezogen hat. Bei einer ersten Erwähnung im Jahre 1898 bezeichnet Freud ihn als „klarsten Kopf unter den heutigen philosophischen Schriftstellern".[104] Auf dem 3. Internationalen Kongress für Psychologie (4. bis 7. August 1896) hatte Lipps einen programmatischen Vortrag zum Thema „Der Begriff des Unbewussten in der Psychologie" gehalten, in dem er die These vertrat, dass die Frage des Unbewussten in der Psychologie „weniger eine psychologische Frage als die Frage der Psychologie" sei.[105] Freud hatte mit dem Gedanken gespielt, zu diesem Kongress nach München zu reisen,[106] dann aber auf die Reise verzichtet. Von einer persönlichen Begegnung zwischen Freud und Lipps ist nichts bekannt.

Wie drei Briefe an Fließ aus dem Jahre 1898 zeigen, fühlte sich Freud durch Lipps' Buch „Grundtatsachen des Seelenlebens" in seiner „keimenden Metapsychologie" des Unbewussten bestärkt. Im ersten Brief schreibt er: „Es geht bis jetzt mit Verständnis und Übertragung in meine Annahmen recht gut".[107] Im zweiten Brief äußert er, er habe „die Grundzüge meiner Ansicht ganz klar wiedergefunden, [...]. Auch in den Einzelheiten ist die Übereinstimmung groß, vielleicht kommt später die Gabelung, von der aus mein Neues ansetzen kann. Ich habe etwa ein Drittel durchgearbeitet".[108] Und im dritten Brief heißt es: „[...] in seinem Dialekt sagt er gerade das, was ich mir ausspekuliert über Bewusstsein, Qualität u. dgl.".[109]

Als Freud in der „Traumdeutung" das Unbewusste als Zentralbegriff der Psychoanalyse einführte, bezog er sich explizit auf Fechner und Lipps.[110] Dort heißt es: „Das Unbewusste muss nach dem Ausdrucke von Lipps als allgemeine Basis des psychischen Lebens angenommen werden. Das Unbewusste ist der größere Kreis, der den kleineren des Bewussten in sich einschließt; [...] Das Unbewusste ist das eigentlich reale Psychische".[111] In dem Buch „Der Witz und seine Beziehung zum Unbewussten" findet man sogar eine ganze Fülle von Bezugnahmen auf Lipps. Dessen Buch „Komik und Humor" verdanke er „den Mut und die Möglichkeit", sein Projekt über den Witz zu realisieren.[112] Im weiteren sah er sich veranlasst, „auf die ausführlichere Behandlung des Unbewussten in meiner ‚Traumdeutung' und auf die mir höchst bedeutungsvoll erscheinenden Arbeiten von Lipps zu verweisen. Ich weiß, dass wer im Banne einer guten philosophischen Schulbildung steht oder entfernt von einem sogenannten philosophischen System abhängt, der Annahme des 'Unbewusst Psychischen' in Lipps' und meinem Sinne widerstrebt und dessen Unmöglichkeit am liebsten aus der Definition des Psychischen beweisen möchte."[113] Noch in zwei seiner letzten Arbeiten erinnerte er daran, dass es erst nach der Erweiterung des Psychischen um das Unbewusste möglich gewesen sei, „eine umfassende und zusammenhängende Theorie des seelischen Lebens zu schaffen". Diese Neuerung sei nicht der Psychoanalyse zuzuschreiben: „Ein deutscher Philosoph, Theodor Lipps hat mit aller Schärfe verkündet, das Psychische sei an sich unbewusst, das Unbewusste sei das eigentlich Psychische".[114] Lipps erscheint demnach als der erste, der den Begriff des Unbewussten im wissenschaftlichen Sinne zu „verwenden" wusste. Die Psychoanalyse habe sich dann „dieses Begriffs bemächtigt, ihn ernst genommen, ihn mit neuem Leben erfüllt".[115]

Freud hat aber auch Abgrenzungsarbeit im Verhältnis zu Lipps geleistet. Seine eigene Konzeption des Unbewussten decke sich nicht mit dem Unbewussten der Philosophen, „auch nicht mit dem von Lipps".[116] Das Innovative, das sich aus der psychoanalytischen Neurosentherapie und Traumdeutung ergeben habe, bestehe darin, dass „das Unbewusste – also das Psychische – als Funktion zweier gesonderter Systeme vorkommt und schon im normalen Seelenleben so vorkommt" – des bewusstseinsfähigen *Vorbewussten* und des eigentlichen *Unbewussten*.[117]

Im Unterschied zur eher rationalistischen Bewusstseinspsychologie Brentanos gelangte Lipps zu einer dreifachen Stufung im psychischen Bereich: der Bewusstseinssphäre, die als lückenhaft aufgefasst wird, dem psychisch Unbewussten und dem physiologischen Bereich. Die von ihm hoch bewertete Introspektion erfasse nur den ersten Bereich des Bewusstseins mit seinen Vorstellungen, die von Kräften, Strebungen, Interessen begleitet sind.[118]

Trotz dieser konträren Position standen sich Brentano und Lipps in ihrer grundsätzlichen Einstellung zur Psychologie durchaus nahe. So wandte sich auch Lipps gegen die einseitige Ausrichtung der Psychologie an naturwissenschaftlichen Methoden. Auch er gründete psychologisches Wissen in erster Linie auf innere Erfahrung. In den 1880er Jahren schloss er sich einer von Brentano initiierten Bewegung an, die gegen die überkommene, vorwiegend passive Assoziationspsychologie gerichtet war, und trat für eine Aktpsychologie ein, die von einem aktiven Ich mit Wünschen und Intentionen ausging.[119]

Wie Brentano hat sich auch Lipps skeptisch über einen Brückenschlag zwischen Psychologie und Physiologie geäußert: „Das Heil der Psychologie und damit zugleich das Heil der Psychophysiologie wird davon abhängen, dass die Psychologie sich mehr und mehr auf ihre eigenen Füße stellt, durch nichts beirrt auf ihren eigenen Wegen ihren eigenen Zielen zustrebt. In dem Maße, als sie dies tut, wird ihr die

Psychophysiologie zu folgen, aber auch nur zu *folgen* vermögen, langsam, vorsichtig und jederzeit mit voller psychologischer Sachkenntnis. Vielleicht dass dann auch das Unbewusste der Psychologie für sie greifbarere Gestalt gewinnt."[120]

Auch Lipps gehörte zu den akademischen Psychologen, die für eine Emanzipation der wissenschaftlichen Psychologie von der Mutterdisziplin Philosophie plädierten. Dabei vertrat er eine tendenziell psychologistische Position. Die Psychologie war für ihn die Grundwissenschaft der Logik, Ästhetik und Ethik. So hielt er logische Schlüsse oder Urteile für psychische Phänomene: „Die Logik ist eine psychologische Disziplin, so gewiss das Erkennen nur in der Psyche vorkommt, und das Denken, das sich in ihm vollendet, ein psychisches Geschehen ist."[121]

An diesem Punkt lässt sich eine Brücke zu Edmund Husserl schlagen. Bemerkenswert ist nämlich, dass sich Husserl in seiner Psychologismus-Kritik in erster Linie gegen Lipps und Mill wandte.[122] Lipps war von Husserls Generalabrechnung mit dem Psychologismus so beeindruckt, dass er umschwenkte. Die Logik bezeichnete er nunmehr als „apriorische Wissenschaft vom überindividuellen Ich", die den Hauptfehler des Psychologismus, die Verwechslung von Inhalten und Gegenständen vermeide.[123] Damit konvertierte er zu einer Art metaphysischem Psychologismus. Das nach 1900 beliebte „Gesellschaftsspiel deutscher Philosophen", alles unter Psychologismusverdacht zu stellen, machte Lipps aber nicht mit.[124]

Lipps' Annäherung an die Phänomenologie wird auch daran deutlich, dass sich in seinem Münchner Umfeld ein Philosophen-Kreis bildete, dem Max Scheler, Alexander Pfänder, Moritz Geiger sowie Adolf Reinach angehörten. Diese Gruppe hat sich später unter der Führung Schelers der von Husserl in Göttingen gegründeten „Philosophischen Gesellschaft" angeschlossen. Anlässlich des 60. Geburtstags von Lipps erschien 1911 eine Festschrift für ihn, an der sich maßgebliche Vertreter der Phänomenologie mit Beiträgen beteiligten. Darin findet sich auch ein Aufsatz von Else Voigtländer über die Psychoanalyse.

Wie sein Schüler Georg Anschütz schreibt, trat bei Lipps zunehmend „das Bestreben nach einer rein phänomenologischen, systematisch, aber möglichst unbefangen beschreibenden Wiedergabe der Erscheinungen hervor." In der 3. Auflage des „Leitfadens der Psychologie" (1909) sei dieses Moment dann so stark geworden, dass er sogar den – in der herbartianischen Tradition stehenden und metaphysisch vorgeprägten – Begriff der „psychischen Realität" fallen ließ und „sich auf eine phänomenologische Beschreibung zu beschränken" suchte.[125] Anschütz ist der Auffassung, dass „die gesamte Phänomenologie nichts ist als ein Verlassen der alten Bahnen der Logik und Erkenntnistheorie und eine wesentliche Hinneigung zu dem, was Lipps mit ‚erleben' meinte".[126]

Auf die Thematik der Psychologismus-Kritik Husserls ist Freud meines Wissens nie explizit eingegangen, worin man ein grundlegendes Problem sehen kann.[127]

Abschließend sei noch erwähnt, dass sich in Freuds Bibliothek acht philosophische und psychologische Bücher von Lipps befanden.[128] Es handelt sich dabei allerdings nur um Bücher, die im Zeitraum von 1883 bis 1902 erschienen waren. Dies lässt darauf schließen, dass sich Freud hauptsächlich in den Jahren von 1897 bis 2002 mit Lipps beschäftigte.

4 Verschmelzung von psychoanalytischen Grundgedanken mit der Phänomenologie – Ludwig Binswangers Auseinandersetzung mit Freud und Husserl

War Brentano ein Lehrer Freuds und Husserls, und Lipps nur wenige Jahre älter als Freud und Husserl, mit seiner Habilitation und Professur karrieremäßig aber deutlich weiter, so gehörte Binswanger zu deren Schüler-Generation.

Ludwig Binswanger (1881–1966) schloss 1906 sein Medizinstudium mit einer psychiatrischen Dissertation ab, in der er die Assoziationsstudien seines Doktorvaters C. G. Jung weiterführte. Danach verbrachte er ein Assistentenjahr an der von Eugen Bleuler geleiteten Klinik „Burghölzli" in Zürich. C. G. Jung, der dort als Oberarzt tätig war, machte ihn auf die Psychoanalyse aufmerksam und nahm ihn im März 1907 zu seinem ersten Besuch Freuds in Wien mit. Als Sohn Robert Binswangers, des Leiters der renommierten psychiatrischen Privatklinik „Bellevue" in Kreuzlingen, und Neffe Otto Binswangers, des Ordinarius für Psychiatrie in Jena, war er „ein Vorzeigeschüler Jungs und durch die Assoziationsstudien auch ein Adept der Psychoanalyse".[129] Gerhard Fichtner hat auf „die große Kongruenz der beiderseitigen Erwartungen" Freuds und des 25 Jahre jüngeren Binswangers hingewiesen: „hier die Hoffnung auf ein Durchbrechen der Mauer zwischen der offiziellen Psychiatrie und der Psychoanalyse sowie auf Anerkennung und Gewinnung eines weiteren Mitstreiters im Ausland – dort die Hoffnung, unter ‚väterlicher' Anleitung in vorderster Linie bei der Durchsetzung einer neuen und zukunftsträchtigen Lehre helfen zu können."[130]

Nach seinem zweiten Besuch Freuds im Januar 1910 konstatierte Binswanger erstaunt, „ein wie geringes metaphysisches Bedürfnis der als Spekulierer verschriene Freud besitzt. Man sollte doch annehmen, dass der beste Kenner des Unbewussten sich auch metaphysische Gedanken macht über das Unbewusste z. B. à la [Eduard v.] Hartmann. Aber nichts von alledem. Zwischen Hartmann und Freud gibt es keine Brücke. Freud ist und bleibt der gewissenhafte Naturforscher, der nicht mehr sagt, als ihm die Erfahrung gibt. Das wiederum bestätigt zu finden, war der größte Eindruck meiner [zweiten] Reise."[131]

Nach dem plötzlichen Tod des Vaters musste der knapp 30jährige Binswanger im Dezember 1910 die Leitung des Bellevue übernehmen, die er bis 1956 inne hatte.

Seine über 30jährige Auseinandersetzung mit Freud und der Psychoanalyse hat Binswanger selbst in fünf Etappen eingeteilt. War die erste Etappe eine Auseinandersetzung „im Sinne des *Lernens*, der lernenden Erfahrung ihrer Lehren durch Schrift und Wort ihres Begründers",[132] so galt die zweite Etappe der „*Erprobung* des Gelernten am lebendigen Menschen", d.h. an eigenen Therapiefällen, die er psychoanalytisch zu behandeln suchte.[133]

In der dritten Etappe untersuchte Binswanger „jeden einzelnen, der in Freuds Definition der seelischen Erscheinungen genannten Ausdrücke auf seine psychologische Sachhaltigkeit und auf deren Verschiedenheiten untereinander. Das geschah durchweg im Hinblick auf die Bedeutung, die diese Ausdrücke in anderen psychologischen Lehren und Auffassungen gefunden hatten, so in erster Linie im

Hinblick auf die heute besonders aktuellen Beziehungen der Freudschen Begriffe der Tendenz sowie die Absicht oder intentio zu der ganz anders orientierten Lehre Brentanos und Husserls von der Intentionalität, [...].“[134]

Im August 1917 fühlte sich Binswanger veranlasst, Freud den Stand seiner „Arbeit über die Psychoanalyse“ mitzuteilen: „Die ganze Arbeit zerfällt in zwei Teile: der erste, 200 Schreibmaschinenseiten umfassende, ziemlich fertige Teil behandelt allgemeine psychologische Fragen, wie die Definition des Psychischen, die psychologischen Grundbegriffe, die verschiedenen wissenschaftlichen Behandlungsarten des Psychischen usw., alles anhand historischer Beispiele. Erst im Anschluss daran folgt dann als zweiter Teil eine Würdigung und Analyse der Psychoanalyse, d.h. des rein psychologischen Teils derselben.“[135] 1922 erschien Binswangers Buch unter dem Titel „Probleme der Allgemeinen Psychologie“. Erst auf Nachfrage äußerte Freud dazu: „Ihr Buch hat mir sehr imponiert – mich allerdings auch enttäuscht, denn es ist nicht das, worauf Sie mich durch mehrfache Mitteilungen vorbereitet hatten. Ich erwartete, dass Sie die Brücke zwischen der klinischen Psychiatrie und der Psychoanalyse bauen und in einem zweiten Band auch selbst über sie gehen würden.“[136]

Bemerkenswert ist, dass Binswanger in seiner „Allgemeinen Psychologie“ ausführlich auf Brentanos Lehre von den psychischen Phänomenen[137], Husserls Phänomenologie und seine Lehre von den psychischen Erlebnissen[138] und Lipps’ Lehre von den Bewusstseinserlebnissen[139] einging. Im selben Jahr äußerte er in einem ersten Vortrag „Über Phänomenologie“, sie sei „zwar selbst ein wissenschaftliches Lehrgebäude“, habe aber „das Gute, dass sie uns mit größter Energie zurückführt auf die schlichte einfache Betrachtung der Phänomene, uns lehrt, nur das gelten zu lassen, was wir wirklich gesehen haben, in sinnlicher oder kategorialer Anschauung, und uns zu hüten vor der Vermengung des Geschauten mit jedweder noch so fundierten Theorie.“[140] Und weiter heißt es: „In der phänomenologischen Schulsprache spricht man im Anschluss an Brentanos Definition der psychischen Phänomene (1874) von einer wahrnehmenden *Intention*; den wahrgenommenen Gegenstand nennt man den intendierten, in der Wahrnehmung gemeinten oder vermeinten Gegenstand. Die Welt der vom Bewusstsein überhaupt irgendwie erfassten oder erfassbaren Gegenstände nennt man die *intentionale* Welt, die Welt der intentionalen Gegenstände, Dabei muss man sich klar sein, dass Intentio und alle Ableitungen davon nichts zu tun haben mit Attentio, mit Aufmerksamkeit, Aktivität, Streben oder dergleichen.“[141] Im August 1923 kam es dann zu zwei Begegnungen mit Edmund Husserl; beim zweiten Treffen im Bellevue hielt Husserl seinerseits einen Vortrag über „Das Wesen der Phänomenologie“.[142]

Noch im selben Monat kündigte Binswanger in einem Brief an Freud an, dass er in seinem nächsten Buch die Psychoanalyse und „das, was ich an theoretischen Kenntnissen mir seither angeeignet habe, miteinander in Berührung bringen will, so den ursprünglichen Plan verwirklichend, den ich schon bei Ihrem hiesigen Besuch hatte und zu dem mir damals nur noch die theoretischen Kenntnisse fehlten.“[143] Der angekündigte zweite Band, der der Psychoanalyse gewidmet werden sollte, erschien aber nie. Dies lag nach Binswangers eigener Einschätzung daran, dass „ich auf Grund der Beschäftigung mit der Phänomenologie Husserls (und später der Ontologie

Heideggers) sehr bald über meine in diesen Untersuchungen befolgte Methode hinausgewachsen war. Sie bewegte sich noch allzu sehr auf begrifflichem und methodologischem Boden, so dass sie Freuds Auffassung und Lehren vom Seelischen und vom Menschenwesen überhaupt nicht an der Wurzel fassen konnte."[144]

Zur vierten Etappe rechnet Binswanger seinen Festvortrag zu Freuds 80. Geburtstag im Jahre 1936. Für „Freuds Auffassung des Menschen im Lichte der Anthropologie" sei „die Idee des homo natura" maßgeblich. Diese Idee dokumentiere sich in Erscheinungen wie „Lebenstrieb, Lustbefriedigung (Aufgabe eines kleineren Vorteils für einen größeren), Hemmung durch Zwang oder Druck von seiten der Gesellschaft, als deren Prototyp die Familie gilt, Entwicklungsgeschichte im Sinne der onto- und phylogenetischen Verwandlung von äußeren in inneren Zwang und der Vererbung dieser Umwandlung".[145] Die Sicht des Menschen als eines rein natürlichen Wesens stehe im Gegensatz zu dem traditionellen Menschenbild eines „homo aeternus" oder „homo coelestus", aber auch zur Idee des „homo existentialis" (Herder, Dilthey, Heidegger) oder anderen naturalistischen Konzeptionen wie denen Rousseaus, Novalis' und Nietzsches. Freuds Antwort auf den Vortrag fiel skeptisch aus: „Natürlich glaube ich Ihnen doch nicht. Ich habe mich immer nur im Parterre und Souterrain des Gebäudes aufgehalten – Sie behaupten, wenn man den Gesichtspunkt wechselt, sieht man auch ein oberes Stockwerk, in dem so distinguierte Gäste wie Religion, Kunst und andere hausen. Sie sind nicht der einzige darin, die meisten Kulturexemplare des homo natura denken so. [...] Aber wahrscheinlich reden wir doch aneinander vorbei, und unser Zwist wird erst nach Jahrhunderten zum Ausgleich kommen."[146]

In der fünften Etappe begründete Binswanger seine eigene Anthropologie, die ‚Daseinsanalyse'. In seinem Vortrag zum 100. Geburtstag Freuds im Februar 1956 mit dem Titel „Mein Weg zu Freud" nahm er an, zu einem vertieften Verständnis von Freuds „Naturalismus" vorgedrungen zu sein: Mit seiner Lehre von der „unbewussten Intentionalität" habe Freud „den Menschen *der* Welt und die Welt *dem Menschen nähergebracht.*" Er habe gezeigt, dass wir „auch ‚unbewusst' *in der Welt sind, Welt haben und über Welt verfügen.*" Freud habe „den Frieden dieser Welt gestört, indem er uns zeigte, wie beschränkt diese Welt ist und wie wenig Macht wir über sie haben."[147]

5 Offene Fragen

Wenn Freud die Psychoanalyse als Naturwissenschaft konzipierte und daraus eine „Psychologie ohne Philosophie" machen wollte, so lag dies in erster Linie an seinem – nicht aufrecht zu erhaltenden – empiristischen Wissenschaftsverständnis und abbildtheoretischen Wahrheitsbegriff.[148] Für eine wissenschaftlich orientierte Psychoanalyse kommt es gerade darauf an, dass sie „Philosophie im Sinne einer ständigen Selbstreflexion ihrer Grundlagen" ist.[149]

Aus psychoanalysehistorischer Sicht erscheinen die in diesem Artikel angesprochenen Verbindungen Freuds zu den deskriptiv, intentional und phänomenologisch orientierten

Psychologien Brentanos, Lipps' und Binswangers keineswegs hinreichend erforscht. Bemerkenswert ist, dass sich Binswanger in „Probleme der Allgemeinen Psychologie" auf der Suche nach einer genaueren erkenntnistheoretischen Erfassung der Psychoanalyse in drei zentralen Kapiteln gerade mit den „nicht-naturwissenschaftlichen" Lehren Brentanos, Husserls und Lipps' auseinandergesetzt und damit Freud in die Nähe dieser von ihm und seinen Nachfolgern weitgehend verleugneten Denktradition gerückt hat.

Während Freuds Begegnung mit Brentano in den Jugendjahren stattfand und offenbar tiefere Spuren hinterlassen hat, als im allgemeinen angenommen wird, erfolgte seine Lipps-Rezeption in der Konstitutionsphase der Psychoanalyse und war in erster Linie durch dessen öffentliches Eintreten für die wissenschaftliche Erforschung des psychisch Unbewussten ausgelöst. Die freundschaftliche Beziehung zu Binswanger begann erst in der Institutionalisierungsphase der Psychoanalyse und hielt bis zu Freuds Tod im Jahre 1939 an. Man hat allerdings nicht den Eindruck, dass die Korrespondenz zwischen Freud und Binswanger zu einer tieferen Verständigung oder gar einem Umdenken Freuds geführt hätte.

Umgekehrt wäre zu untersuchen, über welche Vermittler Husserl mit Freud und der Psychoanalyse in Berührung gekommen ist. Welche Rolle haben dabei Brentano und Binswanger gespielt? Weiterhin könnten Verbindungen von Freud und Husserl zur neueren kognitiven Psychologie[150] und zur Philosophie des Geistes[151] hergestellt werden.

Die um die Wende zum 20. Jahrhundert einsetzende Spaltung zwischen Wissenschaft und Philosophie hat zu einem Jahrzehnte währenden „gegenseitigen Berührungstabu" geführt. Aus dem Trennungsprozess zwischen Psychologie und Philosophie, an dem Freud als Antimetaphysiker und Husserl als Antipsychologist beteiligt waren, haben sich beide Disziplinen eine „Reflexionsblockade" eingehandelt, an deren Folgen sie noch heute laborieren.[152] Es gibt aber hoffnungsvolle Anzeichen dafür, dass beide Disziplinen wieder in eine Bewegung der Annäherung kommen können.[153] Wichtig für die Zukunft wäre eine wechselseitig bereichernde Öffnung und Kommunikation zwischen diesen höchst bedeutsamen und doch so verschiedenen Denkwelten.

Notes

1. Vgl. Wittels 1931; Herzog 1988.
2. Vgl. Gödde 1991 u. 2006, 23 f.
3. Vgl. Sandler 1983; Polanyi 1985; Buchholz 2007.
4. Vgl. Ricoeur 1965; Lorenzer 1970 u. 2002; Sulloway 1979.
5. Freud 1985c, 165 u. 190; Briefe vom 1.1. und 2.4.1896 an Wilhelm Fließ. Die bibliographischen Angaben zu Freud orientieren sich an der Freud-Bibliographie von Meyer-Palmedo u. Fichtner (1999).
6. Freud 1969a, 116; Brief v. 1.5.1873 an Emil Fluß.
7. Freud 1989a, 82; Brief v. 8.11.1874 an Eduard Silberstein.
8. Freud 1933a, 171 ff.

9. Freud 1927a, 290.
10. Vgl. Eckstein 1936, 21.
11. Freud 1989a, 30; Brief v. 16.7.1873.
12. Ibid., 82; Brief v. 8.11.1874.
13. Ibid., 109; Brief v. 7.3.1875.
14. Ibid., 115; Brief v. 13.3.1875.
15. Vgl. McGrath 1986; Gödde 1991 u. 1999, Kap. II.
16. Lange 1875, 592.
17. Vgl. Reicheneder 1990.
18. Siehe Fußnote 5.
19. Freud 1885c, 124 u. 129; Briefe v. 28.3. u. 27.4.1895.
20. Freud 1950c.
21. Freud 1985c, 153 f. u. 357; Briefe v. 8.11.1895 u. 22.9.1898.
22. Ibid., 329; Brief v. 10.3.1898.
23. Ibid., 131, 181 u. 325 f.; Briefe v. 25.5.1895, 13.2.1896 u. 9.2.1898.
24. Ibid., 354 u. 356; Briefe v. 26.8. u. 31.8.1898; s.a. 360; Brief v. 27.9.1898.
25. Vgl. Gödde 1999, Kap. VII.
26. Nunberg u. Federn 1962, 141.
27. Nunberg u. Federn 1967, 27 f.
28. Vgl. Freud 1912-13a, 96; 1960a, 389, Brief v. 30.1.1927 an Werner Achelis. Siehe auch Wucherer-Huldenfeld 1994, 366 ff.
29. Freud 1913b, 407.
30. Rank u. Sachs 1913, 100.
31. Vgl. Putnam 1911, 101 f.; 1912, 527.
32. Vgl. Binswanger 1936, 1956 u. 1957.
33. Weitere Belege finden sich in Lou Andreas-Salomés Tagebuchaufzeichnungen von 1912/13 (1958, 60 f. u. 106 f.), in Freuds Briefen an Andreas-Salomé v. 30.7.1915 (Freud 1960a, 323) und an Groddeck v. 5.6.1917 (Freud 1960a, 333 f.) sowie Oskar Pfisters Brief an Freud v. 24.11.1927 (Freud u. Pfister 1963, 122 f.).
34. Vgl. A. Schmidt 1980, 266.
35. Freud 1925d, 84.
36. Vgl. Gödde 1999, Kap. IX-XII.
37. Freud 1933a, 172 f.
38. Lohmann 1998, 106.
39. Vgl. Giampieri 1990, 41 ff.; Fischer 1995.
40. Vgl. Wittels 1931; Herzog 1988; Gödde 2006.
41. Schöpf 1978, 254.
42. Freud 1940a, 80.
43. Freud 1923b, 239.
44. Freud 1923b, 242 Fn. 1.
45. Stegmüller 1989, 1.
46. Freud 1900a, 110–126.
47. Freud 1896b, 379 u. 383.
48. Husserl 1919, 79 f.
49. Ibid., 87.
50. Brentano 1874a, 3 ff.
51. Brentano 1874a, 3 ff.
52. Freud 1989a, 116 f.; Brief v. 15.3.1875.
53. Vgl. Fischer, 1995, IX ff.
54. Brentano 1874b, 112.
55. Ibid., 125.
56. Ibid., 128.
57. Ibid., 203.

58. Ibid., 219.
59. Brentano 1956, 154 f.
60. Brentano 1974b, 129.
61. Ibid., 137.
62. Ibid., 143. Die Annahme eines ‚Unbewussten' in der Tradition der Romantik, Schopenhauers, v. Hartmanns und Nietzsches lehnte er strikt ab.
63. Ibid., 148.
64. Ibid., 151.
65. Freud 1900a, 616–620.
66. Freud 1985c, 131, Brief v. 25.5.1895; vgl. Gödde 1999, 176 ff.
67. Jerusalem 1922, 25.
68. Schorske 1982, 4.
69. Freud 1917a, 11.
70. Rapaport 1960, Barclay 1964, H. Hartmann 1964, Ricoeur 1965, Wucherer-Huldenfeld 1967, Schafer 1976, Fancher 1977, Schöpf 1982, Kerz-Rühling 1986, McGrath 1986, Kimmerle 1986, 1997, Brauns u. Schöpf 1989, Frampton 1991 u.a.
71. Pongratz 1984, 129.
72. Husserl 1900, II/1, bes. 363–425 ("Bewusstsein als intentionales Erlebnis").
73. Vgl. Schöpf 1982, 136.
74. Vgl. Gödde 1999, 196 ff.
75. Vgl. Buchholz 2006, 96 ff.
76. Freud 1900a, 1.
77. Ibid., 100.
78. Ibid., 126.
79. Ibid., 123, 126, 151.
80. Ibid., 166.
81. Freud 1901b, 171, 303 f., 306; 1905c, 9 f., 59, 146, 154.
82. Freud 1916–1917a, 53–61.
83. Ibid., 63 f.
84. Ibid., 186.
85. Ibid., 254, 260, 270, 277.
86. Ibid., 402.
87. Eine Anknüpfung kann man darin sehen, dass er "psychische Akte" bzw. "seelische Phänomene" in Brentanoscher Manier von körperlichen abgrenzt. Ibid., 55.
88. Brauns u. Schöpf 1989, 69.
89. Vgl. Hirschmüller 1978, 50, 65, 129 f.; Breuer 1978, 293–323 (drei Briefe Breuers an Brentano).
90. Ibid., 62.
91. Schöpf 1982, 135.
92. Kimmerle 1986, 86. Vgl. auch Kimmerle 1997.
93. Vgl. Mertens 1981.
94. Hartmann 1972, 270.
95. Vgl. Schafer 1976, 36 ff.
96. Schafer 1976, 31.
97. Ricoeur 1965, Drittes Buch.
98. Lorenzer 2002, 59.
99. Vgl. Günzel u. Windgätter 2005; Gondek 2006.
100. Gekle 2000, 96.
101. Husserl 1900, II/1, 5. Logische Untersuchung und Husserl 1913.
102. Vgl. Fuchs 2008, 33 f.
103. Vgl. Drüe 1963, 307 ff.; Fellmann 2006, 38 u. 73.
104. Freud 1985c, 354.
105. Lipps 1897, 146.

106. Ibid., 178; Brief v. 6.2.1896.
107. Ibid., 354.
108. Ibid., 356.
109. Ibid., 360.
110. Freud 1900a, 546 und 616 ff.
111. Ibid., 617.
112. Freud 1905c, 5, Fn.1.
113. Ibid., 184.
114. Freud 1940b, 146 f.; vgl. 1940a, 80.
115. Freud 1940b, 147.
116. Freud 1900a, 619.
117. Ibid., 619 f.
118. Vgl. Lipps 1983, Kap. VII u. VIII.
119. Kanzer 1981, 393.
120. Lipps 1896, 163.
121. Lipps 1893, 1 f.
122. Husserl 1900, I, 50 ff.
123. Vgl. N. Schmidt 1995, 90.
124. Ibid., 92.
125. Anschütz 1915, 5.
126. Ibid., 9.
127. Nach Kimmerles Auffassung gehört es "zu den unübersehbaren Mängeln aller bisherigen Versuche, eine eigenständige Psychoanalytische Erkenntnistheorie zu entwickeln, dass sie die von Husserl entfachte Psychologismusdebatte, die den szientistischen Zirkel in allen einzelwissenschaftlichen Begründungen von wissenschaftlichem Denken aufdeckt [...], nicht zur Kenntnis nimmt" (1997, Fn. 205).
128. Vgl. Davies u. Fichtner 2006.
129. Fichtner 1992, XI.
130. Ibid., XVIII.
131. Freud u. Binswanger 1992, 261.
132. Binswanger 1957, 207.
133. Ibid., 208.
134. Ibid., 210.
135. Freud u. Binswanger 1992, 154 f.; Brief v. 10.8.1917 an Freud.
136. Ibid., 184; Brief v. 7.2.1923 an Binswanger.
137. Binswanger 1922, 113–134.
138. Ibid., 135–158.
139. Ibid., 158–172.
140. Binswanger 1923, 24.
141. Ibid., 26.
142. Fichtner 1992, XXII; Freud u. Binswanger 1992, 188 f., Fn. 6.
143. Ibid., 188; Brief v. 27.8.1923 an Freud.
144. Binswanger 1956, 86 f.
145. Binswanger 1936, 162.
146. Freud u. Binswanger 1992, 236; Brief v. 8.10.1936 an Binswanger.
147. Freud 1957, 224 f.
148. Vgl. Mertens u. Haubl 1996; Kimmerle 1997.
149. Nagel 1990, 131 u. 146.
150. Vgl. Mertens 2005.
151. Vgl. Cavell 1993; Giampieri-Deutsch 2002.
152. Vgl. N. Schmidt 1995, 9.
153. Vgl. Kadi, Keintzel u. Vetter 2001; Buchholz u. Gödde 2005; Fellmann 2006; verschiedene Beiträge in "psycho-logik", dem neuen Jahrbuch für Psychotherapie, Philosophie und Kultur, u.a. Rinofner-Kreidl 2006 und Fuchs 2008.

References

Andreas-Salomé, L. 1958. *In der Schule bei Freud. Tagebuch eines Jahres (1912/1913)*. Frankfurt/M./Berlin/Wien: Ullstein, 1983.
Anschütz, G. 1915. Theodor Lipps †. *Archiv für die gesamte Psychologie* 34: 1–13.
Barclay, J.R. 1964. Franz Brentano and Sigmund Freud. *Journal of Existentialism* 5: 1–35.
Binswanger, L. 1922. *Einführung in die Probleme der Allgemeinen Psychologie*. Nachdruck, Amsterdam: Bonset, 1965.
Binswanger, L. 1923. Über Phänomenologie. In *Ausgewählte Vorträge und Aufsätze*, Hg. Ders., Bd. I, 13–49. Bern: Francke, 1947.
Binswanger, L. 1936. Freuds Auffassung des Menschen im Lichte der Anthropologie. In *Ausgewählte Vorträge und Aufsätze*, Bd. I, 159–189. Bern: Francke, 1947.
Binswanger, L. 1956. *Erinnerungen an Sigmund Freud*. Bern: Francke.
Binswanger, L. 1957. Mein Weg zu Freud. In *Freud in der Gegenwart. Ein Vortragszyklus der Universitäten Frankfurt und Heidelberg zum hundertsten Geburtstag*, Hg. F. Alexander u.a., 207–227. Frankfurt: Europ. Verlagsanstalt.
Brauns, H.-P. and A. Schöpf. 1989. Freud und Brentano: der Mediziner und der Philosoph. In *Freud und die Akademische Psychologie*, Hg. B. Nitzschke, 40–79. München: Psychologie Verlags Union.
Brentano, F. 1874a. Über die Gründe der Entmutigung auf philosophischem Gebiete. In *Über die Zukunft der Philosophie*, hg. von O. Kraus, 2. Aufl., 83–100. Hamburg: Meiner, 1968.
Brentano, F. 1874b. *Psychologie vom empirischen Standpunkt*, hg. v. Oskar, Kraus. Hamburg: Meiner, 1973.
Brentano, F. 1956. *Die Lehre vom richtigen Urteil*, hg. v. F. Mayer-Hillebrand. Bern: Francke.
Breuer, J. 1978. Drei Briefe an Franz Brentano. In *Physiologie und Psychoanalyse im Leben und Werk Josef Breuers*, Hg. A. Hirschmüller, 293–323. Bern: Huber.
Buchholz, M. 2006. Vorlesungen und einführende Schriften. In *Freud-Handbuch. Leben – Werk – Wirkung*, Hg. H.-M. Lohmann and J. Pfeiffer, 94–103. Stuttgart: Metzler.
Buchholz, M. 2007. Entwicklungsdynamik psychotherapeutischer Kompetenzen. *Psychotherapeutenjournal* 6(H. 4): 373–382.
Buchholz, M., and G. Gödde. 2005. *Das Unbewusste in aktuellen Diskursen. Anschlüsse. Das Unbewusste II*. Gießen: Psychosozial.
Cavell, M. 1993. *Freud und die analytische Philosophie des Geistes. Überlegungen zu einer psychoanalytischen Semantik*. Stuttgart: Klett-Cotta, 1997.
Davies, J.K., and G. Fichtner. 2006. *Freuds Bibliothek. Vollständiger Katalog*. London/Tübingen: Freud Museum (edition diskord).
Drüe, H. 1963. *Edmund Husserls System der phänomenologischen Psychologie*. Berlin: de Gruyter.
Eckstein, F. 1936. *„Alte unnennbare Tage!" – Erinnerungen aus siebzig Lehr- und Wanderjahren*. Wien: Reichner.
Fancher, R.E. 1977. Brentano's psychology from an empirical standpoint and Freud's early metapsychology. *Journal of the History of the Behavioral Sciences* 13: 207–227.
Fechner, G.Th. 1860. *Elemente der Psychophysik*, 2 Bde, 2. Aufl. Leipzig: Breitkopf u. Härtel, 1868.
Fellmann, F. 2006. *Phänomenologie zur Einführung*. Hamburg: Junius.
Fichtner, G. 1992. Einleitung. In *Sigmund Freud und Ludwig Binswanger: Briefwechsel 1908–1938*, Hg. Ders, IX–XXXI. Frankfurt/M.: Fischer.
Fischer, K.R. 1995. Einleitung. In *Das goldene Zeitalter der Österreichischen Philosophie*, Hg. Ders, IX–XIX. Wien: WUV-University.
Frampton, M. 1991. Considerations on the role of Brentano's concept of intentionality in Freud's repudiation of the seduction theory. *International Review of Psycho-Analysis* 18: 27–36.
Freud, S. 1893f. *Charcot†*. GW I, 21–35.
Freud, S. 1895d. *Studien über Hysterie* (ohne Breuers Beiträge). GW I, 75–312.
Freud, S. 1896b. *Weitere Bemerkungen über die Abwehr-Neuropsychosen*. GW I, 379–403.

Freud, S. 1900a. *Die Traumdeutung*. GW II/III, 1–642.
Freud, S. 1901b. *Zur Psychopathologie des Alltagslebens*. GW IV.
Freud, S. 1905c. *Der Witz und seine Beziehungen zum Unbewussten*. GW VI.
Freud, S. 1912–1913a. *Totem und Tabu*. GW IX.
Freud, S. 1912g. *Einige Bemerkungen über den Begriff des Unbewussten in der Psychoanalyse*. GW VIII, 430–439.
Freud, S. 1913j. *Das Interesse an der Psychoanalyse*. GW VIII, 389–420.
Freud, S. 1914d. *Zur Geschichte der psychoanalytischen Bewegung*. GW X, 43–113.
Freud, S. 1916-1917a. *Vorlesungen zur Einführung in die Psychoanalyse*. GW XI.
Freud, S. 1917a. *Eine Schwierigkeit der Psychoanalyse*. GW XII, 3–12.
Freud, S. 1920g. *Jenseits des Lustprinzips*. GW XIII, 1–69.
Freud, S. 1921c. *Massenpsychologie und Ich-Analyse*. GW XIII, 71–161.
Freud, S. 1923b. *Das Ich und das Es*. GW XIII, 237–289.
Freud, S. 1925d. *„Selbstdarstellung"*. GW XIV, 31–96.
Freud, S. 1926d. *Hemmung, Symptom und Angst*. GW XIV, 111–205.
Freud, S. 1926e. *Die Frage der Laienanalyse*. GW XIV, 207–286.
Freud, S. 1927a. *Nachwort zur Frage der Laienanalyse*. GW XIV, 287–296.
Freud, S. 1927c. *Die Zukunft einer Illusion*. GW XIV, 325–380.
Freud, S. 1930a. *Das Unbehagen in der Kultur*. GW XIV, 419–506.
Freud, S. 1933a. *Neue Folge der Vorlesungen zur Einführung in die Psychoanalyse*. GW XV.
Freud, S. 1935a. *Nachschrift 1935* [zur *„Selbstdarstellung"* (1925d)]. GW XVI, 31–34.
Freud, S. 1940a. *Abriß der Psychoanalyse*. GW XVII, 63–138.
Freud, S. 1940b. *Some elementary lessons in psycho-analysis*. GW XVII, 139–147.
Freud, S. 1950c. *Entwurf einer Psychologie*. GW Nachtr., 387–477.
Freud, S. 1960a. *Briefe 1873-1939*, ausgew. u. hg. von E. und L. Freud. 3., korr. Auflage. Frankfurt/M.: Fischer, 1968.
Freud, S. 1969a. Jugendbriefe an Emil Fluß (1872–74). In *„Selbstdarstellung". Schriften zur Geschichte der Psychoanalyse*, hg. u. eingeleitet von I. Grubrich-Simitis, 103–123. Frankfurt/M.: Fischer.
Freud, S. 1985c. *Briefe an Wilhelm Fließ 1887-1904*, hg. von J.M. Masson. Bearbeitung der deutschen Fassung von M. Schröter; Transkription von G. Fichtner. Frankfurt/M.: Fischer.
Freud, S. 1989. *Jugendbriefe an Eduard Silberstein 1871–1881*, hg. von W. Boehlich. Frankfurt/M.: Fischer.
Freud, S., and O. Pfister. 1963. *Briefe 1909–1939*, hg. von E.L. Freud u. H. Meng. Frankfurt/M.: Fischer.
Freud, S., and L. Andreas-Salomé. 1966. *Briefwechsel*, hg. von E. Pfeiffer. 2. Aufl. Frankfurt/M.: Fischer, 1980.
Freud, S., and L. Binswanger. 1992. *Briefwechsel 1908–1938*, hg. von G. Fichtner. Frankfurt/M.: Fischer.
Freud, S., and S. Ferenczi. 1993. *Briefwechsel 1912–1914*, Bd. I/2, hg. von E. Brabant, E. Falzeder, P. Giampieri-Deutsch u. A. Haynal. Transkription von I. Meyer-Palmedo. Wien/Köln/Weimar: Böhlau.
Fuchs, Th. 2008. Leibgedächtnis und Unbewusstes –Zur Phänomenologie der Selbstverborgenheit des Subjekts. *psycho-logik. Jahrbuch für Psychotherapie, Philosophie und Kultur* 3: 33–50.
Gekle, H. 2000. Bewusstsein. In *Handbuch psychoanalytischer Grundbegriffe*, Hg. W. Mertens and B. Waldvogel, 92–98. Stuttgart: Kohlhammer.
Giampieri, P. 1990. Freud und die österreichische Philosophie. In *Philosophie und Psychoanalyse. Symposium der Wiener Festwochen*, Hg. L. Nagl, H. Vetter u. H. Leupold-Löwenthal, 41–54. Frankfurt/M.: Nexus.
Giampieri-Deutsch, P. 2002. *Psychoanalyse im Dialog der Wissenschaften*, 2 Bde. Stuttgart: Kohlhammer.
Gödde, G. 1991. Freuds philosophische Diskussionskreise in der Studentenzeit. *Jahrbuch der Psychoanalyse* 27: 73–113.
Gödde, G. 1999. *Traditionslinien des Unbewussten. Schopenhauer – Nietzsche – Freud*, 2. Aufl. Tübingen/Gießen: edition diskord/Psychosozial, 2009.

Gödde, G. 2000. Die Öffnung zur Denkwelt Nietzsches – eine Aufgabe für Psychoanalyse und Psychotherapie. Psychoanalyse. *Texte zur Sozialforschung* 4(H. 7): 91–122.

Gödde, G. 2001. Das Unbewusste als Zentralbegriff der Freudschen Metapsychologie und seine philosophischen Wurzeln. In *Traum, Logik, Geld. Freud, Husserl und Simmel zum Denken der Moderne*, Hg. U. Kadi, B. Keintzel u. H. Vetter, 33–60. Tübingen: edition diskord.

Gödde, G. 2006. Freud und seine Epoche. Philosophischer Kontext. In *Freud-Handbuch. Leben – Werk – Wirkung*, Hg. H.-M. Lohmann and J. Pfeiffer, 10–25. Stuttgart: Metzler.

Gödde, G. 2008. Der Kraftbegriff bei Freud. Physiologische und psychologische Verwendungen. In *Zeichen der Kraft. Wissensformationen 1800–1900*, Hg. T. Brandstetter and C. Windgätter, 228–246. Berlin: Kadmos.

Gondek, H.-D. 2006. Philosophie. In *Freud-Handbuch. Leben – Werk – Wirkung*, Hg. H.-M. Lohmann and J. Pfeiffer, 348–372. Stuttgart: Metzler.

Günzel, S., and C. Windgätter. 2005. Leib/Raum: Das Unbewusste bei Maurice Merleau-Ponty. In *Das Unbewusste in aktuellen Diskursen. Anschlüsse. Das Unbewusste II*, Hg. M. Buchholz and G. Gödde, 582–613. Gießen: Psychosozial.

Hartmann, H. 1927. *Die Grundlagen der Psychoanalyse*. Stuttgart: Klett, 1972.

Hartmann, H. 1972. *Ich-Psychologie. Studien zur psychoanalytischen Theorie*. Stuttgart: Klett.

Herzog, P. 1988. The Myth of Freud as Anti-philosopher. In *Freud: Appraisals and Reappraisals*, Hg. P.E. Stepansky, 2 vols, 163–189. Hillsdale: The Analytic Press.

Hirschmüller, A. 1978. *Physiologie und Psychoanalyse im Leben und Werk Josef Breuers*. Bern: Huber.

Husserl, E. 1900. *Logische Untersuchungen*, Bd. I–II. 7. Aufl. Tübingen: Niemeyer, 1993.

Husserl, E. 1913. *Ideen zu einer reinen Phänomenologie und phänomenologischen Philosophie*. Tübingen: Niemeyer, 2002.

Husserl, E. 1919. Erinnerungen an Franz Brentano. In *Das goldene Zeitalter der österreichischen Philosophie*, Hg. K.R. Fischer, 79–89. Wien: WUV-Universitätsverlag, 1995.

Jerusalem, W. 1895. *Die Urteilsfunktion. Eine psychologische und erkenntniskritische Untersuchung*. Wien: Braumüller.

Jerusalem, W. 1922. Selbstdarstellung. In *Gedanken und Denker*, Hg. Ders, 1–35. Neue Folge. Wien u. Leipzig: Braumüller.

Kadi, U., B. Keintzel, H. Vetter, Hg. 2001. *Traum, Logik, Geld. Freud, Husserl und Simmel zum Denken der Moderne*. Tübingen: edition diskord.

Kanzer, M. 1981. Freud, Theodor Lipps and „Scientific Psychology". *Psychoanalytic Quarterly* 50: 393–410.

Kerz-Rühling, I. 1986. Freuds Theorie der Einsicht. *Psyche* 40: 97–123.

Kimmerle, G. 1986. *Anatomie des Schicksals*. Tübingen: edition diskord.

Kimmerle, G. 1997. *Der Fall des Bewusstseins. Zur Dekonstruktion des Unbewussten in der Logik der Wahrheit bei Freud*. Tübingen: edition diskord.

Lange, F.A. 1875. *Geschichte des Materialismus*, Bd. 2. Frankfurt/M.: Suhrkamp, 1974.

Lipps, T. 1883. *Grundtatsachen des Seelenlebens*. Bonn: Cohen und Sohn.

Lipps, T. 1893. *Grundzüge der Logik*. Hamburg/Leipzig: Voss.

Lipps, T. 1897. Der Begriff des Unbewussten in der Psychologie. *International Congress Psychology* 3: 146–164.

Lipps, T. 1898. *Komik und Humor*. Hamburg: Voss.

Lipps, T. 1903. *Leitfaden der Psychologie*. Leipzig: Engelmann (2. Aufl. 1906, 3. Aufl. 1909).

Lohmann, H.-M. 1998. *Sigmund Freud*. Reinbek: Rowohlt.

Lorenzer, A. 1970. *Sprachzerstörung und Rekonstruktion. Vorarbeiten zu einer Metatheorie der Psychoanalyse*. Frankfurt/M.: Suhrkamp.

Lorenzer, A. 2002. *Die Sprache, der Sinn, das Unbewusste*. Stuttgart: Klett-Cotta.

McGrath, W. 1986. *The politics of hysteria*. Ithaca/London: Cornell University Press.

Mertens, W. Hg. 1981. *Neue Perspektiven der Psychoanalyse*. Stuttgart: Kohlhammer.

Mertens, W. 2005. Das Unbewusste in der Kognitionspsychologie – wird damit Freuds Unbewusstes hinfällig? In *Das Unbewusste in aktuellen Diskursen. Anschlüsse*, Hg. M. Buchholz and G. Gödde, 264–309. Gießen: Psychosozial.

Mertens, W., and R. Haubl. 1996. *Der Psychoanalytiker als Archäologe*. Stuttgart: Kohlhammer.
Meyer-Palmedo, I., and G. Fichtner. 1999. *Freud-Bibliographie mit Werkkonkordanz*. 2. Aufl. Frankfurt/M.: Fischer.
Nagel, S. 1990. Psychologie ohne Philosophie – Zu den Versuchen, aus der Psychoanalyse eine Naturwissenschaft zu machen. In *„Wer sich nicht bewegt, der spürt auch seine Fesseln nicht …". Anmerkungen zur gegenwärtigen Lage der Psychoanalyse*, Hg. S. Zepf, 129–154. Frankfurt/M.: Nexus.
Nunberg, H., and E. Federn, Hg. 1962. *Protokolle der Wiener Psychoanalytischen Vereinigung, Bd. I, 1906–1908*. Frankfurt/M.: Fischer, 1976.
Nunberg, H., and E. Federn, Hg. 1967. *Protokolle der Wiener Psychoanalytischen Vereinigung, Bd. II, 1908–1910*. Frankfurt/M.: Fischer, 1977.
Polanyi, M. 1985. *Implizites Wissen*. Frankfurt/M.: Suhrkamp.
Pongratz, L. 1984. *Problemgeschichte der Psychologie*. 2. Aufl. München: Francke.
Putnam, J.J. 1911. Über die Bedeutung philosophischer Anschauungen und Ausbildung für die weitere Entwicklung der psychoanalytischen Bewegung. *Imago* 1: 101–118.
Putnam, J.J. 1912. Antwort auf die Erwiderung des Herrn Dr. Ferenczi (Philosophie und Psychoanalyse). *Imago* 1: 527–530.
Rank, O., and H. Sachs. 1913. *Die Bedeutung der Psychoanalyse für die Geisteswissenschaften*. Nachdruck, Amsterdam: Bonset, 1965.
Rapaport, D. 1959. *Die Struktur der psychoanalytischen Theorie*. 3. Aufl. Stuttgart: Klett, 1973.
Reicheneder, J.G. 1990. *Zum Konstitutionsprozeß der Psychoanalyse*. Stuttgart-Bad Cannstatt: frommann-holzboog.
Ricoeur, P. 1965. *Die Interpretation*. Frankfurt/M.: Suhrkamp, 1969.
Rinofner-Kreidl, S. 2006. Krisis und Gnosis – Grundlinien einer „Archäologie des Sinnes" (Husserl und Freud). *psycho-logik. Jahrbuch für Psychotherapie, Philosophie und Kultur* 1: 48–76.
Sandler, J. 1983. Die Beziehungen zwischen psychoanalytischen Konzepten und psychoanalytischer Praxis. *Psyche* 37: 577–595.
Schafer, R. 1982. *Eine neue Sprache für die Psychoanalyse*. Stuttgart: Klett-Cotta.
Schmidt, A. 1980. Materialismus und Subjektivität. Ein Gespräch mit B. Görlich. In *Der Stachel Freud. Beiträge und Dokumente zur Kulturismus-Kritik*, Hg. B. Görlich, A. Lorenzer u. Alfred, Schmidt, 195–296. Frankfurt/M.: Suhrkamp.
Schmidt, N.D. 1995. *Philosophie und Psychologie. Trennungsgeschichte, Dogmen und Perspektiven*. Reinbek: Rowohlt.
Schöpf, A. 1978. Die psychoanalytische Kritik Freuds am Philosophieren. *Perspektiven der Philosophie* 3: 251–274.
Schöpf, A. 1982. *Sigmund Freud*. München: Beck.
Schorske, C.E. 1982. *Wien. Geist und Gesellschaft im Fin de Siècle*. Frankfurt/M.: Fischer.
Stegmüller, W. 1989. *Hauptströmungen der Gegenwartsphilosophie. Eine kritische Einführung*. Bd. I. Stuttgart: Kröner.
Sullivan, J.J. 1968. Franz Brentano and the problems of intentionality. In *Historical roots of contemporary psychology*, Hg. B.B. Wolman, 248–274. New York: Harper & Row.
Sulloway, F.J. 1979. *Freud. Biologe der Seele. Jenseits der psychoanalytischen Legende*. Köln-Lövenich: Hohenheim, 1982.
Voigtländer, E. 1911. Über die Bedeutung Freuds für die Psychologie. In *Münchner Philosophische Abhandlungen*, Th. Lipps zu seinem 60. Geb., gewidmet von früheren Schülern, 294–316, Leipzig, 1922.
Wittels, F. 1931. Der Antiphilosoph Freud. *Almanach der Psychoanalyse* 6: 16–48.
Wucherer-Huldenfeld, A. 1967. Freud als Philosoph. In *Ursprüngliche Erfahrung und personales Sein*, Hg. Ders, 159–178. Wien/Köln/Weimar: Böhlau, 1994.

Edmund Husserl and Jacques Lacan: An Ethical Difference in Epistemology?

Andrzej Leder

Abstract The text of Andrzej Leder examines Husserlian phenomenology and Lacanian psychoanalysis under the presumption that philosophical concepts and theories can be read as expressions of moral attitudes. It presupposes that putting aside the tangle of different terminologies and theoretical backgrounds, we can find similar constructions for describing the implicit structure of experience. Nevertheless, the phenomenological and psychoanalytic methods can be readily distinguished according to their respective attitudes towards what is being experienced. That is to say that ethics rather than epistemology divides these two fields. This difference could also be restated in terms of the optimistic confidence of phenomenology in the possibilities of human thought, in contrast to the careful apprehension of psychoanalysis concerning its limitations or inherent failures.

Husserl was able to attain the realm of pure consciousness through the procedure of the phenomenological reduction (*epoché*), in which essence was cut from any existential or empirical judgments and could therefore be studied with absolute confidence. The basis for the cognitive confidence of phenomenology was trust in the adequacy of the subjective and objective poles of the intentional act. Following Husserl, we must affirm that objectivization preserves essence. With Husserl we believe this and we approve of this order of things. It appears evident, that the phenomenologist has to adopt the attitude of trust and confidence.

Freudian psychoanalysis introduced the returned *epoché*, which turned consciousness into the great unknown. Given that Freud was as interested as Husserl in preserving trust in our cognitive capacities, he introduced a rescue mechanism – the unconscious as the given source of meaning that permits us to decrypt the sense of experience.

A. Leder (✉)
Institute of Philosophy and Sociology of the Polish Academy of Sciences,
Warsaw, Poland
e-mail: aleder@ificspan.waw.pl

D. Lohmar and J. Brudzińska (eds.), *Founding Psychoanalysis Phenomenologically*,
Phaenomenologica 199, DOI 10.1007/978-94-007-1848-7_7,

With Lacan we face a double *epoché*. Consciousness is not "the given", nor is the unconscious, as the later must always be retroactively "reconstructed" from a given meaning, which is the product of the aforementioned "catastrophe". Are we then facing a kind of skepticism? After all, Lacan is often read as a modern skeptic. Andrzej Leder's proposal is that the problem is more complex. The dynamics of his research doesn't lead in the direction of skeptical doubt, but rather towards the realization that we face a crisis of the purely cognitive attitude towards experience. As in Kafka's saying: *"daß das Erkennen als solches Trost ist"*, epistemology appears here as a way of dealing with depressive, post-traumatic position. Different epistemological attitudes – the one of Husserl, of Freud, of Levinas and of Lacan – represent different ways of transcending this position. '-- End of Abstract'

1

The following text examines Husserlian phenomenology and Lacanian psychoanalysis under the presumption that philosophical concepts and theories can be read as expressions of moral attitudes. Putting aside the tangle of different terminologies and theoretical backgrounds that underlie both trajectories of thought, we can find similar constructions for describing the implicit structure of experience.[1] Nevertheless, the phenomenological and psychoanalytic methods can be readily distinguished according to their respective attitudes towards what is being experienced. That is to say that ethics rather than epistemology divides these two fields. Accordingly, the fundamental difference between Lacanian psychoanalysis and Husserlian phenomenology is moral in character – "moral" in the sense given to the word by the French, implying a general attitude or initial position determining the chain of thoughts that follow.

As Helmut Vetter has remarked:

> For the phenomenologist, freedom is the *telos* of any meditation. For Lacan, conditions which prevent freedom from becoming actual are of the highest interest.[2]

This difference could also be restated in terms of the optimistic confidence of phenomenology in the possibilities of human thought, in contrast to the careful apprehension of psychoanalysis concerning its limitations or inherent failures.

At the outset of any comparative study juxtaposing the moral attitude of the philosopher and the psychoanalyst, we ought to ask about the legitimacy of such an exercise. Can we meaningfully compare transcendental phenomenology, with its aim of giving laws to cognition as a normative science, and psychoanalysis, which is a practice intended to relieve suffering?

We are justified in responding to this question in the affirmative, provided that we recognize a common motivation sustaining the work of Husserl, Freud and Lacan. As we know, Freud wanted to relieve suffering. He produced his "talking cure" in order to achieve this end, which consisted in making individuals conscious of the constitutive structure of this or that phenomenon of experience. This awakening of consciousness was intended to dissolve the illusions that displaced and hid the realities of psychic life behind various symptoms. Formulated in these terms, the approach of Husserl is strikingly similar to that of Freud. Husserl also found himself faced by a patient – European culture of the late nineteenth and early twentieth centuries. He was convinced that the patient suffered from misleading and illusory convictions, and therefore published his work *Logical Investigations*, which was supposed to demonstrate to the European philosophical elite the nature and extent of their errors. Husserl's expectations suggest that he was not taking into account the power of resistance, which was only discovered by Freud after many years of work. Perhaps this is why Husserl wrote *The Crisis of European Sciences* nearly 30 years later – to recommence therapy from the beginning. In short, what the founders of phenomenology and psychoanalysis shared was an abiding preoccupation with the well being of their respective patients. In what follows, we will try to show that it is from this common ground that important differences in their attitudes emerge.

Before proceeding, we ought to note that this attitude of care might be considered the general characteristic of "the philosopher". Was Plato not attempting to cure the weaknesses of ancient Athenian democracy by projecting his rather terrifying vision of the political community? Perhaps it is in this way that we ought to understand Heidegger's description of intentionality as concern (*die Sorge*). Following the proposal of Levinas, perhaps the relation-to-anything must be ethical before it is cognitive? Maybe every philosopher is the psychoanalyst of his time?

2

Consciousness is always the consciousness of something – an object. This statement is the founding principle of phenomenology. The self-presentation of an object marks the initial condition for the philosophical attitude of phenomenology, in which respect for the experience and intuitively given realm of the "lifeworld" is coupled with confidence in the capacity of our mind to grasp "what is given." It is hard not to see the basic optimism of this attitude, which finds expression in many of Edmund Husserl's writings. Even in his later reflections of *Crisis*, the father of phenomenology writes:

> Den Glauben an die Möglichkeit der Philosophie als Aufgabe, also an die Möglichkeit einer universalen Erkenntnis, können wir nicht fahren lassen.[3]

Nevertheless, we might suspect that something casts a shadow across this optimism. After all, Husserl's phenomenology was primarily a response to the reductionism of the late nineteenth century – empiricism was the main object of its critique. If our ability to sense phenomenon was contingent and conditioned by some natural process, then it would seemingly be necessary to abandon the sphere of consciousness in our quest for absolute truth or at least the ideal of absolute truth.

However, the challenge that empiricism posed to our epistemic capacities was rather mild. The strongest attack on the postulates of rationality came from the "masters of suspicion," as Paul Ricoeur has called them. These thinkers were foremost defined by their denial of the significance of phenomena and to postulate the existence of an autonomous sphere, which can be called "the source of *significance*".[4] For Nietzsche, this sphere was the will to power. By contrast, Marx defined this sphere as the whole of social reality. Finally, Freud defined this sphere as the unconscious. These constructs were defined foremost by their impenetrability, the opaque character that kept them out of awareness. They were accessible only to the holders of adequate interpretative theory. The living world was turned into a "living illusion", while the truth, reality, was hidden behind it.

Consequently, this epistemological attitude provoked an important turn in philosophy and in the broader culture of approximately the first 60 years of the twentieth century. The first step was the critique of the phenomenon, which was followed by the quest for the source of meaning hidden behind the phenomenon. This source was substantialized and became the most important reference for both theory and practice. The living world and individual experience lost their relevance, as they had to be interpreted as mere symptoms of a supposedly hidden reality.[5]

Freud's concept of the unconsciousness evolved in the same way. Still, in *Traumdeutung*, the unconsciousness is defined mainly in epistemological terms, which means that it remains outside of our awareness at any given moment; it is resistant to our cognition and can be reached only through a theoretical reconstruction. However, Freud substantialized the unconscious in his meta-psychological writings, where it became something like the real psychic "being" responsible for quasi-causally determining the sphere of phenomenal consciousness.

This marks the most extreme point of distance between psychoanalytic "suspicion" and phenomenological "confidence" with respect to consciousness. Ricoeur has called the Freudian attitude "returned *epoché*".[6] If consciousness becomes the only necessary evidence in the Husserlian *epoché*, it appears in Freud as the main illusion, and working through this illusion is the main task of cognition. It is on this point that Sartre formulated, from the phenomenological perspective, his well-known critique of the psychoanalytic interpretation of the unconscious. As nothing beyond consciousness could causally determine the significance of phenomenon, the legitimacy of the substantial concept of the unconscious, including the drive and its representation, were irredeemably undermined. At the same time, Sartre noted that the job of the psychoanalyst must have been in essence phenomenological, given that it consisted of studying the structures responsible for conditioning the process of becoming aware.[7]

The explosion of structuralism profoundly shifted the intellectual horizons in which the previously described conflict took place. All three major "philosophies of suspicion" were reformulated structurally. Gilles Deleuze proposed a new way of reading Nietzsche, while Louis Althusser proposed a new way of reading Marx. Martin Heidegger's fundamental ontology and structuralist linguistics inspired

Jacques Lacan to reformulate the Freudian concept of the unconscious in a way that deprived it of the attribute of substantial being. "The unconsciousness has the structure of the language", this well-known sentence became the slogan of Lacanian theory. However, this French analyst made another statement that was likely of greater importance: "l'inconscient – c'est que ce n'est ni être, ni non-être, c'est du non-réalisé".[8] Lacan contested the ontological primacy of the unconscious. As his contemporary interpreter Slavoj Žižek has written, Lacan showed that the unconscious is not hidden in some inner depths. It is always here; we face it on the surface of the phenomenal world.[9] For Lacan, there is therefore nothing like an unconscious object, which might emerge on the surface of consciousness.[10] As a matter of fact, the structure of the unconscious always has to be built retroactively and it is the phenomenon – given as *le symptome* – that serves as the starting point for this process.

Nevertheless, the structural reading of Freud, freeing the unconscious from ontological premises, changes the manner in which it stands opposed to phenomenology, not the fact that it is inherently anti-phenomenological. This reading has only changed the direction of the strike. According to Hans Georg Gadamer, the phenomenological project is built on the assumption that there is intimate closeness between the subject and the object of the cognitive act, which is guaranteed by the notion of intention.[11] Vincent Descombes showed that the predominance of structuralist thought made this claim the primary point of contention between phenomenology and anti-phenomenological currents.[12] Therefore, the question of the adequacy of the subjective and the objective poles of experience became extremely relevant for this controversy.

3

Given that all existential judgments are "suspended" in Husserl's philosophy, the only guarantee of the truth is the adequation between the intentional act and its object. Moreover, only the postulate of this adequacy can maintain belief in the accessibility of universal rationality. So the question of adequacy therefore becomes the cornerstone of the phenomenological project.

Although the notion of adequacy is fundamental for Husserl, it is also problematic. It is clear that transcendent cognition is never fully adequate. So how do things stand with immanent cognition? In the first book of *Ideen*, Husserl maintains the assertion that undoubted certainty about the existence of pure consciousness is parallel to confidence about the adequacy of knowledge of this consciousness. Nevertheless, he begins to express some doubts as the book continues. For instance, he remarks that even the immanent cognition of individual experience cannot be fully adequate, as this experience is always part of a stream of pure consciousness, which cannot be fully grasped.[13] Consequently, adequacy is only possible in transcendental subjectivity.

However, in *Cartesian Meditations*, Husserl differentiates between certainty about the "givenness" of transcendental subjectivity and confidence about its adequate cognition. Certainty is higher in rank than confidence. As Husserl himself points out, this observation is directed at the transcendental experience of the self and he explains it by again utilizing the metaphor of the stream, just as he did in *Ideen*:

> Bewußtseinserlebnisse haben nicht nur vermöge unserer unvollkommenen Erkenntniskraft für derartige Gegenstände, sondern apriori keine letzten Elemente und Relationen, die sich der Idee fester begrifflicher Bestimmbarkeiten fügten [...]

as

> das Reich der Bewußtseinsphänomene so recht das Reich Heraklitischen Flusses ist.[14]

Even if we accept, as Ernst Tugendhat suggested, that the apodictic certainty of the existence of transcendental subjectivity can be completed with its adequate cognition only on the level of the most general structures,[15] the level of *eidos,* we have to take into account the remark of Thomas Seebohm that even transcendental essential cognition is cognition of an object, since *the expression of subjectivity is possible only through objectivization.*[16]

One can add that questions and doubts about "objectivization" were present in Husserl's research from the beginning of his philosophical journey. In his early *Logical Investigations* Husserl asks:

> [...] When we pass over from naively performed acts to an attitude of reflection, or when we perform acts proper to such reflection, our former acts necessarily undergo change. How can we rightly assess the nature and extent of such change? How indeed can we know anything whatever about it, whether as a fact or a necessity of essence.[17]

The problem of adequacy therefore appears in the shape of this very question: Is objectivization an innocent operation? In other words, if cognition is only adequate as the cognition of subjectivity, and if subjectivity must become an object to be grasped – does "objectivization" preserve the essential significance of what is "objectivized"?

This is the point at which numerous important criticisms of the Husserlian project have been raised. In *Voice and Phenomenon*, Jacques Derrida argues that the mediation of self-awareness is only possible through the voice. Moreover, in his interpretation of phenomenology, consciousness is actually the voice.[18] In which case, consciousness is implicated in the complex network of relations between and within speech, language and text – the fields of Derrida's work.

The Lacanian answer to the problem of objectivization is apparently quite similar to that of Derrida. Our experience is always mediated by the symbolic structure of language, called "the Big Other". However, the Lacanian approach is unique in that the condition of possibility for objectivization is not directly synonymous with the system of language. "*Le réel*" – left as undefined as the Kantian *Ding an sich*, in its Lacanian usage – always transgresses the symbolic. Therefore, subjectivity cannot be considered equivalent with the symbolic system; it is rather a failure, gap or an empty space that deforms the very system it inhabits. "*Achoppement, défaillance, fêlure*"[19] wrote Lacan. If subjectivity cannot be understood as some structure, how then can it be understood at all?

Slavoj Žižek formulates this question in a way somewhat similar to the phenomenological tradition:

> What, then, is the status of this subject before the subjectivisation?

His answer:

> The subject tries to articulate itself in a signifying representation; the representation fails; instead of a richness we have a lack, and this void opened by the failure *is* the subject of the signifier."

comes as nothing else then the place of failure in the process.[20]

4

Nevertheless, there is a subtle but important difference between the question asked by phenomenology and the question asked by Lacanian psychoanalysis. Whereas the phenomenologist asks about the objectivization of subjectivity, the psychoanalyst asks about the process of becoming a subject, which is pre-subjective. The significance of this difference can be better appreciated by way of direct comparison. For the phenomenologist, subjectivity is always given. By contrast, subjectivity is never given for the Lacanian psychoanalyst – it must emerge as a result of the failure of this process of becoming a subject. The effective experience is a correlate of a lapse.

In this concept we can distinctly see the stress put on the negative meaning of subjectivity – negative in the strong sense. The strength of this sense is readily apparent when compared with the status of negativity in phenomenology.

This comparison is necessary because the idea of consciousness as a form of negation has its own tradition in phenomenology – particularly manifest in the work of Jean-Paul Sartre. According to Sartre, the nothingness of consciousness is the transcendental condition of awareness, of becoming aware. However, it is unnecessary to reference Sartre or even Heidegger. We can easily grasp the same intuition in Husserl's own treatment of the notion of intentionality.

An intention, particularly the signitive intention, may be seen as an empty space, which is in need of being filled with intuition.

> [...] Signitive intentions are in themselves 'empty' and they 'are in need of fullness'. Or "purely" signitive acts are, however, 'empty' [...].[21]

Such formulations by Husserl bring to mind the idea of a certain *absence*, the negation of a specific fulfillment. Since intentions themselves are empty and "waiting" for phenomena, the web of these intentions produces the image of an empty intentional field, or space, which cannot be anything specific.

However, between the emptiness of the intentional web and its fulfillment, we can detect a certain presupposition of adequacy, similar to that which unites the key and the keyhole. The keyhole is a "negative" of the key, but there is an intimate correspondence between every part of the key and the keyhole.

> All perceiving and imagining is a web of partial intentions, fused together in the unity of a single total intention. The correlate of this last intention is the thing, while the correlate of its partial intention are the thing's parts and aspects[22]

Then again, what is the guarantee of this adequacy, which is the condition of correspondence for subjectivity before and after objectivization? There must be some similarity between immanent consciousness and its correlate. Therefore, we have to again ask: what kind of similarity would it be? Something must remain unchanged when transgressing the abyss that separates transcendental subjectivity and its correlate. We know that here the idea of essence, the *eidos,* is indispensable. In phenomenological nothingness – essence, identical to itself, hides.

5

For Husserl, essence is attained through imaginative variation. The privileged field of this operation is fantasy. In *Logical Investigations* variation is quite simple – it is the free transformation of a given object to define its constitutive features. The individual object is approached here mainly as an example of a particular species. This means that there is an *eidos* of the object, which is the essence of the signitive intention and is intuitively attainable through the imaginative variation of the object. Thus, the adequacy of the subjective and the objective is guaranteed.

For psychoanalytic thought, this reasoning cannot be accepted. Imaginative variation would simply lead from one collapse to another. In other words, it would produce an infinite chain of objects, much like the process of free association, which could never be linked with any particular idea of essence. It is at this point that we approach the distinction that separates the concept of negativity in Husserl and Lacan.

For the phenomenologist, even if the web of intentions is "negative" it has a determinate structure, which conditions possibility according to the fundamental rule that determines every possible sense – the logical principle of non-contradiction. It is precisely for this reason that imaginative variation allows us to obtain the complex of non-contradictory constitutive features of an object that correspond with its essence.

The negativity of psychoanalytic thinking is far stronger, going beyond the principle of non-contradiction. The objectivization of subjectivity or rather the subjectivization of the pre-subjective is understood as the correlate of an antagonism. Furthermore, the correlate of a contradiction is not susceptible to any mediation. This is why the process of objectivization is always a failure and subjectivity is precisely the nothingness that marks contradiction at its most unthinkable point – furthest from any mediation. As Žižek puts it:

> [Consciousness] emerges in order to solve some fundamental antagonism through putting its terms in conformity with the sequence of temporal succession [...][23]

In Žižek's interpretation, the necessary condition of any experience is the slit that is subjectivity, the pure negativity of a contradiction that is not suitable for any representation, even the most symbolic abstractions. It is a figure always in pursuit of representation that leaves behind a trail of objects, evidence of successive failures and micro-catastrophes.

At this point in our comparative study it is again possible to think that we have reached the point where the differences between Husserlian eidos and the Lacanian failure of the symbolization process are clearly demarcated. Describing the structure of becoming aware, phenomenology and psychoanalysis could be seen as absolutely foreign to each other. At the logical level, the former starts from the point of pure possibility, the only limit of which is exclusion of the contradiction. By contrast, the latter treats even pure and empty possibility as some kind of positivity, hiding conflict – Heraclitean *polemos*. Psychoanalytic thinking logically starts from contradiction, and it studies unsuccessful mediations of this contradiction.

However, even this style of thought is not completely unknown to Husserl. If we closely follow the evolution of the concept of imaginative variation, we find some astonishing sentences that testify to the idea that contradiction is the basis for every essence. In the latter *Erfahrung und Urteil*, prepared by Ludwig Landgrebe, we find that imaginative variation requires a specific operation, which is the condition of essential intuition. This operation gives us a "hybrid unity" (*Zwittereinheit*). The signitive representation of the general, essential, is fulfilled or achieved in this operation. How?

> Was [...] als Einheit im Widerstreit erschaut wird, ist kein Individuum, sondern eine konkrete Zwittereinheit sich wechselseitig aufhebender, sich koexistential ausschliessender Individuen.[24] (What is intuitively seen [...] as the unity in contradiction is not any individual, but a concrete hybrid identity of individuals, which mutually disallow and coexistentially exclude each other [...]

By simply changing the language, we might easily attribute Husserl's remarks to Lacan, since contradiction in the symbolic sphere is the condition of any experience for him. Even the metaphor being used could be adapted to psychoanalytic discourse. Husserl writes about "hybrid units", while Lacan states:

> j'aurais pu parler de ce que, dans les constructions de la Gnose, on appelle les etres intermediaires – sylphes, gnomes, voire les formes plus élevés de ces mediateures ambigues[25]

6

Hence, the method of reading that we have suggested locates a strange affinity between the two authors in the pure description of the process of constitution. In the work of both theorists we find the idea of an overabundance of contradictory acts and unity appearing as an intuitive manifestation of this contradiction. Along the same lines, there is some structural order to consciousness, which conditions the appearance of a given fulfillment and eliminates the excess of the intentional field. However, what is philosophically significant is that despite finding strong similarities in their descriptions, the attitude of the two thinkers towards their results is completely opposite.

As for Husserl, even if the condition of the general (essential) is *Zwittereinheit* – unity in contradiction – the result is positive and adequate to the signitive intention, as shown in Tugendhat. To cite Husserl's own words:

> In the texture of conscious, intentional experience, there are many possibilities of pointing selection of acts and act-complexes, which remain for the most part unrealized.[26]

That which is realized is that which was intended. In other words, something is identical even in the contradiction of unities and this identity is the very condition of "overlapping synthesis" (*Deckungssynthesis)*. Again, as Tugendhat has put things, we believe that the idea of the truth is attainable: "in the infinity of *possible* acts of the same essence."[27]

For Lacan, as we previously stated, objectivized subjectivity is always a failure in synthesis. The resulting object that appears at the moment of failure is the material trace of this defeat, which fills the empty space of the subject.[28] In the language of phenomenology, immanent cognition never provides us with a simple signitive intention. According to Husserl, there is a complex of acts that "coexistentially exclude each other". The result is not a positive adequate synthesis of a species, but rather an artifact that is foreign to the intentional web of which this very artifact is a trace. In other words, the metaphor of the keyhole is no longer adequate. There is a key, but we will never find the keyhole – we can only try to create it retroactively.

Furthermore, with Lacan we must disavow the Freudian claim that there is another realm of adequate truth hidden beneath experience. Not only we doubt the adequacy of our subjectivity and the objectivity of lived experience. We doubt that objectivization preserves any essential character of objectivized subjectivity. This is what Lacan means in his formula concerning the predominance of the signifier.

This difference in attitude can be illustrated by interpreting one of the major figures in Franz Kafka's writings. His hero can be seen as a person who tries to see essence – to meet God, face to face. His unfinished journey through dark corridors and abandoned rooms becomes a metaphor for the dramatic truth – there is no essence, belief in its presence was an illusion and in its place there can only be emptiness.

However, as Žižek has pointed out, this is clearly a "modernist" interpretation, given that it overlooks a simple fact that is clearly perceived by Husserl and Lacan. We never meet emptiness; we meet phenomenon, experiences and objects. Consciousness is always consciousness of something. Kafka's hero never encounters emptiness. Instead, he meets judges lying in beds, their perverted servants, killers in suits, etc. At this point the phenomenologist and psychoanalyst are still fellow travelers. However, beyond this point they must part. The phenomenologist would try to persuade Kafka's hero that his effort is meaningful. Perhaps suggesting that if the hero's effort is strong enough, he might eventually see His face. By contrast, the Lacanian would respond that by trying to find God the hero will never face him directly, but will instead find himself passed by strange characters and accidental persons. And these traces are the only essence that he can face. As a matter of fact, these characters are seen only because the hero is trying to see the One hidden beneath them. Although what the hero seeks will never be seen, it is thanks to this twist in his gaze that he can glimpse anything at all. If the hero tried looking directly, forgetting the unattainable, he would see nothing.

7

Husserl was able to attain the realm of pure consciousness through the procedure of the phenomenological reduction (*epoché*), in which essence was cut from any existential or empirical judgments and could therefore be studied with absolute confidence. The basis for the cognitive confidence of phenomenology was trust in the adequacy of the subjective and objective poles of the intentional act. Following Husserl, we must affirm that objectivization preserves essence. In the last chapters of *the Cartesian Meditations,* exposing the fundamental naivety of the positive sciences, Husserl confesses to another kind of naivety – apodictic naivety,[29] which is characteristic for the phenomenological attitude:

> Wir haben ihr vertraut dank ihrer ursprünglich durchlebten Evidenz und haben auch in ähnlicher Weise der Evidenz der prädikativen Deskription aller transzendental wissenschaftlichen Erfahrungsweisen überhaupt vertraut.[30]

It appears evident that the phenomenologist has to adopt an attitude of trust and confidence. Despite the risk of finding ourselves seduced into naivety, we long for trust and confidence.

Freudian psychoanalysis introduced the returned *epoché*, which turned consciousness into the great unknown. Given that Freud was as interested as Husserl in preserving trust in our cognitive capacities, he introduced a rescue mechanism – the unconscious as the given source of meaning that permits us to decrypt the sense of experience.

With Lacan we face a double *epoché*. Consciousness is not "the given", nor is the unconscious, as the later must always be retroactively "reconstructed" from a given meaning, which is the product of the aforementioned "catastrophe". Are we then facing a kind of skepticism? After all, Lacan is often read as a modern skeptic.

Our proposal is that the problem is more complex. The dynamics of our research doesn't lead in the direction of skeptical doubt, but rather towards the realization that we face a crisis of the purely cognitive attitude towards experience.

It is not merely coincidental that the most "epistemological" book of Freud, *Traumdeutung*, begins with the vindictive words of Virgil's Juno: *Flectere si nequeo superos, Acheronta movebo.* (If heaven remains locked for me, I will move and raise hell). Within the fundamental attitudes of psychoanalysis we find a deep experience of harm and repudiation. In fact, we might venture that this attitude was the source of Freud's most original and fruitful ideas: repression, the Oedipus complex and the unconscious itself. We may therefore risk the statement that the act most characteristic of psychoanalysis, disputing the dominance of consciousness, is rooted in ethics rather than epistemology. Freud's standpoint is that of the defeated, repudiated, unknown and secretive. As Jacques Derrida has stressed, he is always in conflict with the radiant sovereignty of presence:

> Cette souveraineté, le premier geste de la psychanalyse aura été de l'expliquer, pour rendre compte de son inéluctabilité, tout en projetant d'en déconstruire la généalogie qui passe aussi par du meurtre cruel.[21]

The source of the critique of cognition is therefore an ethical attitude. By giving the repressed a place in the realm of experience, psychoanalytic practice can be seen as the fulfillment of the ancient sentence of Anaximander – the sentence that linked ontology and ethics through the rule of nemesis. This sentence speaks about the inevitable punishment that falls on everything that has managed to come into existence. It is punishment for the harm that underlies the very fact that things are the way they are. What exists has stifled other forms of existence, simply because it has taken in the realm of being the place that could have been taken by them.[32]

Both, consciousness and subjectivity are always guilty and must pass through the sufferings of psychoanalysis in order to let the repressed, the repudiated and the excluded find their place. That is why Freud writes in *Wege der psychoanalytischen Therapie*:

> Wir müssen, so grausam es klingt, dafür sorgen, dass das Leiden des Kranken in irgendeinem wirksamen Maße kein vorzeitiges Ende finde. Wenn es durch die Zersetzung und Entwertung der Symptome ermäßigt worden ist, müssen wir es irgendwo anders als eine empfindliche Entbehrung wieder aufrichten (...)[33]

Psychoanalysis should then be understood as constant thinking in the fields of suffering and trauma, the permanent search for a position in which thought is able to face these two challenges.

The next question we should obviously raise concerns how to understand phenomenology in relation to trauma. To do so, we ought to turn to the pages of *Crisis*, where we can feel a struggle between hope and despair in Husserl's words:

> Damit allein entscheidet sich, ob das dem europäischen Menschentum mit der Geburt der griechischen Philosophie eingeborene *Telos*, ein Menschentum aus philosophischer Vernunft sein zu wollen und nur als solches sein zu können – in der unendlichen Bewegung von latenter zu offenbarer Vernunft [...] ein blosser historisch-faktischer Wahn ist, [...]; oder ob nicht vielmehr im griechischen Menschentum erstmalig zum Durchbruch gekommen ist, was als Entelechie im Menschentum als solchem wesenmässig beschlossen ist.[34]

Perhaps this latent feeling of despair is responsible for the surprising turn in the last fragments of the *Cartesian Meditations,* where Husserl looks to the other to find legitimacy for the universal importance of conscious cognition. Criticizing Kant's transcendentalism, Husserl claims that something is missing between the transcendental aesthetics and analytics, the two pillars of the objective cognition. And in the fifth meditation he writes:

> In das erste diese "transzendentale Aesthetik" übersteigende Stockwerk gehört die Theorie der Fremderfahrung, der sogenannten "Einfühlung"

And this theory is necessary, as

> [...] wie auch nie erkannt worden ist, wie sich die Fremdheit des "Anderen" auf die ganze Welt als ihre "Objekvität" überträgt, ihr diesen Sinn erst gebend.[35]

Emmanuel Levinas has provided commentary that helps to develop this thought further. As a matter of fact, he uses this thought to construct the foundations of his position that any objective experience is conditioned in meeting the Other. That is to say that objective experience is ethically conditioned:

> this analysis dissimulates, in each of its stages which are taken as a description of constitution, mutations of object constitution into a relation with the Other – which is as primordial as the constitution from which it is to be derived.[36]

Husserl closes his *Meditations* with the confession borrowed from Augustine: *Noli foras ire, in te redi, in interiore homini habitat veritas.* It seems reasonable to interpret this borrowing as an unambiguous signal that Husserl located the sources of universal cognition in transcendental reason – not the other.

We may therefore accept that Husserl and Levinas each offer two opposite possibilities concerning the source of objective truth in phenomenology. Husserl locates it *in interiore homini*, whereas Levinas locates it in the relation with the absolute transcendence of the other. Nevertheless, surprising similarities emerge when we look at these two poles from within "the field of trauma."

In some ways, their respective beliefs in the possibilities of founding rationality and absolute truth may be understood as attempts to avoid experiences of harm and despair – mourning. Despite their different methods, they both wanted to preserve confidence. Nevertheless, there are prices to pay for such continued optimism. Husserl pays in the form of an almost solipsistic phenomenology, while Levinas always stands at the edge of sacrificing individual autonomy.

Psychoanalysis offers us a third way that remains within the field of trauma. It represents a conscious renouncement of any mediation that we might idealize. Consequently, this renouncement represents a severe ban on the search for any particular *eidos*.

While the most morally discriminating, this attitude is ambiguous. The historical experience of the twentieth century has provided particularly troubling commentary. Any rationality is endangered when the feeling of harm becomes the only touchstone of thought, in which case any event, even the most apparently innocent, can be seen in a dark light. From this perspective there can never be a place for rationality, given that there is no harm that could be "explained" or justified by rational reasoning. Any logical argument trying to explain harm appears as nothing more than a ruse meant to exclude or hide some element of suffering that escapes *logos*. Rationality becomes rationalization.

But we can stress another, perhaps more radical, point. Is this attitude – the renouncement of any idealization in the process of thinking – possible to maintain? Even if, from the psychoanalytic point of view, we consider the confidence of Husserl (and Levinas) as a kind of fantasy, we must remember the role that fantasy plays in the construction of reality. As Slavoj Žižek has made clear:

> Here we can see clearly, how fantasy is on the side of reality, how it sustains the subjects' "sense of reality": when the phantasmic frame disintegrates, the subject undergoes 'a loss of reality' and starts to perceive reality as an unreal, nightmarish universe [...]; this nightmarish universe is not 'pure fantasy', but, on the contrary, *that which remains of reality after reality is deprived of its support in fantasy.*[37]

With his fascinating gift of precision, Franz Kafka formulates a similar thought in a simpler way:

> Ist es möglich etwas Untröstliches zu denken? Oder vielmehr etwas Untröstliches ohne den Hauch des Trostes? Ein Ausweg läge darin, daß das Erkennen als solches Trost ist.[38]

It appears that even if it is morally tempting in its maximalism, a fully consistent attitude is impossible for the psychoanalyst. Maybe this is what makes us sensitive to the charms of the phenomenological project, even if we know that it rests on naïve trust in the *ursprünglich durchlebten Evidenz*.

Notes

1. An interesting discussion could be had on this very point. Can we find anything having the features of similar "constructions", or even something less determined that we might call "trajectories of thought", in two different theories based on two different discourses? Here we follow the advice of Jacques Derrida, who asks in his essay *The Pit and the Pyramid* if it wouldn't be pure naivety not to notice "long sequences and chains of predicates" which persists even after the transference of a concept from one system of thoughts to another. We mean exactly the Derridians "sequences and chains" when we use the notion of a "trajectory of thought".
2. Helmut Vetter, "Lacan Between Freud and Heidegger," in *Filozofska Istrazivanja*, 32–33 (1989), 1701–1710, polish trans. Jan Miziński, *Lacan między Freudem a Heideggerem*, Colloquia Communia, Nr 3–6/1989, 35.
3. Edmund Husserl, *Die Krisis der europäischen Wissenschaften und die transzendentale Phaenomenologie* (Hamburg: Felix Meiner Verlag, 1992), 15.
4. Marcel Gauchet, *Le désenchentement du monde* (Paris: Gallimard, 1985). We owe the notion of *significance* to Jacques Derrida.
5. It is not necessary here to speak about the horrible absurdities of these "epistemologies" in totalitarian societies. This pattern of thinking is intimately connected with the features of modernity, which Reinhart Koselleck labeled as the drift of the expectations horizon away from the space of experience. Reinhart Koselleck, "„Erfahrungsraum" und „Erwartungshorizont"– zwei historische Kategorien," in *Vergangene Zukunft. Zur Semantik geschichtlicher Zeiten* (Frankfurt a. M.: Suhrkamp, 1979), 349–375.
6. Paul Ricoeur, *De l'interprétation* (Paris: Éditions du Seuil, 1965), 136.
7. J-P. Sartre, *L'etre et le neant* (Paris: Gallimard, 1994), 502.
8. Jacques Lacan, *Le seminaire. Livre XI, (1964), (Les quatres concepts fondamentaux de la psychanalyse)* (Paris: Éditions du Seuil, 1973), 38.
9. Slavoj Žižek, *The Plague of Fantasies* (London/New York: Verso, 1997), 3.
10. Jacques Lacan, *Les quatres concepts...*, 32–33.
11. Hans Georg Gadamer, *Wahrheit und Methode. Grundzüge einer philosophischen Hermeneutik* (Tübingen: Mohr, 1975), 231–236.
12. Vincent Descombes, *Le même et l'autre. Quarante-cinq ans de philosophie francaise (1933–1978)* (Paris: Éditions de Minuit, 1979), 97.
13. Es liegt an der Eigentümlichkeit des Bewußtseins überhaupt, ein nach verschiedenen Dimensionen verlaufendes Fluktuieren zu sein, so daß von einer begrifflich exakten Fixierung eidetischer Konkreta und aller sie unmittelbar konstituierenden Momente keine Rede sein kann. *Ideen zu einer reinen Phänomenologie und phänomenologischen Philosophie*, M. Nijhoff, Den Haag, 1976, 156 (140).
14. Edmund Husserl, *Cartesianische Meditationen und Pariser Vorträge* (den Haag: M. Nijhof, 1950), 86.
15. Ernst Tugendhat, *Der Wahrheitsbegriff bei Husserl und Heidegger* (Berlin: Walter de Gruyter, 1967), 206.
16. Thomas Seebohm, *Die Bedingungen der Möglichkeit der Transzendental-Philosophie* (Bonn: Bouvier, 1962), 140.
17. Edmund Husserl, *Logical Investigations*, trans. J. N. Findlay (London/New York: Routledge and Kegan Paul/Humanities Press, 1970), I:255.

18. Jacques Derrida, *La voix et le phénomène. Introduction au problème du signe dans la phénoménologie de Husserl* (Paris: Presses Universitaires de France, 1972), 83–90.
19. J. Lacan, *Les quatres concepts...*, 33.
20. S. Žižek, *The Sublime Object of Ideology* (London/New York: Verso, 1989), 175.
21. E. Husserl, *Logical Investigations*, Vol. II, 728, 744.
22. E. Husserl, *Logical Investigations*, Vol. II, 701.
23. S. Žižek, *The plague of...*, 10–11.
24. E. Husserl, *Erfahrung und Urteil: Untersuchungen zur Genealogie der Logik* (Hamburg: Felix Meiner, 1972), 417.
25. J. Lacan, *Les quatres concepts...*, 38
26. E. Husserl, *Logical Investigations,* Vol. II, 703.
27. E. Tugendhat, Der Wahrheitsbegriff..., 53, 54.
28. Lacan, *Les quatres concepts...*, 36.
29. Nur daß wir es vorgezogen haben, die ungeheure Problematik der ersten in ihrer Art selbst noch mit einer Naivität behafteten Phänomenologie (der apodiktischen Naivität) [...] in Umrissen zu zeichnen, [...] E. Husserl, *Cartesianische Meditationen...*, 177.
30. E. Husserl, *Cartesianische Meditationen...*, 177.
31. J. Derrida, Interview in: *Le monde* de 09/07/2000.
32. „εξ ϖν δε η γενεσιζ εστι τοιζ ουσι, και την φθοραν ειζ ταυτα γινεσθαι κατατο χρεων διδοναι γαρ αυτα δικην και τισιν αλληλοιζ τηζ αδικιαζ κατα την του χρονου ταξιν, ποιητικωτεροιζ ουτωοζ ονομασιν αυτα λεγων." Anaximander, in: G.S. Kirk and J.E. Raven, *The Presocratic Philosophers. A Critical History with a Selection of Texts* (Cambridge: University Press, 1957), 117.
33. Sigmund Freud, *Wege der psychoanalytischen Therapie,* 1918, GW XII, 188.
34. Edmund Husserl, *Die Krisis der europäischen Wissenschaften ...*, 15.
35. Edmund Husserl, *Cartesianische Meditationen...*, 173.
36. E. Levinas, *Totality and Infinity, an Essay on Exteriority,* trans. Alphonso Lingis (The Hague/Boston/London: Kluwer Academic Publishers, 1979), 67.
37. S. Žižek, *The Plague of ...*, 66.
38. F. Kafka, Oktavheft G (II, 2), http://www.kafka.org/index.php?ohg.

Psychoanalysis and the Logic of Thinking Without Language. How Can We Conceive of Neurotic Displacement, Denying, Inversion etc. as Rational Actions of the Mind?

Dieter Lohmar

Abstract Freud's psychoanalysis proposes the thesis of a powerful and lasting unconsciousness and it also calls our attention to the action of „neurotic displacement" that affects our behavior and can be redone only with the help of a psychoanalytical hermeneutics. Thus, from a philosophical point of view, psychoanalysis incorporates the alarming insight that our consciousness is opaque. My starting point is a phenomenological analysis of human non-linguistic thinking that is centered on the mode of scenic phantasma we commonly identify with daydreams. I will consider the idea that daydreams may be an old form of (non-linguistic) thinking about the present world, about our former experiences, or about our wishes and future plans. Daydreams turn out to be the medium to bind my former experiences with possible future actions and possible events. It reveals as a problem-solving activity even in the specific forms of neurotic displacement. From this point of view, some enigmas of our wakeful daydreams may be solved and turn out to be quite rational processes. '-- End of Abstract'

Freud's psychoanalysis presents more than one enigma to the philosophy of consciousness. Psychoanalysis proposes the thesis of a powerful and lasting unconsciousness, which is out of reach of conscious thinking. Furthermore, psychoanalysis also calls our attention to the action of the human mind, called „neurotic displacement" (Verschiebung), that in a variety of ways encodes the experienced contents. Although the original contents are difficult to decode, they have effects on our behavior. Neurotic displacement has different forms: shifting, denial, inversion, compression of contents, etc. One can reconstitute the displaced activity only with the help of a psychoanalytical hermeneutics. This hermeneutics helps one find the original contents. The success of the analytical

D. Lohmar (✉)
Husserl-Archive, University of Cologne,
Albertus Magnus Platz, D 50923 Cologne, Germany
e-mail: Dieter.Lohmar@uni-koeln.de

D. Lohmar and J. Brudzińska (eds.), *Founding Psychoanalysis Phenomenologically*, Phaenomenologica 199, DOI 10.1007/978-94-007-1848-7_8,

process (the curing effect) as well as the sudden insight and revitalized memories of the patient convinces as one of the success of this procedure.

Thus, from a philosophical point of view, psychoanalysis incorporates an alarming insight, viz., the insight that our consciousness is opaque and that in the self-obscuring activity it is oriented to rules that we do not fully understand in their sense and aims. Looking from the point of view of a subject who understands himself as lucid and rational, this enigmatic activity is a thorn in the flesh of reason.

In my contribution, I would like to make some of the above-mentioned enigmatic aspects more comprehensible. My starting point is a phenomenological analysis of human non-linguistic thinking that is centered on the mode of scenic phantasma we commonly identify with daydreams. Since we regularly suppose that most performances of thinking are bound to the use of language, my starting point calls for some explanations.[1]

With this treatment, I will by no means claim a comprehensive understanding of all psychic events in correlation with daydreaming. Such a claim would be disproportionate when compared with my limited knowledge of the psychoanalytical theory-formation. I will consider a hypothesis, according to which daydreams may be interpreted as an old form of (non-linguistic) thinking, i.e. a form of thinking that humans probably use before the full development of verbal language abilities. From this point of view, some enigmas of our wakeful daydreams may be solved and turn out to be quite rational processes. Nevertheless, we might take an opposite every-day view and suppose that wakeful fantasies deal only with irreal fantasy-worlds and never concern the real world. This view needs to be given up if daydreaming turns out to be an old, non-linguistic mode of thinking about the present world, about our former experiences, or about our wishes and future plans (or even the plans of others). Already in virtue of this change of our point of view, I can easily understand the characteristic changeability of the scenes and phantasms in which I treat former and future events in daydreams. Thus daydreams turn out to be the medium in which I bind my former experiences with possible future actions and possible events. Daydreaming thus functions as a problem-solving activity. The characteristic transformations also include denying of former events (while still holding on to them in the form of negation), inverting activities, or transferring my former and future activities to other persons and other objects, etc. Because of such far-reaching transformations, which nonetheless preserve the lessons of former experience while opening up particular future possibilities, I see in this discussion a contribution to the epistemological founding of psychoanalysis.

We must first have a rough idea of non-linguistic thinking in its modes and its performances to be able to understand that its performance is almost the same as that of linguistic thinking, even though it is based on a quite different set of rules. However, non-linguistic thinking has some specific limitations and deviations when compared to language-based thinking: Non-linguistic thinking can preserve our experience (whether it is pleasant or not), recall and modify it, and transform it into a form that permits its use in further actions. Human non-linguistic thinking proceeds mostly in the mode of (sometimes highly emotional) phantasmatic scenes with which we are well acquainted from our daydreams. It might seem that these phantasmatic scenes only repeat a former unpleasant event or a challenging future event. But this thinking proceeds in the mode of repetitions (a kind of replays) of a particular scene in our consciousness. It is important not to overlook that in each repetition the particular scene undergoes a slight modification. This means that the circumstances, situations and sometimes even the acting and suffering persons are slightly modified in their constellation, activities and motives. The result of this thinking activity is a kind of „characteristic scene", which may be regarded as an advantageous but fake memory of my past experience (because it avoids more or less and other emotionally painful aspects). But it is more appropriate, with regard to its overall function, to consider this modification as a useful idea of my future actions based on former experience.

Perhaps we may think of a kind of a video clip (resp. a narrative scene) that briefly presents a possibility regarding how, for instance, a painful and passive experience could have been turned into a successful active mastering of experience. To give an example: Had I been pressed hard by an impertinent and aggressive bully and had I given way to his demands due to the situation and circumstances, the annoying situation would repeatedly and furiously reemerge in my daydreams. Everyone knows this type of daydreaming. But these seemingly identical reappearances would each time introduce slight modifications and in the end engender the right solution to get rid of aggressive demands. Suddenly I gain the insight: This would have been the right reaction; had I done this, it would have stopped him!

This resulting characteristic scene need not be accurate in all its details regarding the actual experience. Its central function is to keep the decisive „lesson" for the future (from the experience made), but at the same time to transform it in a way that one could memorize it without difficulties and emotional pains and easily make productive use of it in future challenges. But keep in mind that non-linguistic thinking is only useful for the solitary inner thinking. It does not have to adjust to the external demand of accuracy in a communicating society. While the demand of accuracy makes good sense within the public forms of communication, it is not necessary for the solitary non-linguistic thinking.

In non-linguistic non-public thinking we are capable of learning the most central lessons of experience; but precisely with such an aim in mind, it may make good sense to change some features of the former experience. Especially if an experience connected with painful and frightening emotions (bodily pains, humiliation etc.), or with strong defensive reactions like fear, disgust etc., then it can be of decisive importance to change particular elements in order to be able to make use of this experience. In the case of a mere repetition of the critical situation, we might remain completely paralyzed with fear or disgust. By displacing particular elements of experience, we preserve our ability to act effectively without unnecessary hindrance.

All of these modifications and transformations are not to be interpreted as lies, because non-linguistic thinking is not happening in a communicative framework. Moreover, the slight modifications in non-linguistic thinking are not even cases of self-deception because the sense of a self-deception carries a social and communicative sense. Understanding some displacements of contents as a self-deception asks for the contribution of other persons who could show me that my memory is not fully accurate but changed and improved.[2]

To give some examples: I do not have to keep in mind the painful memory of rape so as to hold on to the essential lesson I have learned from this experience, which enables me to avoid such an event with some security. Similarly, if a robber or a dangerous animal has threatened my life, I do not need to memorize the situation in its full thrilling anxiety. It is enough to remember that „something like this“ once has happened to „other persons“ to avoid places, situations and persons that entail particular dangers (and this is already possible in the scenic mode of non-linguistic thinking). This might be interpreted as a first partial step to what we call generalization on the conceptual level.

To hold on to the essential lesson of experience, I may even forget that it was I who suffered the unbearable humiliation and violation. Even more, it is helpful to forget the seemingly central elements of my former experience so as to make successful use of it without being paralyzed by anxiety. The non-linguistic mode of thinking, by introducing slight modifications of my experience, enables me to act without such hindrances.

In regard to the essential lessons of experience, there is always a set of equivalent memories (characteristic scenes). We may regard different characteristic scenes as „equivalent“ if they portray the central lesson of experience and also enable us to use this experience in future situations without anxiety. We may therefore paradoxically say that we must be able to forget parts of our experience to become able to hold on to and make further use of the central lessons of our experiences.[3]

One great advantage of the non-linguistic mode of thinking is to start the theoretical understanding of neurotic displacement by analyzing normal and psychologically healthy persons. The special characteristics of non-linguistic modes of thinking can be analyzed phenomenologically through self-observation and reflection. Analysis of non-linguistic thinking in the context of everyday situations enables us to understand why and how neurotic displacement, inversion, denying etc. is possible, and why it makes sense in the broader context of evolutionary functions. Thus the general strategy of my approach is a kind of „approximation“ of the phenomenon of neurotic displacement from the functioning of non-linguistic thinking in normal persons. But besides this positive function, non-linguistic thinking also offers negative possibilities. The special mode of non-linguistic thinking also enables us to go beyond the limits that are determined by its function to preserve experience and make it usable in the future. This is the case of serious psychological diseases that are based on the function of neurotic displacement.

In the first part of my presentation, (1) I will discuss the philosophical difficulties in understanding our enigmatic ability for neurotic displacement, denying, inversion etc. In the second part, (2) I will delineate the central characteristics of non-linguistic thinking and present some arguments for the existence of this kind of thinking in humans. Finally, in the third part, (3) I will try to solve some of the puzzles of psychoanalytical theory with the help of the concept of non-linguistic thinking.

1 The Enigmas of Neurotic Displacement (Verschiebung)

I am not an expert in psychoanalytical theory, therefore it may happen that I will present some of its parts in a too simplified way. But let me start with the philosophical difficulties: There are some logical rules of thinking that we believe to be universally valid, but these rules are obviously violated by neurotic displacement, denying, inversion etc. For example we demand that the objects of our thinking remain identical throughout the argumentation, that subjects and objects of actions remain the same (and also the direction of the activities), that a proposition keeps the same truth-value through the whole argumentation etc. Nearly all of these rules are broken by neurotic displacement. Denying negates what has in fact happened. Neurotic displacement assigns an action or a property to another person or object: It wasn‘t I who did the deed but this other person. Inversion reverses the direction of an action: it wasn't I who was treated badly, but rather, I was the one who treated him badly, etc.

Here we tend to ask: Is this already a kind of lying, of false reality? Is it a kind of self-deception? But if this is the case, then we might also ask who possibly benefits from this deception. Paradoxically, two actors appear with the same name: I the deceiver and I the deceived. And if this is in fact a case of self-deception, then we have to ask whether such an action is possible at all in reasonable thinking. Is it not a kind of wrong thinking? Is it already a malfunction in thinking? What point of view could make a good sense of such a distortion?

If one only take into account the standards of discursive logic, one notices that in neurotic displacement the principle of identity is broken. This happens in nearly all the cases of neurotic displacement. Moreover, denying presents a violation of the principle of contradiction: one claims that A is true and one also believes in not-A. If one gives absolute privilege to the logical point of view, one has to interpret neurotic displacement as a malfunction of the mind. Furthermore, one has to make rules to forbid a process, which in fact is regular, without the slightest indisposition. But the whole of this problematic constellation lets us suspect that neurotic displacement has a good sense from a certain point of view, even though we do not have the right access. Situations like this often call for a consideration in terms of evolutionary function analysis. Let us see whether this is possible.

Therefore, I would like to start with the following question: Why is it so easy for consciousness to think by seriously violating the principles of logic? In my opinion, we can only find a solution for this puzzle if we realize that the „logic" we take as a standard is by no means basic and obligatory to all types of thinking. It is obligatory only to propositional thinking that is useful for public communication. „Beneath" this layer of linguistic thinking, there is another powerful layer of non-linguistic thinking, which follows completely different rules. To address the puzzles of neurotic displacement, it may be helpful to take into account this non-linguistic type of thinking and its rules.

2 Non-linguistic Thinking

To make my thesis of non-linguistic thinking clearer, I will first try to establish the concept of a „symbolic system of representation". This expression denotes a general concept, and our language is only one single case of it. Nevertheless, this general idea is best exemplified by language: A system of representation enables us to form an idea of a state of affairs or of an event without having a corresponding intuition of them. We usually do this with the help of linguistic expressions. However, language is only one system of representation, and we can conceive of other (non-linguistic) systems of representation.

In my view, Husserl's phenomenology offers a refined theory of meaning and this theory leaves open the possibility of non-linguistic systems of representation. Here I will not discuss this item extensively but only delineate the argument.[4] There are also arguments based on human evolution, which suggest that humans must necessarily have non-linguistic systems of representation. However, arguments for the possibility and necessity of non-linguistic thinking remain not fully convincing if they do not entail detailed intuitive evidence that humans are in fact using such non-linguistic systems.

I will thus initiate a phenomenological analysis of the non-linguistic systems functioning in us. It is especially fruitful to investigate the scenic mode of day-dreaming as a central form of non-linguistic mode of thinking. This analysis gives evidence that a non-linguistic system of representation is still functioning in our own consciousness.

Human thinking can use conceptual language. There are some very useful phenomenological descriptions of how we think with the help of concepts. Most basic in this regard is the insight into the function of acts that are dedicated to give intuitive evidence of states of affairs. Husserl names them categorial acts. Other acts, that are dedicated to connect this intuition with elements of a representational system, for example language, are called by Husserl meaning-bestowing (bedeutunggebende) acts. In the complex interplay of meaning-bestowing and intuitive acts that provide the evidence for categorial objects, the most important component is that of adjusting the expression to the intuition and not the other way around.[5]

We are able to interpret spoken language in terms of words and sentences that points to the intuition usually connected with the sentence. We thus can discover the intuition at which words and judgments aim. This shows that language and the intuition of states of affairs are not inseparable. Language is a certain system of representation of the originally intuited states of affairs. But this originary intuition, when compared with linguistic representation, turns out to be more basic, originary and independent. With the help of language we are able to conceive the same state of affair that we have had intuitively before, and this is possible even in the absence of intuition. This is, generally speaking, the central function of a system of representation.

But as we realize the difference between words and intuitions of the state of affairs, sometimes we even realize the difficulty of adjusting linguistic judgments to the intuitive evidence (and also vice versa of judgments understood to their corresponding intuition). This gives us a clear hint that spoken language is only one of several possible systems of representation for cognitive contents operative within our thinking. We can find arguments for this in Husserl's theory of meaning.[6]

There is a broadly spread opinion that thinking is closely bound with language. In this connection, I would like to show that Husserl's analyses of the relation between intuitive knowledge (Husserl's *kategoriale Anschauung*) and the connected act of meaning-bestowing (and eventually also the linguistic expression based on this meaning-bestowing) leaves room for alternative conceptions. There can be meaning-bestowing acts, which do not employ language as a medium of expression. In such cases, I will speak of non-linguistic systems of representation.

Husserl conceives of the cognitive act as an independent intuitive act. My argument rests on Husserl's insight that while it is true that the meaning-bestowing acts are usually closely connected to the act of categorial intuition, the meaning-bestowing acts are not a necessary element of thinking and cognition, understood as independent intuition. Thus there remains a difference between categorial intuition and meaning-bestowing acts[7] which use, for example, language. This difference allows one to perform the meaning-bestowing acts in other mediums of expression.

In Husserl's theory of knowledge, categorial intuition is conceived as an intuitive source. Categorial intuition is a fulfilled intention directed at states of affairs or relations; it is an insight into the event's causal effects, or of the object's value and use. This kind of intuitive intention of cognitive contents, which entails the ability to intend a cognitive content as well as to have the same content intuitively, determines the broadest sense of thinking which I will use from now on.

In normal cases, a categorial intuition is always already accompanied with a meaning-bestowing act and mostly also with an act of expression. Both are often closely connected, one could even say "melted together". But this statistically normal connection of categorial intuition with a meaning-bestowing act does not imply any kind of necessity. Moreover, it is not necessary that language should be the expressive medium used in meaning-bestowing acts. Just as we may use another language (i.e. not our mother tongue) for this function, so we may also use another symbolic medium.

Cognition's true symbolic expression should only allow one to *think* the same insight again; this repeated cognition can either take place in solitary thinking or, as happens in the case of public communication, it can be also thought by another person. This quite general description of a principal function cannot determine whether language is the only possible symbolic medium. We thereby realize clearly the basic, primary and independent performance of categorial intuition. Thus the question which symbolic medium is used to fulfill this demand is not that important.

Categorial intuition can be expressed in a variety of ways. I will name its three basic types: (1) Language and codified gesture languages (ASL, ...) enable public communication and for thinking; (2) Non-codified gestures together with mimics and pantomime enable public communication without language; (3) Scenic phantasma of past and future events are suitable for their representation in solitary thinking even though they cannot be used for public communication. Such scenic phantasma are exemplified not only by nightly dreams but also by daydreams.

The connection of language and thinking is generally not as narrow and firm as we tend to believe. We express our insights in different languages; we can think in a language that is not our mother tongue. Most of us are familiar with the following experience: after spending some days in a foreign country where a foreign language is spoken which is nonetheless known well by us, our thinking takes on the form of this other language. It becomes clear in this easy change of symbolic language that the level of language is very close to the surface of the whole phenomenon of thinking and expression. The most basic level is the special form of cognitive intuition (categorial intuition).

Regarding the loose connection between thinking about cognitive contents and language, we might ask ourselves: Is categorial intuition indeed to such an extent primary and independent that there is no real use for a symbolic medium to keep the information and to enable the hypothetical manipulation of this intuitive cognition? This question should be answered negatively. We can indeed hold on to the intuition of state of affairs only for a short time. After this we need a symbolic medium to hold on to the meaning of our cognition. The intuition gets thereby to be transformed into a firm conviction (which also obtains a symbolic form) that this state of affairs is the case. This is even more evident in regard to the hypothetical manipulation of future states of affairs that we embark upon while considering our options.

Thus the symbolic carrier of a conviction is the presupposition for the three essential performances of thinking: (1) the ability to awaken and to retain in mind the same object of cognition; (2) the ability to engender other cognitions from this one; (3) the ability to manipulate our future possibilities (and also different hypotheses concerning the course of history in the past). These central performances allow me to manipulate the possible future of an object or event in different situations, ponder possible consequences, obstacles and solutions of problems. Essentially, thinking is an active treatment of the contents of our cognition.

If we understand thinking as the ability to awaken, hold onto and manipulate the contents of cognition even in the absence of the intuition of the states of affairs, then we cannot deny that thinking must have a medium of symbolic representation. The latter, however, need not be language. Yet language gives us a hint about the most important feature of such a system of symbolic representation: I must be able to produce the material carriers of symbols at any time. For example, I must be able to produce spoken or written words at any time either in public speech or in inner speech. But in regard to solitary thinking in a phantasmatic mode the same is true for phantasmatic scenes. I am able to "think" in this broadest sense only if the symbolic carrier is present all the time. This carrier must achieve its meaning in a meaning-bestowing act based on the intuitive cognition (categorial intuition). This is true for language as for all other non-linguistic systems of representation. In this regard, the use of non-linguistic symbols follows the pattern of Husserl's theory of meaning.

Thus we may conclude what we already know: Language is a usable carrier of cognitive meaning, it makes thinking and public communication possible because I can speak audibly any time. In regard to inner thinking, I can let my inner voice function as the carrier of thinking. But our conclusion can go also beyond this trivial insight because now I know at least one general feature of symbolic systems useful for thinking: I must be able to produce the carrier of symbols at any time – either in inner – or in outer-sensibility. Thus there can also occur internal carriers of meaning that enable thinking but do not enable public communication. Moreover, there may be also carriers of symbols that enable both, such as language, gestures and pantomime. But it is obvious that language need not be the carrier in all these cases;

alternatives are always present. All of the above allows us to see the possibility of a non-linguistic system of representation.

Now I would like to take a completely other view on the question of non-linguistic thinking, taking into account some arguments from evolutionary theory. In my view, these arguments allow one to conclude that there must necessarily be non-linguistic systems of representation in humans. The argument for this thesis centers on a problem of human evolution. A gap in our understanding of human evolution stems from the insight that spoken language and concepts cannot be older than 120–150,000 years. The decisive finding is that up to now there are no older findings of the human tongue-bone (Zungenbein), i.e. the bone that enables refined phonetic languages and cannot be found in primates and older anthropoid species living before modern humans (*homo sapiens sapiens*).

On the other hand, we know from the analysis of the lifestyle of early hominids that there must have been powerful mental means for the organization of cooperation 2, 5–1, 8 million years ago. The basis for this conclusion is the knowledge that *homo erectus* settled the whole world at this time. Settling regions like deserts, tundra or northern Scandinavia presupposes foresighted thinking, disciplined and flexible cooperation, social institutions and an extensive tradition of expert knowledge. All this has been possible without the use of spoken language.

We cannot avoid the conclusion that there must have been non-linguistic systems of representation used for thinking and also for public communication. An influential line of thought in modern theory of evolution suggests that it was gesture language that allowed public communication in these early hominids.[8]

Now the question arises whether these non-linguistic modes of thinking and communication are still functioning in humans today, or whether they have simply vanished with the emergence of language. If they still function in human consciousness – and this is my opinion – then we should be able to reveal this by means of phenomenological investigations. In my view, this non-linguistic system of representation of cognitive contents operates with scenic phantasma and feelings (as well as co-feelings).[9] I would now like to concentrate my analysis on this non-linguistic system of phantasmatic scenes still operative in humans. This system entails different elements centered on scenic images or "characteristic scenes" that are enriched by emotions and co-feelings of others.

The scenic phantasma may sometimes seem to be reducible to only static pictures that do not entail any kind of narrative or idea of the self. Consider in this regard the case of someone just grinning at me or looking sorrowful. But scenic phantasma are not to be thought of in terms of pictures through which objects are mediated; they are more like scenes that appear in the same way as though the person was really looking at me. Thus I am also somehow there, right in this scene, but as the spectator who is incorporated in a special perspective. Scenic phantasma are not static: nearly all of them have a narrative element, even though this element may sometimes be hidden in a move of emotions or other dimensions of the scene that do not affect the visual dimension. For example, I begin a particular activity with self-confident optimism, yet I notice a skeptical look of a close friend that says: this is no good way to act, think it over.

Co-performing his emotional valuing, I overwrite and correct the positive view of my inconsiderate plans.

But scenic phantasma are not the only powerful non-linguistic systems we are using. A brief glance at gestures will confirm this. Our ability to communicate with gestures and pantomime is broadly underestimated. Let me give you an example: Imagine that you are in a foreign country and you cannot speak the local language but you have to go to the airport. Imagine you meet a taxi driver whom you need to inform about your urgent wish, but without language: In a situation like this one, we immediately start communicating our wishes with the help of gestures, onomatopoetic means and pantomime. This behavior is very informative about our non-linguistic systems of representation. We start without further thinking and we are certain about our attempt to communicate in this way. This reveals that this non-linguistic mode of communication is constantly alive even when we use language, for we do not have to wonder about the "how" of this gestic-pantomimic communication. We do not wonder whether it may work, we simply start with it. We are behaving as if we have tacitly done this kind of communication all the time. This is only an example of public communication without language.

Now I would like to concentrate on the central and most important non-linguistic system of representation using scenic phantasma: We are using scenic phantasma as expressions of our wishes and fears in our daydreams and thus they function as representations of cognitive contents. It is always a state of affair that we wish for or are in fear of. But we do not simply express our preferences and our views of the state of affairs by these means. It turns out that daydreams are also a kind of action on this problem, a mental action.

At first sight we might object that in our daydreams we are completely free to imagine whatever we like. Daydreams seem not to be bound to reality and the problems of reality. But if we remain truthful to our own experience of daydreaming, we have to confess that in fact we are not completely free in the formation of our daydreams. We know that we are somehow bound if we continuously repeat the humiliating scene of an emotional defeat in everyday interactions. We might try to make a distinction between wish-daydreams and fear-daydreams (or daydreams of humiliations) and we might suppose that at least in the daydreams that form our wishful hopes into phantasmatic scenes we are free. And in opposite to this, we are only bound in daydreams expressing our fears. But both are not true, both kinds of daydreams may turn out to be bound, because daydreams are designed to solve lasting, urging problems and find ways to realize lasting, essential wishes. And as these wishes, impulses and motives last, the same themes impose themselves on me in daydreaming in constantly different modifications.

Perhaps it is this felt difference (feeling urged – feeling free to perform the fantasies) that makes the difference in the quality of the contribution of our non-linguistic thinking to problem solving. In the aftermath of humiliation, it may be helpful for a moment to imagine freely beating up the one who humiliated me. Through such self-modifying imagination, I may find out about a clever active variation of my future action that evades the problems caused by my former actions: Perhaps I should change my habit of speeding or of driving provocatively slow on highways to avoid such consequences. Thus in most of our daydreams we are not in a fantasy-world, but in the real world pondering our possibilities and the probable outcome of different behavior of myself and others.

This alternative is also to be found in Freud, who often interprets wakeful fantasies as a kind of flight from reality, as a regressive way of satisfying insatiable wishes or as a phantasmatic comprehension (compensation) of humiliating experiences by free formation of my fantasies of being mighty. But in Freud there is also a distinct recognition of scenic fantasies as a forceful means of reshaping and imaginatively modifying urgent wishes while facing unavoidable obstacles.[10]

In my view, in daydreams, no matter whether they reflect humiliation, fear or fun, we are playing out possible solutions to a problem, mentally testing our options, their usefulness for a solution and their respective consequences. This life of scenic phantasma constitutes an important part of our conscious life, no matter how rarely we reflect on this fact. Here are a few every-day examples known to everyone: Worries about urgent challenges or uncertainties that makes us sleepless at night. There are many fantasies of having success. I would like to mention also empirical-psychological research that suggests that most grown up males think of sex every few minutes, and the mode of this thinking is definitely not conceptual.[11] In these scenic episodes of our conscious life, linguistic expressions emerge in the background in favor of phantasmatic elements.[12] I am not denying that we can also think about our wishes and problems by means of language and that in daydreams both are often merged, but what I want to emphasize is that we also use non-linguistic systems of representation.

Feelings constitute an important element of the non-linguistic phantasmatic system of representations. I think that we cannot interpret emotions as an independent system of representation because we always have to presuppose another kind of representation in which we have in mind things or (possible) events that are the object of feelings. Emotions can easily grant the most important request for a system of representation for we can have them in an actual situation and we can "produce" them (but mostly not arbitrarily) also in the absence of the intuitive situation, only by imagining it. The feeling of fury is moving me violently in a certain situation but also in mere thinking of the same situation later on. In both cases the feeling "tells" me something about the value of the event; it is a part of my inner "expression" that has a certain meaning. In thinking about a nice experience the pleasant feeling "means" the desirable quality of the event.[13]

Thus daydreams together with emotions perform a consistent representation of our wishes and fears. They mirror our personal order of significance between the two poles of events, viz., those that should never happen and those that should happen at any costs. They do not ask for a refined psychoanalytical hermeneutics – at least at the first glance. Daydreams additionally respect the identity of objects, the causality of events and their order in time, while nightly dreams do not respect this. Also from this point of view daydreams can be accepted as a thinking activity with past, present and future reality.

The framework of our order of relevance in possible events makes us also understand better why special daydreams are repeatedly experienced as long as the urgent needs and fears remain the same and unaltered. But we have to be attentive to small modifications in these repetitions that represent our possible options in real action.[14]

To return to my first example: Had I been pressed hard by an impertinent and aggressive bully and had I given way to his demands due to the situation and circumstances, this annoying situation would furiously reemerge in my daydreams many times. This reappearance would also engender the right solution to get rid of his aggressive demands: This should have been the right reaction; had I done this, it would have stopped him! Nevertheless, this insight is irreal and it cannot change the past, but it is a kind of action on reality that enables me in a future similar situation, if it were to recur, to act appropriately and to resist the unjust demands.[15] Thus the result of my thinking activity in daydreaming may appear as an advantageous fake memory (or as an arbitrary fantasy helping me in depressed moments, but not in reality), yet regarding its function, it appears like a plan for future action in similar circumstances.

Thus the special scenic mode of daydreams allows for an interpretation of daydreaming as an old mode of thinking. If I am worried in the mode of daydreaming then things and persons are occurring in scenic representation and language shifts into the background. The content of my worries is represented in scenic phantasma, but in every repetition with small modifications. And in these modifications we sometimes realize successful solutions to our problems: Winning in a lottery will solve in an easy way the pressing financial concerns; working hard or suffering for some time from some privations will work as well; driving my youngest daughter to the party and picking her up in the evening will diminish my worries that keep me sleepless, etc. This shows clearly the function of the daydreaming as a non-linguistic mode of thinking that can, so to speak, lead all problems in thoughts towards their possible solution.

I am not denying that in turning back from our inner life of scenic phantasma to other members of our group we will immediately change to a language-mode of communication, but this shift will only expresses what was already found with scenic means before. Also, language-based information is often influential on, for example, my sorrowful daydreaming concerning new dangers that my children face, etc.

From a very general point of view, there is only a limited set of themes that human as well as non-human primates living in groups have to be able to think about: (1) Objects, their past, present and future properties, states and use (for example as a tool), as well as their value in my personal estimation and their value in the view of the community, i.e. the cultural value. (2) Events in present, past and future, their probable effects and felt value. (3) Other persons with their sensings, feelings, convictions, valuing and their practical intentions related to me and other members of the group. I will leave it to you to find examples for the first two themes. I will directly turn to the last group of intentions of other persons.

At first glance, it seems difficult to imagine a scenic image of the character of a person and of his or her probable behavior towards me, especially within complex constellations with others who are involved in the action. But scenic phantasma offers a simple solution to this apparent difficulty. In remembering a brutal former classmate, I see his face looking at me with evil eyes, with clenched fists, and ready to give me a beating. But this "image" is not simply an image of him; it is a characteristic scene within which I am present, still in pain from his beating and in fear of further beatings. This scene presents central aspects both of his character and of his future behavior.

But scenic presentation of the attitude and the behavior of a person need not be so one-dimensional as in the case mentioned, since normally there are multiple facets of the character of other persons that we are able to present. Thus the question arises: How can I think a multitude of (changing) attitudes in a scenic mode? Think of a colleague with whom you work together successfully in most cases, but who occasionally appears with an air of high-nose arrogance. Both "faces", i.e. both aspects of his character, may be represented in scenic phantasma, one after the other, or, even, as mixed in a changing way, which results in an uncertain base for your plan-making. The character of possibility and uncertainty is thus present in the changing and merging faces of your colleague. We might interpret this changing image as a non-linguistic form of the logical „or".[16] His attitude towards other persons and other situations may be represented in a similar way since you can easily extend the characteristic scenes.

The value and the use of objects can change, which is also reflected in the characteristic scene. For instance, if I own a car that usually breaks down and thus has to be towed off and repaired, the characteristic scene within which I am positively excited about my car is modified, and converted to one that is negative. The emotional aspects of this bad experience are especially mirrored in the characteristic scene: I no longer imagine the car with the joyful expectation of reliable use, but with the cheerless expectation of future harm, expense, and inconvenience. In this way, the two sorts of characteristic scenes – i.e., the characteristic scene that involves other subjects and the characteristic scene that involves objects or events – are analogous, insofar as both scenic presentations will change on the basis of the underlying scenic phantasma that give them their ground.

There are also means of presenting the possible assessment of esteemed members of the group on my planned actions. If I am thinking about a risky plan of mine that may also endanger the interests of others, I may suddenly see the sympathetic but sorrowful faces of close friends, looking at me, expressing something like "your plans will probably cause us great sorrow because they will endanger your recognition within the community."

Now we have discussed scenic phantasma in daydreams as a special system of representation for cognitive contents, characterizing this process as an "old mode of thinking" employed by humans (and probably also by primates).

As a consequence of our analyses, the significance of language for human thinking is delimited in clear way. Language is by far not the only possible means of thinking and, moreover, it is not the only system of representation operative in the human consciousness. It is probable that the real basic performance of cognition and our conception of reality is based on the more simple phantasmatic systems of representation that are still operative in our mind.

Thus non-linguistic thinking is by far not a peripheric performance of our consciousness but a very central achievement. In my view, the most essential performances of thinking are already done on a non-linguistic level. One consequence of this theory is a transformation it introduces into our estimation of language that shows a limitation regarding the meaning of linguistic thinking: It now seems to be the case that language is a relatively superficial phenomenon which only transforms insights we have already gained on a deeper level into another system of representation.

3 Forget to Remember

Up to now I have only discussed examples of non-linguistic thinking which, despite the slight modifications they introduce, still hold on the identity of the most important agents such as acting and suffering persons and central objects. In so far this thinking remains more or less truthful to its objects. Now I will go beyond this limitation and take into account cases in which this borderline is crossed, i.e. cases such as neurotic shifting, where there is a change of persons or an inversion of the direction of activity. This is in principle possible because non-linguistic, solitary thinking does not have to respect the rules of communicative actions. We already know that it does not preserve the exact circumstances but now we learn that it must not even preserve the identity or the sense of activity. The decisive function of non-linguistic thinking is to preserve the most important lessons of my experience and enable a further effective use of it.

This means that the modification of an experience in a characteristic scene can be quite drastic because all kinds of vindicating, pain- and anxiety-avoiding transformations are possible. But all of this makes sense because these transformations enable me to take into consideration the central lesson of my former experience in the next and perhaps similar situation, without being paralyzed by pain or invincible anxiety. Thus under the point of view of preservation of the essential lesson of experience, even a change in the acting person is not dysfunctional or troublesome. Not even the denial of my own experience had to be an obstacle of my use of experience, as long as I keep the lesson of my experience in the very general mode of „sometimes something like this happen to other persons".

If we still want to speak of a modification of the same experience or the identical core of experience (even if semantically and grammatically it is something different), we have to choose a special point of view that asks for closer explanation. Only the point of view of the effective pragmatic influence on my actions[17] enables me to regard different insights like „my life was threatened, because I stayed in a dangerous area of the city after midnight" and the insight „someone was attacked in this area after midnight" to be equivalent. In both cases of knowledge, I would be extremely cautious to enter this area at night. A slight feeling of anxiety starts to rise when I am only thinking of this area of the city. If I had to go there, I would only feel well in a forceful group of other persons.

But even the identity of influence on my further actions does not characterize the full sense of identity we have to aim at: It is the evolutionary point of view of function that allows one to see the identity of the result of the thinking modification of my experience. This decisive function of keeping the central lesson of experience in a useful form allows for neurotic displacement. Even if acting persons and circumstances are changed in a drastic way, the central lesson of experience may be preserved.

I have left to discuss two possible objections. The first concerns the inversion, because it is not from the start obvious why a change of the sense of activity may conserve the central lesson of experience and make it applicable. The second objection concerns what I would like to call the „exceeding neurotic displacement". This should denote a neurotic displacement that changes the situation, the acting persons and actions themselves in such a far-reaching way that the original lesson of the experience is no longer preserved. For example, think of Freud's analysis of the „kleiner Hans" where the anxiety caused by the casual thread with castration by the mother is transferred to the horse.

To start with inversion, is this still a modification that preserves the lesson of experience? I think one must answer with a "yes," but to gain this insight we have to take into consideration the special character of human constitution. Man is at the same time an effective hunter and a possible victim of violence of other hunters. Therefore, the lesson of a past experience must be helpful for violent hunters and for possible victims striving to escape at the same time. Even if the original experience violently endangered my life, yet I managed to get away alive as an anxious victim, a man as a hunter (beast of prey) needs to modify this lesson of experience so as to see that he is the merciless hunter who tries to trap and hurt his victim. For this reason, inversion may also count for a modification that preserves the central lesson of experience. From the point of view of evolutionary function, it makes perfect sense that I should not only keep this experience from the perspective of the victim but also enable myself to become an effective hunter. Thus, if I plan for an attack, I know that it would be done best in that dangerous area in the dark and it would be even better for me to be much stronger than the victim. If I were paralyzed with fear when I remember the former dangerous and humiliating experience in its passive original form, then I would face an obstacle for the effective use of my experiences.

Up to now we have discussed displacement, denying, inversion, etc. as the basic tools of non-linguistic thinking. As far as we know, any further combination and iteration of these modifying tools is possible. Yet where are the precise limits of modification, which cannot be stepped over if one is to retain the lesson of experience? We certainly know that there are such limits. This problem does not yet arise when the original experience is no longer identifiable semantically; as we saw, even in such cases the central lesson of experience may still be preserved, usable and even recognizable by reflection. But this is not the case in neurotic displacement that does not lead to the change of behavior, which makes good sense in regard to the central lesson of experience.

How can we understand the fact that neurotic displacement often transcends this limit of modifications, characterized by preservation of the central lesson of experience? Many neurotic displacements drift away in a completely different, pathological direction and cannot preserve the change of behavior that makes sense from the functional point of view, that may even lead to a pathological blocking of my activities. Is there no natural limit for the iteration of neurotic displacement? I do not think so.

The tools of neurotic displacement are used iteratively until the scenic phantasma is no longer frightening, humiliating, disgusting etc. These emotions are the restless motor of shifting contents in the non-linguistic mode. Think of Freud's description of the "kleine Hans" who displaces the mother's more or less casual threatening with castration onto the horses on the street, which he fears to be bitten by.[18] There is no real protection against such border-crossing displacements. And this process seems to stop only when the subject feels able to go along with the emotional threatenings still connected with the modification. Thus the "limit" is individually determined and depends on the "strength" of the subject and his tolerance in face of emotional threatenings.

I have concentrated my analysis of the grounds of the possibility of neurotic displacement on the basis of non-linguistic thinking in the phantasmatic mode. But this older non-linguistic system of representation for cognitive and volitive contents in humans is by no means completely independent from language. Both systems are representations of the matters of fact, fears and wishes in concern of the world of our experience, and both ultimately rest on our ability to have states of affairs in an intuitive form (categorial intuition). Thus we do not really have a problem of translating one system into the other but a well established relation between each of the systems of representation and its basis in intuitive givenness of cognitive and volitive contents. And this relation runs *there* as well as *back* for both systems. Therefore, the way of translation runs via the intuitive basis more or less without difficulties. And both systems also allow for empty intentions, i.e. an idea that has not yet an adequate intuitive mode.

Thus there is not only the possibility to speak about something that we have worked through in non-linguistic thinking but also the opposite possibility. And in language we are often confronted with words that signify states of affairs and relations that we in principle cannot have intuitively. Think, for example, about relevant states of affairs that relate to events before my birth. If a child hears about "sexual act", "adopting" or "illegitimate child," he or she faces the challenge to somehow imagine the contents in question.[19]

Let me conclude: We can discuss neurotic displacement, denying, inversion, condensing etc. from the point of view of a non-linguistic solitary thinking. This thinking preserves the central lessons of experience (and their usability) even in those modes in which the experience itself is no longer identifiable. For non-linguistic thinking not all the norms of public communication are valid. Thus non-linguistic thinking is not in the first line oriented to objective truth that is valid for all. It is more bound by its evolutionary function and thus by the law to preserve the central lesson of experience in a form that has effective influence on my further behavior.

We may thus understand the different forms of neurotic displacement, denying, inversion, transfer etc. as a kind of toolbox of non-linguistic thinking which has to deal with experiences that are emotionally highly threatening. In spite of this, an acting creature such as a human being must be able to preserve the most important lessons even from dangerous experiences. In the slow process of modification that is characteristic of non-linguistic phantasmatic thinking, we have an appropriate means to reach useful and applicable scenes, which can effectively guide our further actions. Therefore, the toolbox of neurotic displacement is part of the complete ability to preserve the lesson of experience in the non-linguistic form of phantasmatic thinking, and all of the single tools have a good sense in the framework of this function. But this does not form a limiting function, which would hinder displacement that goes beyond this sense. Displacement continues until fear and pain connected with the formation of the characteristic scene are tolerable for the person. It might even happen that the good pragmatic sense of this modification in non-linguistic thinking is overstepped.

The only limitation of this modification is the strength and stability of the person and his or her tolerance of fear and other emotional threats. If a traumatic experience – even in a drastic modification – remains connected with too much emotional threat, everything depends on the ability of the individual person to tolerate this.[20] Thus even if the danger of pathological neurotic displacement remains, the basic ability of displacement in all its modifications makes perfect sense in the framework of non-linguistic thinking that should be able to preserve the central lesson of experience in persons without linguistic means.

Notes

1. This starting point arises in the framework of a broad analysis of the central functions of phantasy in our consciousness. As a consequence of this approach, there lies an extension of the concept of thinking to non-linguistic thinking. Cf. D. Lohmar, *Phänomenologie der schwachen Phantasie* (Dordrecht/Heidelberg, 2008). I would like to thank Dr. Saulius Geniusas for his kind help with the English text.
2. This also means that we do not have to solve the enigma of a subject who decides to deceive himself and may even be successful in this action.
3. The concept of non-linguistic thinking is obviously also of some use to understand thinking in animals. Cf. D. Lohmar, "How Do Primates Think? Phenomenological Analyses of a Non-language System of Representation in Higher Primates and Humans," in *Husserl and the Non-human Animal,* ed. Christian Lotz and Corinne Painter, 57–74 (Dordrecht: Springer, 2008). The decisive point in my analysis is that humans are using language and the older non-linguistic mode of thinking. And this is the ground of our possibility to manipulate the characteristic scene, and somehow also to manipulate our memories but in doing this to keep the central lessons of our experiences.
4. I have argued more explicitly for such a view in: "Denken ohne Sprache", in *Meaning and Language: Phenomenological Perspectives,* ed. F. Mattens, 169–194 (Dordrecht: Springer, 2008).
5. For Husserl's theory of meaning cf. his 1. and 6. Logical Investigation in Hua XIX/1 and Hua XIX/2 and D. Lohmar, "Husserl's Concept of Categorical Intuition," in *Hundred Years of Phenomenology,* eds. D. Zahavi, F. Stjernfelt, 125–145 (Dordrecht: Kluwer, 2002).
6. Cf. D. Lohmar, "Denken ohne Sprache", in *Meaning and Language: Phenomenological Perspectives,* ed. F. Mattens, 169–194 (Dordrecht: Springer, 2008).
7. Thus the relation of categorial intuition and meaning-bestowing acts for Husserl is characterized by a difference and a striving: language should be a true and faithful expression of categorial

intuition („treuer Ausdruck", Hua XIX/1, 313 u.). But this aim is not easy to reach. Husserl coins a special concept of truth for exactly this trueness-relation between expression and categorial intuition: rightness („Richtigkeit"). This incorporates a one-way striving: The expression should become appropriate to the intuitively given cognition, i.e. this intuition is the primary and self-standing guiding principle for my striving to rightness, cf. Hua XVII, § 46.

8. Cf. M.C. Corballis, "The Gestural Origins of Language," in *American Scientist Vol. 87,* 138–145 (2/1999). This thesis was discussed in the seventeenth century by Condillac and recently by Gorden W. Hewes. Recently Michael Tomasello has taken up this argument in *Origins of Human Communication* (Cambridge: MIT Press, 2008).
9. There is another central question in this regard: How can we conceive of the interplay of different systems of representation in one and the same subject? The thesis that in human consciousness there are two different but closely related processes, which have the same mental performance has been posed already in 1975 by P. C. Wason and J. St. B. T. Evans. Cf. the contributions of P. C. Wason and J. St. B. T. Evans, "Dual Processes in Reasoning?," in *Cognition 3*, 141–154 (1975), Johnathan St. B. T. Evans: *The Psychology of deductive Reasoning*, Chap. 12 (London: Routledge & Kegan Paul, 1982); Jonathan St. B. T. Evans, "In Two Minds: Dual-Process Accounts of Reasoning," in *Trends in Cognitive Science,* vol. 7 (2003), 454–459. A good overview about the different dual-process theories offer Keith E. Stanovich and Richard F. West, "Individual Differences in Reasoning: Implications for the Rationality Debate?," in *Behavioral and Brain Sciences,* 22(5) (2000), 645–726, Ch. 6. The first process is a *low level-system*, that is *phylogentically old; relatively simply structured* and *less trouble-prone*. It enables quick perceptions and insights, thus it also enables quick and self-assured acting. This *low level-system* is not language based and we have it in common with most of higher organized animals, whereas the *high-level*-system rests on the use of language and concepts. Therefore the *high-level*-system is *relatively slow* because it makes use of *complex rules* and *dependencies*. With the help of this conceptual system we are able to constitute new abstract objects and higher level concepts. But most of our cognitive, emotional and volition performances we are also able to perform in the *low-level-system* which we share with many higher animals.
10. Cf. for example the impressive analysis of the three phases modifying the characteristic scene in: „Ein Kind wird geschlagen", (S. Freud, *Gesammelte Werke*. Bd. XII, 197–226). Cf. also the elucidating Discussion of this text by R. Bernet in this volume (R. Bernet, *Phantasieren und Phantasma bei Husserl und Freud*, part 2.3).
11. Cf. P. Cameron and H. Biber, "Sexual Thought Throughout the Life Span," in: *Gerontologist* 13 (1973):, 144–147; T. Hicks and H. Leitenberg, "Sexual Fantasies About One's Partner Versus Someone Else: Gender Differences in Incidence and Frequency," in: *Journal of Sex Research* 38 (2001): 43–50.
12. This is true also for nightly dreams, cf. Donald Symons, "The Stuff That Dreams Aren't Made of: Why the Wake-State and Dream-State Sensory Experiences Differ," in: *Cognition* 47 (1993): 181–217.
13. Another aspect that can be partly be expressed by feeling is the dimension of time: fearing an event points to the future character of an event, regret to past.
14. This compulsion for repetition may perhaps mirror a limitation in the performance of the non-linguistic phantasmatic system of representation: It cannot find definite solutions and no fixation in concepts, like in language.
15. The result of this slow modification in the phantasmatic non-linguistic mode of thinking is a kind of ideal version under given conditions, but nevertheless Humans tend to communicate this result as a true description. In this way many lies of children rest on true scenic phantasma.
16. Some readers may miss a general discussion of logical functions in this non-language system of representation. These tools of thinking belong to the second group of necessary topics in the life of group-living primates: Events in present, past and future and their felt value for me (and others) and their probable following events.

17. This point of view is inspired by W. James' pragmatism.
18. Cf. S. Freud *Analyse der Phobie eines fünfjährigen Knaben [Der kleine Hans].* In: S. Freud, GW, Bd. VII, 243–377.
19. Cf. the Discussion of R. Bernet concerning this topic in Freuds „Der Familienroman der Neurotiker" in his contribution in this volume.
20. For example I may modify like this: I was attacked and humiliated in this mean part of the city. Things like holdups happen sometimes there. Violence and other worrying things may happen at dark and lonesome places.

The 'Unconscious' in Paranoid Delusional Psychosis: Phenomenology, Neuroscience, Psychoanalysis

Aaron L. Mishara

One falls so easily into the mistake of being abstract (Husserl 2005, Hua Mat VIII, 350)

Abstract In this contribution I present three overlapping approaches to the phenomenology of the unconscious (Conrad, Binswanger, Husserl). Conrad and Binswanger challenge the classical view that the delusional perception in schizophrenia is an abnormal symbolic meaning attached to an otherwise intact percept. Rather, a perceptual aspect or expressive (physiognomic) quality, detached from its visual context, becomes salient and develops into the delusion. Both believe that the delusional object involves a transformation of perceptual Gestalt-meaning on a "lower" unconscious phase of its development but they apply different methods. Conrad appeals to contemporary experimental work on microgenesis (*Aktualgenese*). Binswanger applies Husserl's "genetic" phenomenology. Conrad describes the delusional object as a pre-Gestalt (Vorgestalt), a physiognomic-expressive Gestalt-quality arrested at an earlier phase in the development of meaning which "normally" remains unconscious so far as consciousness remains intact. For Binswanger, the "delusional object" is formed from a sensory profile-aspect (Abschattung) released during the loosening of the perceptual object's internal structure (it's "internal horizon" of meaning). The phenomenological unconscious (Husserl) is two-pronged: it is both what underlies the lowermost background of any emergent Gestalt in the present, but it is also the past, the night of the unconscious, into which every

A.L. Mishara (✉)
Department of Psychiatry, Clinical Neuroscience Research Unit, Yale University School of Medicine, CMHC 339-A, 34 Park St, New Haven CT 06519, USA

Department of Psychiatry, Brain Mapping Unit, University of Cambridge, Downing Site, Cambridge CB2 3EB, UK
e-mail: Aaron.Mishara@Yale.edu

D. Lohmar and J. Brudzińska (eds.), *Founding Psychoanalysis Phenomenologically*, Phaenomenologica 199, DOI 10.1007/978-94-007-1848-7_9,

emergent saliency passes. Time-consciousness is not the passive self-affection of pre-reflective self-awareness (M. Henry) but requires the unconscious relationship between present and past selves in the ongoing movement of self-transcendence. It is this self-transcendence which is both compromised and preserved by the metaphoric meaning of the delusional object in schizophrenia. '-- End of Abstract'

1 Introduction

Founded by the mathematician turned philosopher, Edmund Husserl (1859–1938), phenomenology is the rigorous, methodical description of conscious experience. It is applied to study general mental structures in human experience and how these are disrupted in neuropsychiatric disorders. In this contribution, I examine how the phenomenological approach to paranoid delusions in schizophrenia requires reopening the question of the unconscious. For this purpose, I discuss Husserl's and the phenomenological psychiatrists, Conrad and Binswanger's different "phenomenologies of the unconscious." I begin with Conrad, whose work on the unconscious, as far as I know, has not been discussed (in English or German). I then consider Binswanger's own decision to apply Husserl's genetic phenomenology to schizophrenic delusions as, in part, a response to Conrad. I close with some remarks about how Husserl's theory of self as a hidden unity supports Binswanger's and Conrad's approaches.[1]

Prior to their work on delusions, both authors had published on the unconscious and dreaming. Conrad studied his own hypnagogic hallucinations while falling asleep. Binswanger proposed that the private universe (*idios kosmos*) of dreaming shares features with psychosis. Only by tackling the challenge of schizophrenic delusions as they experienced it in the clinic, however, the need for a more systematic, "phenomenologic" understanding of the unconscious became apparent to them. Conrad did not avail himself of the technical vocabulary of philosophic phenomenology but preferred direct description. Not unlike Binswanger's close friend, Erwin Straus, Conrad was impatient with the cumbersome phenomenologic terminology and, like Straus, made significant contributions without resorting to this terminology. It was Binswanger, however, who in his systematic, plodding manner, made use of the more technical philosophic phenomenology (i.e., Husserl's genetic phenomenology) to disclose unconscious processes in paranoid psychosis. Binswanger was one of Freud's few close friends able to maintain their friendship after breaking with classical psychoanalysis. Freud warmly teased Binswanger as being in the "clutches of a philosophic demon."[2] At different stages in his own thinking, Binswanger returned to examining how the phenomenology of lived-bodily experience could lead to a constructive revision of the psychoanalytic unconscious.[3]

Although Husserl's knowledge of psychoanalysis and depth psychology was, at best, sketchy,[4] it was Husserl – among the three discussed here – who most directly approached the psychoanalytic concepts by analyzing how "screen memories" and unconscious "repression" could take place phenomenologically.[5] Moreover –as the contributions in this volume elegantly demonstrate – Husserl's approach may be used to supply phenomenological foundation to psychoanalytic concepts such as defenses, primary process, drive, or the therapeutic relationship.[6] This contribution examines Conrad's, Binswanger's and Husserl's overlapping but differing approaches to the "genesis" of unconscious meaning.

2 Klaus Conrad's Phenomenology of the Unconscious: Delusion as Physiognomic Pre-Gestalt (Vorgestalt)

Not well-known in the English-speaking world, Klaus Conrad's (1905–1961) monograph[7] provides "one of the most impressive descriptions ever written concerning early schizophrenia."[8] Conrad also conducted introspective experiments concerning his own hypnagogic (i.e., between waking and sleep) imagery proposing that the unconscious is "a phenomenological problem."[9]

Conrad bases his phenomenologic study of delusions in beginning schizophrenia on the Gestalt-psychological concept of "holistic properties," his own phenomenological approach to treating patients as peers or collaborators in the clinical interview,[10] and his observations of anomalous conscious experiences, including the introspective study of his own hypnagogic hallucinations when falling asleep. In addition, he integrates the following approaches: the experimental procedure, microgenesis (*Aktualgenese*) which examines how perceptual meaning is formed in definable developmental stages; the English neurologist, Sir Henry Head's distinction between different forms of sensibility; and the neurologist and "founder" of psychosomatic medicine in Germany, Viktor von Weizsäcker's concepts of Gestalt-circle and the pathological *change* of the Gestalt-experience in neuropsychiatric disorders.

As director of a neurologic military hospital, Conrad (1958) interviewed and carefully documented the reports of a large sample of soldiers (n = 107) experiencing beginning schizophrenia. From these reports, Conrad developed a "stage model" (similarly to his contemporary, Binswanger) for the formation and maintenance of delusions in beginning schizophrenia. The following case exemplifies this model and how Conrad was able to integrate the above listed diverse approaches in his phenomenology of the unconscious in delusions.

Case history. Due to psychosis, a 32 year-old first-class private, Karl B., is brought to Dr. Conrad's hospital. In his interview with Conrad, the patient reports that "everything begins" one morning as his unit breaks to leave camp. When the sergeant asks him for the key to his quarters, it is suddenly clear to him that it is a ploy to "*test*" him. While departing in the bus, he notices that his comrades are behaving strangely: they knew something that he was not supposed to know. One of his comrades asks *conspicuously* if he has any bread. At mid-day, they arrive in a town to relieve units positioned there. A few in his company are charged with finding quarters for the rest of them. This is only a ruse for the few to receive instructions in how to deal with him, while he waits with the others in the motor coach. One after another, groups of men leave the coach only for the others to return. "It is clear that they are all receiving their instructions" about him. The patient is unable to explain how he sees this. He simply "sees it." He straightens the quarters assigned to him and then goes below to buy cigarettes. He proceeds through a garden, where many non-commissioned officers, the staff sergeant and some women are sitting. They are surprised to suddenly see him there and are planning that the women fabricate something with him that evening. One of the officers then drives off [...] to inform the superiors about him [...] In the pub that evening, the music, the woman selling cigarettes, the conversations have been prearranged to "test" whether he notices. Everyone is instructed and knows exactly what to do.

Due to Karl B.'s failure to follow orders, which is another "test," the staff sergeant transports him by car to the psychiatric hospital. Everything along the road, e.g., piles of stone, construction sites, sheep, is arranged to test whether he notices. While looking out the window, the staff sergeant observes whether he correctly notes all of this. Later he thinks, "There must be some kind of peculiar effect emanating from me. Other people are under my influence as if under a spell." That is, the persons who experience his gaze, i.e., his looking at them, exhibit a distorted facial expression or bodily behavior, indicating the tension they receive from him (*omnipotence*).

When he reaches Conrad's military hospital, the delusions have *progressed* from external space to the inner space of his body. The patient reports that a "wave apparatus" controls his movements from some distance through electric current. Adjusted by a dial, the current changes from having negligible control over his movements, preserving his "free will," to having complete control, at which point, the machine "inputs" commands. (Conrad 1958, my trans and paraphrasing).

While the patient does not exhibit typical paranoid delusions, he exemplifies many changes of subjective experience which belong to the phenomenological structure of delusions:

1. Prior to delusions, a prodromal *delusional mood* or *atmosphere* may last for days, months, or even years.[11] The patient experiences increasingly oppressive tension, *a feeling of non-finality* or expectation. Although the experience is varied, there is a marked change of *emotional-motivational* state, which eventually pervades the patient's entire experiential field. The patient feels excitement, "intoxicated" anticipation, but also, suspiciousness, fear, depressive inhibition, guilt, alienation, and often, a combination of these. She/he performs abrupt, senseless actions. Nothing in particular has changed in the experiential field and yet it has changed in its "physiognomic-qualitative" totality in a hitherto unexperienced manner. Something is "in the air," but one is unable to say what. Conrad calls this initial, expectational phase, *Trema* (stage fright) as the patient has the feeling that something very important is about to happen. She/he has a crucial "*role*" to play, but the role remains undefined. The patient has the feeling that the world will end (*Weltuntergangserlebnis*), or has fundamentally changed (as in Karl B.'s case). The patient's changed internal motivational-emotional state, the delusional mood, imbues the entire field of experience with a transformed "*physiognomic*" quality (i.e., a sense of potential revelation/threat accompanied by affective tension due presumably to underlying neurobiological changes).

Nevertheless, the subject does not attribute the changes to his/her own state but externalizes them to some, yet to be understood process in the world.[12] Karl B. is unable to state what in the others' behavior allowed him to see that they received instructions about him. He simply "*sees* it." When walking with a small flashlight at night in the forest, the timorous hiker is not so much concerned with what the flashlight reveals with its small beam but what remains hidden in the background, the lurking dangers.[13] When suspiciously jealous, it is not what the other person says or does, but what she/he does *not* do or say that becomes thematic. "The background acquires entirely new characteristics. Previously, we did not pay any heed to it. It lay in its nature that we had no reason to pay attention to it." "Everything which lies in the periphery to one's attention, what is behind, *not* part of one's current thematic focus [...]" (Conrad 1958, 41) becomes a potential threat, such that there is a spreading of the physiognomic quality of threat (or in K.B.'s case, artificiality) to the entire experiential field. This means that what is *not yet* noticed in a potential orienting, takes on *saliency even before we orient to it.*

2. The next stage is the emergence of the delusions themselves. Often, these bring relief to the increasing delusional mood, appearing as an *Aha-Erlebnis*, or sudden "revelation" concerning what had been perplexing during the delusional mood. Karl B. *realizes* that everything is being arranged to test him. Random occurrences have special meaning directed towards the patient. Conrad calls this stage *apophany* (revelation) in which the patient finds meanings in things that are not normally there. Here there is a "lawful" change of the patient's entire field-experience, which has its own *formal* structure. "We coined this term [apophany] on the basis of Jaspers' observation that 'the immediate, obtrusive knowing of significant meanings' occurs as revelation. This is essential to primary delusion." (Conrad 1958, 46, my trans). However, Conrad extends Jaspers' abnormal consciousness of meaning (*abnormes Bedeutungsbewusstsein*) to the formation of the Gestalt perception itself in terms of its holistic qualities (see below). He writes: "In apophaneous delusion, illusory misinterpretations or hallucinations may break in, as the feverous child who sees grimacing faces in the carpet." (Conrad 1960, 392). When perceptual processing is diminished or disrupted, we impose 'meaningful' order on the ambiguous sensations. *Apophany* indicates that "the experiential structure is transformed such that each aspect of the patient's field starts to be related back to the patient [...] Similar to a neurologic symptom, we find the same *monotonous* formal structure in each clinical case [...] Borrowing from ancient Greek, the *artificial* term *apophany* describes this process of repetitively and *monotonously* experiencing abnormal meanings in the entire surrounding experiential field, e.g., being 'observed, spoken about, the object of eavesdropping, followed by strangers."[14] Karl B. exhibits *bi-directional* delusions of causal influence: (1) he is able to *influence* other people's facial-expressions simply by looking at them; (2) his own movements are *controlled* from a distance by an electric "wave machine."

By being unable to shift "frame of reference," the delusional patient exhibits a failure to transcend (*übersteigen*) the current perspective. "We perform this exchange of perspectives *without the slightest effort* innumerable times each day" (Conrad 1958, 49, my trans). *The transition from delusional mood to the Aha-Erlebnis of the delusional revelation occurs precisely at the moment of loss of the patient's ability to transcend*: "As long as the patient is still able to achieve an exchange of reference frames or perspectives, that is, to consider the situation – even if only temporarily – with the eyes of others, [...] he is not yet ill" (Conrad 1958, 43, my trans). However, it is not possible for the clinician or patient to determine the precise moment of transition from the delusional mood to delusion. The patient "is not conscious of this loss of the ability to transcend" (Conrad 1958, 43, my trans). "The most central kernel of human experience, what distinguishes human from non-human animals, is attacked: it is the I – the ability to reflectively transcend. We thereby gain some indication of what the underlying changes of neural substrate must be. It must be a 'functional change' (*Funtionswandel*) of those components of cerebral organization, which enable humans to distinguish themselves from the highest non-human primates" (1958, 162, my trans).[15] Binswanger demonstrates that the concretization of metaphors in the delusional meaning of the (perceptual) object is nevertheless an implicit way of preserving a minimal self in its compromised ability to transcend (see below).

Conrad illustrates this loss of self-transcendence (i.e., spontaneously self-decentering by adaptively shifting frame of reference) in delusion: (1) I hear my name called out on the street. After looking, I realize that the call was *intended* for someone else. *Here, the shift in reference-frame requires that I inhibit the initial self-reference*. (2) A train-passenger whimsically decides to attribute the movement outside to the passing landscape. "How one perceives or judges what is at rest and what is moving depends on one's reference point" (Conrad 1958, 49, my trans). Suppose our passenger is unable to *inhibit* this fantasy by *shifting back* to consider the train's movement (and by extension, his own movement) as the source of motion and thereby, no longer experiences his bodily-self as capable agent.[16] Rather, he becomes the sole stationary point in the universe which now revolves about him, what Conrad calls the Ptolemaic position, or *anastroph* (the "turning back" on himself as middle-point).[17] In beginning schizophrenia, patients often report that "everything appears to *revolve* about me." Wherever Karl B.'s glance falls, every "component of his experiential field," appears to stand in special relation to him, e.g., the "instructions," "preparations," "being staged." "His 'world' transforms itself into a singular field specifically meant to 'test' him (*Prüffeld*)." (1958, 53, my trans). Once the apophany takes over, no aspect of the field remains untouched. Then, "*everything becomes conspicuously salient* (*auffällig*). The patient often interprets the course of events as if a film were being made or a theater-piece performed" (1958, 53, my trans).

Conrad's and Binswanger's respective stage models of delusional psychosis were profoundly influenced by the experimental and theoretical work of their contemporary, V. von Weizsäcker: each stage (as response to increasing underlying neurobiological disturbance) is the subjective reorganization of meaning with the view of preserving subject's "vital" relationship with the environment (mediated by what v. Weizsäcker calls a Gestalt-circle, *Gestaltkreis,* or perception-action cycle).[18] "These transitions in perceptual organization are rapid and ballistic in that each new organization appears to emerge on its own without precedent in the prior organization."[19] Weizsäcker found that the subject's ability to maintain coherent perceptual-Gestalten is disrupted in definable stages of self-world relationship. By experimentally inducing vertigo, he discovered the Gestalt-circle, the forming of the Gestalt (as preserved coherence) in the ongoing balance between perception and movement. In a typical experiment, the subject is surrounded in an otherwise darkened room by an illuminated rotating cylinder (an 'optokinetic drum') with vertical stripes. As the drum's speed increases, the subject experiences dizziness and nausea. Optokinetic nystagmus begins. *The subject makes unwitting turning movements of the head, torso and arms in the direction of the drum's movement.* However, "if the subject holds a resting object before the eyes and fixates on that instead of the paper-cylinder, the subject suddenly experiences the cylinder at rest, but the subject's own body appears to move in the opposite direction" (v. Weizsäcker 1950, 9, my trans). With this "illusion of self-movement (vection), the drum appears stationary" (ibid.) Even today, many researchers believe that vection arises solely from the visual information from the moving optic-flow. However, this would not account for the subject's prior, compensatory involuntary movements. The illusion of self-movement illusion does not arise solely from the visual "information" but from an embodied subject who, as bodily-self embedded in the situation, maintains the coherence of his ongoing experience in terms of the balance between perceptual and motoric systems. Critically, the "coherence" of the subject's experience is preserved by a spontaneously new organization of experience (i.e., "improvisation") in which the organizational *components* become redistributed by (dialectically) reversing relationship (e.g., world and self, perception and movement).

For Conrad and Binswanger, delusions involve a similar effort to maintain coherence of self-world relationship in the face of the increasingly disturbing background emotional-motivational state of the delusional mood and its underlying neurobiology. Experimental vertigo models the delusional "Ptolemaic" position because the patient experiences the self to be at rest but everything else (in his perceptual field) as revolving about him as its center-point. This is coupled with the inability to transcend the vertigo, *the inability to go back and reverse reference frames by inhibiting the current one* (as in Conrad's two illustrative examples). Similarly, Binswanger describes psychosis as the mountain climber's vertigo, "Verstiegenheit" (sometimes translated as extravagance), the inability to either proceed upwards or return back, i.e., to "step over" (*übersteigen*) one's current perspective.

2.1 Unconscious Meaning in the Transformation of Gestalt in Delusional Psychosis

In classical descriptive psychopathology (K. Jaspers, H. Gruhle, K. Schneider), delusional interpretations of perception, i.e., "delusional perceptions" (*Wahnwahrnehmungen*), are two-tiered: an *abnormal meaning* attaches to an otherwise intact perception without understandable reason or cause (*ohne Anlass*, Gruhle).[20] The lack of "understandable" relationship between the reported perception and its symbolic interpretation makes the delusion "primary" (i.e., pathognomic of incipient schizophrenia). For Jaspers, "delusions only arise in the process of thinking and judging."[21]

Matussek challenges the classical view as relying on a faculty "psychology of elements" in its assumption that the underlying percept is intact in delusional perception. It separates perception from the abnormal symbolic meaning putatively grafted onto it by the delusional judgment. For Matussek, the perceptual-Gestalt is part of, and thus organized in terms of the total organization between self and world. He proposes that the delusional "symbolic" meaning is not something first derived from thought but experienced directly in the percept.[22] The organization of self-world relationship (and the preservation of its coherence), as v. Weizsäcker (1950) had demonstrated, is mediated by the *dynamic* Gestalt meaning of the perception.

In their analysis of delusional perception, Matussek and Conrad apply the Gestalt concept of holistic-properties (*Ganzeigenschaften*). Although characterizing the whole Gestalt, these properties are separable into: (1) structural properties (*Struktur, Gefüge*); (2) textural-material properties (*Ganzbeschaffenheit*); (3) expressive-essential properties (*Ausdrucks-* or *Wesenseigenschaft*), immediately experienced physiognomic-qualities, e.g., artistic style, a person's character. Least "objective" of the three Gestalt-properties, the expressive-essential properties are *experienced* as residing "within" the object as its ownmost "essential" meaning (thus, *Wesenseigenschaften*). Although all three properties are intrinsic to the perception, they may compete with one another and achieve some independence.[23] *It is the third expressive-physiognomic quality, however, which becomes exaggerated in the delusional perception.* To the extent that the structural or material properties are reduced, we rely more on the object's expressive qualities. In delusion, these accentuated perceptual expressive-qualities stand out against a diminished or changed background.

Matussek postulates that a loosening of the "natural" connectedness between objects in scene-based vision (*Auflockerung des natürlichen Wahrnehmungszusammenhangs*) results in the "releasing" of the object's expressive-physiognomic qualities in the delusion. The contextual constraints that normally *bias* object perception towards shared conventional intersubjective meanings (common sense) are no longer present.[24] Only with great effort, the patient is able to momentarily restore the natural context.[25] It is not merely that the details fascinate or captivate the attention, but the patient experiences *an inability to look away* from them. Looking away requires too much *effort* (*Das Wegschauen kostet Mühe*). It is easier to remain transfixed on the same aspect, i.e., perceptual rigidity (*Wahrnehmungsstarre*). Matussek's view that a perceptual-expressive quality becomes salient in the delusion is elaborated by Conrad and Binswanger, but in different ways. Both believe that the delusional object involves a transformation of perceptual Gestalt-meaning on a "lower" *unconscious* phase of its development but they apply different methods to arrive at this conclusion. Conrad appeals to the experimental work of "microgenesis." Binswanger applies Husserl's "genetic" phenomenology.

For the delusional patient, mere *similarity is taken as identity* allowing a new context to restructure the loosened qualities and previously unexplained saliencies in the delusional epiphany. He experiences *delusional identification* between living beings or landscapes because he experiences their shared physiognomic qualities as identical (*auf Grund gleicher Wesenseigenschaften*).

Conrad (1958) finds that the *delusional-misidentification* of persons, a symptom of neurologic disorders, also occurs in beginning schizophrenia and is rooted in delusional perceptions.[26] Of the 107 schizophrenia patients Conrad interviews, 17 report misidentifications. Most are "positive misidentifications" in that a stranger, or unfamiliar person, is perceived as known (*misplaced familiarity*).[27] For example, the patient perceives a detail in a stranger's face, e.g., a scar or crooked tooth that represents the expressive quality "rugged." However, it is *not* the actual scar or tooth but rather its "ruggedness" which allows the patient to delusionally misidentify the new person *as being the same person* as some previous person also experienced as "rugged." This quality may be experienced in the stranger's voice, or even in the way he makes a *single* movement or gesture (Conrad 1958).[28] The physiognomic similarity between beings, and not their "objective" structural or material Gestalt properties, allows for their *identification* in the delusional perception.

Conrad describes a patient with incipient schizophrenia placed temporarily in a guardhouse before transport. Being a former carpenter, the patient finds that the door, windows, floorboards and bed-frame in the cell have a "familiar" quality. He sees all at once that he himself is the carpenter of these objects. They look so familiar. They were removed from his old workshop. The windowsill has scratches on it, which he made as a child and has been removed from his childhood home. Everything revolves about the patient (*anastrophe*). The *familiar, expressive quality* of his own workmanship emerges from each object he encounters in the cell and spreads (with *monotonous* repetition) to his entire perceptual field (*misplaced familiarity of delusional misidentification*).

In delusional misidentification, the structural Gestalt properties recede and the patient relies on their physiognomic-expressive qualities. During a night walk, I see a tree trunk as a crouching robber (Conrad 1958, 183). Here, the impoverished perceptual structure contributes to the Gestalt's prevailing expressive physiognomic quality. The physiognomic similarities become more striking than normally. The shadowy tree-trunk is not a differentiated Gestalt-perception but what Conrad calls a pre-Gestalt (*Vorgestalt*). When unable to recall a name, for example, there is the feeling of it being on the 'tip of the tongue.' We access the word's expressive qualities (e.g., short or long, Italian or French, soft or harsh), a provisional pre-Gestalt, but its structure remains unconscious.

Since we experience the expressive properties as *inhering in the object*, we are not always directly conscious of them *per se*. During waking experience, the multiple qualities are integrated into or suppressed by the perceptual context and remain *unconscious*. They "form an essential part of what has been termed unconscious components of subjective experience, which otherwise become released in dreaming" (Conrad 1960, 378). "Although the properties are constantly in our field of vision, they nevertheless remain concealed and only become salient under certain conditions" (Conrad 1957, 66). While a few predominant qualities prevail in discursive, waking-consciousness, the *moment we relax conscious control* in "day-dreaming," sleepiness, or hypnagogic transitions to sleep, the numerous, hidden qualities become evident and overpower the perception. *The Gestalt's expressive qualities predominate precisely when the structural organization which conscious, goal-directed effortful processing imposes is reduced or when the perceptual conditions themselves interfere with apprehending a complete and clearly defined Gestalt.*[29]

The delusional patient experiences the enhanced expressive physiognomic qualities of the *Vorgestalt* as salient. When healthy subjects are presented perceptual objects in impoverished or reduced conditions, they report similar experiences. The experimental method, "microgenesis" interrupts or diminishes the percept by means of tatiscopic presentation (often too briefly to be consciously experienced), reduced illumination of the field, diminishing the size of the stimulus, or presentation in peripheral vision (Conrad 1953, 67).[30] These impoverished conditions lead to a loosening of the object's perceptual binding (*gelockerten Reizbindung*) (Conrad 1958).

Impoverishing the stimulus, or interrupting perceptions truncates the perceptual complexity which normally contributes to our everyday experience of complete objects. It accesses "the sequence of events [...] assumed to occur in the temporal period between the presentation of a stimulus and the formation of a single, relatively stabilized cognitive response (percept or thought) to this stimulus."[31] The developmental (genetic) processes forming the finalized percept or thought occur outside awareness, i.e., automatically.[32] Since we generally do not have introspective access to how our experiences, goals and desires are developmentally composed of phases, we only access the phases by experiment or reflective method (i.e., genetic phenomenology).[33]

In the first phase of a microgenetic experiment, the stimulus is presented in the most attenuated manner, i.e., as a diffuse, undifferentiated or vague background (*Ganzfeld*). A "non-determinate something" is sensed but not directly seen. In the next microgenetic phase, the stimulus is presented with more illumination for somewhat longer tatiscopic durations, etc. Figures may be differentiated against the background but *continuously flicker* in non-stability. The physiognomic-expressive qualities continue to dominate over the figure's structural articulation. It's primitive differentiation emerges but disappears again (*Primitivgliederung*). The subject has an anxious feeling of non-finality (*Nichtendgültigkeits-tönung*), yet experiences a feeling of being *transfixed, unable to look away* (Matussek's *Wahrnehmungsstarre*). Unable to voluntarily distance, or reflect critically, the subject suffers the experience in a receptive, non-critical attitude and remains *emotionally* engaged. For Conrad, this phase most accurately reproduces in the healthy, awake subjects, the delusional patient's or dreamer's experience.[34] In a final phase of the microgenetic experiment, the healthy subject recognizes suddenly, with relief and surprise, the actual Gestalt. The delusional patient, on the other hand, remains attached to the earlier, arrested phase of meaning.[35] This marks a stable, and sometimes relatively permanent loss of the capacity to shift frame of reference (i.e., the ability to test reality) as "the subject is unable to shift back from the previously passive-receptive to a critical attitude." (Conrad 1957, my trans).[36]

As the delusional process progresses from outer world to his body, Karl B. reports a *wave*-generating apparatus, which controls his movements from a distance.

The role of the *Vorgestalt* (and its accentuated expressive qualities) in the *delusional wave-generating apparatus*, acquires "metaphoric" meaning, as Conrad puts it. This meaning is no longer anchored in the delusional perception, but reflects the structure of the self as a self-transcending process preserved minimally in metaphors of self in the delusion. That is, the delusional meaning has become separated from the original perceptual experience (Binswanger, see below).

2.2 *Delusion as the Protopathic Functional Change of the Vorgestalt: Head and von Weizsäcker*

Citing Sir Henry Head and Viktor von Weizsäcker, Conrad observes that the *Vorgestalt* informing the delusion is not merely an earlier, unconscious phase of the perception – exposed during psychosis, dreaming or microgenetic experiment – but actually undergoes *a pathologic change of meaning*. Because Head found his patients' reports of *qualitative changes in sensation* following peripheral afferent nerve-trauma imprecise and influenced by his questions, the soon to be famous, British neurologist elects to have 'first-hand' (an ill-advised pun) experience. In 1903, Head permits the surgically division and suturing of the radial nerve of his own forearm. For 5 years, he and his colleague, W. J. Rivers, carefully document the returning sensibility during regeneration in the affected arm and hand.[37] Immediately after surgery, Rivers touches the affected areas with various probes (cotton wool, von Frey hairs, pin prick, etc.). Head feels nothing on the skin surface. Due to preserved "deep" sensibility, however, he senses the pressure on the arm and hand.[38] After a while, Head experiences the return of cutaneous sensations, but these have a peculiar character. Only "spots" on the skin surface (with "spaces between") are sensitive to heat or cold (*punctate sensibility*). Moreover, the temperatures applied must be more extreme than normally perceived (*raised threshold*). With his eyes closed, Head reports "diffuse" sensations remote from the point of stimulation (*radiation or referral*),[39] which have an *all or none* character. Insensitive to light touch, he "overreacts" to more strongly applied stimuli, experiencing excessive pain (*hyperalgesia*). Unpleasant sensations are experienced as "exaggerated," "more vivid" than normally (*intensification*). After ca. 1 year, 'normal' sensations return. *Critically, when the hand regains sensibility to light touch, the diffuse tingling and radiating pain disappear.* These give way to well-localized sensation, two-point discrimination (compass test), appreciation of intermediate temperatures and differences in size (i.e., the 'Gestalt' of the probe object).

Head and Rivers interpret the two distinct recovery phases as reflecting two underlying systems: (1) protopathic; (2) epicritic.[40] The protopathic (Greek, proto-, 'first, primitive' + pathos, 'suffering, feeling') returns first and is more "primitive" phylogenetically, "capable of producing qualitative changes in consciousness."[41] It's discriminations of heat, cold, and pain are coarse and non-localized. Radially extended and referred in an all or none manner, it requires a raised threshold and produces an exaggerated, inordinate response (disproportional to the actual stimulus intensity).

The epicritic innervation (Gk., *epikritikos 'giving judgment over,'* from *epi 'upon or over' + krinein 'to judge')* is more recent evolutionarily, producing localized, gradated, and proportionate (tempered), fine spatial discriminations. When epicritic sensibility returns, the 'primitive,' tingling, diffuse, exaggerated and referred painful responses disappear. Inspired by their predecessor, Hughlings Jackson, Head and Rivers conclude that the more evolved, epicritic functions are more vulnerable to disorder (*dissolution*) and thus, the first lost in pathological conditions. "Normally," they impose hierarchical, *inhibitory* control over the less evolved, protopathic functions.

Head played a key role in reviving interest in Jackson's work. Both Freud and Head's colleague, Rivers saw Jackson's relevance for the psychoanalytic unconscious. Nevertheless, Head's observations were subsequently criticized as overly "theoretical" and "abstract." Our concern here, however, is Conrad's application of Head's experimental conclusions to the transformation of unconscious meaning in paranoid psychosis. Conrad finds that the Jacksonian "release" of pathological behaviors of the earlier stage of perceptual-meaning (i.e., the microgenetic "*Vorgestalt*") cannot be said to be merely a component of the later process but is its own productive or *positive* transformation.[42] Conrad calls the delusion a *protopathic* "functional change" (*Funktionswandel*) of the *Vorgestalt*. For Head, cutaneous sensation changes when epicritic sensibility – due to pathologic dissolution – no longer dominates/inhibits its protopathic counterpart. For Conrad, it is only when epicritic, waking-consciousness is relaxed that the expressive-physiognomic Gestalt qualities come "most purely" to expression, "namely in the state of dreaming" (Conrad 1959a, 184, my trans). Also in the delusional state, the epicritic function is lost. The *Vorgestalt* is now experienced according to different (reduced) criteria of what constitutes a *meaningful* object.[43] Nevertheless, Conrad reconceptualizes Head's concept of release of the protopathic symptom in terms of von Weizsäcker's concept of "functional change" as Gestaltkreis.

Von Weizsäcker observes that symptom-formation (whether neurologic, psychiatric or psychosomatic) brings about a "functional change" on both the neural and cognitive levels:

> When correctly grasped, symptomatic 'functional change' (*Funktionswandel*) is a Gestalt-circle (*Gestaltkreis*) [...] It involves the forming of the Gestalt, or rather its reforming (*Umgestaltung*). This is not only a material-physiologic change, but, at the same time, cognitive. By using the phrase 'at the same time,' I borrow from our everyday experience of time to describe what otherwise remains inaccessible. For example, reaching for an object involves both active grasping and palpating its shape. [The motoric side is efferent, centripetal, and accomplished in terms of a body-centered, egocentric frame of reference. The touching-palpating on the other hand is afferent and centrifugal, and accomplished in terms of an object-centered, allocentric frame of reference. Nevertheless, the motoric and perceptual sides of the act "mutually condition" (i.e., presuppose) but also mutually exclude one another: the hand both feels and grips. This is the Gestalt-circle.] In (pathological) functional change, the same achievement [i.e., result] is accomplished *by taking a different path* so that the new structure substitutes by standing in (*stellvertretend*) for the previous one. Here the material substrate obtains, as it were, a cognitive function, and conversely, what had been cognitive is now materialized. This mutuality only occurs through a circular process as a Gestalt-circle. The biological study of such acts requires introducing the [concept of] subject.[44]

With his concepts of *functional change* and *Gestalt-circle* (*Gestaltkreis*), v. Weizsäcker introduces a new way of thinking about how subjectivity informs the organization of the experiential field as a totality in which the embodied subject experiences *both* being embedded within the field *and* transcending beyond it. Conrad proposes that this view surpasses Head and Hughlings Jackson. Conrad, Binswanger, Blankenburg, Ey, Wyss and other phenomenologically oriented psychiatrists of the time were indebted to v. Weizsäcker's critical appraisal of the "metaphysical" oppositions which continue to uncritically inform the research of neuropsychiatric disorders: mind/body, inner / outer, self/other, I/illness, conscious/ unconscious. These are rethought in terms of a mutually-dependent/mutually-exclusive *Gestaltkreis*.[45]

3 Binswanger's Phenomenology of Unconscious: The Concretization of Self as Metaphor in Failed Self-transcendence

While Conrad acknowledges that Binswanger's "Daseinsanalytic" approach to the schizophrenia patient's being-in-the-world (modeled after Heidegger's analysis) has much to say about the *individual existence* of the mentally ill, he finds it unable to make general claims about delusions in schizophrenia. Daseinsanalysis describes the transformation of the schizophrenia patient's total existence, but it does not access the putative unconscious processes present in the delusions.[46]

Impelled by this critique and his experience of Heidegger's preference for the Swiss psychiatrist, Medard Boss, as rejection, Binswanger returns to Husserl's phenomenological method in a final phase of his thought. In his earlier debate with Jaspers about the importance of psychoanalysis (1910s – mid 1920s), Binswanger employed Husserl's phenomenology of the body to provide a foundation for a revised concept of the psychoanalytic unconscious (Mishara 1997). Still, what is gained by Binswanger's turning to reflective philosophy, specifically genetic-phenomenology, as supplement to Conrad's approach to unconscious meaning in delusions?[47]

Conrad views delusions as the protopathic functional change of the *Vorgestalt* as demonstrated by the microgenetic, experimental method. He believes that little is gained by turning to Binswanger's more philosophic approach.[48] At first this view appears justified: Philosophic phenomenology's sole access to experience is reflection. Our measurement of conscious experience or other cognitive and neural processes occurs, by definition, in the real time of neural events.[49] Phenomenology, however, is unable to access the cognitive or neural processes measured by experimental science in "real time," i.e., which is only possible by accessing and measuring the subject's responses.[50] Starting with experiences as they are "given" in awareness, genetic phenomenology *reflectively* removes layers of meaning as conditions of possibility for the genetically *later* complete-meanings in the *subjective* experience of time. The earlier phases accessed through the reflective genetic-phenomenological method, although rigorously obtained, are "abstractions." In principle, they cannot be directly measured in real time. Conversely, microgenesis is unable to directly study internal time-consciousness but only the *accompanying*, experimentally measured neural and psychological processes (accessed through the subjects' *responses* or reports). *These are fundamentally different, mutually exclusive ways of viewing human experience.*[51] Attempts to link the phenomenology of subjective experience with real time responses (accessed experimentally) may be conceptualized in terms of a *Gestaltkreis* (i.e., each perspective mutually excludes, but also presupposes its counterpart). In addition, as the abstractive removing of layers of meaning through a bracketing procedure, phenomenology's "results" are *provisional*, always open to further refinement by going back to the "things themselves," and performing new, related reflective reductions.

There is an additional problem internal to phenomenology itself. Ludwig Landgrebe (Husserl's assistant) expresses it as follows: "the depth dimensions of the process of constitution cannot be attained by the phenomenological reflection."[52] Binswanger's answer is that we rely on psychosis itself as a "natural experiment" in which the phenomenological researcher examines "deeper," otherwise inaccessible unconscious levels of processing. It is as if layers of our experience were suddenly exposed. That is, psychosis and other forms of neuropsychiatric disorder are able to perform "phenomenologic reductions" that we are unable from the standpoint of reflection.

To elucidate Binswanger's approach, I present his case, Suzanne Urbanne (pseudonym). The patient learns in an abrasive manner from an urologist that her husband is diagnosed with cancer. "Meanwhile, the urologist turns his back to my husband. He gives me a hopeless grimace. [...] presses my hand [...] that I should be careful not to let my feelings show to my husband. It was this insincere gesture which was most horrible."[53] In the emergent *delusional mood*, she *reexperiences* the "hopeless grimace of the doctor" which provides the content for subsequent delusional elaboration. Binswanger[54] describes how one perceptual aspect (*Abschattung*) (in this case, the doctor's grimace) becomes exaggerated and separated from its background. This occurs in a process of loosening of the delusional theme from its life-historical embeddedness, the "becoming independent of the theme into a delusion."[55] As this theme becomes the patient's exclusive focus, her previously frantic activity during the prodromal delusional atmosphere evolves into an ever more passive attitude of resignation. She feels herself to be the passive middlepoint of a 'delusional stage' (*Wahnbühne*).[56] Suzanne is now convinced that not only the doctor wants to "martyr her family." The "delusional schema" of his insincere hopeless expression (now separated from the original scene (*Urszene*) of its occurrence) *generalizes* to (anonymous) others: "the police are martyring my entire family." Still "others" have the ability to listen in on her conversations from afar by means of unknown, technical devices. The sounds of "paper crinkling" in a nearby room indicate to her that her thoughts are simultaneously stenographer. Hidden wires under the earth transmit electricity to her body.

During delusional mood, fragments of experience stand out against a transformed or diminished background and are no longer synthesized in the continuum of "natural experience." They leave 'gaps' appearing not to occur in ordinary time. *The nontemporalized, impressional fragments or partial aspects of perceptual objects collect and start to coincide in terms of one physiognomic-expressive feature* (e.g., the intent to martyr). The disengaged impressional-fragments collect and gather around the new meaning-core of the delusional perception bringing provisional stability to the delusional mood. From out of the fragments, the patient has an *Aha-Erlebnis*, a sudden insight into the situation (Conrad's apophany). This relieves the increasing distress due to the gaps in the natural successive organization of this experience in time. The seeming 'insight' of the delusion imposes a *retroactive* organization on the collected, nontemporalized fragments. *The perceived coincidences seem to restore an illusory continuity of experience.* As in dreaming, objects are accepted as meaningful or complete when viewed from only one side or perspective, i.e., in terms of the immediate expressive aspect originally given in sensory awareness (i.e., a *Vorgestalt*), given 'ready-made' to conscious thought as if they were fully constituted objects[57] (paraphrased from Uhlhaas and Mishara 2007, 147–8).

Binswanger's theory of delusion relies on the phenomenological theory of meaning: The intentional experience of 'object' requires the underlying – nonconscious passive 'synthesis' of its spatial and temporal aspects or profile adumbrations (*Abschattungen*). For example, our *expectations* about objects based on past experience play an implicit, largely unnoticed role in the continuity of experience. Husserl writes, "When we see a dog, we immediately anticipate its additional modes of behavior: its typical way of eating, playing, running, jumping, and so on. We do not actually see its teeth, but [...] we know in advance how its teeth will look – not in their individual determination but according to type, inasmuch as we have already had previous and frequent experience of 'similar' animals, of 'dogs'."[58] That is, we perceive the not yet known in terms of the known, i.e., in terms of the general type that is activated in the particular perception.[59] With each view, there is built a reference to the next anticipated view based on past experience of this and similar objects. *The references between aspects are anticipatory constraints, which are nevertheless open to revision or cancellation (i.e., prediction error) in their structure so that each aspect prefigures its successor in seamless transition as belonging to the same perceptual object.* When viewing the cup of coffee that I am about to grasp, there is a rear side of the cup that is not available to the current view. Nevertheless, the aperture of my grasp correctly anticipates the 3-dimensional volume of the object about to be grasped. This is based in part on my current view of the object's surface (including textural cues) and in part on my previous experience with this and similar objects.

In the phenomenological theory, a type (Binswanger's 'mnemic schema') provides the principles of organization, i.e., rules for synthesis of aspects of the perceptual object in its inner structure. Object perception requires the ongoing synthesis or binding of (1) the currently experienced aspect with (2) the aspects not available to current perception and (3) a totality or unity of aspects that is never actually given in terms of the one aspect, i.e., never directly experienced. The type or schema implicitly organizes the aspects of an object into a coherent relationship of perceptual meaning 'prior' to its conscious perception. The fact that the object type or schema is already activated at this level of object recognition and is responsible for the inner mutual coherence of aspect-views (*Abschattungen*, as variants of the object's core but invariant perceptual meaning) allows for the seamless transition from an object's pre-lexical identification in visual perception to its linguistic expression in conscious explicit judgments. (However, conscious awareness of the object does not require this transition to verbal naming.) Because the type is *anticipatory*, it provides the rules by which each partial view is in turn synthesized into an object, a totality that is never apprehended by just one view. It is not possible to experience the perceptual object in terms of all its aspects at once. The perception of a thing is relative to the standpoint of the observer (paraphrased from Uhlhaas and Mishara 2007, 147–148).

Matussek and Conrad view the delusional perception as a "loosening" of the natural visual context, which "releases" the object's physiognomic-expressive qualities. These dominate over the structural-material ones in the perception of a non-finalized Gestalt. In contrast, Binswanger attributes the delusional object's meaning transformation to a "loosened mnemic schema." Leaving aside Binswanger's novel terminology,[60] the perceptual object is constrained as meaningful in terms of the interconnecting profile-aspect-adumbrations around an *anticipated* noematic core of meaning, the object's pre-linguistic structural eidos or type. For Binswanger, it is not the object's outer perceptual context (Matussek, Conrad), but rather, employing Husserl's genetic phenomenology, its "inner horizon" that is disrupted in delusions.[61]

Binswanger gives the example of dreaming about an approaching boat, which suddenly becomes a dolphin riding the waves. Here, the "mnemic schema," i.e., the constraining "references" to an *anticipated* core meaning (expectancies, Bayesian "priors") by which each passing sensory profile aspect contributes to a unified objective-meaning, is not absent. It is merely *loosened*. That is, the constraining prescriptions for the image (*Bildbildungsvorschriften*), i.e., what remains identical in each metamorphic *transition* of the image (i.e., how the passing retentions, or priors, group around an 'anticipated' core meaning) is *not directed to a complete object*. Rather, the core-meaning is a single *quality*, the "approaching, moving to and fro through the waves."[62] There is a "failure of the schema to remain rigid, a failure to follow the reference to natural objects as constraining prescriptions. [...] As in dreaming, the delusional person is at the mercy of his/her own impressions."[63] *The delusional mnemic schema is loosened but also "monotonously" rigid by prescribing the one expressive quality*. As Corlett and colleagues write, "while delusions are fixed they are also elastic and may incorporate new information without shifting their fundamental perspective."[64]

The delusional "object" (e.g., the invisible powers or devices that control one's thoughts and actions) is not fully constituted in perception or conscious judgment but remains an incomplete saliency, a partial object (*Vorgestalt*, mnemic schema) that is elevated to the epistemological status of a complete object 'pregiven' with the "presumptive evidence" of world experience.[65] Following Matussek, Blankenburg proposes (paradoxically) that it is "not pathological belief but a pathological absence of belief" that is fundamental to the formation of delusions.[66] Generally, we presume that experience will continue more or less in the same manner that it has up till now (Binswanger 1994). In our 'certainty' that tomorrow will come, v. Weizsäcker observes, lurks an assumption no less "delusional" than the patient who believes the world will end.[67] In schizophrenia, there is a loss of *trust* with regard to the continuity of experience and the underlying automatic processes of perceptual meaning (e.g., common sense) that support this continuity. Contrary to the conventional view, delusion is not a form of belief but something more fundamental, what Merleau-Ponty calls "perceptual faith" or "flesh" through which we as subjects are able to have an embodied relationship to the world at all.[68]

For Binswanger, human being is "condemned" to an ongoing process of self-transcendence as openness ("prospective vulnerability")[69] to an unknown future, which, although in part anticipated, displaces the current perspective. Self-transcendence (the reflexive "I move myself" as a *Gestaltkreis*) is the condition for the ability to *distance from or transcend one's current experience*.[70] For Binswanger and Conrad, the *deformation* of Gestalt perception in early schizophrenia reflects the loss of the self's ability to transcend experience. As in dreaming, *the self in the acute psychosis of schizophrenia, is captivated in the present moment (a "temporal shrinking" (Schrumpfung) of past and future (Binswanger)), which compromises the ability to transcend.*

Binswanger proposes that the anticipatory, prospective aspect of perceptual binding (i.e., passive synthesis) is compromised in schizophrenia with the loosened, but nevertheless rigidified mnemic schema in dreaming and psychosis. The monotonous insistence of the mnemic schema of the delusion is not prospective but replaces expectation. Corlett and colleagues (in press) write, "With sufficient reconsolidation [what we are calling here the forming of the delusional mnemic schema in its repeated, monotonous reiterations], the priors become so strong as to be resistant to contradictionary evidence" (16, my insertion).[71]

Patients with schizophrenia delusionally refer to themselves in inhuman, "thing-like" terms, e.g., as "machine," "computer," or "apparatus" whose sole function is to "register" impressions. This concretization of metaphors of self is nevertheless an implicit way of preserving minimal self in its compromised ability to transcend the present perspective. That is, the metaphoric description of self as a "registering apparatus," or Karl B.'s wave apparatus controlling his movements, at once testifies to the patient's compromised ability to transcend current experience but, at the same time, preserves a distance (no matter how minimally) to this experiencing by enabling the patient to (metaphorically) describe, and thus, transcend by use of the metaphor (no matter how concretely interpreted). Just as v. Weizsäcker's concept of the symptom as forming, creating an "it" which, in its very opposing the "I," provides a "detour" or alternative path (the *Es-bildung* of *Funktionswandel*), the very delusion of experiencing oneself as a passive "registering apparatus" or computer, unable to plan or experience a personal future, a mere "it," provides the occasion to transcend itself but only through the continued reinstantiation (and thus *reconsolidation*[72] of mnemic schema) of the delusion.

4 Husserl's Phenomenology of the Unconscious: The Streaming-Standing of the Living Present and Past Self

Despite readings inspired by Derrida that there is "no unconscious" in Husserl, several studies[73] definitively pointed to an unconscious in his phenomenology. If the automatic processes of passive synthesis are "unconscious" in terms of being pre-affective (i.e., not reaching or "affecting" consciousness), then it is possible to examine a "dynamic" unconscious in terms of an embodied, intersubjective field formed by the syntheses (Mishara 1993).

4.1 Husserl's Most Radical Reduction: The Enigma of the Living Present

Husserl's "apodictic" *re-duction* (a 'leading back' from Latin, *re- 'back'* + *ducere 'lead'*) to the "living present," consists in a "deepened epoché, in which the horizons of the past and future of world-experiencing life are bracketed."[74] This involves the systematic removing of phases of complete-objects in their constitutive meaning, starting with the most conscious ones first – as if peeling the layers of an onion – to see what layers remain underneath. These layers, or genetic phases become separated 'abstractly' in reflection, but may not be said, as mere conditions of possibility, to 'exist' on their own and, as we have already indicated, are not directly measurable in real time. Recalling Husserl's admonition against abstraction cited at the beginning of this paper, and the previous discussion concerning the advantages vs. disadvantages of pursuing Binswanger's more "philosophic" approach, we should be wary of succumbing, or becoming overly attached, to our own abstractions. However, if we are to examine the 'depth dimensions' of the living present, we must reflectively access what is itself non-experiencable, what is pre-egoic (in the mundane sense), and pre-temporal (Held 1966). Therefore, we are advised to proceed carefully in our descent to this "underworld,"[75] as our abstract approach may lead us either to precipitous conclusions or irresolvable aporias.

In this reduction, Husserl discovers "originary association" (*Urassoziation*), the association of coexistent hyletic (from ancient Greek, *hyle*, matter or material) data in the living present. Husserl distinguishes, 'pre-affective' from 'affective' syntheses or associations in the Urassoziation. Preaffective-syntheses of hyletic data remain "unconscious." Affective-syntheses, on the other hand, are conscious, or on the way to becoming conscious. Affection 'awakens' the I, stimulates it into activity. Once awoken, the I attends to the greatest prevailing contrast value relative to the others in the sense-fields. It is not the stimulus itself which determines the magnitude of attractive force it exerts on the I, but rather its 'relative' height of contrast, or Gestalt-saliency (*Abgehobenheit*), with respect to the other hyletic stimuli present in the field at any given moment. When the I is first awoken by a contrasting affective force, it is at the "mercy" of the hyletic forces. Just as the Freudian ego is not master of its own house, so the I "is not master of its own field. It can be completely overpowered by it," as in traumatic experiences.[76] The I is attracted or repulsed by 'instinctual preferences' for sudden contrasts in the very becoming conscious of them. *The first relationship of the I to its field is neither neutral nor voluntary, but one of exposure and vulnerability.* Affection is above all a "function of contrast" (Hua XI, 149). The living present is divided into a relationship of foreground and background which is shaped from moment to moment by the competing contrasts and where the I attends. However, *the Husserlian 'unconscious' is not the background, but the underlying pre-affective syntheses which make the foreground/background relationship first possible* (what Husserl identifies as initially "affectively null", see below).[77]

By turning to audition, Husserl finds evidence for the unconscious. As we know from its role in processing music and language, audition is particularly geared to exhibiting successive relationships. Let us imagine Husserl sitting, busily at work, at his writing desk. There is a background sound, a hammer-blow, which Husserl does not consciously heed nor bother to identify. An indefinite period of time elapses before he hears a second hammer-blow. The interim, however, exceeds the temporal window required for maintaining retention of the unheeded stimulus in the present field of consciousness. Husserl not only notices the second hammer-blow, but, *all at once*, identifies both this and the prior sound, which has passed out of awareness, as *two successive hammer-blows*. It is only by being brought into relation with each other in a backwards-radiating identity synthesis that *both* terms become identifiable as belonging to the same class of things, "hammer-blows." Husserl is able to demonstrate in auditory successive synthesis the existence of *an unconscious, preaffective organization*: "It is clear that an awakening of the *concealed* plays its role here across gaps or distances (*Weiten*) of successive syntheses" (Hua XI, 176, my trans). The "backwards-radiating affective awakening" (*rückstrahlende affektive Weckung*) proceeds from the second blow to the first in a "unifying" operation. Nevertheless, the first blow is no longer materially present within the present field as primal-impression, or its fading retention.[78] It is "clouded over (*vernebelt*), having more or less forfeited the effectiveness of its particular content" (Hua XI, 176, my trans). How, then, is it recovered from unconscious concealment?

Each retention passes out of awareness and sinks into a "horizon of forgetfulness," whether the retention was initially heeded or not. It passes out of awareness by means of an *empty retention* which *replaces* the fading retention. As the retentions pass off, they *lose their inner articulation, crowding into one another*, before disappearing altogether into the obscurity of the unconscious night. The empty retention "*shrouds*" the retention by progressively diminishing its "raised" surface-aspects, contours against a background, by which it affects awareness in terms of its contrast saliency (*Abgehobenheit*). Understandably so, as room must be made for the fresh original impression. However, it is by virtue of such an empty retention that the retention of the initial, unheeded blow (already passed outside awareness) is awoken in the backwards-radiating *affection*. What is awoken is not the material content of the already faded retention, which has sunk into unconsciousness, but rather *its structural sense, which is accessed through the empty presentation.*[79] The retentional process "is a process of identifying synthesis across and through which passes the selfness of the objective sense" (Hua XI, 171). However, the retentions as they first emerge "in their originality, have no intentional character" (Hua XI, 77). The empty presentation has the ambiguous function of being simultaneously present and absent to consciousness. It is present to consciousness in preserving *momentarily* the affective force of the passed retention in its felt sense, and yet absent in preserving the retentive content for an indefinite period after it has left 'immediate' awareness.[80]

The competing contrast-saliencies of each impressional, living present sediments beneath the present one as a kind of 'dead' geological layer. "It is to this underworld or subterranean region of sedimented layers ordered by their successive occurrence that the affective awakening of the empty presentation must proceed in order to surface recollections. It does so in a leaping or springing (*sprunghaft*) manner, by leaping across layers of the buried, sedimented past presents. In Husserl's 'underworld of memory (*Gedächtnisuntergrund*),' deceased retentions dwell as shades cut-off from the light of consciousness and all life, only to be momentarily stirred by an empty presentation for brief appearances on the stage of consciousness." (Mishara 1990a, 48).

The retrospective grasping of the two hammer-blows indicates that there are gaps of discontinuity over which the 'backwards-radiating' affection 'leaps', enabling syntheses of identity. There is discontinuity, or a gap of indefinite, though "not arbitrary duration," between the successive-syntheses across which the *awakening*, the *becoming conscious of their relationship*, must leap backwards in time (via the empty presentation) to an unconscious target. Despite variant morphological-structures and uniqueness of position (*Zeitstelle*) within successive time, this operation treats the two hammer-blows as equal in their *ideal* meaning, belonging to the *type*, hammer-blow (paraphrased from Mishara 1990a).

Husserl gives the example of looking down into the valley during an evening walk into the Loretto Heights. Suddenly, "a row street lamps is illuminated below in the Rhine Valley. [...] The fact that the series of lights is affective as a whole in one swoop *(mit einem Schlag)* evidently lies in the pre-affective conformity to laws of the formation of that unity" (Hua XI, 154). That is, the affection can arise on its own from any point in a sense-field and propagate itself (*Fortpflanzung*) as an *already articulated unity, a Vor-Gestalt* with its own surface contours, *prior to becoming conscious*. "If the propagation or spontaneous spreading of the affection from a new 'local' surface point in the sense field accumulates enough affective force relative to the other surface contrasts, it will awaken the ego to a corresponding kinesthetic activity of noticing." (Mishara 1990a, 41). That is, the *at first* unconscious pre-affective-syntheses of similarity need not merely adhere to association by contiguity but may traverse both simultaneous and successive distances in their awakening force from a distance (*Fernweckung*). These leap over the first gaps marked by discontinuous separations in either space or time and *form rudimentarily meaningful Gestalt unities prior to awareness.*[81]

4.2 The Three Source Points of Experience in Present Streaming Consciousness and the Phenomenological Unconscious

The phenomenological unconscious is two-pronged: it is both the lowermost stratum of the *Urimpression* of the living present, the pre-affective-syntheses *underlying* the background of any emergent Gestalt, but it is also the past, the "night" of the unconscious, into which every emergent saliency passes, progressively loosing its affective contours and ability to attract awareness. To understand this self-dividing (*Entzweiung*) of time-consciousness as a self-displacing totality required for the memory of a past self, we must first examine the unconscious of the living present.

There are three *starting points* with each new now phase of "fresh" primal-impression:

1. The living present: The primal-impression comprises a beginning point (*Anfangsphase*, Hua X, 199) of conscious experience which is itself abstract and non-experiencable (Held 1966).
2. The beginning spreading affection: At first unconscious, it allows for unities to become organized according to the laws of genetic association prior to Gestalt awareness. As a race which starts with a gunshot, all points in the topographic *surface* (*Gesamtrelief*) of each new impressional present start out affectively as null; however, the propagation of affective-syntheses spreads from one (previously non-determinable) point in the field. In this strife, each affective saliency competes with every other for awareness by posing the greatest contrast (standing out the most) relative to the others. This differs from # 1 where the original impression in its totality, i.e., including the pre-affective-syntheses, never reaches consciousness.
3. The kinesthetic-noeses (Ancient Gk., *noesis*, the operation of *nous*, or mind): these orient to the emergent affective contrast-saliencies and are accompanied by the "kinesthetic sensations" (proprioceptions). Every kinesthetic orienting begins with what is currently being attended while a yet to be conscious spreading affection may flare up in another part of the field.[82] Here the kinesthesis always starts as *null-point* relative to where it eventually orients in the emergent affection of the contrast saliencies.[83]

The three source-points are initially *independent* but eventually converge in the becoming conscious of perception or other meaning. For perceptual awareness, the affection and the kinesthetic orienting, which start from divergent source points with each fresh impression, must eventually converge. However, there is always a "delay" between the start points and their convergence.[84]

The phenomenological self is both the kinesthetic-noetic orienting to an emergent affective saliency in its own field but also the totality which transcends the current moment. That is, it is both the living present and the transcendent past as *one* totality of streaming consciousness, but how is this possible?

We experience our consciousness as an obligatory displacing itself with each new now, a "standing in the streaming" (Held 1966). Husserl writes that the "self" *is* the "streaming consciousness *in itself*" (*das Ansich des Bewussteinsstroms*) as a totality "*transcendent*" to current conscious experience. This ongoing process of a self-displacing present involves both conscious and *non-conscious, automatic processes,* "passive syntheses," which underlie each now-point (in successive syntheses of transition, *Übergangssynthese*). The "transcendent self" (as the *totality* of streaming consciousness) can "[...] only [be] incompletely and approximately given in any particular recollection" of a past now (Hua XI, 204, my trans). When we remember something, the memory occurs in the present but refers to a past that transcends this present. That is, each past memory is not only itself (its own "self-givenness") but also part (*Mitglied*) of a larger totality, the transcendent past (of which we can never be completely conscious in any given memory). The past continues to "enrich itself" (*sich stetig bereichende*), expanding with each new experience up to the present (XI, 207). As such the past is *both* immanent to present consciousness in making available *individual* memories that occur at the moment, but also a transcendent "realm of Being in itself," which any particular remembering presupposes.

The *self* as the totality of the streaming is *both* the present moment (with its unconscious strata of emergent, contrast-saliencies eventually "affecting" consciousness, provoking the kinesthetic orientings) *and* the transcendent past. Any present moment passes off as retention into this "underworld of the unconscious," but we must also appeal to this same unconscious to retrieve any past now in a recollection. The past (as immanent "object") is continuously instituted anew in the present (*immer neue Urstiftung in sich vollzieht*), but precisely as that which transcends the present as its *own realm of Being*.[85] It is through this same past that streaming consciousness constitutes *itself* as "true Being" (*wahres Sein*) (*ibid.*) and to which we owe the "*idea of a true self*" (*die Idee eines wahren Selbst*). "Before any activity of the I," consciousness "objectives" itself as past, as no longer *I* but retrospectively *me* (Hua XI, 210). Paradoxically, the *self* as the streaming totality is transcendent to present consciousness as its past, but also (in a way that remains *hidden*) *is* this consciousness.[86]

Husserl writes: "In empathizing, having others in a co-present, [...] I am with them in feeling as an 'I' with a 'thou,' an other I. This is similar to how I am to myself in remembering, I am in a communal-sharing of consciousness of the past I with the present I."[87] That is: "The transcendental I is, in outline, already *plurale tantum*."[88]

Does this mean that the I only achieves pre-reflective connection with itself as both being a present and having a past through a pre-reflective self-awareness, or so-called passive self-affection (Michel Henry), which, in turn, enables the unitary experience of present and past selves? Quite the contrary, the connection between current and past self is only possible through the retention's disappearing, its being covered over by the empty retention, by the unconscious relationship between present and past selves as a self-transcending. As v. Weizsäcker writes: "The subject is not a firm possession but must be acquired anew at each moment to "possess" it" (1950, 173, my trans). That is, self-transcendence, becoming oneself occurs paradoxically by giving oneself up in the *hidden* unity between a present and (unconscious) past self.

Recently, commentators have interpreted Husserl's phenomenology in terms of the French philosopher, Michel Henry. However, as suggested here, time-consciousness is not the passive self-affection of pre-reflective self-awareness (M. Henry) but the unconscious relationship between present and past selves in the ongoing movement of self-transcendence. For Henry, the "life" which the Freudian unconscious is unable to grasp is its own manifestation precisely in feeling it, a being gripped by itself in passive self-affection. This, however, is not the "life" that Husserl uses metaphorically when he speaks about the "living present" of the primal-impression and its retention, which suffer a "death" sinking into the unconscious "underworld." The living present is already past the moment we are *affected* by it, or become reflectively aware of it.[89]

5 Conclusions

In this contribution, I outlined how a phenomenology of paranoid delusions leads to the revision of the psychoanalytic and cognitive neuroscientific concepts of the unconscious and unconscious, automatic processing, respectively. By taking the patient's subjective experience of paranoid psychosis seriously, Conrad and Binswanger propose that the "delusional object" is formed in terms of automatic meaning processes that "normally" remain unconscious and which they compare to dreaming. It is not merely that there is a "release" of the unconsciously formed meaning but there is a pathological transformation of its Gestalt-meaning which at once disrupts but also preserves the experience of self as an ongoing process of self-transcendence. There is a "shrinking" of temporal experience (Binswanger) in that the mnemic schema of the delusional object is loosened, detached from the context of the original scene of its occurrence (*Urszene*). However, by replacing natural protentive expectation, the schema is applied monotonously, at once disrupting but also holding together the patient's experience. Husserl's genetic phenomenology provides a conceptual revision to the unconscious, proposing an embodied intersubjective field in which the self is both embedded and beyond this embeddedness as the ongoing self-transcendence (self-displacing, standing in the streaming) of the present moment. Time-consciousness is not the passive self-affection of pre-reflective self-awareness (Henry) but requires the unconscious relationship between present and past selves in the ongoing movement of self-transcendence. It is this self-transcendence which is both compromised and preserved by the metaphoric meaning of the delusional object in the paranoid delusions of schizophrenia.

Notes

1. I have discussed Binswanger's and Husserl's phenomenologies of the unconscious in previous publications: *L'Inconscient chez L. Binswanger. Phénoménologie, Psychiatrie, Psychanalyse.* In: P. Fedida, ed. Paris 1986; "Husserl and Freud: Time, memory and the unconscious." *Husserl Studies* 7 (1990a): 29–58; "The Problem of the Unconscious in the Later Thought of L. Binswanger: a Phenomenological Approach to Delusion in Perception and Communication." *Analecta Husserliana* 31 (1990b), 247–278; "Die Phänomenologischen Grundlagen der

psychoanalytischen Theorie." *Analecta Husserliana* 39 (1993): 413–438; "Binswanger's psychiatry." ed. L. Embree et al., *Encyclopedia of Phenomenology* (Dordrecht:Kluwer Academic Publishers 1997), 62–66. Once a work is cited, I cite it subsequently by author and year (followed by a letter in alphabetic order, if more than one text in a particular year is cited).

2. See G. Fichtner, ed., *The Sigmund Freud – Ludwig Binswanger Correspondence*, 1908–1938 (New York: Other Press, 2003).
3. A. L. Mishara, 1997.
4. Freud's *Über Psychoanalyse* (1909), and *Selbstdarstellung* (1936) were found in Husserl's library, but show no signs of being read. Husserl did underline his copy of C.G. Jung's *Versuch einer Darstellung der psychoanalytischen Theorie* (1913), especially passages concerning how Jung's "association experiment is helpful in disclosing the repressed unconscious." Elmar Holenstein, *Phänomenologie der Assoziation* (Den Haag: Nijhoff 1972), 321, my trans.
5. A. L. Mishara, 1990a.
6. See also A. L. Mishara, 1993.
7. Klaus Conrad, *Die beginnende Schizophrenie. Versuch einer Gestaltanalyse des Wahns* (Stuttgart: Thieme, 1958).
8. M. Hambrecht and H. Häfner, "Trema, Apophänie, Apokalypse"– Ist Conrads Phasenmodell empirisch begründbar? *Fortschr Neurol Psychiatr* 61 (1993): 418–23, my trans.
9. He writes, "the psychoanalytic results can be 'translated' into the language of phenomenology." Klaus Conrad, "Das Unbewusste als phänomenologisches Problem," in *Fortschr Neurol Psychiatr* 25 (1957), 56–73; "Das Problem der Vorgestaltung," *Das Unvollendete als künstlerische Form* . Ed. J.A. Schmoll., (Bern: Eisenwerth, 1959a), 35–45.
10. D.W. Ploog, "Autobiographical Sketch," *History of Psychiatry* 13 (2002): 358–360.
11. A.L. Mishara and Klaus Conrad (1905–1961), "Delusional Mood, Psychosis and Beginning Schizophrenia," *Schizophrenia Bulletin* 36(1) (2010): 9–13.
12. "Anosognosia" (J. Babinski, "Contribution à l'étude des troubles mentaux dans l'hémiplégie organique cérébrale (Anosognosie)", in *Revue Neurol* 27 (1914): 845–848), lack of insight, is the unawareness/denial of a deficit, e.g., in hemiplegia or blindness. Conrad describes a progressive "spreading" of the delusional mood from the envinroment's most salient features to the entire perceptual field. As if "protecting" the self, the delusions, at first, concern external space. But as illness progresses, the bodily self is affected as in Karl B.'s delusions of control. The prodromal feelings that unexplained changes in the environment are related to self in the delusional mood reflect the underlying neurobiological processes of beginning psychosis, which progressively disrupt the "binding" processes of perception, agency and self-experience. The patient's very feeling of being alive and world as she/he knows it are threatened with ending, by literally 'coming apart'.
13. The narrow beam of light creates a "wall" of darkness on all sides. "Here, nothing is any longer to be 'taken for granted.' Nothing is 'natural' any more. Something completely undefined is present. It is the quality of lurking itself." (Conrad, 1958, 41, my trans).
14. K. Conrad, "Gestaltanalyse und Daseinsanalytik." *Nervenarzt* 30 (1959b); 405 my trans). Similarly, Binswanger describes the "monotonous" insistence and spreading of the delusion to ever-increasing realms of the patient's experiencing, but as the delusion's "loosened mnemic schema." More recently, we interpreted the monotonous-repetitiveness of the delusion to be the "reconsolidation" phase of impaired learning about rewarding events (presumably mediated by dysregulated dopamine and related glutamatergic and/or GABAergic signaling abnormalities): unexpected events, prediction errors, are registered inappropriately in an eventual shifting of control from goal-directed learning to the "striatal-habit" system. See: A.L. Mishara and P.R. Corlett, "Are Delusions Biologically Adaptive? Salvaging the Doxastic Shear Pin," in *Behavioral and Brain Sciences*, in press.
15. See also K. Conrad, "Die symptomatischen Psychosen," in *Psychiatrie der Gegenwart*, vol. II, ed. H.W. Gruhle, et al. (Berlin, 1960), 369–436. Following Binswanger's view that both dreaming and psychosis involve a loss in the ability to transcend (sich übersteigen) current experience or flexibly assume a new or critical perspective, Conrad concludes that dreaming is indicative of the kind of Gestalt-transformation which occurs in delusional psychosis. Conrad,

Binswanger, and other phenomenological psychiatrists at the time proposed that *psychosis is similar to dreaming in its inability to distance or disengage from incomplete meanings*, i.e., absent the complete intentionality of awake consciousness (see microgenesis, below). This view is incompatible with the popularizing "Apollonian" hyper-reflexive approach to schizophrenia as involving excessive, "morbid rationality" or "hyper-reflexivity." For reviews, see A.L. Mishara, "Missing links in phenomenological clinical neuroscience? Why we are still not there yet." *Curr Opin Psychiatry* 60 (2007): 559–569; *Kafka, paranoic doubles and the brain: Hypnagogic vs. hyper-reflexive models of disruption of self in neuropsychiatric disorders and anomalous conscious states*. In: Philos Ethics Humanit Med, in press a; *The phenomenology wars: self, psychopathology and neuroscience*. In: Philos Psychiatr Psychol, in press b.

16. Interestingly, I. Feinberg and C. D. Frith later develop the related hypothesis that the schizophrenia patient's loss of a sense of agency or ability to monitor one's own actions results from an impairment in the efference-copy of the movement. Conrad relies here on v. Weizsäcker's "Gestalt-circle" for his phenomenological analysis of delusions, which predates von Holst and Mittelstaedt's efference-copy/reaffference and Sperry's corollary-discharge models.
17. From the ancient Greek anastrophē (ana- 'back' + strephein 'to turn'). The modern Copernican view that the earth revolves about the sun requires *relinquishing* the older Ptolemaic view that the earth (or self) is motionless (passive) center of the universe.
18. By founding with his assistant, Alexander Mitscherlich, the Heidelberg psychosomatic institute, von Weizsäcker helped reestablish Freudian psychoanalysis in post-WWII Germany.
19. P. Uhlhaas and A.L. Mishara, "Perceptual Anomalies in Schizophrenia: Integrating Phenomenology and Cognitive Neuroscience," *Schizophrenia Bulletin* 33 (2007): 142–156.
20. Delusions may be related to perceptions or autochthonous (German, Wahneinfall) occurring directly in thought. For K. Schneider, the autochthonous delusion is single-tiered, while the delusional perception is two-tiered, i.e., the intact perception and its delusional interpretation.
21. K. Jaspers, *General Psychopathology*, 7th ed. (Chicago: University of *Chicago* Press 1963), 95.
22. "The abnormal significance of the delusion is [...] neither discovered, thought or otherwise 'dredged up by thinking'. Rather, it is experienced immediately in the object on the basis of the changed perceptual world." P. Matussek, "Untersuchungen über die Wahnwahrnehmung. 1. Mitteilung." *Arch Psychiatr Zeitschr Gesamte Neurol* 189 (1952): 279–319, my trans.
23. The Gestalt-psychologist, Metzger (Matussek's and Conrad's source) classifies the Ganzeigenschaften: (1) "Structural properties" contribute to the Gestalt's overall organization or goodness (Prägnanz) (e.g., round, jagged, color, course of movement, or melody for tones); (2) "Textural-material properties" (e.g., transparency, rough, smooth, soft, hard, and shrill); (3) "Expressive-essential properties" (sometimes referred to as "tertiary qualities") whereby both animate and inanimate beings are experienced as having physiognomic character (e.g., friendly, sinister, stunning), and are evocative of feelings. W. Metzger, *Psychologie*. (Dresden: Steinkopff, 1975. The physiognomic-expressive properties are not the result of attribution, predication or judgment imposed on the perception but are (following Scheler and Klages) part of the perception itself. As von Ehrenfels' Gestalt-qualities, the global-properties remain "invariant in transposition," e.g., a change of key of a melody.
24. Cf. W. Blankenburg, *Der Verlust der natürlichen Selbstverständlichkeit* (Stuttgart: Enke, 1971); "First steps toward a 'psychopathology of common sense'." Trans by A. L. Mishara, *Philosophy Psychiatry Psychology* 8 (2001), 303–315.
25. Phenomenological psychiatrists at the time (e.g., Binswanger, Blankenburg, Conrad, Ey, Wyss) emphasized that normal Gestalt-perception requires effortful, awake conscious processing. In delusion, dreaming or trance, there is a 'relaxing' of current goal directed, effortful processing and attendant executive functioning, which, in neuropsychological terms, provides the context of relevant, goal directed activity through "working memory," known to be disrupted in schizophrenia.
26. Prior to Conrad, Scheid reports delusional person-misidentification (as delusional perception) in early schizophrenia: "The misidentification is immediately given in the experience of the perception, and is therefore, phenomenologically speaking, a delusional perception." W. Scheid, "Über Personenverkennung, " *Z ges Neurol Psychiatr* 157 (1936): 7–8, my trans.

27. Ramin Motjabai, "Misidentification Phenomena in German Psychiatry," *History of Psychiatry* 7 (1997): 137–158.
28. The 'Aha' of the delusional-perceptual-misidentification is rapid. Recently, I interviewed a schizophrenia patient with intractable erotomanic delusions, who maintains that a young man, "P," had fallen in love with her during her adolescence and controls parts of her life by reappearing in various men she later encounters. She identifies one man as "P" simply because over the phone he had, for a moment, the same tone of voice as P.
29. Sleep-deprivation "resembles" psychosis by leading to a disinhibition of the objects's multiple expressive meanings by "releasing" the "cloud" or "halo" of multiple expressive, physiognomic-meanings that surrounds each object or person but normally remains suppressed in the awake perception (Conrad, 1958). It may serve as "a non-drug, psychotomimetic model" for delusions. P. Corlett, C.D. Frith, and P.C. Fletcher, "From Drugs to Deprivation: a Bayesian Framework for Understanding Models of Psychosis," *Psychopharmacology* 206 (2009): 515–30.
30. The émigré, Austrian psychologist, Heinz Werner coined the term "microgenesis" as translation of the German, *Aktualgenese*.
31. J.H. Flavell and J.A. Draguns, "A Microgenetic Approach to Perception and Thought," *Psychological Bulletin* 54 (1957): 197–217.
32. H. Werner, "Microgenesis and Aphasia," *Journal of Abnormal Social Psychology* 52 (1956): 347–353.
33. Tononi writes, "the time scale of neurophysiological interactions needed to integrate information among distant cortical regions appears to be consistent with that required by psychophysical observations (microgenesis) [...]. No matter how hard you try, you cannot speed up experience to follow a movie accelerated a hundred times, nor can you slow it down if the movie has decelerated. Studies of how a percept is progressively specified and stabilized – a process called microgenesis – indicate that it takes up to 100–200 milliseconds to develop a fully formed sensory experience, and that the surfacing of a conscious thought may take even longer." G. Tononi, "An Information Integration Theory of Consciousness," *BMC Neuroscience* 5 (2004): 1–22.
34. These observations do not support the "Apollonian" hyper-reflexive view of psychosis as an emotionally reduced, objectifying, morbid intact rationality, which places the patient at a distance from the experience.
35. Conrad, 1959a, 36–7.
36. The Vorgestalt-qualities resemble hallucinations of a double (autoscopy). So far as the hallucinatory experience is believed, the motoric body-schema and not merely the predominantly visual body-image is engaged or implicated. A.L. Mishara, "Autoscopy: Disrupted Self in Neuropsychiatric Disorders and Anomalous Conscious States," in *Handbook of Phenomenology and Cognitive Science*, ed. S. Gallagher and D. Schmicking (Berlin: Springer, 2010).
37. WHR Rivers, H. Head, "A Human Experiment in Nerve Division," *Brain* 31 (1908), 323–450; H. Head, *Studies in Neurology* (London: Oxford University Press, 1920).
38. Deep sensibility (Sherrington's "muscular sense") is subserved by afferent fibers of muscular nerves and thus, not affected by the disrupted cutaneous sensibility, and informs Head and Holmes' later distinction, body schema/ body image.
39. Cotton wool produces a peculiar "radiating," "tingling" sensation.
40. Head (1920) thought the 2 systems were subserved by anatomically different peripheral "end-organs" (i.e., receptors), respective nerve fibers and (subcortical vs. cortical) central mechanisms.
41. H. Head, W.H.R. Rivers, and J. Sherren, "The Afferent Nervous System from a New Aspect," *Brain* 28 (1905): 99–115.
42. Conrad writes, "In sleep, there is radical dismantling (Abbau) of higher functional levels [...] this characterizes the negative side of the phenomenon. At the same time, we find in dreaming the expression of the release of deeper [...] levels of functioning as positive symptoms of this occurrence." Referring to his French contemporary and friend, Henri Ey, he continues: "Without previous knowledge of Ey's efforts, I repeatedly referred to the dream as a typical

state of protopathic transformation of Gestalt-meaning of the total mental field." K. Conrad, "Über moderne Strömungen der französichen Psychiatrie," *Nervenarzt* 25 (1953): 114–118, my trans). Ey's classification of the different mental disorders according to the depth of "dissolution" (Jackson) of consciousness nevertheless intrigued Conrad.

43. Flavell and Draguns' (1957) observe that schizophrenia is "a condition in which early cognitive formations intrude into consciousness and get expressed as though they were completed thoughts."
44. V. v. Weizsäcker, "Funktionswandel und Gestaltkreis," *Deutsche Zeitschrift für Nervenheilkunde* 164 (1950): 43–53 (my trans, paraphrasing and insertions). Our current medical model views illness in terms of underlying physiological processes, not acknowledging that they are inseparable from the person's life. *The symptom indicates both organic change but also what this means for the person.*
45. Metaphors such as lower = earlier/more primitive, or inner = deep inform our folk psychology and, as a result, current models of brain (and self) in neuroscience and neuroanatomy. A.L. Mishara, "The disconnection of external and internal in the conscious experience of schizophrenia," *Philosophica* 73 (2004): 87–126.
46. Conrad writes: "it seems important that this kind of analysis should not only be applied to the sum total of our existence, but also to its subordinate parts, which are in themselves wholes, or gestalts, in the narrower sense" (1952, 243).
47. Binswanger states that his later genetic-phenomenological approach is consistent with his earlier Daseinsanalysis. For more complete discussion, see Blankenburg, 1971; A.L. Mishara, 1990b; 1997.
48. Conrad asks "Why does one need the unduly brittle terminology of the philosophers? [...] The view that the person, as mentally ill, lives in his own world is not new." (Conrad, 1958, 45, my trans).
49. See Tononi's (2004) description, cited above.
50. Neuroscientific method measures subjective processes and experiences indirectly in terms of the subject's responses (verbal, non-verbal, neural). These inevitably involve a "delay" in real time between the experience and the response. Even so-called more direct measurements of neural 'responses' (e.g., fMRI, PET, EEG) inevitably involve a temporal, artifactual delay between what occurs in the brain and the preferred method for measuring it. See Mishara, in press a; in press b.
51. Despite recent claims to experimentally study inner time-consciousness, the measurement of *subjective experience of time* in real time relies on, as just noted, the subject's responses (verbal, behavioral, neural). *It does not directly access the subjective experience except through the mediation of these responses which artifactually introduce a delay in real time and the non-coincidence between subjective experience and its measurement* (see Mishara in press a; in press b).
52. L. Landgrebe, *The Phenomenology of Edmund Husserl, Six Essays*, ed. D. Welton (Ithaca: Cornell U.P., 1981), 52. Landgrebe writes "without [sensory] impressions, there are no achievements constituting time and without kinaestheses there are no impressions [...]", 59. That is, different reductions lead to different fundamental abstract levels.
53. L. Binswanger, *Schizophrenie* (Pfullingen: Günter Neske, 1957), 383, my trans.
54. L. Binswanger, *Wahn*. Reprinted in: Ludwig Binswanger, *Ausgewählte Werke*, Bd 4, *Der Mensch in der Psychiatrie*, ed. A. Holzhey-Kunz (Heidelberg: Asanger, 1994), 429–539, originally published 1965.
55. W. Blankenburg, "Die Verselbständigung eines Themas zum Wahn." Reprinted in W. Blankenburg, *Psychopathologie des Unscheinbaren, Ausgewählte Aufsätze*. ed M. Heinze. (Berlin: Parados, 2007), 25–68, originally published 1965.
56. Cf. Conrad's *anastrophe*.
57. Cf. Flavell and Draguns' (1957) observation cited above.
58. E. Husserl, *Experience and Judgment, Investigations in a Genealogy of Logic* (Evanston: Northwestern University Press, 1973), 331.
59. Binswanger reinterprets Conrad's "misplaced familiarity" in delusional misidentification in schizophrenia as the "monotonous" insistence of the delusional schema which takes over ever increasing realms of the patient's experiencing.

60. Binswanger's close collaborator and friend, W. Szilasi, suggests the term, "mnemic schema" (referring to Husserl's inner horizon of object-type as eidos), which has roots in Aristotle, Kant, Heidegger, Head and Bartlett. See also, Dieter Lohmar, "Husserl's Type and Kant's Schemata, Systematic Reasons for their Correlation or Identity," in *The New Husserl: A Critical Reader*, ed. D. Welton (Bloomington: Indiana University Press, 2003), 93–124.
61. The loosened mnemic schema becomes "independent" from its original context (Urszene) in "inner life-history" (i.e., autobiographical-narrative memory).
62. Binswanger, 1994, 446, my trans. The referential connections (Verweisungs-zusammenhänge) between successive profile aspects of the experienced object form themselves (sich bilden) with regard to an anticipated core meaning. In dreaming and psychotic delusions, these are shifted from complete objects to the dominating physiognomic-qualities of the perceptual fragments (Conrad's Vorgestalt).
63. *Ibid.* Cf. Conrad's assertion that the dreamer or psychotic individual is unable to detach from the incomplete object-meanings of the Vorgestalt which are experienced in a receptive, non-critical attitude.
64. P. R. Corlett, J.H. Krystal, J. R. Taylor, and P.C. Fletcher, "Why Do Delusions persist?," *Frontiers in Human Neuroscience* 3 (in press).
65. L. Binswanger, "Über das Wahnproblem in rein phänomenologischer Sicht," *Schweiz Arch Neurol Neurochir Psychiat* 91 (1963): 85–88. Here, Binswanger cites Husserl (Hua I, 96).
66. W. Blankenburg, 1971, 7. (See also Uhlhaas and Mishara, 2007).
67. V. von Weizsäcker. *Pathosophie*. (Göttingen: Vandenhoeck & Ruprecht, 1956).
68. M. Merleau-Ponty, *The Visible and the Invisible*, trans A. Lingis (Evanston: Northwestern University Press, 1968) (Original French: 1964).
69. Mishara, 2005.
70. Binswanger describes being-in-the world as a process of self-transcendence or "Gestalt-circle" as the "hidden unity" between perception and action, disrupted in schizophrenia.
71. For the reduction of expectational, protentional processes in schizophrenia, see T. Fuchs, "Psychopathologie der subjektiven und intersubjektiven Zeitlichkeit," *Journal für Philosophie & Psychiatrie* 2 (2009).
72. Corlett et al., in press.
73. H. Drüe, *Edmund Husserls System der phänomenologischen Psychologie*. (Berlin: De Gruyter, 1963); Holenstein, 1973; Mishara, 1984; 1990a; 1990b, 1993; T. Seebohm, "The New Hermeneutics from the Standpoint of Transcendental Phenomenology," in *Continental Philosophy*, ed. J. Sallis, et al. (Pittsburgh, 1985), 64–89. T. Seebohm, "The Preconscious, the Unconscious, and the Subconscious: A Phenomenological Explication," *Man and World* 25 (1992): 505–520.
74. K. Held, *Lebendige Gegenwart* (Den Haag: Martinus Nijhoff, 1966), 62 (my trans).
75. Both Husserl and Kafka borrow the metaphor of the unconscious as underworld from their German romantic predecessors. For Kafka's relationship to Husserl on the unconscious "hidden unity of self" as "doubling" (*Entzweiung*) see Mishara in press a.
76. T. Seebohm 1985, 186.
77. Paraphrased from Mishara 1990a, 38–39.
78. Paraphrased from Mishara 1990a, 46.
79. Husserl describes the disappearance of the originary impression and its retention in forgetting in 'optical' terms as "vanishing" into a "horizon of the past," losing ever more of its articulated surface detail. Passing into the "underworld" of the unconscious, it is no longer "constitutively living," but suffers a death, obscured by the shrouding-cloaking function of the empty presentation. Mishara, 1990a.
80. Paraphrased from Mishara 1990a, 45–47, 51. N.b., by employing Husserl's concept of empty presenation as the felt-sense of unconscious meaning, we may elaborate on Conrad's account of the tip of the tongue experience.
81. The affection "skirts along (entlang gehen)" the topographic surface (Gesamtrelief) of the incoming sensations (Hua XI, 164). As for von Weizsäcker, each present field organization is *de novo* "improvisation" (i.e., self-organizing).

82. Husserl discusses how the new-born infant has a 'temporal past' with its own habitualities of kinesthetic orienting: "The first act-what is its foundation? [...] The living wakens the unliving. The primal infant (Urkind) - how is it able to orient to the first datum, in what does this 'instinctive habituality' consist?" (Hua XV, 604, my trans).
83. Husserl's insight anticipates neuroscience, e.g., K. Shimono, A. Higashiyama, W.J. Tam, "Location of the Egocenter in Kinesthetic Space," *Journal of Experimental Psychology: Human Perception and Performance* (2001, Aug 27(4)): 848–861.
84. The two systems, kinesthetic and perceptual, are organized in terms of two different reference-frames or coordinate systems. These are egocentric, or body-centered, and allocentric, or object-centered, respectively, and are implicated in the neurologic opposition (proposed by Head, 1920) between body schema and body image. See S. Gallagher and J. Cole, "Body schema and body image in a deafferented subject," *Journal of Mind and Behavior* 16 (1995): 369–390. Husserl observed that any new attended to location in the field is prospectively (but nonconsciously) structured by anticipatory "kinaestheses" of ocular-motor response required to reorient optimally to the novel target are computed relative to the current "null point." The orienting "kinaestheses" (i.e., eye-centered coordinates) are not themselves conscious prior to, or during the viewing of things the orienting makes possible. U. Claesges, *Edmund Husserls Theorie der Raumkonstitution* (Den Haag 1964).
85. "Sure enough, this being in itself of the stream of consciousness is entirely its own sphere of Being by virtue of the fact that its future is conversely not 'in itself'" (Hua XI, 208, my trans), i.e., 'prospectively open.'
86. Reflecting on experience itself occurs within the temporal passing of consciousness and is subject to the same "laws" of "time consciousness" as the originally reflected on experience: "Admittedly, the moment I begin to reflect, the naïve perceiving by the self-forgetting 'I' is already past. I am only able to grasp this by reaching back, in the reflecting, into what has 'remained in consciousness' as retention, an immediate memory which attaches itself backwards to the original experience" (Hua VIII, 88, my trans). The splitting into present and past 'selves' (Ichspaltung) occurs passively or automatically in spontaneous doubling (*Entzweiung*), Mishara in press a.
87. Husserl, Ms. E III 9 (1931), 84, cited by Held, 1966, 166, my trans. Husserl states, "I am in a dialogue (Zwiegespräch) with myself, a dialectical conversation with myself" (Hua XV, 416, my trans).
88. Latin for "in plural only."
89. Henry critiques the Freudian unconscious as being both a product of, but also lying outside the metaphysics of representation. It is rather the body as alive. Here, self is given to itself in the immediacy of life feeling itself. There is no gap between self and its own autoaffection as the instantiation of being alive at the moment, an interiority *immediately* intimate with itself. He proposes that the problem of ultimate grounding rests with the structure of appearing itself in that all intentionality refers back to the ecstatic appearing in which it itself unfolds. M. Henry, "Phenomenology of the Unconscious," *Stanford Literary Review* 6 (1989): 149–169. Henry's concept of "life" is not what v. Weizsäcker (1950) means in his oft-cited statement: "one must participate in life to understand it." If life is feeling itself to be alive, what v. Weizsäcker calls the "pathic," it is also not pre-reflective self-awareness, nor immediate self-manifestation, but the hidden (unconscious) unity of the subject with itself and its environment in a perception action cycle (Gestaltkreis) vital for self-preservation (Mishara and Corlett, in press).

The Phenomenological Psychology of Gender: How Trans-Sexuality and Intersexuality Express the General Case of Self as a Cultural Object

Ian Rory Owen

Abstract Transcendental phenomenology identifies ideal enabling conditions that permit something to happen or exist unlimited by ideas of what constitutes the world (Hua IX, 305, 328, 334, 336, 341–5). Intersubjectivity for Husserl names the conditions for knowledge to be social. For him, phenomenological psychology interpreted conscious experience and explained the creation of meaning in its social habitat as part of a biological, psychological and social whole as reality. In this light, the conscious meanings and experiences of gender are considered. The terminology employed is that "gender" refers to intersubjective (or psychosocial) aspects of culturally-defined identity and roles; whilst "sex" refers to physical aspects of the body. The relation between physical sex and intersubjective gender is explored to show how people find and place themselves within pre-existing codes of cultural objects and their manifolds of meaning. The usual assumption is that gender follows a simple binary classification of there being two mutually exclusive sexes. But the assumptions concerning mutually-exclusive gender and sex are challenged by a full attention to the evidence. The focus is not on Husserl exegesis but showing how being trans-sexual and intersexual are part of the way in which people create and express their identities. Specific comments on trans-sexuality have been derived from first-person accounts that are interpreted in a Husserlian way. Trans-sexualism is where persons feel themselves to be, in part or in whole, of a different combination of gender characteristics to their sex. People who are "primary" trans-sexuals help explain the nature of psychological meaning concerning roles, identity and culturally-constituted meanings. Intersexuality is where people have biological aspects of both sexes. The region of evidence for consideration is the set of the cultural objects of gendered behaviour and identity. '-- End of Abstract'

I.R. Owen (✉)
Leeds Partnerships NHS Foundation Trust, Leeds, UK
e-mail: ianrory@hotmail.co.uk

D. Lohmar and J. Brudzińska (eds.), *Founding Psychoanalysis Phenomenologically*, Phaenomenologica 199, DOI 10.1007/978-94-007-1848-7_10,

1 Introductory Remarks

The inquiry starts with defining the variation in sex and explains trans-sexuality where physical males feel themselves to be female and physical women feel themselves to be male, to varying degrees and in varying ways. Second, a brief three-way comparison is made between psychological science, psychoanalysis and phenomenological psychology. Scientific psychological research is briefly recapped. Then three psychoanalytic positions are critically discussed. A Husserl-inspired interpretation of being trans-sexual is provided. It takes trans-sexuality as a meaningful construction. The next section explains some of the shared problems for psychoanalysis and phenomenological psychology. The emphasis is explaining the differences and commonalities between the two. Conclusions on being an intersubjectively-situated self are provided.

The whole of sex includes intersexuality where people have male and female aspects. People who are intersexual may have both male and female genitals in some cases. Or in other ways they might have the genitals of one sex, for instance, but have female and male chromosomes (or other physical aspects). Because of intersexuality, sex is a continuum of male, female and intersexual. When viewed as a whole, there is no binary classification of sex.[1] This is contrary to the assumption that there are only two sexes. However, the force of the binary assumption is that intersexual people have been routinely given sexual reassignment surgery as infants and small children, contrary to the wishes of the person as a teenager and adult. Let us begin to consider the link between signified gender and sex.

Overall, gender identity and behaviour is a biopsychosocial whole. In human development on average, the sense of gender identity forms at about 24 months. For the majority, there is congruence between intersubjective gender identity and behaviour – and sex. Gender is often assumed to be obvious and not problematic. Trans-sexuality is the expression of observable gender behaviour and identity that is incongruent with sex, in children or adults. There are a number of similar types of trans-sexuality. But behaviour, identity and the declared felt-sense of gender may or may not coincide with the wish to change sex. The term "primary" trans-sexualism is used for persons who have always innately felt themselves to be predominantly of a gender different to their sex. The desire of the primary trans-sexual is not just to "pass," to be accepted by others as being, or at least looking as though they were of a gender different to their sex. The primary trans-sexual may completely identify with the chosen gender and be committed to this identity to the degree of having surgery and on-going hormone treatment.

But there is more than one form of trans-sexuality. "Secondary" trans-sexualism refers to persons who might wish to change their sex through surgery but never felt themselves to be of a different gender to their sex when they were children and may have previously had a gender identity congruent with their sex in their youth. During adolescence and adulthood, they might have begun to question their gender identity and experiment with their gender behaviour. But for reasons other than those of primary trans-sexuals, they come to identify with the chosen gender in adulthood and midlife. In summary, primary and secondary trans-sexualism is intersubjective in the sense that self is expressed through clothing, hairstyle and the accoutrements of the chosen gender. Accordingly, trans-sexuality is an intersubjective expression of gender behaviour in-line with the felt-sense of gender identity and the consequent investment of belief in such a conclusion.

An important distinction needs to be made. The type of trans-sexualism discussed as a phenomenon in these pages is not fetishistic transvesticism but primary trans-sexuality. Within transvesticism there may be further types still and it might be the case that some persons prefer to show themselves to the world as differently gendered for a variety of psychological reasons. These reasons include never having identified with the parent of the same sex as children, or due to early trauma, or conflict with the parent of 'opposite' sex. Neither types of trans-sexual are fetishists who obtain sexual satisfaction through cross-dressing. Transvestites might choose cross-dressing for a number of psychological reasons, some of which might be versions of sexual narcissism or the use of pleasure as a defence or coping strategy, or as a means of bolstering a weak or endangered sense of identity. Other possibilities exist for the refusal to identify with the parent of the same sex in childhood. One form of transvesticism is the creation of a gendered identity as a sexualised distraction from problems or as a means of overcoming a sense of emptiness concerning the sense of self. Psychological defences concern the ability to cope with ordinary living and participate in intimate attachment relationships. Interpreting defences concerns understanding that they have both positive intentions and consequences (self-defence and protection) but because of their over-use they also inevitably entail problems and negative consequences. Most often, the positive intent is to stave off a fear, prevent disappointment or some anticipated failure.

2 Some Findings from Psychological Scientific Research into Gender Identity and Sex

This section recaps some further findings on sex before considering the intersubjective meaning of gender. Firstly, primary trans-sexuality might have a biological cause in neurological differences.[2] Primary male trans-sexuality might be a form of intersexuality because the brains of trans-sexual people may have features usually belonging to the female sex. Other scientific findings on the biopsychosocial whole of gender follow.

The behavioural science of gender behaviour and identity relates average individual differences in behaviour to hereditary biological cause by estimating what proportion of the variation can be explained by genetic cause. Beijsterveldt, Hudziak and Boomsma conclude that children of both sexes display gender behaviour that can be classed as male and female. For most, the amount of cross-gender behaviour decreases with age. They found a decrease of opposite gender behaviour between the ages of 7 and 10. Specifically, the amount of cross-gender behaviour and identity for boys decreases from 3% to 2% for boys; whilst the amount of the same falls from 5% to 3% for girls.[3] They cited evidence that gender behaviour itself is 70% genetic. Therefore, the motivation to be congruent or incongruent with sex, according to genetic research, seems to be biological in 70% of cases on average with the remaining 30% coming from intersubjective influence alone. This means that there could be two types of cause present. The felt-sense of gender identity and its accompanying role-behaviour could be biologically caused; or intersubjectively-influenced due to psychological meaning and social learning (and due to defensive choice). The same authors found no hormonal influence in the womb, when one twin was of a different sex to its co-twin. What they did note is that in different countries, the rate and age at which children are referred for treatment for gender identity problems varies a great deal. The overall trend is heavily against the expression of girlish behaviour in boys; and a remarkable tolerance for boyish behaviour in girls.

The finding for the amount of heritability of cross-gender behaviour has also been estimated by Iervolino et al.[4] who used a different methodology. But this study did not take into account the influence of parenting style on the children it studied. What these authors found was that boys were more sensitive to parenting style and more aware of the taboo against female behaviour. The gender behaviour included in this study included considerations of choice of toys, play activities and personality. The influence of parenting style is important because in a family and cultural setting where there is much enforcement of highly differentiated male and female roles, then it would be expected that there would be much greater conformity to role. In a more egalitarian household and culture, there would be less enforcement, so if there was cross-gender behaviour or identity expressed, there would not be a problem and censure would not be forthcoming.

Knafo, Iervolino and Plomin[5] studied the degree to which male and female gender behaviour exists in relation to sex amongst children. They found that children can be bi-gendered because they express behaviour that is both male and female to the eyes of their parents. They called this behaviour "partly atypical" because it expresses male and female qualities. They also noted children who were "fully atypical" in that they expressed 'opposite' gender identity (which is similar to being trans-sexual in an adult). Of the girlish boys, none of them were as girly as the typical girls. Their finding was that being a fully atypical, boyish girl was genetically inherited; whereas partly atypical boyish girls had a much lower level of heritability. Their estimate for the girlish boys showed that 49–67% of their total biopsychosocial environment, from the womb onwards, was responsible for their behaviour.

Now that some of the scientific evidence about the relationship between gender and sex has been laid out, the attention now turns to interpreting intersubjective meaning, identity and human development. Firstly, the attention is turned to psychoanalysis then to phenomenological psychology.

3 Comments on Psychoanalytic Interpretations

Herman Drüe[6] has noted that there can only be an antagonistic relationship between psychoanalysis and phenomenology because they are "divergent". This paper is in the spirit of imagining and empathising with the first-person experiences of trans-sexual people, so something can be first noted in Freud's favour, before following it with something against the tradition of interpretation that he began. Before 1926 Freud noted repression[7] as a universal a priori necessity in the development of human beings. Repression occurs in two stages. First in infancy, it is initiated to repress infantile sexuality. Secondly thereafter, repression is a compromise that is maintained by repressing ideas over repressed material and this is used to explain obsessive compulsive disorder as the ego acting to repress its guilty self-reproaches about its sexual preferences from infancy. In a wider scope, and in the light of changes after 1926, repression concerns the relationship to identity, sexuality and aggression that are on-going necessary parts of human development. Taken in the wider sense, repression is part of development in family, culture and society, in being civilised and adapted with others. If full expression was given to every wish and impulse, there would be chaos rather than the highly predictable normality and stereotype-adherence that most often do occur.

Freud's original thought on the matter of sexuality was influenced by his tendency to assume epiphenomenalism and eschew conscious phenomena in favour of theory.[8] Indeed, Freud seems only to have considered the case of fetishistic cross-dressing. For Freud, sexual paraphilias, "perversions," are a psychological answer to sexual frustration and unconscious conflict. For him, paraphilias serve as defences in order to regress to an alleged stage of non-genital sexual orientation that was claimed to have been achieved during infancy.

Fenichel[9] took the same type of argument a step further when he concluded that fetishism is part of a means of achieving orgasm and decreasing anxiety, rather than using a defence mechanism of a non-sexual sort. Fetishism is the defensive use of pleasure, rather than the neurotic-defensive achievement of unpleasure or distress. For Fenichel, repression in the paraphilias is 'incomplete' in that infantile sexuality re-appears; whereas for other types of defence, infantile sexuality does not re-appear because of a more complete repression. So the idea of repression can be seen to play a role in adaption to intersubjective cultural and societal norms, according to various contexts for role, sex, age and other relevant factors. Three more contemporary psychoanalytic positions on trans-sexualism are as follows.

Loeb[10] takes the view that unconscious fantasy is causative of psychological problems. For instance, she claims that the genitals are sufficiently fear-inducing to cause shock and denial in some children. This causes trans-sexual adults to require repetitive actions to wipe out the unconscious fear that psychoanalysis interprets them to have governing their behaviour, conscious experience and choices. It is claimed that this process is particularly a problem for boys because they fear their penis might get damaged or fall off. For phenomenological psychology, this reasoning typifies what is wrong with the psychoanalytic way of making sense of conscious phenomena.[11] Loeb makes no reasoned showing of how gender comes to exist, particularly in the case of people who have a gender identity different to their sex. Nor does she make any reference to what primary trans-sexual people feel, think or believe.

Volkan and Greer[12] believe that trans-sexualism is a version of transient psychosis. The phenomena they focus on are trans-sexual people who have large amounts of surgery. But this confuses the issue. Volkan and Greer cite no evidence to show how trans-sexuals are temporarily psychotic. Volkan and Greer allege that trans-sexuals suffer a delusion in their belief that they have a different gender to their sex. They argue that surgery serves the function of a hoped-for guarantee against depression and aggression. They conclude that trans-sexualism is really fetishistic transvesticism that exists for the defensive purposes of becoming a perfect self and staving off depression, anger and helplessness. They argue that trans-sexual persons believe that surgery and hormones will produce a new, ego-constant sense of self that will overcome the previous lability of emotion and lack of the sense of self that occurs for people who have transitory psychoses.

Stoller[13] takes a more enlightened position but still holds the central tenet that transvesticism is due to unconscious conflict. Whilst Stoller is clear that there are people who are primary trans-sexuals, who have always felt themselves to be of the 'opposite' gender, he also notes that trans-sexualism can occur amongst siblings who share the same parenting and genetic influence, which might be evidence for the biological cause of trans-sexualism and it being a form of intersexuality. Stoller believes transvesticism is unconsciously caused because sexually attractive objects are chosen due to 'unconscious emotions' of fear and danger. He further hypothesises that a sexually- or gender-traumatised infants become adult survivors who make similar attacks on themselves. Specifically, and in the case of a male transvestite, secondary trans-sexualism is interpreted as the persisting need to protect the penis that originated in the little boy that lives on in the adult and is achieved by cross-dressing as part of sexual excitement.

These three contemporary analysts share interpretative positions that are faulty for phenomenological psychology: Contemporary psychoanalytic hermeneutics prefers explanations of unconscious conflict and universal cause. Such certainties are established prior to empirical research and prior to attending to conscious experiences. Because the objects, meanings and causes are interpreted as *unconscious*, such conclusions are by definition, asserted *despite* conscious evidence.[14] Accordingly, psychoanalytic hermeneutics is opposed to the hermeneutics of phenomenology.

For phenomenology, oxymorons of the sort unconscious object, unconscious cause, unconscious intention, unconscious emotion and unconscious identification are never acceptable in the sense that these senses and objects are permanently unconscious. It is not clear what an unconscious fantasy is because it can never appear for the person who holds it. Nor is it clear what a system of permanently unconscious objects is because only conscious and preconscious objects can appear. For phenomenological psychology, interpretations can only be argued by stating the theory used and the conscious evidence involved: The root of the problem is ignoring first-person accounts and mis-interpreting the evidence of the conscious meanings and experiences of trans-sexual people.

4 Trans-Sexualism as a Cultural Object

Phenomenological psychology as Husserl conceived it, is a theoretical enterprise for grounding any psychological method (Hua IX, 284–287, 321–327). Its guidelines are a set of theoretical rules that could produce new emphases in psychology, psychoanalysis and the psychotherapies. In this section, Husserl's concepts are explained concerning cultural objects and how psychological meanings exist. Most generally, people have an intentional relation to themselves (Hua I, 81) as well as to the meanings of cultural objects for self and other people. However, the physical substrate enables the intersubjective constitution of meaning (Hua IX, 109). The physicality of the body is what enables human beings to indicate their personality and gender identity through gendered behaviour and placing themselves in family, culture and society. Moreover, people have a relation to others and themselves because of the sense they have of being gendered. This is a specific and central case of what it means to have a sense of self, an ego, identity or personality. For phenomenological psychology, the contributory factors overall are biological, psychological and intersubjective. The following remarks are conclusions taken from a reading of first-person accounts of male to female and female to male trans-sexuality.[15]

Iso Kern summarises Husserl's position on the relation between self and other.[16] These comments can be added to others from Marbach[17] and the details of the cultural object and Sects. 16 and 45 of *Phenomenological Psychology* (Hua IX, 110–118, 228). Together these shine light on psychological meaning and identity: For trans-sexual people, the inner gendered sense of self is incongruent with sex but connected to the identity of the gender of choice, so additions need to be made to express the inner sense. The motivational experience of trans-sexual persons is that their felt-bodiliness and self-reflexive self-presence is female when they are male, for instance. The empathised and real relation to other people is the sum total of retained experiences in connection with anticipations about the current interaction.

The 'equation' that trans-sexuals and transvestites follow is that their physical body is added to the cultural objects of the gender of chosen identity to create a new whole: producing an intersubjectively-recognisable person of the chosen gender. In dressing or through surgery, these acts emphasise and express the chosen gender, despite its incongruence with sex. Through cultural objects, trans-sexuals create themselves by de-emphasising aspects of their sex (the extreme of this is having surgery) and using cultural objects to portray themselves as being of the chosen gender identity. What then occurs is the achievement of positive self-esteem. The internal dialogue is of the sort: "This is the truth. This is me. I like being me". However, even after surgery and hormone treatment, there is still a residue of the sex of birth. Even if the intersubjective role is fully convincing to the public, the personal history of having been incongruent with sex in the past, can never be totally absolved. The social place achieved by successful surgery for primary trans-sexuals should lead to greater satisfaction and a relaxation of the tension they had felt previously.

However, because of breaking a taboo, trans-sexuals are faced with a dilemma concerning how to be. Some of their choices can be summarised as the following mutually exclusive directions:

- Repress the chosen gender identity and behaviour and limit the expression of self to the identity, role and behaviour appropriate to sex.
- Express the trans-sexual gender identity and dare to be congruent with the felt-sense of gender in public and be openly full-time trans-sexual but not have surgery.

- Express the trans-sexual identity in roles, places and contexts that are not antagonistic but supportive of a part-time trans-sexual identity. But expressing sex-congruent role, clothing and behaviour in other contexts.
- Have surgery to alter sex to become congruent with the felt-gender identity.

These options revolve around being able to judge what is egoic (authentic, ego syntonic) about the sense of self as gendered. This is particularly difficult when the roles of men and women are in flux. Since the rise of feminism, there has been a move to equality of opportunity for both sexes. In some areas of life, there is still a division between the sexes so that some roles are kept specifically for people who are physically male or female. For instance, females might only be allowed to be nursery school teachers, midwives or gynaecologists in some countries.

What these intersubjective and physical processes show are codes of non-verbal meaning that co-exist with similar and opposed types of non-verbal meanings. Such codes of meaning accrue across social history and the changing ways in which men and women express gender and other attributes according to the style of the times. Because of staying at a level of abstraction, definitions of male and female gender have not been provided. But if conformity to expectation is not met, then there is confusion and social rules of an unwritten sort are broken. The response to breaking taboos shows what the general population believe should happen.

5 Shared Problems for Psychoanalysis and Phenomenology

There are a number of shared difficulties for any school that wishes to interpret conscious experience, let alone unconscious mental objects and the processes that form them. In fact, there is common ground between the empirical and a priori theoretical approaches. The empirical disciplines of psychoanalysis, psychotherapy and psychological science could benefit from further philosophical-theoretical clarification to enable them to be better focused on meaning and experience in its social habitat. The a priori disciplines of transcendental philosophy, psychological hermeneutics and phenomenological psychology comment on empirical everyday experience. These disciplines share common problems. There are at least five difficulties in moving from the empirical to deriving a priori theory – and difficulties moving from theory to its application.

1. There is the permanent inability to have the experiences and perspectives of others as they have them. There is the empathic possibility of quasi-experiencing the experiences or perspective of other persons through social learning (Hua XIV, 249) and verbally expressing the understandings gained about them, so that they can confirm or disconfirm what has been understood.
2. There is great difficulty in remembering one's own childhood or understanding the experiences of infants. Adults can learn to grasp non-verbal and para-verbal expressions and empathise the experiences and perspectives of infants with accuracy.

But it is only with difficulty that it is possible to interpret how infants empathise their carers.

3. The ability to empathise imaginatively another's experiences is limited according to the breadth of one's social and cultural experiences (cf Hua XIV, Number 6, Appendices XII–XIV, Hua XV, Numbers 10, 11, 35, Appendices VII, IX–XI, XIII).
4. The early history of childhood is not immediately apparent for understanding the domain of adult development. What is apparent are the current influences and inter-relationship between the ego, social context and family influences – on self-esteem and mood. Adults' memories of their own childhoods can mis-represent that stage of life. There is difficulty in knowing what sort of human experience to include, and hence, how to capture the whole of a region, in relation to the greater wholes around it. Husserl classed his analysis of what appears, in relation to intentionality, as a theory-making procedure not an empirical one.
5. There are problems of justifying any means of interpreting lived experience. Consensus about justifications is necessary in order to account for the reasoning used in an explicit way, for colleagues of the same and different schools of thought. Interpretation necessitates a justified psychological hermeneutics. Particularly when interpreting the nature of intentionalities and combinations between types of active and passive intentionality do not appear and must be argued with respect to conscious experience.[18]

The matters above could be explored in greater detail. One philosophical question that arises from the five difficulties above is to wonder to what extent the a priori-empirical distinction is tenable for thinking about psychological matters. For instance, Kant and Husserl made psychological a priori arguments by deriving universal conclusions from everyday experience. The questions that arise are "to what degree can such universal a priori become separate from the empirical regions that they are about?" And "how can any such claims about empirical reality be shown to be universal, when there could be the possibility of finding an empirical case that disproves a universal claim?" The question concerns the degree to which a priori conclusions have actually escaped the realm of the empirical. Despite Husserl's own advice to attend to what appears and make conclusions based only on differences in givenness, perhaps he was unduly guided by his early experience in mathematics in focusing on an ideal view of meaning.

What the region of current conscious experiences about gender and sex show for phenomenological theorising is that there is a need to be clear about how personality types amongst trans-sexual and non-trans-sexual people vary, according to the parameters of being introvert and extrovert, for instance, and the quality of self-esteem. Such meaning-oriented analyses should occur without consideration of theorising about biopsychosocial causes and the possibility that there might be neurological causes for intersexuality and trans-sexuality.

One therapeutic question that arises from the selection above is to wonder about the extent of the free will and the degree of choice of the ego. Adult selves could change most of their behaviour and role, if they wished to do so. Despite the existence of free will, some persons seem to be unwilling or unable to understand and change some aspects of themselves that others might. Accordingly, there is differing inertia to change, for some persons and not for others. How does this happen? How do the effects of biological inheritance actually meet with the intersubjective influences on the ego that have been accumulated over the lifespan? These are the sort of questions that are common to psychoanalysis, psychotherapy and phenomenological psychology. Husserl noted that the world should be approached neutrally, "without being tested and also without being contested" (Hua III, 57). This is particularly difficult when the evidence for one's sense of self is immanent and made through comparison to others.

For phenomenological psychology, what is interpreted are conscious experiences, meanings, motivations and intentions. The way to understand these experiences *is from within the inherent differences of a specific region of experiences*. Not primarily by reference to thinking about cause and effect, but by attending to the differences that appear, in order to interpret the intentionalities at work in relation to their conscious senses (Hua III, 269–273, 313–318). This latter more general process of the expression of the sense of self as a cultural object is a general aspect of expressing any aspect of self and the relationships that self has to others, meanings and cultural practices. This will be revisited below. Husserl's advice on the psychology of intentionality is that it must map the ways in which the different types of object givenness appear in the all-encompassing sphere of the perceptual original temporal field of the present moment, including the other types of temporal givenness and types of semiosis. The specific case of the semiosis of gender is like pictorial presentation and signitive presentation. The specific case of signifying links to the traditional binary opposition of male and female occurs through the physical association between items of clothing of a specific style. Wearing an item means adopting the role and identity of the gender of the wearer as indicated by the cut of the garment. The associative connection is between the piece of clothing and the ideal sense of the binary meaning existing as a cultural object. What appears in the style of a garment is the perceptual presence of the item that indicates and connects to the depicted gender-ideal.

If it is accepted that the being of consciousness and relationship between persons are adequately addressed by Husserl's ideas of intentionality, intentional implication and intersubjective intentional implication (Hua VI, 111–112, 166–167, 170–171, 258–260). It remains to be seen how the nature of psychological reality as shared, temporal and meaningful can be empirically disclosed. Josef Perner[19] and colleagues have begun an empirical approach to intentionality in child development. The difficulties in arriving at a consensus of theory and practice mean there is a proliferation of schools and a lack of standardised ways in agreeing stances and methods. The consequence is that the inevitable variance in dealing with meaning leads to differences in the actions that follow. However for phenomenology, the areas noted above are capable of supporting schools of justification about what is psychologically and perceptually given, on the proviso that theory and reasoning concern the given.

6 The Wider Implications

A conclusion is now provided. Logically, a man wearing women's clothes does not make him into a woman. Similarly, a woman who wears women's clothes does not make her into a woman either. But from the view point of meaning, trans-sexualism shows something important and common about non-verbal expression. Trans-sexualism shows how pre-existing intersubjective codes of meaning and the semiotics of expression are appropriated in becoming gendered. The more abstract point is that *similar processes occur in expressing any identity or role*. The overall appropriation of cultural objects explains the interaction that occurs between inner and outer, in expressing what is inward in a dynamic relation to the outer. The mode of expressing for a trans-sexual self is the same for those whose gender is congruent with their sex: in order to place any self within the psychological universe, self has to appropriate the already existing cultural order to identify itself with respect to the dominant 'discourses' of the local symbolic order.[20] This appropriation is required to be any self, belong to a group or occupy a role.

The Husserl-inspired analysis above shows psychological phenomena concerning human identity. The nature of the ego is related to non-perceptual meanings that are mediated by cultural objects and practices. These meanings are intersubjective, temporal and distributed across society and history. The key element is showing who one is by appropriating cultural codes. For instance, for persons to indicate themselves as female, the feminine display is increased by taking female clothing, grooming, decreasing and controlling body hair and using cosmetics to create a female appearance, irrespective of sex at birth. This is no different to being physically female. Women whose gender is congruent with their sex also use clothing, control body hair and apply cosmetics to emphasise their sex and gender. Alternatively, they could wear bland clothing and adopt a non-verbal demeanour and speech that would de-emphasize their sex and create a different type of gender identity. The equation of expressing gender identity as *physical body plus cultural objects* of the chosen gender holds for non-trans-sexual people who dress congruently with their sex and the cultural conventions concerning the assumed binary opposition of gender. The standard outcome is producing a congruent whole of appearing as a human being with the bodily adornments and grooming worthy of role, age, cultural group and personal style.

The intersubjective expression of chosen gender identity by trans-sexual persons is one case of a much more general process of semiotic expression through appropriating suitable cultural senses and cultural objects concerning other aspects of identity, lifestyle, choice, status and role. The type of proposition that is most basic is that *any object-meaning in the psychological universe has its meaning in contradistinction to other objects and categories of object-meaning*. For the Husserlian tradition of interpretation, these meanings are identical and identifiable regularities of ideal sense that are found against the wider backdrop of other types of meaning, as these comprise the totality of meanings of the psychological world-whole, the universe of psychological sense. Expressing gender identity is one amongst many characteristics within society that are apportioned on the basis of bodily physicality like race, disability, height, weight and age. In this view, the more fundamental ability is appropriating and expressing culturally-maintained codes of expression as part of non-verbal and verbal communication. Clothing, bodily expression and hairstyle show meanings of specific communal and communicational sorts. They create a non-verbal frame or context for understanding the position of the speaker who positions him or herself among the pre-existing codes: Like actors choosing props in order to express their roles more credibly, the general public becomes the audience for witnessing the performance of roles, narrative and drama taught by culture and improvised in the moment.

At a greater level of abstraction still, any role in society requires the semiotic expression and appropriation of suitable cultural objects in order to signify specific meanings to show that persons have adopted a role or identity according to cultural and social expectations. Congruence with cultural expectations promotes stereotypy. For instance, lecturers look, speak and act like lecturers. Men who dig holes in the roads wear big boots are ready to do physical work in all weathers. Mothers with new babies have coffee mornings and get involved socially with other new mothers. The stereotypical performances of social roles are a non-verbal code that may or may not have ever been explicitly taught by culture or family. But the cultural objects and attitudes pertinent to any specific role are what people in society expect.

Because the realm of any meanings and cultural practices are intersubjective, they are difficult to enforce and control. Trans-sexuals appropriate pre-existing gender codes in order to express themselves like anybody else. During the twentieth century, the female sex appropriated previously male sexual roles, permissions and power and a greater degree of commonality began for the sexes. There is also a great deal of variation cross-culturally when considering what appropriate gender behaviour is for sex. In matriarchal societies, possessions and other rights pass only through women, for instance. For phenomenological psychology, this shows that pre-existing semiotic codes and conventions of expression are necessary enabling conditions for the creation of self. In the broader phenomenological psychology view, more detail is required. Three leading questions are "what is the nature of psychological meaning?" "How are psychological meanings originally made?" "And how are they maintained?" Given that human beings are intersubjective as well as material (Hua IV, 158, 311), the wider case is that people appropriate already existing cultural codes in occupying a role. Husserl defined cultural objects as historically-accruing manifolds of meanings that are deployed and re-deployed by groups of persons over time (Hua IX, 115, 118).

Understanding cultural objects requires understanding semiotic links to social contexts and meanings that are not currently present but form part of the general background of intersubjective experience in society. Using cultural objects creates links between users and the reference groups to whom the objects belong. Expressing gender identity is one case of self-creation by adopting the current non-verbal, semiotic systems of signs and codes, and gaining connection to these meanings to *show* and *place self* within the full spectrum of gendered behaviour. The most general expression is encoding followed by decoding. Behaviour is adopted to indicate a position within the realm of gendered identity. In a more abstract view, people might want to indicate their wealth by driving an expensive car, dressing in the latest fashion or having the latest technological devices. The general principles used are associations of sense from a person to a cultural object, a brand name, lifestyle or type of identity. For instance, a cultural object such as a brand can be linked to famous people to indicate its desirability and suggest the meaning that it would confer on its purchasers.

7 Conclusion

The phenomenon of trans-sexuality is where people of one sex feel themselves to be of a different gender. This is not a uniform phenomenon but happens in different degrees. The intersubjective psychological world is gendered and has pre-established social rules and expectations about how men and women can be, largely in-line with the assumption that there are only two, mutually-exclusive types of sex and only two, mutually-exclusive types of gender. But people who are trans-sexual and intersexual aid understanding the whole of what it is to be gendered and sexed. They are part of the larger whole of what it is to express all aspects of self and connect with cultural and societal groups.

Because physical masculinity and feminity include intersexuality, in the senses of being both "among" and "between," then there is no universal opposition between male and female: for gender or sex. One tendency has been for culture and society to enforce its assumption of the mutual exclusivity between male and female. This is particularly evident in discouraging boys to be feminine; whereas girls have gained greater access to what used to be exclusively male roles, behaviours and identity. As regards gender roles, they are currently in a state of flux and vary ad hoc across history and cultures. What seems to be widespread in the west is a taboo against traditionally feminine behaviour and roles for men, although the reasons for this have not been explored. Given that there has been an emancipation of women in the twentieth century, perhaps it is time for an emancipation of men, to consider the question of what it means to be a man.

Notes

1. Sharon Preves, *Intersexuality and Identity: The Contested Self* (Piscataway: Rutgers University Press, 2003).
2. Frank Kruijver, Jiang-Ning Zhou, Chris Pool, Michael Hofman, Louis Gooren, and Dick Swab, "Male-to-Female Transsexuals Have Female Neuron Numbers in a Limbic Nucleus," *The Journal of Clinical Endocrinology and Metabolism* 85 (2000): 2034–2041.
3. Toos van Beijsterveldt, James Hudziak and Dorret Boomsma, "Genetic and Environmental Influences on Cross-Gender Behaviour and Relation to Behaviour Problems: A Study of Dutch Twins at Ages 7 and 10 Years," *Archives of Sexual Behavior* 35 (2006): 647–658.

4. Alessandra Iervolino, Melissa Hines, Susan Golombok, John Rust, and Robert Plomin, "Genetic and Environmental Influences on Sex-Typed Behaviour During the Preschool Years," *Child Development* 76 (2005): 826–840.
5. Ariel Knafo, Alessandra Iervolino, and Robert Plomin, "Masculine Girls and Feminine Boys: Genetic and Environmental Contributions to Atypical Gender Development in Early Childhood," *Journal of Personality and Social Psychology* 88 (2005): 400–412.
6. Herman Drüe, Psychoanalysis, in *Encyclopedia of Phenomenology,* ed. L. Embree et al., trans. W. Wittenstein, 568–572 (Dordrecht: Kluwer, 1997).
7. Sigmund Freud, *Repression,* SE XIV, 156–158. GW X 250 (1915d).
8. Sigmund Freud, *Introductory Lectures on Psychoanalysis,* SE XV 67, GW (1916).
9. Otto Fenichel, *The Psychoanalytic Theory of Neurosis* (New York: W.W. Norton, 1945).
10. Loretta Loeb, "Childhood Gender-Identity Disorders," in *Sexual Deviation,* ed. I. Rosen, 3rd ed, (New York: Oxford University Press, 1996), 134–157.
11. Eugen Fink, "Beilage XXI," in Die Krisis der europäischen Wissenschaften und die transzendentale Phänomenologie. Eine Einleitung in die phänomenologische Philosophie, ed. W. Biemel (Hague, 1956), 473–475. Simone De Beauvoir: La deuxième sexe, 2 tomes. Paris 1949.
12. Vamik Volkan and William Greer, "True Transsexualism," in *Sexual Deviation*, 3rd ed., ed. I. Rosen (New York: Oxford University Press, 1996), 158–173.
13. Robert Stoller, "The Gender Disorders," in *Sexual Deviation*, 3rd ed., ed. I. Rosen (New York: Oxford University Press, 1996), 111–133.
14. Ian Rory Owen, *Psychotherapy and Phenomenology: On Freud, Husserl and Heidegger* (Lincoln: iUniverse, 2007).
15. Jennifer Boylan, She's not There: A Life in Two Genders (New York, 2004); Mildred Brown and Chloe Rounsley, True Selves: Understanding Transsexualism – for Families, Friends, Co-workers, and Helping Professionals (New York: Jossey-Bass, 1996); Jason Cromwell, Transmen and FTMs: Identities, Bodies, Genders, and Sexualities (Illinois, 1999); Tracie O'Keefe and Katrina Fox, Finding the Real Me: True Tales of Sex and Gender Diversity (New York, 2003); Henry Rubin, Self Made Men: Identity, Embodiment and Recognition Among Transsexual Men (Nashville, 2003); Peggy Rudd, Who's Really from Venus? The Tale of Two Genders (Katy, 1998); Veronica Vera, Miss Vera's Finishing School for Boys Who Want to Be Girls (New York, 1997).
16. Iso Kern, "Intersubjectivity," in *Encyclopedia of Phenomenology*, trans W.R. McKenna, ed. L. Embree et al. (Dordrecht: Kluwer, 1997), 355–359.
17. Eduard Marbach, "Two Directions in Epistemology: Husserl and Piaget," *Revue Internationale de Philosophie* 36 (1982): 435–469.
18. Eduard Marbach, *Mental Representation and Consciousness: Towards a Phenomenological Theory of Representation and Reference* (Dordrecht: Kluwer, 1993).
19. Josef Perner, *Understanding the Representational Mind* (Cambridge, MIT Press, 1993).
20. Claude Lévi-Strauss, *Sociologie et anthropologie* (Paris: Presses Universitaires de France, 1950).

Self-Deception: Theoretical Puzzles and Moral Implications*

Sonja Rinofner-Kreidl

Abstract Analysing the logical structure of self-deception requires to mark the difference between normal, that is interpersonal deception and self-deception. Equally, we have to distinguish simple errors with regard to oneself from proper cases of self-deception. The latter obviously are of a more complicated structure. Persons who fall prey to self-deception seem to harbour antagonistic tendencies. Occasionally, these tendencies were analysed in terms of simultaneously held incompatible beliefs. Theoretical approaches that consider self-deception as some kind of cognitive deficiency typically take this view. Contrary to this, the author argues that a phenomenological description endorses a deflationary conception of self-deception akin to Alfred Mele's pioneering analyses. A phenomenological approach steers clear both of presuming unconscious processes (in terms of a Freudian theory of the unconscious) and of referring to contradicting beliefs. Accordingly, phenomenologists neither unduly strengthen the irrational components of human life (Freudian interpretation) nor do they defend a strongly rationalized account of human action (cognitivist interpretation). Instead, it will be argued that in a garden-variety of cases self-deception amounts to an emotionally motivated temporary suspension of our will to acquire knowledge or true belief. This special type of avoidance behaviour obviously has interesting moral implications. The latter centre round the issues of truthfulness, self-control, and responsibility. '-- End of Abstract'

---

*The first draft of this paper was done on occasion of the *Philosophy, Psychiatry and the Unconscious Colloquium,* February 8–10, 2006, at the Bioethics Center, Dunedin School of Medicine, Dunedin/New Zealand. I would like to thank Grant Gillet and the other participants of this conference for discussing my paper. I am indebted to Monica Clark-Grill and Sebastian Luft for their accurate linguistic correction of the original conference submission. The remaining linguistic and other errors, without exception, rest with the author.

S. Rinofner-Kreidl (✉)
Department for Philosophy, Karl-Franzens-University Graz, Heinrichstrasse 26/6, 8010 Graz, Austria
e-mail: sonja.rinofner@uni-graz.at

D. Lohmar and J. Brudzińska (eds.), *Founding Psychoanalysis Phenomenologically*, Phaenomenologica 199, DOI 10.1007/978-94-007-1848-7_11,

1 Freud's Stake in Self-deception

According to Freud, phenomena of self-deception are frequent. Although states of self-deception are quite normal in terms of their frequency, it readily happens that persons to whom such states are ascribed slide into pathological situations. Psychoanalysts commonly expect that their patients may be caught in some specific kind of obstinate self-deception. Persons with a psychological disorder can be said to be, in some special sense, "split apart." They suffer from a more or less threatening uneasiness about how they behave and how they perceive themselves and others, but nevertheless are unable to change their modes of behaviour and their attitudes. Assumed to underlie the various symptoms of psychological illness are past traumatic experiences which needed to be transferred to the unconscious ("suppressed") because of their very intensive negative affective implications. From a psychoanalytical point of view, self-deception results from the fact that conscious and unconscious intentions come into conflict with each other. Consequently, we should argue that phenomena of self-deception cannot be explained unless we make reference to a sphere of unconscious forces that Freud tried to systematically describe in his so-called first and second topic.

The issue of self-deception, especially when analysed in terms of unconscious desires and intentions, inevitably touches on the problem of agency. Tacitly or overtly, the latter is implied in every reference to an unconscious sphere of our psychic life. Within the framework of psychoanalysis, describing situations of self-deception requires to assume that the person in question is split into two parts, a conscious and an unconscious one, which both behave, respectively, as if they were independent agents. If we agree to this view, the knotty point, of course, is how we should imagine these agents to be re-united in a single consciousness.[1] This very tersely sketched psychoanalytic approach is compatible with another view on self-deception that is famous among philosophers. We may call it the cognitivist interpretation of self-deception. Before we turn towards it, we should take notice of some conceptual distinctions.

2 Error, Deception, and Self-deception

Errors occur unintentionally. They slip in. If I knew that I was about to make a mistake, I certainly would try to avoid it, and, therefore, presumably succeeded in avoiding it. According to our common usage of the word "error", it is impossible that someone *intends* to make an error. If one does, we are faced with some kind of deception. Deceptions are errors that are deliberately produced in order to mislead someone else. Deceptions require some interpersonal relation. They are, by definition, interpersonal. The person who has the intention to deceive and the person who is deceived (and is meant not to know that she is) are different persons. Deceptions can only occur under the following circumstances:

(i) There is someone who has the intention to deceive.
(ii) There is someone who is deceived, i.e., who is wrong about some aspect of reality because she believes what someone else wants her to believe.
(iii) The person who has the intention to deceive and the person who is deceived are not identical.
(iv) The person who has the intention to deceive knows how things really are. Otherwise, he could only accidentally (instead of: intentionally) deceive someone else. Consequently, he himself could not know whether or not, in a particular case, he really is deceiving someone else.
(v) The person who has the intention to deceive someone else knows about the fact that he has this specific intention and expects the other person not to know that he has.

If we consider self-deception instead of deception, we obviously have to replace (iii) by

(iii^0) The person who has the intention to deceive and the person who is deceived are the very same person.

However, introducing (iii^0) we face some difficulties. In case of normal deceptions, i.e., interpersonal deceptions or deceptions by others, it is unproblematic to state that deceptions require both the intention to deceive and the knowledge about how things truly are because of (iii). On the other hand, self-deceptions, according to (iii^0), seem to be based on an impossible connection: namely, that I myself know the truth but, nonetheless, deceive myself with regard to the very same state of affairs. This is the mysterious and ticklish character of self-deceptions that has been rightly called "the static puzzle (or: paradox) of self-deception" (Mele 1998, 2001, 50–75). Whenever someone deceives herself she induces herself to be wrong with regard to some particular state of affairs, although she has knowledge about the truth. Consequently, we should refer to actually conflicting intentions in order to explain phenomena of self-deception. In other words: we should expect the person in question to simultaneously hold incompatible states of belief. On the one hand, she must be wrong insofar as she successfully deceives herself. On the other hand, she must know the truth, since otherwise she could not even deceive herself. According to (iv): Every intentionally produced error requires to assume that the person who is engaged in this activity knows the truth. Following this approach we should say: A person suffering from self-deception is wrong (succeeds in deceiving herself) and is not wrong (knows that she deceives herself).

Referring to the phenomena considered above, the distinction between how things really are and how they appear to be, or the distinction between truth and error, is of utmost importance. Making errors implies, as we said above, that the person who is mistaken does not know the truth, although talking about "errors" would not make sense in general, if *nobody* were able to know the truth. Successful deceptions require that the person who deceives knows the truth, whereas the person deceived does not. Hence, phenomena of self-deception seem to imply that I (who is the only person involved) both know the truth and do not know the truth. Here we face a very peculiar situation that includes an irritating coincidence of antagonistic tendencies. On the one hand, it is obvious that a person who falls prey to self-deception does not know what she really does, that is, what her real intentions are. Otherwise we could not consider this to involve a deception. On the other hand, if "self-deception" means that there must be a more or less hidden intention to deceive oneself, it seems unavoidable to concede that the very same person, in this way or another, does not only know about her hidden intentions, but equally about the fact that she tries to conceal them, while simultaneously, in some sense, this concealment must be effective. 'Being effective' here requires that the concealment must even conceal itself.[2] There must be some kind of knowledge about the difference between reality and appearance with regard to the mental states of the person at issue. Otherwise, the relevant deception could not be considered self-referential.

It is worth noting that self-deception cannot simply be identified with lacking knowledge or errors concerning oneself. Normally, such errors do not imply self-deception. Suppose that I was involved in a serious accident and the doctors decided to put me into a coma for 10 days in order to stabilize my physical functions. If I do not remember what happened when I recover consciousness, it is correct to say that I, at least to a certain extent, lack knowledge with respect to myself. Although in this situation I am, to a certain extent, mistaken with regard to my own person, it certainly would be inadequate to consider this a self-deception unless we suppose that I myself deliberately gave rise to my post-traumatic amnesia. If someone, temporarily or generally, does not have the cognitive abilities to recognize that she has been caught in an illusive view on how things really are, we cannot blame her for self-deception although we still can say that she is wrong with regard to herself. What can we learn from this apart from the fact that it is not at all clear whether or not we might be justified in blaming someone for her self-deceptions (see below, Sect. 5)?

First, there is a clear and distinct difference between situations of self-deception and situations of deception (errors or fallacies). The latter are due to various cognitive deficiencies like unusual conditions that are detrimental to accurate reasoning (e. g., illness, drug abuse, lack of necessary information, mental disability). Whereas errors refer to the issue of *truth*, and can only be recognized on the basis of the idea of truth, self-deception is not a matter of true or false statements. As I shall argue below, it refers to the issue of *veracity* which does not affect the objective state of the world. Veracity rather concerns the issue whether or not my actions und thoughts correspond to my true convictions and desires. Striving to recognize the truth is quite a different thing than striving to recognize one's own true desires, motives and attitudes. However, it is in the latter case that our practical engagement is of fundamental interest. It is quite a normal situation that, notwithstanding the fact that I am motivated by a (philosophical) will to achieve true insight, I fail to do so. With regard to veracity, things are different. Here, in order to attain my purpose, it suffices to have the clear and decided will to attain it. Whenever I am really determined to behave in a veracious way, I shall succeed in doing so. Veracity is a matter of subjective motivation; truth is not.

Secondly, self-deception, contrary to "normal" deceptions, needs to be maintained in a certain sense. It requires some amount of psychic energy, some kind of practical engagement to permanently persist in a state of self-deception. We must have a stake in deceiving ourselves in order to be successful in doing so. (This is due to some peculiar implications of self-deception that will be analysed later.) The same could not be said about errors lacking self-referentiality. On the contrary, errors often occur although we try to avoid them. Thirdly, self-deceptions do not happen to me in the same way as when I make a mistake. Self-deceptions do not occur in a neutral, objective mode. They are typically based on some kind of emotional bias (see Mele 1987, 1995). This is a crucial point to which I will come back soon.

So far we have outlined the rather complex situation we enter when talking about self-deception. *Cognitivist interpretations* focus on one of the issues mentioned above, namely the issue of truth or (conflicting) states of belief, respectively. According to a widespread view, self-deceptions should be described as follows (see Davidson 1982, 2004, Chaps. 11–14). A person who suffers from self-deception simultaneously is in two states of belief that exclude each other. Or: she simultaneously acknowledges two contradictory statements. Logically viewed, it is impossible that two contradicting statements are both true (according to our classical conception of logic). Epistemically, it is impossible that one and the same person simultaneously holds two beliefs that exclude each other if both these beliefs are distinctly grasped. The only available and plausible explanation of how this could be done (granted that we are not faced with a case of mental insanity), seems to be to assume that the person in question is unaware of one of the beliefs or statements at issue, in that at least one of them remains unconscious. Of course, arguing in this manner gives rise to additional problems. To whom should we ascribe unconscious states of belief, unconscious convictions, and unconsciously acknowledged statements? Under what conditions is it possible to recognize states of self-deception? Who is able to recognize them from what point of view? It is one of the intriguing aspects of self-deception that, while trying to analyse this phenomenon, we are directly led to think about the position we have to take in order to be able to recognize it at all. Obviously, we can claim to do this from a third-person-perspective or from a first-person-perspective. The former is a methodical constituent of the scientific approach, the latter, if interpreted in a specific mode, is characteristic of a phenomenological approach (Rinofner-Kreidl 2004a, b). What is at stake here, are not different interpretations of the same phenomena. The moot point, rather, is that the methodical approaches differ in such a manner that the given objects, i.e., phenomena, cannot be said to be identical.

3 Naturalistic Versus Phenomenological Approaches

If we proceed from a folk psychological understanding of self-deception (as we did above), it is obvious that the scientific approach, which tries to explain conscious phenomena solely with reference to physiological facts and natural laws, cannot grasp the very phenomenon of self-deception. Instead, it redefines it and substitutes it by some kind of theoretical construction exclusively involving relations of natural facts and generalizations referring to these facts. Yet, phenomenology does not seem to fare any better. A phenomenological, that is, intentionalistic approach obviously cannot cope with phenomena of self-deception if it is true that such an approach is bound to a first-person-perspective and that we cannot go wrong with regard to our present experiences. How could I ever misconceive my intentions if I am immediately acquainted with the experiences I actually live-through and if this mode of immediate acquaintance, as Husserl and other phenomenologists maintain, implies that I am immune to error? (This is what sometimes has been called the Cartesian or solipsistic bias of phenomenology.)

Let us, for the time being, ignore the phenomenological predicament and follow the policy of neutral observation that is typical for a "positivistic" idea of science. Taking this to be our guiding idea of science, we should ask what it means, under this condition, to describe the situation that a deception turns out to be a proper case of self-deception. I suppose that describing self-deception, according to a scientific approach, means to explain the occurrence of this phenomenon by referring to certain natural causes that, normally, are unknown to the person who actually suffers from self-deception. In case of errors concerning the way persons are in contact with their natural and social environment, the causes in question are external stimuli that are misinterpreted by the organism at issue. If we argue along the lines of a naturalistic account, criteria of misinterpretation refer to insufficiencies or failures of adaptive behaviour. For the present purpose, I do not distinguish scientific and naturalistic accounts (see Rinofner-Kreidl 2003a). Scientific theories offer a causal or functional interpretation of those intentions and motives that are involved in human behaviour. Consequently, there is no conceptual room for distinguishing errors, deceptions and self-deception as we did above. What is distinctive is solely the extensional character and spatial location of the causes that bring about the effects in question. In case of errors and deceptions, these causes are not, or at least not exclusively, part of the organism in question; in case of self-deception they are (although, in particular cases, it might be difficult to supply the relevant evidences in a way that does not rule out the claim to intersubjective verifiability or falsifiability, respectively, and to succeed in presenting complete explanations). Freud's approach to the issue of self-deception is compatible with such an account, although he did not try to show how all those psychic forces that psychoanalysis supposes to exist could be localized in (or supervene on) brainphysiological processes. Doing this was not his prime interest. Nonetheless, Freud certainly was driven by something like a vision of naturalistic reductionism. And he is clear about the fact that approaching self-deception psychoanalytically, we have to take a third-person perspective and to assume a sphere of efficient unconscious tendencies. Taking a scientific approach, we obviously should consider *every* human behaviour to be, in a certain sense, illusive. This is due to the fact that human behaviour normally occurs without any accompanying knowledge of the necessary physiological conditions lying beneath the behaviour at issue: the person who behaves in this or that way normally does not have any knowledge about these conditions. What is more, he does not stand in need of a relevant knowledge *in order to be able to (smoothly) act*. Whereas I definitely cannot realize a particular intention without being aware of the fact that I am in a specific mental state, causes bring about their effects independent of someone knowing them or being aware of them. In terms of referring to conditions of human behaviour that do not belong to its intrinsic meaning, a scientific approach rules out the idea of agency and declares human behaviour, in principle, to be illusive since it is neither actually concerned with its physiological conditions nor interested in them. Consequently, scientists argue that what persons consider to be their intentional experiences and actions truly are effects of natural causes which are adequately represented by theories referring, for instance, to the architecture and functions of the human brain.[3] According to this view, we should say that we do not know what we really want and what we actually do. Whenever human actions occur, what really happens is that some kind of complex physiological reaction takes place.

Let us pause for a moment. Granting that the above considerations are correct, we obviously arrive at an impasse. We are faced with two alternative views, neither of which seems to be satisfying. Whereas a phenomenological view, as sketched above, holds that conscious behaviour cannot be self-deceptive on principle, a scientific view, on the contrary, results in the thesis that human behaviour, *as it is experienced by the agents themselves*, is illusive on principle (in the specific sense explained above). This being the case, we should argue that both approaches fail to give an adequate account of a widespread and common experience such as self-deception. Yet, in order to not jump to conclusions we should reconsider the above argumentation. Let us, once again, take a look at the phenomenological approach.

Given that a phenomenological approach is bound to our first-person perspective, it is not easy to see how this approach could offer effective analytical tools to explain instances of self-deception. There is a simple experience that corroborates this view. It is impossible to intelligently and truthfully utter the following sentence and, thereby, pretend to state a truth: "I presently suffer from a self-deception." It is only retrospectively that I may say (and that it makes sense to say): "When I thought of, or behaved in this or that way, answering to a particular situation, I was subject to self-deception, as I can see now." It is possible, and presumably more frequent than we like it to be, that at a certain moment in the past we intended to do x and believed that we intended to do x, and afterwards discover that what we really did and intended to do was something else. Recognizing this to be so is tantamount to recognizing that this former misunderstanding of our own intentions was motivated in some specific sense. It did not happen accidentally or without reason. What does that mean in terms of a possible contribution on the part of phenomenology to clarify the issue of self-deception?

A phenomenological approach is able to descriptively grasp self-deception if we do not restrict this approach to stating the actual content of someone's consciousness and if we do not reduce intentionality to act-intentional behaviour but, instead, consider diverse forms of so-called passive intentionality as well, which have been painstakingly investigated by Husserl and other phenomenologists. There is, for instance, the dynamic structuring of our perceptual field according to the distinction of figure and background that represents a continuous and unobtrusive achievement of marking relevancies and effecting selections. This kind of passive intentionality is constitutive for what we perceive, although it does not result from and is not reducible to explicit, i.e., act-intentional activity. Here, 'passive' refers to those aspects of intentional relations we are usually unaware of. Nonetheless, these very aspects are not unconscious in terms of psychoanalytic theory. Relating to the *actual* content of consciousness we argued above that it rules out self-deception. Yet, arguing in this manner, we ignored that referring to a present mental content there is, strictly speaking, no self. A self can only be identified by means of varying modes of behaviour showing themselves over the course of time. Hence, self-deceptions cannot be described unless we consider reflective references directed at our own past experiences. This implies that consciousness is taken into account not only with regard to the present moment, but as covering a certain span of time. It is obvious that we can be mistaken with regard to our past experiences (or: modes of behaviour). If such mistakes occur, they are subject to the same criteria we are used to rely on concerning errors that do not refer to our own psychic life. For instance, I may be wrong in believing that I saw a parrot in a zoo in Switzerland 2 years ago. It might be that I was in Switzerland at that time together with a friend who went to the zoo and spoke to me lively about his impressions there. It sometimes happens that past experiences are confounded with fantasy experiences or stories told by others. It equally happens that we confuse real experiences and dreams. These are errors that concern the reflective reference to particular contents of our own consciousness. Relating to this, there is no privilege of the first-person perspective. Another person's knowledge about my past experiences and modes of behaviour is, on principle, no less reliable than my own knowledge about myself. On the contrary, it is a frequent experience that others are able to make judgements about our lives more adequately because they are not afflicted with those particular motives lying beneath the misconceptions of our own behaviour (although they are equally liable to be mistaken with regard to the driving forces of *their* behaviour). This is an important issue with regard to psychoanalysis as well. Self-deceptions, on principle, are accessible to and often require interpersonal corrections. Whereas discussing the basic intersubjective accessibility and corrigibility of self-deceptions is a matter of philosophy, we shall draw on psychological guidance in order to trace out the specific extent to which interpersonal corrections are feasible and required in particular cases of (pathological) self-deception. Of course, taking account of the role other persons may play with regard to discovering and eradicating self-deceptions does not touch upon, and should be carefully distinguished from, the possible involvement of an agent's social life with regard to the peculiar contents of her self-deceptions. Although self-deception does not necessarily, i.e., by definition, have a considerable social impact in this respect, it is evident that more often than not self-deceptions occur on the occasion of social conflicts and involve distorted views on our social relations.

4 Phenomenological Description: A Deflationary Conception of Self-deception[4]

Is it possible to accurately describe self-deceptions and, thereby, to go beyond a cognitivist conception of self-deception as well as a scientific re-interpretation of the phenomena in question, including Freud's supposition of unconscious processes? What does a phenomenological approach achieve with regard to self-deception? Let us take a realistic example, which is frequently mentioned in the literature.

Self-deception often occurs when someone commits adultery. This is an interesting case because it enables us to see how in real social life deception and self-deception, notwithstanding their clear structural distinction, often are intertwined and tend to mutually reinforce each other. Suppose there were conspicuous evidence that should induce me to doubt my husband's fidelity and, under normal circumstances, would suffice to actually provoke this doubt. However, I am very afraid of the painful conflicts and quarrels that would result if I accused my husband of fraudulent behaviour. And I am very afraid of changing my life, which I consider unavoidable in case that I put my cards on the table. What happens? Objectively viewed, there is enough relevant information arousing suspicion and justifying some resolute reaction. Let us suppose that no reaction follows. Instead of confronting my husband, I resort to some kind of self-deception. That seems to be, in terms of frequency (not in terms of psychic health or good moral luck), a normal reaction to adultery. How do I succeed in resolving this situation given that we do not trust in the cognitivistic interpretation that expects me to simultaneously hold conflicting states of belief or to simultaneously maintain contradictory statements? What is actually very likely to happen is a selection from or a mixture of the following attitudes. I may ignore the relevant evidences. I may take notice of them in a quite selective manner.[5] I may find interpretations that either are trivial or harmless or that can otherwise easily be refuted as irrelevant or unreliable. Among the many varieties, which should be traced out in cases like that, belongs the difference between (i) refraining from collecting all relevant evidences that, altogether, would corroborate a true though practically fatal and therefore undesired belief, and (ii) encouraging or manufacturing a belief that is incompatible with present evidences.[6]

Behaving like that, my present self-deception cannot and need not be described in terms of contradictory statements or incompatible states of belief.[7] This is due to the fact that I do not allow myself to gain any distinct view on my husband's behaviour. What really happens is that my emotional disposition obviates a sober cognitive evaluation of the situation. When we said above that the evidences at hand would be sufficiently conspicuous to doubt my husband's fidelity "under normal circumstances", this clearly involved an idealization that still seems to be prevalent in philosophy of action. It consists in supposing that persons primarily and mainly are rational agents whose behaviour is determined by their cognitive abilities. Phenomena of self-deception unveil this to be an illusive view on human persons. It is not that an average agent could not distinguish cognitive and emotional abilities or that she regularly would consent to a collapse of rational behaviour in favour of some kind of emotional reaction. Rushing into extremes, we often lose sight of reality. Cognitive abilities cannot be reduced to emotional tendencies. Yet, neither are our cognitive abilities, if we consider their modes of realization, entirely independent from and unaffected by our emotions.[8] In a vast majority of cases, self-deception rests on the fact that our cognitive and emotional tendencies are not in accordance with each other. This drifting apart regularly results in some kind of impairment of our cognitive relation to the world that turns out to be emotionally biased.[9] One possible effect of this is my very peculiar way of ignoring or interpreting those evidences that convincingly corroborate my suspicion. Since I do not feel strong enough to stand the reality as it shows itself in the light of these evidences, the only way out, from an emotional point of view, is to avoid taking notice of the evidences in an unrestricted and undistorted manner. It goes without saying that my (partial) ignoring or re-interpreting of the evidence suggesting my husband's involvement in some escapade, must not be described in terms of a *decision* to ignore or re-interpret the facts in question. If I decided to do so, I must have known about my husband's behaviour and then somehow tried to neutralize this knowledge, i.e., offer some kind of rationalization with regard to my husband's behaviour. This description certainly falls back on the cognitivist account.

A deflationary conception of self-deception centres on the idea that the latter cannot be considered as analogous to the deception by others. Following this view, we had to endorse some dubious double-self theory as if someone else were "located" within my psychic life and tried to deceive me. To be sure, even if we take a deflationary view and, on that account, try to accurately describe typical cases of self-deception, there is plenty of room for interpretations and discussions. For instance, it normally does not involve a straightforward case of self-deception if someone turns out to be susceptible to insinuations on a large scale. Nonetheless, we can suppose that if someone easily falls prey to deception by others, she may equally tend to easily give in as far as self-deception is concerned. Yet, in some important sense it is less problematic and "easier" to be deceived by others than to deceive oneself. It requires weaker conditions to be deceived by others than to deceive oneself. For being liable to deception by others it suffices to take a certain uncritical attitude towards my fellow men's opinions and actions. States of self-deception require more than this kind of naivety. Moreover, in case of deceptions the person who is deceived usually does not have any presumption or suspicion of how things truly are. States of self-deception do not occur unless the agent shows some greater amount of activity on her side. In order to succumb to self-deceptions I, to some extent and in some more or less subtle way, have to exercise an influence on how the relevant evidences are taken into consideration. Contrary to this, my liability or readiness to being deceived by others typically manifests itself in an entirely passive attitude towards the other person's mode of presenting and interpreting the state of affairs at issue. Note that this passivity, for purely conceptual reasons, cannot be grasped by arguing that it means to *tolerate* being deceived by others. Since it is hard to see how I could tolerate something without knowing that it is in some sense a problematic demand or even an affront, we can use the term "tolerate" only in post-hoc statements about situations of deception. Of course, this kind of passivity may be involved in situations of self-deception, too.[10] Nevertheless, it never can be a sufficient condition for the occurrence of self-deceptive behaviour.

According to the above description, self-deception, at least with regard to typical cases, manifests itself in blocking a knowledge one might gain from purely emotional reasons. Or, it consists in adhering to a belief that immediately turned out to be misguided if the relevant evidence would be given due attention. Falling prey to self-deception does not mean to suppress a knowledge we already have at our disposal. It means to forestall gaining knowledge because we could not bear to face the truth. It is in this sense that I deceive myself. However, the fact that I do not allow for an objective evaluation of the evidences at issue, and that I have to make (hard) efforts not to try to achieve knowledge (which, as we may suppose, runs counter to a "natural" inclination of human beings), indicates that there is some kind of more or less vague presumption of how things really are. This presumption remains latent. It is not an adequate description of the above case of self-deception to say that I waver between consenting to the statement "my husband cheats me" and the contradictory statement "my husband does not cheat me". Self-deception, at least in a wide variety of cases, is not a matter of conflicting beliefs or contradictory statements. It, rather, is a matter of suspending our attempt to acquire clear and distinct beliefs and to formulate clear and distinct statements with regard to some *important* state of affairs. Therefore, self-deception may be described as a state of blurred beliefs. It is only by going beyond this state, that we can become aware of possible conflicts or contradictions implied in our belief system. In other words: self-deception rests on temporarily suspending our will to acquire knowledge or true beliefs.[11] Contrary to a cognitivist approach, a phenomenological description argues that the knowledge or belief involved in self-deception (if any) remains latent. To dispense with any attempt to corroborate or refute a latently present presumption is, from a logical and epistemological viewpoint, neither paradoxical nor unintelligible. It, rather, is a psychological fact that human creatures tend to behave in this manner under certain circumstances. Following the present approach, typical cases of self-deception can be described (a) without referring to logical or epistemological paradoxes and (b) without referring to an elaborated idea of the unconscious that is methodically committed to a natural scientific approach. In terms of (a) and (b), I consider the above description, which deviates both from a cognitivist and a psychoanalytic interpretation, a deflationary conception of self-deception.

5 Moral Implications

At least in one respect it seems to be justified to associate self-deception with deception by others. Given suitable circumstances the former is equally blameworthy as the latter. Normally, we do not hesitate to expect a self-deceiver to take responsibility for his way of shaping his behaviour and his opinions about himself.[12] This expectation does not automatically diminish in accordance with the supposed actual inaccessibility of the relevant moods and ideas. This is due to the fact that, unless there are obvious indications of mental disease, we assume persons to have a temporally unfolded, more or less consistent practical identity. Persons, from time to time, fall prey to more or less profound self-deceptions. We nonetheless take for granted that self-deceptions are, on principle, recognizable and corrigible. Otherwise the agent could not be considered responsible for what she does and, to some extent, for what she is.[13] What does that mean? Taking morality serious requires to hold a long-term perspective on human agents or persons. This is the natural view we assume with regard to issues of morality. A deflationary conception of self-deception that focuses on its dynamic structure may deliver strong evidences in favour of this long-term perspective by asking for the moral implications of self-deception. Relating to this, we do not ask any more how an agent's consciousness must be structured in order to enable her to suffer from self-deceptions. From the point of view of morality, the guiding question is: how can we acknowledge self-deception as a natural and undeniable part of human life without thereby abandoning the moral status of the agent? This question triggers another one: how can we meet the following conditions, namely, first, that typical instances of self-deception are not based on firm and explicitly stated decisions or intentional acts of some other kind; secondly, that we nevertheless, under normal circumstances, consider agents responsible for their self-deceptive modes of behaviour?[14]

Mutually acknowledging each other as moral agents, among others, requires that we are not indifferent to our propensity for indulging into self-deception. This is not to deny that processes of self-recognition and self-correction are fallible and only gradually successful. Yet, we have to trust in our capability of self-knowledge. From the point of view of morality, a self-deceiver cannot be entirely ignorant and is not entirely innocent. Otherwise we have to consider him a helpless bystander of his own actions and modes of behaviour. As long as we respect him as a person, we cannot entirely exonerate him from what he does as well as from what he allows to be done to him. This is necessarily so although the realm of his responsibility cannot be sharply delineated. The latter includes, among others, specific types of the above-sketched interplay of interpersonal deception and self-deception that clearly go beyond the "inner", private life of the agent. Typical cases of self-deception do have social implications; they cut across the line of demarcation between our private and public sphere. Equally, we cannot assume our personal and social identity to represent neatly separated dimensions of life. There is a great variety of experiences that testify in favour of their inextricable intertwining. It may, for instance, occur that someone starts to actually identify with a social role she has grudgingly played for a fairly long time just for the sake of ensuring peace and harmony in her social environment. Accordingly, someone may stumble into believing those lies he has told others a hundred times. Since it is impossible to sharply delineate the private and the public sphere in terms of distinctly separated types of motives, it will be equally difficult to single out ("pure") cases of exclusively "internally directed" self-deceptions that do not, in some sense, involve the social relations of the person concerned. This being the case, it is all the less surprising that we are faced with an extensive area where lying, latent complicity, manipulation, injured self-respect, avoidance behaviour, bootstrapping and self-deception melt into one another.

Referring to this area, we may wonder whether seeking refuge in self-deception could be a promising way[15] of coping with feelings of impotence and a loss of self-respect due to aggression, violence, sexual abuse and other threats to one's personal integrity that entail thoroughly negative or highly ambivalent social relations to others. Especially in cases of violence and abuse, self-deception seems to be a suitable option in order to maintain affectively threatening social relations that could not be maintained otherwise. In many less afflicting cases, it seems to be evident that persons allow for being affected by self-deception because this enables them to avoid settling delicate issues with others or with themselves. (In the latter case self-deceptions seem to suppress the "inner" voice of conscience.)[16] To be sure, these persons do not *decide* to avoid the outburst of pending conflicts. They simply overlook suitable occasions to have it out with someone; they do not react in a sensitive way if they are invited to enter discussions; they are so busy that nobody could reasonably expect them to face conflicts. There are innumerable ways of dispensing with a knowledge that could easily be gained if suitable efforts would be made.

As argued above, self-deception can be described in terms of the motivational structure of human behaviour. Accordingly, self-deception involves a temporary suspension of our will to acquire knowledge and, since this suspension does not happen accidentally, a concomitantly occurring desire to prefer partial ignorance. This quite peculiar motivational situation concerns the agent's intellectual and emotional attitudes and, in the long run, her practical identity as a person who struggles to integrate these different spheres. Consequently, an impairment of the agent's striving for knowledge simultaneously manifests itself as an impairment of her intention to behave truthfully (given that we are not faced with pathological situations). This correlation cannot be claimed unless two conditions are met: first, we interpret truthfulness in terms of acting according to one's best possible judgment. Secondly, we conceive of self-deception in terms of a seemingly unnoticed by-passing of one's best possible judgment. Being subject to self-deception, I behave untruthfully insofar as I, occasionally or habitually, refuse to know who I ("really") am.[17] According to the above analysis, self-deception, strictly speaking, is not a matter of being deceived *by myself* if this implied to understand self-deception on the model of interpersonal deception. Rather, it is a matter of concealing oneself. Self-concealments do have moral implications. These implications are interesting although they are not of an immediately and overtly normative nature. Being caught in serious self-deceptions, I can neither take care of myself, e. g., in terms of self-respect[18] or (following Kant: *imperfect*) *duties* referring to myself as a moral person, nor can I comply with moral obligations in general. It is obvious that every possible motivation to overcome a state of self-concealment, ultimately refers to some positive idea of human existence,[19] and, to some extent, contributes to what we may call an individual's practical identity.

Among those who are concerned with unfolding the impact of self-deception on personal integrity is Harry Frankfurt. One issue that is of utmost importance in this respect is ambivalence with regard to one's own (first- or second-order) beliefs and desires: "Ambivalence as such entails a mode of self-betrayal. It consists in a vacillation or opposition within the self which guarantees that one volitional element will be opposed by another, so that the person cannot avoid acting against himself. Thus, ambivalence is an enemy of self-respect." (Frankfurt 1999, 139)[20] At least long-term ambivalence, which is not confined to instantaneous irritations and uncertainties, causes a serious impairment of one's practical identity:

"There is much opportunity for ambivalence, conflict, and self-deception with regard to desires of the second order [...] as there is with regard to first-order desires. If there is an unresolved conflict among someone's second-order desires, then he is in danger of having no second-order volition; for unless this conflict is resolved, he has no preference concerning which of his first-order desires is to be his will. This condition, if it is so severe that it prevents him from identifying himself in a sufficiently decisive way with *any* of his conflicting first-order desires, destroys him as a person. For it either tends to paralyze his will and to keep him from acting at all, or it tends to remove him from his will so that his will operates without his participation. In both cases he becomes [...] a helpless bystander to the forces that move him" (Frankfurt 1998, 21).

Here, Frankfurt reminds us of two pivotal issues. First, ambivalence (as well as any kind of hesitancy, irresolution and self-deception) typically occurs in a gradual mode. Secondly, ambivalence is akin to self-deception insofar as it produces some kind of self-alienation that tacitly undermines the (self-)attribution of responsibility.

Contrary to a still widespread view, the mere existence of strong desires or anxiety that very likely prejudices our assessment of persons, situations, and actions is not incompatible with the demand to realize, at least to some degree, a detached view and thereby being able to duly consider the moral concerns of others. Yet, being tacitly motivated to act by *unacknowledged* desires certainly undermines our moral attitude. Therefore, ethicists rightly put much emphasis on the ability of reflection, i.e., the ability to stop thinking or acting *modo recto* in favour of a *modo obliquo* deliberation that amounts to approvingly or disapprovingly comment on desires and anxieties we actually have. From a moral point of view, we have to consider ourselves free to either give in to our first-order desires and emotional tendencies or to reject them. Rejecting them means not allowing them to become an effective motive of one's actions. Since reflecting upon one's desires and emotional tendencies requires to come to know about their presence and first-order efficiency, it stands to reason that our readiness to acquire the relevant self-knowledge is morally momentous. A person prone to self-deception suffers from a lack of control with regard to her desires and her way of being emotionally involved in situations. This being so, self-deceptions more or less vigorously undermine the agent's practical self-consciousness, i.e., her understanding of herself as the doer of her deeds. In other words: self-deceptions tend to weaken the agent's autonomy by challenging her feeling of authorship and responsibility. By the same token, we may suppose that people provided with strong capacities of autonomy are less liable to self-deceptions (cf. Meyers 1989, 233).

Self-deceptions, in some subtle way facilitate the life of those who fall prey to them, although in the long run this alleviation may turn out to be a fragile illusion of self-control. Notwithstanding this likely failure in the long run, taking serious phenomena of self-deception should prompt us to reconsider usual patterns of thinking about autonomy. Instead of strictly juxtaposing self-control and heteronomy, it seems more adequate to take account of the variety of ways, including occasionally paradox ones, that enable persons to gain a temporary, gradual and instable form of self-control even though this may involve some kind of self-alienation and dependency.[21] (Therefore, it might well be characterized as heteronomous, given that we adhere to the usual juxtaposition of autonomy or absolute self-control, on the one hand, and heteronomy, on the other.) Relating to autonomy, it is misguided to talk about possible options whatsoever. What really is at stake are *relevant* options, choices and projects. Accordingly, we should assess self-deceptions with regard to their range of effects: do self-deceptions affect the whole spectrum of a person's activities and character traits or only certain facets of herself? Do they affect crucial choices and projects or issues of minor importance? Whether or not self-deception in a singular case jeopardizes or annihilates personal autonomy depends on how we judge upon its impact on this person's practical identity.[22]

At first sight it might seem plausible to argue that "self-deception [...] appears as an intrinsic moral fault only if we are ready to make absolute demands to truthfulness that are considered to be context-independent." (Klusmann 2001, 27, translation mine, SR) (This is a viewpoint the author attributes to Kant.) Whether or not it is correct to argue in this manner, ultimately depends on what we take "morality", "moral agent", and "practical self-knowledge" to mean. If we understand self-deception as a process of gradual self-concealment, it is clearly not a matter of absolute demands as against contextual commitments and their relativizing effects. Rather, we are faced with an absolute demand that is due to an original and unchallengeable *contextual configuration of the moral agent*. This demand amounts to not concealing oneself, since behaving as a moral person requires that I am in a peculiar state of self-awareness, namely that I am ready to consider what kind of person I am and what kind of person I would like to become. Concealing oneself (in this specific sense) is not morally faulty in terms of violating some particular moral law or ignoring some qualified rights or claims of persons who are affected by my actions. Rather, concealing oneself is morally faulty because it calls into question our self-respect as moral agents. It does so by means of impairing our ability to adhere to *or* to violate whatever moral law or moral rights and claims. It is as if I cut the ground from under my feet. It is with a view to being responsive to moral demands at all, i.e., being susceptible to the difference of behaving morally good *or* morally bad, that we need to see through our self-deceptions.

What does that mean relating to the individual case of self-deception discussed above? Granted that we approve of the moral practice established in our culture, my husband does me wrong in committing adultery. However, what I do (though not intentionally) if I answer this moral offence by readily falling back on a state of self-deception is even worse than that: I take myself out of the moral game.[23] I withdraw my capacity to act, at least in moral respect. And this is, though in quite another sense than can be said about my husband's infidelity, blameworthy. Preventing oneself from being addressed as a moral agent, is the most fundamental "moral failure" we can be blamed for, although doing so, strictly speaking, cannot be conceived as a moral action. Moreover, behaving in this manner renders more difficult any effort to make good what has happened. As long as I persist in this state, i.e., as long as I, for purely emotional reasons, refuse to take notice of the moral offence to which I am subject, the offender is stigmatised in a double sense. It is not only that he did me wrong. Beyond that, he is guilty of having placed me into my present state of "demoralization". Situating self-deception at this fundamental level of moral agency, we shall not (and need not) consent to the idea that at least those who endorse a non-intentionalistic interpretation of self-deception should generally deny that self-deceivers can be morally responsible for their behaviour (see Levy 2004). Self-deception and moral responsibility are not mutually exclusive. Given this to be so, we can reasonably advance a thesis that has to be carefully scrutinized within the horizon of both empirical investigations and philosophical analyses: Being a moral person calls upon much more than our rational and cognitive abilities in general as well as our act-intentional behaviour, our preferences and explicit purposes.

According to the conception of self-deception introduced above, we should be eager to separate distinct approaches to phenomena of self-deception, none of which seem to be unprejudiced. As far as philosophical approaches are concerned, we may argue that it is our prevalent theoretical interest that determines our descriptions and explanations of self-deception. This is especially conspicuous within ethical contexts. In the foregoing, we tried to show that it amounts to a far-reaching reduction of typical cases of self-deception not to consider their dynamic (temporal) structure as well as their social and moral implications. However, cutting off these aspects is fairly comprehensible given certain theoretical decisions and interests. For instance, those who are occupied with elaborating a consistent theory of action or theory of rationality often are not interested in discussing possible motives, social encouragements and moral aspects of self-deception. Instead, they focus on the logical structure of self-deceptions. However plausible this may be from the viewpoint of a philosopher working within the field of action theory or philosophy of mind, feminist philosophers, for instance, largely identify this approach with a retreat into a sphere of privacy that tends to conceal the social, political and moral implications of the issue at hand. (For this view see e.g. Rich 1993.) It goes without saying that an epistemologist or action theorist will protest against equating logical analysis with a retreat into the private sphere. Yet, this is how their work is likely to appear from the point of view of a feminist philosopher (and others as well). Of course, we can imagine circumstances under which pushing self-deception back to privacy, thereby suggesting that it simply is a psychological matter or a matter of exclusively personal or intimate bearing, may be used to habitualize socially induced forms of self-deceptions and make them invisible for the very persons concerned. In other words: Arguing in favour of privacy or tacitly supporting this view with regard to phenomena of self-deception can be part of a paternalistic strategy of deception. For instance, my husband may try to shame me into concealing and suppressing my dawning hunch about his infidelity.[24]

Referring to ethical concerns, it is remarkable that, first, it depends on our specific ethical approach whether or not we consider self-deception to be a morally relevant issue at all. Secondly, we find ourselves urged to take a somewhat larger view on the issue at hand than the majority of those who follow an action theoretical approach. Relating to the former condition, it has been rightly stated that considering self-deception a morally relevant issue is not at all common sense among ethicists. On the contrary, it is primarily among Kantians and virtue ethicists that we encounter an outstanding interest for recognizing and correcting modes of self-deceptive behaviour (cf. Darwall 1988, 407f). In this context, Stephen Darwall defines Kantian "constitutionalism" as follows:

> Their ideal of character is of a person who assumes responsibility for her own moral integrity by regulating her life by her own best judgment. I call this a constitutionalist ideal of character since its central theme is that moral integrity involves self-government and because its project is to elaborate the 'constitution' for such self-government – the constitution of the moral agent as such. (Darwall 1988, 409)

Following this approach, self-deception is among those experiences that tend to undermine the constitution of the moral agent. Thereby, Darwall stresses the fact that self-deception cannot be understood along the lines of interpersonal deception. Instead, it is "more like a seduction of himself" (Darwall 1988, 413) or a "motivated carelessness" (Darwall 1988, 423). What is interesting about this proposal is, among others, that it reminds us of the fact that self-deception need not be grasped as a purely mental, quasi-solipsistic experience if we reject its explanation on the model of interpersonal deception. Seduction is a genuinely social interaction. Talking about a seduction *of oneself* does not eliminate this social meaning. It leaves ample room for social inducements and social embeddings. There are good reasons to assume that self-deception more often than not is a socially induced experience with a specific dynamic structure including the mutual reinforcement and collusion of interpersonal deception and self-deception as it occurs especially in close social relations. In course of such interactions, the other person is ready to benefit from my readiness to be less than honest with regard to my own past or my present abilities or with regard to the value of my personal relations and my social status. Notwithstanding the fact that my readiness to succumb to self-deceptions can certainly be investigated in purely mental terms, it also has a definite meaning and utility within an encompassing social sphere, including a complex set of moral habits and moral judgments. Ignoring this wider field tends to cut off the intriguing question: why do we have a stake in self-deceptive modes of behaviour? Arguing in favour of a deflationary conception of self-deception within a phenomenological framework helps us regain the wider social and moral field of concern without thereby abandoning the responsibility of the moral agent in terms of a social or natural determinism.

Notes

1. This is what guided Sartre's famous reproach of Freud's theory in his *Being and Nothingness*. It is not by chance that this reproach was articulated on the occasion of presenting Sartre's idea of *mauvaise foi*. The latter is normally, though slightly misleading, translated as "self-deception".

2. A large part of the ongoing debate on self-deception is concerned with specifying the corresponding minimally required complex structure of the human mind that has to be assumed in order to explain or describe phenomena of self-deception. Part of the peculiar nature of self-deception is that, by definition, the person succumbing to it does not know about this very fact. Cf.: "While ordinary pretending is quite consistent with awareness of pretense, self-deception involves as well a second-order pretense that one is not pretending at a first-order level; this second-order pretense deflects cues that might return one from ordinary first-order, playful pretending to the real world. It tends to corrupt, therefore, the self-deceiver's very ability to abandon the first-order pretense. Self-deception is on the way to delusion in a way that innocent play is not" (Darwall 1988, 414).
3. Elsewhere, I have characterized this as *fallacy of latency*. See Rinofner-Kreidl 2003b, 37.
4. The most prominent advocate of a deflationary account in recent debates on self-deception is Alfred Mele who succinctly resumes the benefit of such an account: "If I am right [in endorsing a deflationary account, SR], self-deception is neither irresolvably paradoxical nor mysterious and it is explicable without the assistance of mental exotica." (Mele 1997 91)
5. Cf. "Self-deception is the occupational danger of those capable of selective attention. […] the very thin line between what is an achievement, namely, keeping out of full mental view what it is reasonably judged for the moment best kept dark, or at least blurry, and what is usually a fault or a failure, namely, disowning one's own pushing of these things into obscurity, and so mistaking one's ignoring of them for one's ignorance of them. Self-deception is often the failure to achieve or to maintain consciousness of one's own successes at selective attention. It is then a disowning of one's own mental activities of overlooking and highlighting" (Baier 1996, 54f).
6. For the above distinction see Pears 1984, 33. Since, according to Pears, irrationality is incorrect processing (Pears 1984, 18) it is (ii), which is of outstanding interest with regard to self-deception. (Information that is left out of account is not available for processing.) Given that self-deception is conceived of as motivated irrationality, this "implies that it is the same desire that biases the agent's belief and then produces his action."(Pears 1984, 19)
7. The above approach is suitable only with regard to those cases of self-deception in which counterevidences could easily be gained. It has been argued that these cases are typically distinct from psychoanalytic cases. Cf. Erwin 1988, 237.
8. For an attempt to distinguish (a) self-deception about own emotions ("self-feigning"), (b) emotionally induced distorsions of beliefs, (c) false beliefs about one's own emotions, and (d) false beliefs on which they might be founded, see de Sousa 1988, 328f.
9. With a view to morality, it is the opposite movement that is of utmost importance, namely the attempt to acquire self-control by means of curbing one's spontaneous emotional reactions.
10. This is typically true for all those cases where self-deception goes together with *akrasia*.
11. If there is something paradoxical in this, it does not refer to the special issues implied in self-deception, but to what we may call "Socrates' problem". In order to strive for the truth, I have to know what I am looking for. Consequently, we may argue that in order to strive for the truth we already have to know it. Correspondingly, we may say that in order to effectively hinder the gain of knowledge, this knowledge must, in some sense, be at our disposal. For instance, I have to know what the relevant evidences are in order to grasp them in a distorted way. I do not take this to be fatal with regard to the above argumentation. With a view to both searching for the truth and suspending this search, "in some sense" should be explicated as "being guided by some vague presumption". It is true that I do *not arbitrarily* produce distortions. (Obviously they do not occur purely accidentally.) But neither do I *intend* to produce them.
12. "Normally" should indicate here that the agent's involvement in his specific mode of self-concealment does not amount to a thoroughly pathological character.
13. Assuming the possibility of veracity is not only a practical necessity but a theoretical necessity as well. It does not make sense to talk about deceptions unless we take it for granted that delusion and reality are discernible on principle. Equally, it does not make sense to talk about self-deceptions unless we take it for granted that adequate self-knowledge, i.e., an authentic relation to one's own mental contents and processes, is possible on principle.

14. If we formulate the issue of self-deception in this way, it is obvious that we should relate it to the far more encompassing issue of moral luck. What is at stake here, and what certainly is of central interest with regard to morality, is the idea that we are not able to offer a satisfying answer to the following question: Do we really know exactly what is within our control? Given that the idea of self-control collapses under an overwhelming evidence in favour of external guidance of my decisions and actions, we certainly would have to re-define our understanding of ourselves as well as our understanding of interpersonality and morality. Among those who recently argued along these lines are the so-called situationists. See Doris 2002 and Harman 1999.
15. Given that our deflationary approach is correct, we must not use "strategy" instead of "way".
16. Arguing like this is compatible with a phenomenological approach only if we assume that the agents themselves can retrospectively realize these specific functions of their former self-deception.
17. I take it that occasionally occurring self-deceptions are an unsuspicious part of our normal mental and social life while firmly established, habitual, i.e., long-term self-deceptions that tend to predominate a person's mental and social life are part of pathological biographies. Hence, I assume that (1) people cannot be held accountable for their pathologies, and that (2) it may be difficult to distinguish normal and pathological behaviour in individual cases.
18. Cf. "Not only do defense mechanism and cognitive filters compromise self-respect by blinding people to the realities of their lives, but they also compromise self-respect by preempting self-definition. Promiscuously self-affirming people are not self-respecting. To be self-respecting, one may have to reform oneself by disavowing discredited beliefs, harmful habits, demeaning associations, trivial goals, and so on. Self-respect may require change, but defense mechanisms and cognitive filters often prevent minimally autonomous people from noticing that change is called for. Moreover, change that is imposed from without or unconsciously insinuated from within may again defeat self-respect." (Meyers 1989, 231)
19. This, by the way, is an ethical presupposition of psychoanalysis that cannot be treated in terms of psychoanalytical methods. See Binswanger 1947, Gebsattel 1954, Bonn 1999.
20. Cf. "Where a person is self-deceived there are contradictions and ambiguities in her identifications." (Taylor 1985, 121)
21. For a debate on the *vacillating self* and the *alienated self* as two ideal types of self vulnerability that have a strong impact on moral behaviour see Noam 1993, 225ff and 229ff.
22. Cf. "People are not self-governing, in a sense, when their responses to problems are blind, dictated by neurotic impulses of which they are unaware, shaped by prejudices at odds with the noble sentiments they think are moving them. When we make decisions like this we are divided against ourselves. There is little profit in debating which is the 'true self' – the 'self' revealed in high-minded, consciously adopted principles, or the 'self' of prejudice and neurotic impulse that really determines the outcome; there is no unified 'self' here to govern the decision. While it may be debated whether having a unified personality is in general a moral goal, surely we can agree that it is a morally worthy goal to try to face our important moral decisions with as few as possible of these self-fracturing obstacles." (Hill 1991, 50f)
23. This consideration has a clear impact on psychotherapy insofar as the latter aims at self-acknowledgment. "Avowal of one's engagements is the optimal goal of classical psychoanalysis. Such avowal is the necessary condition of moral action, but it is not itself moral action." (Fingarette 1982, 226) Therefore, the author rightly insists that the medical aim of therapy is "a spiritual aim. It is to help the individual become an agent and cease being a patient; it is to liberate, not indoctrinate." (Fingarette 1982, 227)
24. The self-assessing emotions of shame and guilt are especially involved in diverse brands of *habitual* self-deceptive practices.

References

Ames, Roger T., and Wimal Dissanayake (eds.). 1996. *Self and deception. A cross-cultural philosophical enquiry*. Albany: State University of New York Press.

Baier, Annette C. 1996. The vital but dangerous art of ignoring. Selective attention and self-deception. In *Self and deception: A cross-cultural philosophical enquiry*, ed. Roger T. Ames and Wimal Dissanayake, 53–72. Albany: State University of New York Press.

Binswanger, Ludwig. 1947. *Freuds Auffassung des Menschen im Lichte der Anthropologie. Ausgewählte Vorträge und Aufsätze Band I: Zur phänomenologischen Anthropologie*, 159–189. Bern: Francke.

Boss, Medard. 1999. *Grundriss der Medizin und der Psychologie. Ansätze zu einer phänomenologischen Psychologie, Pathologie und Therapie und zu einer daseinsgemäßen Präventiv-Medizin*. Bern/Göttingen/Toronto/Seattle: Huber.

Darwall, Stephen L. 1988. Self-deception, autonomy, and moral constitution. In *Perspectives on self-deception*, ed. Brian P. McLaughlin and A. Rorty, 407–430. Berkeley: University of California Press.

Davidson, Donald. 1982. Paradoxes of irrationality. ed. Wollheim and Hopkins, 1982, 289–305.

Davidson, Donald. 2004. *Problems of rationality*. Oxford: Oxford University Press.

De Sousa, Ronald. 1988. Emotion and self-deception. ed. McLaughlin and Oksenberg-Rorty, 1988, 324–341.

Doris, John M. 2002. *Lack of character. Personality and moral behavior*, 128–153. Cambridge: Cambridge University Press.

Dupuy, Jean-Pierre (ed.). 1998. *Self-deception and paradoxes of rationality*. Stanford: CSLI Publications.

Erwin, Edward. 1988. Psychoanalysis and self-deception. In *Perspectives on self-deception*, ed. Brian P. McLaughlin and Amelie Oksenberg-Rorty, 228–245. Berkeley: University of California Press.

Fingarette, Herbert. 1982. Self-deception and the 'splitting of the ego'. In *Philosophical essays on Freud*, ed. Richard Wollheim and James Hopkins, 212–227.

Frankfurt, Harry G. 1998. Freedom of the will and the concept of a person. In *The importance of what we care about*, ed. Harry G. Frankfurt, 11–25. Cambridge: Cambridge University Press.

Frankfurt, Harry G. 1999. Autonomy, necessity, and love. In *Necessity, volition, and love*, ed. Harry G. Frankfurt, 129–141. Cambridge: Cambridge University Press.

Harman, Gilbert. 1999. Moral philosophy meets social psychology. Virtue ethics and the fundamental attribution error. *Proceedings of the Aristotelian Society*, New Series vol. 119, 316–331.

Hill, Thomas E. 1991. The importance of autonomy. In *Autonomy and self-respect*, ed. Thomas E. Hill, 43–51. Cambridge: Cambridge University Press.

Klusmann, Dietrich. 2001. Wissensvermeidung und Selbsttäuschung (unveröffentlichtes Manuskript http://zpm.uke.uni-hamburg.de/WebPdf/Wissensvermeidung.pdf. Last visit: 11 Feb 2009).

Levy, Neil. 2004. Self-deception and moral responsibility. *Ratio* XVII: 294–311.

McLaughlin, Brian P., and Amélie Oksenberg-Rorty (eds.). 1988. *Perspectives on self-deception*. Berkeley/Los Angeles/London: University of California Press.

Mele, Alfred R. 1987. *Irrationality. An essay on Akrasia, self-deception, and self-control*. New York: Oxford University Press.

Mele, Alfred R. 1995. *Autonomous agents. From self-control to autonomy*. New York/Oxford: Oxford University Press.

Mele, Alfred R. 1997. Real self-deception. *Behavioral and Brain Sciences* 20(1): 97–136.

Mele, Alfred R. 1998. Two paradoxes of self-deception. In *Self-deception and paradoxes of rationality*, ed. Jean Pierre Dupuy, 37–58. Stanford: CSLI Publications.

Mele, Alfred R. 2001. *Self-deception unmasked*. Princeton/Oxford: Princeton University Press.

Meyers, Diana T. 1989. *Self, society, and personal choices*. New York/Oxford: Columbia University Press.

Noam, Gil G. 1993. 'Normative vulnerabilities' of self and their transformations in moral action. In *The moral self*, ed. Gil G. Noam and Thomas E. Wren, 209–238. Cambridge/London: MIT Press.

Noam, Gil G., and Thomas E. Wren (eds.). 1993. *The moral self*, 209–238. Cambridge/London: MIT Press.

Pears, David. 1984. *Motivated irrationality*. Oxford: Clarendon Press.

Pearsall, Marilyn (ed.). 1993. *Women and values. Readings in recent feminist philosophy*. Belmond: Wadsworth Publishing Company.

Rich, Adrienne. 1993. *Women and honor: Some notes on lying*. ed. Pearsall, 391–395.

Rinofner-Kreidl, Sonja. 2003a. Naturalisierte Erkenntnistheorie. Eine phänomenologische Kritik. In *Mediane Phänomenologie. Subjektivität im Spannungsfeld von Naturalität und Kulturalität*, ed. Sonja Rinofner-Kreidl, 1–20. Würzburg: Königshausen und Neumann.

Rinofner-Kreidl, Sonja. 2003b. Phänomenales Bewußtsein und Selbstrepräsentation. Zur Kritik naturalistischer Selbstmodelle. In *Mediane Phänomenologie. Subjektivität im Spannungsfeld von Naturalität und Kulturalität*, ed. S. Rinofner-Kreidl, 21–55. Würzburg: Königshausen und Neumann.

Rinofner-Kreidl, Sonja. 2004. Representationalism and beyond. A phenomenological critique of Thomas Metzinger's self-model theory. *Journal of Consciousness Studies* 11(10–11): 88–108.

Rinofner-Kreidl, Sonja. 2004b. Das „Gehirn-Selbst“. Ist die Erste-Person-Perspektive naturalisierbar? In Phänomenologische Forschungen, 219–252.

Taylor, Gabriele. 1985. *Pride, shame, and guilt. Emotions of self-assessment*. Oxford: Oxford University Press.

von Gebsattel, Victor E. 1954. Krisen in der Psychotherapie. In *Prolegomena einer medizinischen Anthropologie. Ausgewählte Aufsätze*, ed. V. von Gebsattel, 347–361. Berlin/Göttingen/Heidelberg: Springer.

Wollheim, Richard, and James Hopkins (eds.). 1982. *Philosophical essays on Freud*. Cambridge: Cambridge University Press.

Some Observations on Husserl and Freud

Francesco S. Trincia

Abstract Is there something essential that binds the theme of the unconscious to the philosophies of the twentieth century and to phenomenological inquiries in particular? The issue of the unconscious gets hold of philosophy thanks to a sort of "reaction to the originary" that took place in the last century. As a result of this reaction, it is difficult to find a philosophical sphere in which that theme is absent, overlooked or forgotten.
In my paper I would like to offer some comparative reflections on the relationship between Husserl's inquiry on time-consciousness and Freud's thought in order to push the limits of the concepts of the "unconscious" and a "philosophy of the unconscious" in a productive fashion. '-- End of Abstract'

In a passage of the *Analyses Concerning Passive and Active Synthesis*, Husserl writes: "I do not need to say that the entirety of these observations that we are undertaking can also be given the famed title of the 'unconscious'. Thus, our considerations concern a phenomenology of the so-called unconscious".[1] It is meaningful that Husserl talks about the "unconscious" just when he examines the phenomenon of being noticed or unnoticed in the emergence of the sensible unities. He calls the unconscious "so-called" and this indicates the problematic tension contained in the idea of an "unconscious phenomenon".

The Appendix IX of the Time-Lectures[2] can be useful to understand how time, i.e. the relationship between originary apprehension and retention, justifies Husserl's refusal of the unconscious. The "primal consciousness" passes over into a retentional modification, which is a specific intentionality: the modification performs a retention of that consciousness and of its datum. The core of the Husserlian conception is that the consciousness and its conscious datum *must already be therein*

F.S. Trincia (✉)
University of Rome "La Sapienza", Rome, Italy
e-mail: fstrincia@hotmail.com

D. Lohmar and J. Brudzińska (eds.), *Founding Psychoanalysis Phenomenologically*, Phaenomenologica 199, DOI 10.1007/978-94-007-1848-7_12,

to make thinkable the retention. Therefore the retention is the conceptual instrument by which it is possible to refute the phenomenological possibility of the unconscious, since the latter should come before its "becoming conscious". But, as Husserl writes clearly, "consciousness is necessarily *consciousness* in each of its phases".[3] This means that in each phase one is *conscious* (*Bewusst-sein*).

The retention is called by Husserl an "intentionality *sui generis*", for it does not involve the maintenance of the "impressional data" and thus represents a *specific intentional moment*, which is lacking the feature of "act". To retain means "to hold something in the palm of one's hand", to not lose the *elapsed* phase of a process as an "originary datum", i.e. a *new* phase, emerges. The retention "retains" what is from time to time passed in relation to what is from time to time originary; thanks to the retention a retrospective look on what is flowed out is possible. But because the retention itself is not a retrospective look, it doesn't make this elapsed phase into an object. It means on the contrary to live in the present phase, to which I add the elapsed one: "while I have the elapsed phase in my grip, I live through the present phase, take it – thanks to retention – 'in addition' to the elapsed phase; and I am directed towards what is coming (in a protention)".[4]

The consciousness of the just now elapsed phase is as such consciousness of the serial totality of what is elapsed: "Each phase, by being retentionally conscious of the preceding phase, includes in itself the entire series of elapsed retentions in the form of a chain of mediate intentions".[5] What comes to givenness in "retrospective acts" is the whole "constituted unity" (for instance of the maintained sound) and the series of the "constituent phases", which are all, without any lapses, phases of a retentional consciousness. Husserl therefore affirms that the retention gives us the consciousness as "object".[6]

In this way we come to the point in question concerning the theme of the unconscious. Husserl considers the constitution of a mental process (*Erlebnis*) and wonders himself how things stand with respect to its "beginning-phase." He thus turns his attention to the initial moment of the process, of which he has so far described only one single phase. At this point of the argumentation, Husserl decides to analyze the originary moment of a mental process which is a part of the course where the retention works. It is very telling and relevant that it is just here that he recalls the theme of the unconscious. He asks of this beginning-phase: "does it also come to be given only on the basis of retention, and would it be 'unconscious' if no retention were to follow it?".[7] This question involves the other one: is there an "unconscious phase", which is behind the phase which is reached by the retention? Is there an "older" phase than the one to which the retention is "connected"? Is there, finally, an "unconscious" which is not yet reached by the retention? The Husserlian question evokes Freudian suggestions, but it meets *only partly* Freud's position. According to Freud the unconscious is an "object" of the knowing consciousness, which is unknown as long as the consciousness doesn't light it up; Husserl thinks similarly that the retention is able to reach the "unconscious" phase of what is elapsed. But while Husserl interprets the unconscious as a conjecture which is only formulated to be rejected, Freud thinks that the unconscious becoming an object for the knowing consciousness is the precondition for its interpretation. This is because the coming to givenness of the supposed unconscious phase coincides with its *failing as unconscious*. The interpretation presupposes in turn the recognition of the structural function of the unconscious within the psychical system, that is its *not failing as unconscious*.

Husserl provides a thesis in order to avoid construing the originary moment (what should be called the "now" [*Jetzt*] of the start of the process) as an object and from being given only by the retention. One has to say that "the beginning-phase can become an object only *after* it has elapsed in the indicated way, by means of retention and reflection (or reproduction)."[8] This means that by the temporal sequence it is possible to get in touch *via retention* with what *was* the beginning-phase of the mental process; but it doesn't mean that this temporal sequence implies that the consciousness of the elapsed beginning-phase is possible *only* by retention. It is relevant for my argumentation to stress the reason why it is impossible to assign to the retention the consciousness of the beginning-phase: in this case, "what confers on it the label 'now' would remain incomprehensible."[9] The beginning-phase is the originary "now" of a mental process and that is possible only if such a "now" is in itself *not* unconscious and does not attain existence as consciousness-object thanks to the retention, which should set it free from its supposed hidden-place both *on this side of* and *outside* the consciousness. It is possible to speak of a "now" as a phase of a mental process only if one recognizes that there are no breaks in the presence of the consciousness in each phase. An originary phase thought as *empty* is *not a phase*.

The beginning-phase, with its label of "now," is described by Husserl as "characterized in consciousness in quite positive fashion", it follows that "it is just nonsense to talk about an 'unconscious' content that would only subsequently become conscious".[10] The consciousness doesn't constitute, i.e. doesn't start in a moment of lived time, for it is not a function or a region of the psyche: "consciousness is necessarily *consciousness* in each of its phases". In this way, Husserl unifies, or rather transcendentally identifies, what in Freud has to remain programmatically separate: only thanks to the separation between "consciousness" and "being conscious" does what is not conscious *become* conscious in the consciousness and by the consciousness, and psychical time shows itself as the "place" of the process of the "becoming conscious" which occurs in the psychical. In the following quote, I would like to draw your attention to the first part of the entire passage, where Husserl shows clearly that the originary "now" is already conscious, without an apprehension-act directed to it:

> Just as the retentional phase is conscious of the preceding phase without making it into an object, so too the primal datum is already intended – specifically, in the original form of the 'now' – without its being something objective. It is precisely this primal consciousness that passes over into retentional modification – which is then retention of the primal consciousness itself and of the datum originally intended in it, since the two are inseparably united. If the primal consciousness were not on hand [i.e. if an unconscious content were on hand], no retention would even be conceivable: retention of an unconscious content is impossible.[11]

The primal consciousness passes over into the retentional modification, which is nothing but retention of the consciousness and of its conscious datum, which are inseparable. That is precisely the reason why the retention cannot "meet" an unconscious and therefore make it conscious. The retention presupposes not only the originary consciousness, of which it is retention, but it is in itself only, as retention, retention of a conscious content. At the end of the quoted passage, Husserl himself wonders: what is the "primal consciousness" which we talk about? It is essential to understand that we are not discussing an apprehension-act, which is able to give us the consciousness of content. It is not a sort of apprehension "without consciousness". If one supposes to distinguish "apprehension-act" and "consciousness", there is the risk of a *regressus in infinitum*, for the apprehension-act, which gives us the consciousness of content, is in turn a content which needs a having-consciousness. But the consciousness doesn't follow an apprehension-act. It comes before it as a structure which does not support or authorize the *regressus in infinitum* from the consciousness of a content to the consciousness of the consciousness of a content and so on. Husserl writes: "But if every 'content' is 'primally conscious' in itself and necessarily, the question about a further giving consciousness becomes meaningless."[12]

While Freud assumes a "horizontal" multiplication of the consciousnesses interrupted by voids and arrives in this way at the acknowledgment of the unconscious, Husserl's refusal of that multiplication, in order to avoid the regress, means the refusal of the supposition concerning an unconscious content of consciousness and the reaffirmation of the originally conscious nature of *each* content.

The Husserlian confutation of the notion of the unconscious appears very definite, since it attacks the Freudian theory on the time level, which is quite weak in Freud. In comparison with the inseparable complex between temporality and retention in Husserl, the relationship between conscious and unconscious is constructed by Freud, or at least according to a part of his theory, on the plane of the horizontal contiguity of psychical "spaces" rather than on the plane of the temporal dimension. A central Freudian thesis declares that from the "latency", in which it ended up at a certain moment of the psychical vicissitudes, the repressed unconscious comes out in order to "re-surface". The Freudian unconscious thus originally belongs to a "geographical" conception of the psychic and assumes the features of an organism. For this reason it is not sufficient to ask, from within a Freudian perspective, what the relationship is between the unconscious and its "not-being-time". It is not enough to say that the unconscious "weakens time in itself", since it isolates itself from the time-flow and thus "neutralizes" the time. That's not enough. It seems, really, that just the neutralization of time in the unconscious shows *a contrario* that the flowing time-consciousness persists as the condition of the neutralization itself. I mean that the persisting of the temporal succession in the life-consciousness works as "background" for the escaping of the unconscious contents form their consumption in the time process. Since it is possible to see this escaping only from the point of view of the consciousness, the latter has to be thought of as *continually* outstretched in time. And that is valid also within a Freudian theoretical scheme. In accordance with this perspective, it is possible to try to draw the Husserlian conception of a never absent consciousness close to the Freudian concept (even though implicit and unintentional) of a temporal continuity of the life-consciousness. It involves, of course, admitting the pre-critical (pre-Kantian) notion of the time as "thing" in itself flowing in the psyche.

In this way it is necessary to put in question the key concept of Freudian thought, which claims that the unconscious has to be admitted on the grounds of the establishment of some gaps in the life-consciousness. This concept seems to have been spared from questioning in order that psychoanalytical theory might be saved from a potentially destructive theoretic crisis. I propose to attempt a critical operation provided that it allows avoiding the injunction to keep separate the (presumed) Freudian empiricism and the Husserlian anti-naturalism. I add, *en passant,* that it is not so easy to claim (only) empirical value for the concept of the unconscious; nor is it easy from the point of view by Freud itself.

According to Freud, as I just said, the relationship between conscious and unconscious is thought in spatial terms, that is in terms of *localized* energies, but in reality conscious and unconscious are also *moments* of the psyche, and talking about the idea of a "life" of an organism introduces the theme of the time in any case. It is clear that it is not necessary, within a Freudian perspective, to ask about the relationship between time and consciousness, but this question seems to be virtually present from this perspective. The question has a peculiarly *philosophical* trait, since it does not represent a forcing external to the Freudian thought, but it is the unavoidable prosecution of a philosophical reflection which begins just *within* this thought.

One can formulate the question in the following way: is it possible to give to the psychoanalytical conceptual universe a sort of "phenomenology of time-consciousness"? What are the requirements and the limits of this attempt? Could this kind of philosophical and methodological approach be able to explain on a phenomenological level what happens, according to the psychoanalysis, in the experience of *setting*, that is the fact that the unconscious content *becomes* conscious? And, if so, is it possible to reconcile this psychoanalytical scheme with Husserl's statement that "consciousness is necessarily *consciousness* in each of its phases"? Is it possible to avoid the conflict between what one thinks *will happen* and what one can *say* about it in phenomenological language? Must we choose between the Husserlian *time* and the Freudian *spatiality* or can we reconcile them with each other? In accordance with the consideration above, the temporal continuity of the life-consciousness seems to be a sort of transcendental condition of the being-thinkable of the interruption *of* the time, even better *from* the time, i.e. as concerning the time itself, namely of that interruption which connotes the unconscious.

If we go on to radicalize this attempt, we are forced to decide between the thesis of the *continuity of the life-consciousness* on the one side, and the notion of the unconscious as "gap", "break" of this life itself on the other. If we opt for the former thesis, we face the question of *how* we can imagine the interruption without damaging the continuity on life-consciousness. If we opt for the latter thesis, we should renounce the very way we wish to travel, that is to try *to think of the unconscious no more solely as what is in opposition to the consciousness, but also as a phenomenon which takes place within the temporal horizon and then in the context of the continuity of the life-consciousness.*

I intend to pursue the former thesis in order to preserve my basic assumption, i.e. that the Husserlian reflection on the Freudian phenomenon of the unconscious is far from having no effect on it and spurs a possible redefinition and/or reformulation of it.

It represents a conceptual operation which has its own irreplaceable *Leitfaden* in the idea (though fatal from the Freudian point of view) of the continuity of the life-consciousness.

The unconscious gaps in consciousness involve, within the Freudian thought, the *problem of the truth*; I think this is a paradox for philosophy, because philosophy just is what essentially and originally deals with the truth. Philosophy is implicated in the problem of the unconscious, which in turn seems to exclude programmatically philosophy itself. But it remains to go beyond the mere ascertainment of the paradox and to attain the non-empirical objective level of the truth. So the problem concerns the way to continue advancing in order to outline the project of including the unconscious in a phenomenological theory of the consciousness. We have to face this difficult transit if we wish to reach the "truth", i.e. the *philosophical truth*, of a theory of the unconscious. The question is now the following: how is it possible to retain what Sartre calls in his critique of the Freudian theory of the unconscious the "unity of the psychical act"[13] without renouncing the fact that not two conscious acts, but rather one conscious and the other one unconscious, are connected in this unity *in* time and *as* phenomenological time?

I don't mean it is necessary or even possible to *translate* this or that part of the Freudian thought into the language of philosophy. It is impossible and useless. If this translation into the language of truth is not required, one needs rather a radical *dislocation* of the *whole* Freudian thought into the horizon of philosophy. The philosopher is in front of a clear alternative: accepting the Freudian notion of unconscious in scientific, objective and naturalistic language (to which Ludwig Binswanger[14] paid attention) and renouncing philosophy, or setting the unconscious free from its Freudian interpretation as an "object" of empirical observations and making of it a "phenomenon" in a phenomenology of consciousness.

A practicable road in attempting to close the gap between Husserl and Freud is available by valuing the Husserlian concept of "not rational motivations."[15] These motivations have been shaped in the past by a reason which is now mute and passively settled. I think these kinds of motivations, analogous but non equal to the rational motivations, can help enrich the a-rationality of the Freudian unconscious with at least two elements: the *first one* is the concept of the rational motivation which becomes non-active sediment, a merely "sensible" thing. In this way we obtain a feature of the non-rationality of the motivation, which doesn't mean an immediate and complete reduction of the unconscious to a sort of pre-conscious, and stands for an idea of a "mute" reason, which is mute and material (*sachlich*), but doesn't signify a radical "gap of the consciousness". The not-rational motivation implies an *absence of reason*, but it *does not* suggest an *absence of consciousness*.

The *second* element provides the opportunity to include in the conceptual region of the unconscious something which is obtained by an "analogical" way. Freud believes that the analogical way leads from the consciousness *in others* to the non-consciousness as psychical region *in everyone* and so it has the function of aiding the "justification" of the unconscious. Husserl in turn seems to believe that the analogy indicates a relationship of difference and mutual irreducibility between rational and not-rational motivations. Reading the notion of the unconscious in analogical terms saves it from a "speculative" interpretation and protects its character of "a-rational" reality. Thanks to the analogical approach, this a-rational being maintains its motivational trait, which is just *analogous* (but not identical) to that of reason and which allows it to be discussed as a *motivation.* In this way a sort of "analogical space of the not-reason" grows in the unconscious and the structural relationship with reason remains, as is required by phenomenology, without the concealment of its non-rationality. Reason is absent, but still the absence of reason remains a motivation, which is rationally understandable as a lack *of reason.*

It is not irrelevant that Husserl stresses the analogical nature of the "associative motivations" characterized by passivity. This "passive causality" is in itself not shaped by reason and on just these grounds it can give us an image of the unconscious. Active causality and the passive causality are intertwined in the mechanism of motivation, but they remain distinct, for the latter, the "causality of the backgrounds", is not free and pure like the former, but "it plays its role in the supplying of the original material, which doesn't involve any more implicit thesis." [16] If we accept this kind of reformulation of the nexus which links conscious and unconscious, we obtain a theoretical benefit, which consists of making clear that passive causality, as the "background of association," provides the non-thetical material to the active causality, to which it remains joined. The unconscious can also be a *passive background*, but it is not excluded from the horizon of the "rational requirement" of rebuilding the nexuses. The Husserlian conceptual universe offers a relevant opportunity to re-model the Freudian unconscious. The unconscious presents itself as the extreme, paradoxical outcome of a "motivational law", which in turn has a rational motivation. This gives us a more aware and refined way of understanding that what Freud terms the "legitimacy" of the unconscious involves the decision to search and find "connection" and "meaning" in psychical life.

What is relevant is the fact that this decision, once translated into the Husserlian language, changes from an empirical necessity to fill the empirically observed "gaps" of the psychical life to a phenomenological constitutive intentionality, which is able to find a phenomenology of the unconscious.

In this way, both Husserl and Freud obtain a result: form the point of view of the former, the oxymoron of the "phenomenon of the unconscious" is challenged from the inside, while from the point of view of the latter, the unconscious becomes a philosophical phenomenon and so it is rescued from its psychoanalytical destiny to work as unit of measurement and as a judging principle (psychological and not truth principle) of every discourse about the unconscious itself.

Notes

1. E. Husserl, *Analyses concerning passive and active synthesis*, trans. A.J. Steinbock (Kluwer: Dordrecht, 2001), 201.
2. E. Husserl, *On the phenomenology of the consciousness of internal time*, trans. J.B. Brough (Kluwer: Dordrecht, 1991).

3. Ibid. p. 123.
4. Ibid. p. 122.
5. Ibid.
6. Cf. ivi, p. 123.
7. Ibid.
8. Ibid.
9. Ibid.
10. Ibid.
11. Ibid.
12. Ibid.
13. Cf. J.-P. Sartre, *L'être et le néant* (Paris:Gallimard, 1943), 81–106.
14. Cf. L. Binswanger, *Zur phänomenologischen Anthropologie* (Bern: Francke, 1961).
15. Cf. Hua IV, § 56, pp. 220 ff.
16. Hua IV, p. 224: "nur ihre Rolle spielt für die Herbeischaffung des Urmaterials, das keine implizierten Thesen mehr enthält" (my translation).

Toward a Semantics of the Symptom: The World of Frau D*

Donn Welton in colloboration with Wolfram Schüffel

Abstract This paper arises out of collaborative work between a psychosomatic physician and a philosopher that uses an analysis of a 30-year-old woman suffering from tinnitus to begin framing what we call a semantics of psychosomatic symptoms. We suggest that her symptom has a *truth-bearing* function that can be discovered once we understand the symptom as situated in her *world* and her world in terms of the phenomenological notion of *horizon*. The horizon, to speak generally, consists of a nexus of significance. The notion of significance, however, is polymorphic and can be dismantled into three different structures supporting human engagement, into what we call *setting*, *context*, and *background*. Distinguishing them, we suggest, would make a contribution to the theory of psychosomatic symptoms. The paper then concentrates on the notion of background, the harder of the three notions to capture, and introduces a contrast between the origins and the telos of bodily symptoms. Returning to the case of Frau D, we suggest that the truth of her (and perhaps others') conflict-generated symptoms can be found not just in the history of her conflicts but also in four interlocking functions organized teleologically: delimiting, bordering, gate-keeping, and attaching. '-- End of Abstract'

Frau D is a strong looking woman with pitch-black hair and silver studs in her ears, five in one and one in the other. She is tall and has a penetrating yet open glance. Originally thin, she shows signs of having added weight over the past several years,

---

*A lecture as given at the 19th World Congress on Psychosomatic Medicine, Quebec City, Canada on August 30, 2007. This is the lecture version of a larger paper with the same title, which is itself a work in progress. Critical comments are welcome and can be addressed to: donn.welton@sunysb. edu.

D. Welton (✉)
Department of Philosophy, Stony Brook University, New York 11790-3750, USA
e-mail: dwelton@ms.cc.sunysb.edu

W. Schüffel
Department of Psychosomatic Medicine, University of Marburg, Marburg, Germany

D. Lohmar and J. Brudzińska (eds.), *Founding Psychoanalysis Phenomenologically*, Phaenomenologica 199, DOI 10.1007/978-94-007-1848-7_13,

as is common among working class women. Now 30 years of age, she has been married for about 10 years and has two children, 6 and 4.

This is the fourth time she has been treated for a failure in her hearing and the second time she has been treated psychosomatically, which is itself a source of concern for her. The first three times there was a temporary loss of hearing for which the examining physicians found no ear infections. After the third loss, she spent several weeks in a psychosomatic course of treatment in another clinic. This fourth time her hearing remains but she complains of an unremitting sound persisting in both ears. The sound is uniform and no voices of any kind are heard, she reports. If the *tinnitus*, as it is called, was present in earlier cases, this time it has increased and become so loud that she needs strong sleeping pills at night. She has been wearing an ear device that she believes helps diminish the volume of the tone. Her one prior stay in the hospital did not work, as she puts it. She returned to the same living situation as before and now finds herself back in the clinic. My observations of her were in a group with two other women, led by Dr. Schüffel.[1] This paper grows out of my collaboration with him in the Department of Psychosomatic Medicine at the University of Marburg. I have also been greatly helped by discussions with Dr. Dr. Neraal, who was the primary physician, and Dr. Kolb-Niemann, who also offered valuable insight into this case.

A case like Frau D's tinnitus suggests that this illness is a complex that cannot be sufficiently explained by physical causality alone and that a complementary notion of *motivation* must be included as well. Indeed, it even suggests that neuro-physical causes (micro-level) run their course within complexes (macro-level) having essentially functional and existential significance. To truly understand the illness, larger questions must be asked. Why did Frau D develop this *particular* illness and not another? If one invokes stress, then why does it affect her hearing and not her taste or smell, as in the case of Frau A, another patient? How is this symptom connected to her efforts to navigate her "all too human" environment?

In an effort to understand the case of Frau D, I have divided this paper into five parts. The first part works with the assumption that to understand the case of Frau D is to understand the *world* of Frau D. I will use the concept of significance (*Bedeutsamkeit*) as my point of entry to a notion of world appropriate to psychosomatic medicine. The second part will suggest that various types of significance can be correlated to differences within the concept of world between setting, context and background. The third part will further specify the formation of background. The final two parts will focus on the way the case of Frau D sheds light on what I will call the truth-bearing function of her symptoms.[2]

1 World as Horizon

For the class of psychosomatic illnesses that are forged out of conflict, such as we find in the case of Frau D, we readily say that symptoms arise because a person's involvement with her or his world has become overwhelmingly stressful. But what do we mean by world? Or, better put, what is the notion of world that allows us to understand both the etiology and what I will call the teleology of psychosomatic symptoms? Let me step back from psychosomatic medicine for a moment and go at this question with an approach shaped by phenomenology.[3]

The phenomenological problem of the world arises in reaction to the natural scientific attempt to reduce it to a certain type of natural complex. This reduction is a result of a certain stance or attitude, what Husserl calls the natural attitude. According to him, the sciences do not apprehend the world falsely but "objectivistically", i.e., they are capable of approaching the world only as something having the character of an object. Unfortunately, in psychiatry and psychology as well, Blankenberg complains, "objectifiability [*Objektivierbarkeit*]" also reigns.[4] What confirms this apprehension is that, given a certain attitude (*Einstellung*), the world can appear in this way. In the natural attitude the world can be treated as the set of all facts or as the totality of all things. Sets and totalities are not things, of course, but they are nevertheless objects, *Gegen-stände*. But what allows the world to appear in this way is not itself an appearance. The structure of the world can never be manifest as something having the character of an object and, therefore, never as the field of an object-oriented investigation.

In an effort to capture this difference between an objectivistic and a phenomenological concept of the world, Husserl and then Heidegger characterized the world as *horizon* and horizon as a nexus of *significance* that situates not only our multiple discourses about different regions of the world but also the regions themselves.

But what does this mean? What do we mean by nexus of significance? As someone asked in one of the workshops, what is the meaning of meaning? Does it have an internal structure? In some of the philosophical work that I have done, I have attempted to get at the concept of the horizon by distinguishing between field, context, and background. Does the distinction between background and context have any relevance for clinical understanding in general and the case of Frau D in particular? This paper is an attempt to *begin* to give a few answers. Let us look at the polymorphic world of Frau D.

2 The Polymorphic World of Frau D

2.1 Setting

The illness that Frau D has is, first of all, situated in a particular environment. The environments that psychosomatic medicine studies might better be called settings since they are particular human places in which persons work out their relationships with each other. A setting can, indeed, be given a rather straightforward description. There are a number of facts that Frau D reported, using what we philosophers call claims or propositions. Propositions are sentences that have the standard form of S is p, that refer or fail to refer to facts, and thus can be true or false. The *meaning* of a proposition is carried by the concept(s) expressed by the predicate term(s); concepts, in turn, are publicly shared and *rule-regulated distinctions*. Propositions can be grouped according to the different fields or "regions" to which they belong, with the rules governing meaningful claims in one region overlapping with and differing to various degrees from the rules of another region. Logical coherence and consequences define the relationship between propositions. This is the language of textbooks; textbooks are what transform regions into academic disciplines. But this is also the sort of third person reporting we find in everyday life whenever a speaker offers an objective account of the facts or, lacking sincerity, whenever he or she chooses to deliberately conceal the facts. Much of what Frau D offered were straightforward propositions; taken together they "set the stage" of her own illness. Summarizing we can say that in addition to *general* rules that set formal conditions for meaningful propositions, there are also *regional* rules regulating psychosomatic discourse in contrast to other types, and then *particular* rules that are in play in the case of Frau D's situation. The *setting* is the set of these particular conditions.

Over time the picture of her home situation fell in place. She and her husband have been living in what was originally a pub (*Gaststätte*) owned by his father and mother. The father became a drinker and sent the pub into bankruptcy. In an effort to save the home, the son, Frau D's husband, took out a mortgage, bought the building, and converted the downstairs into living space. To help with the expense of carrying the house, his father and mother, his sister and family, then Herr D and Frau D with their two children all lived there. The home was located in A, which is a strict Catholic village, open only to those born there. A Passion Play is staged periodically, along the lines of the one found in Oberammergau. This is the town from which Frau D's mother stems but Frau D was never really received by her in-laws. She gets along with some individual members, but not all, and certainly not the whole group, she claims. Her father-in-law in particular would constantly demean and verbally abuse her. The husband promised to move the family on several occasions but this never happened. At one point during the 10 years she did leave in frustration for a year and moved some 100 km back to her parents house. But she returned and was living with her family in the unbearable and stressful situation in the old *Gaststätte* at the time she was admitted to the hospital.

2.2 Context

In addition to making different claims *about* various facts in her home setting, Frau D also revealed segments or samples of dialogues that took place *in* that setting. Discussions with her father-in-law and, later, with her husband would be reenacted. Or she would freely talk about her feelings and reactions to her situation as if she were still in the Gaststätte.[5] What we are interested in are the various ways she acts out and "sorts out" her situation. Here we turn our attention not to her third person *reflective* account *about* her situation, as we just did, but to the grammar of her first person *reflexive* discourse *in* her situation.[6] Indeed, the value of transference, as Dr. Schüffel emphasizes, is that it allows the therapist to stand in for a significant person to whom the patient's discourse is addressed. As the patient places the therapist in his or her situation, the therapist gains access to it. This discourse is meaningful but in a way different from propositions. The meaning of the sentences here consists of various *schemata of differentiation* that allow the speaker not so much to reflectively describe but to directly articulate and engage her situation. Here the element of performance prevails. The schemata of differentiation are different (possible) ways of "taking-up" or "taking-on" various persons and facets of the environment. Speech here is not the product of well-formed thoughts seeking words. Rather the "thought" or intention is itself first shaped in the process of speaking.[7] Meaningful terms, in turn, are related not by logical entailment but by *differential implication* or what goes by the unfortunate name of association.[8] The meaning of terms is determined by their relationship to yet other contrasting and opposing signs that can or cannot be used as a speaker engages his or her environment. We could say that the *unity* or identity of a term's meaning is a function of these *differences*. The set of all such relationships of identity and difference give us the system of implications; the set of differential implications is what we mean by *context*.

Notice also that a corresponding change in the referents of the sentences is in play. The facts become *affairs* in which we are entangled, and our speech captures the style of that active participation. This is the kind of talk[9] that carries our practical and emotional involvement in situations. Like farmwomen, we "sing" as we harvest the golden wheat; in periods of drought our songs become sad.

Therapy begins with the setting but is mainly interested in context, for to understand a patient is to grasp the relationships of implication and exclusion in the language that the patient uses. The therapist is interested not so much in the logic of what is said, for she or he has been trained to view that with suspicion, but rather in its illogic, its bending of the rules, its *Unrechtmäßigkeit*. Along with many others, we found two forms of semantic deviation in Frau D's discourse about and with her father-in-law that were especially telling.

Frau D reported feeling very secure in the group session with two other female patients, did not hesitate to speak about her feelings, and offered good insights into the other two patients. Yet even charged group sessions, in which the other two wept deeply and where she talked about her own frustrations, never saw her moved to tears. This seemed related to an important feature of her descriptions. When asked about her feelings and thoughts at the present time, she had great difficulty using the indexical pronoun "I" (*ich*). For example, her frustrations with her father-in-law, who continues to drink, were put like this: "One cannot cope with him at all," which works a little better in German, i.e., "Man kommt mit ihm überhaupt nicht zurecht." She also said that she feels guilty and sad because she had to leave her children and reenter the hospital but expressed this impersonally as well: "one is guilty" ("man ist schuldig"), not "I feel guilty." The I, the "ich," is lost behind the One, behind "das Man."[10]

There is another striking form of grammatical displacement in the case of Frau D. At one point, when talking about the way "du" (familiar form of "you") and "Sie" (formal or polite form) were being used in the group, she candidly admitted that she had never been able to call her father-in-law, even after 10 years of living under the same roof as part of the family, "du", but instead always addressed him as

"Sie." I was astonished, as were the others in group. Of course, a "Sie" implies only a neutral "man sagt," a "one says." It was not she that was speaking but the community of voices. This was a way not of dealing with him but of refusing to deal with him, of being absent, of not being affected. But here it is also the case that a "du" implies a contrasting "ich," a delimited "I" that is sufficiently different from the father-in-law that she can be angry with him without herself becoming the object of her rage. This, we find, is what is missing in her case.

2.3 Background

The analysis of both stage and context has taken its guiding thread from language, as well it should. Therapists begin by talking to patients and most of what therapists know about patients comes from interpreting both their reflective claims about their lives and the pattern of their unreflective discourses and dialogues in their situations. Yet patients also act or fail to act, work or fail to work, move freely in their environments or remain locked in their houses. Thus far we have made no connection to the body and the actions that carry our involvement in various situations. Doing so allows us to discover another type of significance and yet a third type of horizon, what I am calling background. Being rooted in the body, it is preverbal and preconceptual in nature. We must dwell on this for a few moments as the prevailing tendency is to confuse background and context or, in the case of strict social constructionist theories, to collapse background into context.[11]

Context does not stand alone. In addition to our speaking about matters in an environment we are also engaged with them bodily. There are not only acts of speaking but also *actions* in which we take what is spoken about to hand and use it practically. Taking to hand and using objects generates a kind of significance different in kind from what we found in speech. In place of that distance that allows the speech-act to refer to an object, we grasp the object and bring it within the circuit of our body. Indeed, actions can "constitute" the determinations of things apart from or before speech: placing a rock in front of an open door "unfolds" its significance as a door stop; the action of taking the round stick in hand and using it to hit a ball is what determines it as a bat.[12]

It is in this relationship between action and what is ready-to-hand, *zuhanden*, that we discover what we can call primary perception. Primary perception itself is never a mental act of interpreting data or sensations according to concepts, for it is controlled by action, on the one hand, and need or desire, on the other. In primary perception objects appear according to what Kurt Lewin called their "Aufforderungscharaktere," K. Koffka their "demand character", and J.J. Gibson their "affordances."[13] "A handle wants to be turned, a step invites a 2-year-old infant to climb it and jump down from it, chocolate wants to be eaten, a mountain to be climbed."[14] In primary perception, moreover, the way the object is present for action is internally connected to our *affects*. Needs and drives motivate actions. The desire for or an aversion to something calling us to action frames the way it is perceived.

Perception, we can say, employs schemata of *discrimination* facilitating action that are not or not yet the schemata of differentiation animating speech. Let us follow both Husserl and Heidegger and call this kind of significance *sense* (*Sinn*), and let us at the outset not confuse it with *meaning* (*Bedeutung*), which was the focus of our analysis of propositions and everyday talk.

The senses of things, I am suggesting, arise in the course of our bodily actions upon them. While action is often directed by conceptual content expressible in speech, it does not require this, nor is the significance of things ready-to-hand itself produced by the way they are referred to in descriptions. Rather than looking to differential schemata, which we have linked to our speaking about the world, there is another level of organization, schemata of *discrimination*, that is in play, one suggested by the actions of the body and the way perception itself is organized affectively. In contrast to context we have *background*. World as background is a nexus of indicative implications (*Verweisungs-zusammenhang*).

3 The Formation of Background

Let us give up one of the restrictions that we have imposed on the analysis thus far. We have spoken only of actions but actions are generally forms of *interaction*: we work with others, we play soccer together, we dance with a partner, or, in more turbulent times, we strike others in anger. It is crucial to see that our interactions are not always the product of prior thoughts or ready-made intentions. Often intentions arise in the course of an interaction and are shaped by it. Striking another person is often a case of intention-in-action.[15] The body, pushed beyond a certain threshold, reacts. And when she says afterwards "I did not mean to hit you," we should interpret this precisely: there was not a prior act-intention formed before the action and motivating it. Yet, in fact, she did mean to hit him, i.e., her body and its actions formed the intention for her, not her deliberative thinking. Background takes shape, first of all, through forms of intentionality that are rooted in the body and that arise during the course of our actions and interactions.

We also need to root background in affectivity. Well before all of our developed forms of interaction, rich with speech, we find the triadic relationship between child, mother, and father rich with affects. This is the first and most basic field of interaction.[16] This relationship is governed by the dynamics of touch, not vision. Here touching is structured in a way that not only provides an awareness of the physiognomy of the body of the other but also establishes an exchange of feelings that necessarily involves both the parent and the child. The parent touched is also touching, which allows the child doing the touching to sense itself as touching and touched at the same time. Touching, as Husserl also pointed out, "localizes" experience in the body.[17] Here the feelings of the mother or father are directly given in the exchange of touch. Thus to touch the other (mother or father) is simultaneously to experience the affects of the other. Touch introduces a singular type of bodily reflexivity, in play well before there is a developed difference between inner and outer, subject and object, that is missing from vision and even further removed from speech. An analysis of touch leads us to something deeper than intersubjectivity here: we discover the intercorporeal nature of affectivity.

The triadic relationship between child and parents is governed by an economy of needs and gratification, of desires and affection, in short, of an economy of binding.[18] Touch developed over time is what produces holding, and holding that becomes constant leads to what Erikson and Winnicott call "basic trust," its failure to that terrible opposite, basic fault. To fix this terminologically, let us say that at this level the primary mode of the child being related to the significant persons in its environment is clinging (*Anfassen*[19]), the mode of significant persons experiencing the child is embracing (*Umfassen*[20]).[21] The horizon in play here can be thought of as an emerging nexus of senses defined by primary attachments. It is the organization of primary attachments that gives us the deep structure of background.

4 The Origins of the Symptom

Breaking out the notion of world in terms of setting, context, and background, and then deepening the account of background in terms of action and affectivity allows us to return to the question of the origin and function of symptoms. We will attempt to show that the symptom[22] has not only an etiology but also a teleology, i.e., not only formative features, *Gestaltungselemente*, but also purposive features, a certain *Zweckmäßigkeit*. The analysis of both formative and purposive achievements in terms of context and background will give us the key to the constitution of symptoms.

The context sustaining our everyday talk is essentially a social horizon of meanings consisting of shared schemata of expressible differentiations. It allows a subject to articulate not only the matters with which she is engaged but also the feelings and concerns that she has – sometimes directly, sometimes indirectly. Wishes and desires are cast in an ideational form that allows them to meet the conventions and expectations of others. If strong wishes and especially the core need for basic affection are emphatically rejected, they do not die of their own accord but seek to find fulfillment in surrogate objects or people. And if these surrogates fail or are also rejected, tension is redoubled. Once certain thresholds are crossed, the tension is manifest as bodily symptoms. This conversion model, of course, was the one that Freud introduced.[23] As is well known, his notions of wish, censorship, repression, sublimation, and substitution provide a workable account of the oblique and dense nature of the ideational content of symptoms. This account has been modified and extended by Dr. Schüffel's discussion of wishing, warding off, suspending, and solving.[24] Approached from the side of content, what is striking is the way that the symptom and, with it, the speech of the subject introduce a certain *impropriety* into relationships with others that plays off manifest meaning against the underlying sense. The impropriety is found in the fact that collusion with, protest against, and protection from significant others are all in play. Indeed, the manifest meaning as understood by others stands in tension with what they accept as normal or healthy and, in being rejected or judged by others, thereby conceals its sense. But this point already carries us into background, into the domain of affects and interaction. Because the symptom is formed by what Freud called primary and not secondary processes, background is inextricably interwoven with context: the processes of condensation (*Verdichtungsarbeit*) and displacement (*Verschiebungsarbeit*)[25] generating the manifest meaning of the symptom are driven by the vicissitudes of basic drives or affects. Barriers in the way of acting on the basis of needs, wants, and/or desires create a conflict of affects that is *converted* into a symptom to which the body, for its part, lends itself and finds at least a momentary resolution. Yet the fact that the conflicted desires generating the sense are also unknown to and not in the control of the subject turns protest into a pathology from which she cannot escape.

The meaning of the symptom is found in its ideational context; the sense of the symptom is found in its affective content. By means of primary processes they form a single whole. The implications of this for therapy are quite clear. It is only by (re) establishing an affective sense of basic trust, reactivating the affects associated with the underlying conflicts, and tracking the way that they come to expression in the symptom that the therapist and subject will be able to get at the origins of the illness. "Hysterics suffer mainly from reminiscences," Freud and Breuer tell us in their early 1893 *Preliminary Communication*.[26] Mutually discovering and, to some extent, recreating the context and background generating the symptom opens up its *retrospective* significance.

While the distinction between context and background might be new, the notion of conversion and its "mechanisms" are already familiar. What might be novel in our account is the claim that symptoms also have a teleology co-constitutive of their formation.

5 The Teleology of the Symptom

Time does not permit me to deal further with Frau D's relationship to her father-in-law and, thus, the way this seems to involve unresolved Oedipal issues with her own father. And we can only mention her suppressed resentment toward her husband and the way this involves a symbiotic dependence upon him. He has dominated the relationship and determined its space. Conflict-based psychosomatic symptoms are a form of *withdrawal* that allows a subject to process the conflicting desires and affects connected to significant others, yet we can also understand them as forms of *engagement* that grant one enough space to navigate the coming day. They reflect as they deflect a past, but they also make possible action in the future, I want to suggest.

However one decides to interpret the Oedipal dynamics,[27] we are now in a good position to return to the tinnitus. To connect the sense of the symptom to its generation out of action and interaction is simultaneously to understand how the meaning of the symptom is connected to the way the subject *navigates* her all-too-human relationships. In short, the symptom is purpose-driven, though it is not a purpose located in a conscious intention, but rather one shaped by the way its ideational content stands in for the unconscious wishes and desires sustaining the symptom and "works" their "will" on significant others.

If it is the background that dominates the etiology of the symptom, it is the context that dominates its teleology. Symptoms are more than indicators, they are signs: the subject knows, at least tacitly, that the symptom has a certain meaning that in being understood (superficially) by others also moves them in one way or another. The subject's acquaintance with the context allows for a restructuring of the space of her actions and, thereby, the background. The symptom is not only reactive but proactive, not only retrospective but prospective, not only a form of memory but also of anticipation.[28] In *marking* the impossibilities it also *intimates* the possibilities of acting in the environment in which Frau D lives. The symptom, I am suggesting, not only projects a past onto a present; it also protects the present in view of a future. Taken in this way, the tinnitus is rich with significance. It contributes toward a certain "spatialization" of the "I" in at least four interlocking ways.

1. Delimiting, *Abgrenzung*. The tinnitus both draws a line and establishes a difference. On the one hand, it separates the space that belongs to others and that belongs to her. The contrast is in ownership. Her space is not to be touched by other hands. This space is open only to her. She alone has access. She hears the sounds, no one else does, not even the examining physician.
2. Threshold, *Schwelle*. The border between inner and outer is also a threshold between the two. Unlike certain cases of schizophrenia, where the connection to the world has been inverted and the sounds have become internal voices, this is a uniform tone that both blocks what she hears and yet allows her to understand everything. The threshold as well as the intensity of the sound are determined by the affective quality of the relationship with the other. Significantly, when Dr. Schüffel, whom she trusted, deliberately lowered his voice in a group session, which he did without her realizing it, there was no loss in comprehension.
3. Gatekeeper, *Schleusenwärter*. The threshold is also a gate that can be open or closed to others. The symptom causes others to hesitate and sometimes repels them. The element of control is there. During her stay in the hospital she even cut her hair, which otherwise concealed the small device she was wearing to help with her hearing disorder. Now it is open for all to see. It functions like a small, stern gatekeeper that simultaneously assists her even as it obstructs others.
4. Attaching, *Verbindung*. Symptoms of this type are not just ways of gaining control, however imperfectly, over fields of action, but are also ways of reaching out. They communicate, though they are more like icons than words, more like gestures than symbols. They even invite help. She does not want to divorce. The tinnitus keeps the husband connected, if at a distance, by shared issues that they have to come to grips with together. If the gatekeeper usually functions to push away, this invites connection, invites him to enter respectfully what is now becoming her own space.

It is this last function of reattaching – in the face of lost or frustrated primary attachments – that opens up the hope of a new relationship to significant others and gives both the patient and the therapist a future toward which they can work. The fact that symptoms have not just an etiology but also a teleology has clear implications for therapy and points to the importance of rebuilding narratives and developing new *rhythms*, i.e., new ways of integrating affects and styles of action that ground such narratives.

Notes

1. For an overview of the approach to psychosomatic medicine taken by Dr. Schüffel, his colleagues and others in the field (see Schüffel et al. 1998).
2. Let me say in advance that I am frightfully aware of how laconic and incomplete this account will be. Each section that follows is easily a chapter, if not several, in itself. I expect to devote considerable attention to them in a forthcoming book tentatively titled *Bodies of Flesh*.
3. What follows is adapted from "World as Horizon," (Welton 2003).
4. On his appropriation of the Husserlian notion of the reduction (see Blankenburg 1979).
5. What makes the distinction between claims and first person descriptions subtle and hard to grasp is that there need not be any surface difference in the form of the sentences (they can both have the form of S is p) and the fact that even the most straightforward claim always has the implicit operator "I think that," "I believe that," "I feel that," etc., and thus a certain indexicality or occasionality that allows one, especially a skilled therapist, to interpret the claim as expressive not of a fact but of how the speaker is coming to grips with his or her situation.
6. On the difference between reflective and reflexive (see Welton 2003).
7. When that speech repeats or mimics the voice of "man sagt," the schemata of differentiation are simply what a culture teaches us to say and think. Our way of taking-up and taking-on are the product of our society.
8. If this is the case, then the very notion of association must be freed from the emphasis upon contiguity (Hume) and pairing (behaviorism) that prevails in empiricist accounts.
9. It is what Husserl called "occasional" and what we today think of as "indexical" speech.
10. Of course, these are also excuses or justifications, which also have the effect of removing the I (the ich) from the stage.
11. If one collapses background into context we end up with a strict social constructionism in which the body is only a blank tablet on which culture inscribes its structures.
12. "Door stop" and "bat" are, of course, concepts. But we use each here only as placeholder for a sense-structure or what Husserl called a "type," which would have to be characterized in terms appropriate to it.
13. Koffka (1935, 355–357) and Gibson (1986, Chap. 8).
14. Koffka (1935, 553).
15. We need to contrast what we can call intention-before-action to intention-in-action. There obviously are cases where one decides what needs to be done and then goes about doing it. The dishes have been sitting in the sink for a week; I decide that it is time to clean them, from which follows the action of filling the sink with water and washing them. But to get at the concept of action of particular interest to psychosomatic medicine, we need to think about cases where my behavior does not follow from a previous conscious decision but occurs without such, thoughtlessly or automatically, as we often say. The skilled cyclist swerves to the left to avoid touching the wheel of the competitor in front of him. The experienced cabinetmaker moves without hesitation from sawing the leg of the table to chiseling out a mortise and to sanding its surfaces. The sleepy student does not hesitate to put her books on the table and sink

into the chair. These forms of action, in which there are no "prior" intentions, are the more interesting to look at for us as they might eventually give us insight into their neurotic siblings, as we find in obsessive-compulsive disorders, and perhaps even more distant relatives, such as the symptoms of Frau D.

16. It is central to the account we are offering that we place interaction first at this level, both structurally and genetically, and not the level of verbal exchange.
17. Husserl (1952, 144–156) and (1989, 152–163). For an analysis of Husserl's notion of the body (see Welton 1999).
18. On the notion of affection and a critique of Freud's emphasis upon eros (see Welton 1998b).
19. I am playing on the sense in which "an" can mean "up against," "in," "at," and "on." This is the view of the child on the mother's breast, in the father's arms, etc.
20. Not in the sense of "comprehend," as if this is a mental act, but in the sense of "contain" or "cover" or "embrace."
21. Umfassen stands in contrast to the Umsicht that Heidegger takes as basic to action.
22. Keep in mind that we are focusing on conversion-type symptoms, what Freud called hysterical symptoms, leaving open the question of whether this scheme applies to yet other classes.
23. For a recent discussion of conversion that has been of help in our study (see Casey 1998).
24. See Schüffel (2007), Sect. 3.4.
25. See Freud (1900/1972) for these notions.
26. Breuer and Freud (1957, 7). Italics dropped. After Casey (1998, 217).
27. If time allowed, we would go on to speak about the way that the Oedipal story is situated between context and background. It must be located there because it is not just the needs or desires of the child but the actions of the child that meet the culture of the parents, shaped by language (context). Background and context always work together in the "history" of illness. But here I am after the transference of sense between father and father-in-law.
28. As the dominant temporal dimension shifts from the past (memory) to the future (anticipation), spatialization achieves a certain priority. I will take this up in a forthcoming book, *The Spatiality of Consciousness*.

References

Blankenburg, Wolfgang. 1979. Phänomenologische Epoché und Psychopathologie. In *Alfred Schütz und die Idee des Alltags in den Sozialwissenschaften*, ed. Sprondel Walter and Grafthoff Richard, 125–139. Stuttgart: Ferdinand Enke Verlag.

Breuer, Josef, and Sigmund Freud. 1957. *Studies on hysteria* (trans: James Strachey). New York: Basic Books.

Casey, Ed. 1998. The ghost of embodiment. In *Body and flesh*, ed. Welton Donn, 207–225. Oxford: Blackwell Publishers.

Freud, Sigmund. 1900/1972. *Die Traumdeutung. Studienausgabe, Band 2*. Frankfurt: Fischer Verlag.

Freud, Sigmund. 1900/1965. *The Interpretation of Dreams* (trans: James Strachey). New York: Avon Books.

Gibson, J.J. 1986. *The ecological approach to visual perception*. Hillsdale: Lawrence Erlbaum.

Husserl, Edmund. 1952. Ideen zu einer reinen Phänomenologie und phänomenologischen Philosophie. In *Band 2: Phänomenologische Untersuchungen zur Konstitution*, ed. Marly Biemel. Husserliana, vol. 4. The Hague: Martinus Nijhoff.

Husserl, Edmund. 1989. Ideas Pertaining to a Pure Phenomenology and to a Phenomenological Philosophy. In *Book 2: Studies in the Phenomenology of Constitution* (trans: Richard Rojcewicz and Andre Schuwer). Collected Works, vol. 3. Dordrecht: Kluwer Academic Publishers.

Koffka, K. 1935. *Principles of gestalt psychology*. New York: Harcourt, Brace & World.

Schüffel, Wolfram. 2007 "Das Erstgespräch aus ärztlich-phänomenologischer Sicht: Symptomzentriert." (manuscript).

Schüffel, Wolfram, Ursula Brucks, et al. 1998. *Handbuch der Salutogenese*. Weisbaden: Ullstein Medical Verlagsgesellschaft.
Welton, Donn (ed.). 1998a. *Body and flesh*. Oxford: Blackwell Publishers.
Welton, Donn. 1998b. Affectivity and eros. In *Body and flesh*, ed. Donn Welton, 181–206. Oxford: Blackwell Publishers.
Welton, Donn. 1999. Soft smooth hands: Husserl's phenomenology of the lived body. In *The body: Classic and contemporary readings*, ed. Donn Welton, 38–56. Oxford: Blackwell.
Welton, Donn. 2003. World as horizon. In *The new Husserl: A critical reader*, ed. Donn Welton, 223–232. Bloomington: Indiana University Press.

Psychic Reality. Intentionality Between Truth and Illusion

Daniel Widlöcher

Abstract From a psychoanalytical point of view, "unconscious proper" must be reserved for material that can not gain any access to becoming conscious.
Of all the fundamental concepts which we owe to Freud's genius, none more clearly marks his discovery than the concept of psychic reality.
The reality of the unconscious contents of mind, the structural "Unconscious", creates in the mind *illusory* belief.
It derives from a hallucinatory activity issued from the Id which imposes itself on the Ego as reality. The Ego *must* believe in reality of unconscious fantasy as he believes in the external world.
The analyst's understanding results from the associative work that he experiences with the patient. The term "co-thinking" is suggested for linking patient and analyst through this emerging process. '-- End of Abstract'

Wanting to explain how to describe the fundamental rule to the patient, (Freud 1913, 135) advises the psychoanalyst to use a metaphor: "Act as though, for instance, you were a traveler sitting next to the window of a railway carriage and describing to someone inside the carriage the changing views which you see outside." As far as communication between patient and psychoanalyst is a description of what the patient perceives, from the subjective experience, speech is the usual way to communicate the inner perceptions. Speech and subjectivity are therefore closely related. But is it also the case when unconscious thoughts are taken into account? From the "changing views" described by the patient, the psychoanalyst can infer only some unknowable reality. Freud, however, refers yet to the perception of it. "Just as Kant warned us not to overlook the fact that our perceptions are subjectively conditioned and must not be regarded as identical with what is perceived though unknowable, so

D. Widlöcher (✉)
79, boulevard Vincent Auriol, Paris 75013, France
e-mail: d.h.widlocher@wanadoo.fr

D. Lohmar and J. Brudzińska (eds.), *Founding Psychoanalysis Phenomenologically*, Phaenomenologica 199, DOI 10.1007/978-94-007-1848-7_14,

psychoanalysis warns us not to equate perceptions by means of consciousness with the unconscious mental processes which are their object. Like the physical, the psychical is not necessarily in reality what it appears to us to be" (Freud 1915, 171). But does listening to unconscious psychic reality entail the same usual kind of verbal descriptive communication than ordinary conversation (that was suggested by Freud in his 1913th paper) or does it entail a specific way of language or a specific way to listen to it?

It is usually stated that the patient's words are not heard as spoken utterances but perceived as signifiers which refer to a story the patient intends to tell us. We don't pay attention to the words as things but to their meaning, to what is signified by the words. Following Freud's metaphor, the patient describes what he is thinking about, a memory, a conscious fantasy, a mental state, and addresses the analyst to share with him/her a common knowledge and asking from him/her a response. But the question is: "How does the transformation of an intended narrative to its unconscious or shadow narrative take place in the analytic listener and, it is hoped, in the patient?"

In the following comments, I want to stress the fact that the contrast between external and internal worlds results not only from the opposition between external reality and subjective experience, but also from a radical opposition between material reality (the external one) and another kind of reality, another form of coherence, pressure and resistance, comparable to material reality. The unconscious replaces the external by psychic reality: "The phantasies possess *psychical* as contrasted with *material* reality, and we gradually learn to understand that in the world of the neurosis it is psychical reality which is the decisive kind." (Freud 1916, 368). In one sense, the ego must believe in the reality of unconscious fantasy as he believes in the external world.

Too often, this sharp distinction is blurred because the difference between descriptive and structural unconscious is not clearly made. From the dynamic point of view, the "psychical process", which is temporarily or permanently repressed by the "second censorship" (Freud 1915, 160) may be qualified as unconscious (descriptive unconscious). But, from the topical (structural) point of view, "unconscious proper" may be reserved for material that cannot gain "easy access to becoming conscious but must be inferred, recognized and translated into conscious form" (Freud 1940, 160).

As far as the second censorship is removed, descriptive unconscious material becomes part of subjective experience and may be transmitted by the intended narrative. On the contrary, there is no direct access to the unconscious proper material that must be inferred. As I will elaborate later, more precisely unconscious pressure (unconscious act, psychic reality) shifts into a narrative and looses this status of psychic reality. A very mundane clinical example illustrates first repression due to the "second" censorship of material previously suppressed by the conflict between the preconscious and the unconscious, and then the enactment of an unconscious fantasy.

1 Temporary Repression via "Second" Censorship

The patient, a 30-year-old woman who has been in analysis with me for some time, reported in our next session of the week that she had been totally preoccupied over the weekend by the thought of meeting me outside of the office. She had been imagining that she would meet me by attending scientific conferences or art exhibitions, but she eventually realized that she could meet me directly by ringing me up or by staking herself out near my house. She agreed that such behavior is that of a true lover.

She then tried to remember how the previous session, the last one of the week, had ended; I could not see what she was referring to.

Fantasies succeeded one another in this patient, such as the wish to be my daughter. She also brought up various images of fraternal rivalry. A memory came back to her of her mother telling her how happy she was not to have to worry about her for her future.

She then suddenly remembered the end of the previous session. She had been expressing all the interest she now had for her treatment. A little while later, I signaled very abruptly the end of the session by saying the usual "Bien". "Bien" alone, in French, is a wording that expresses either approving what has been said (this is the meaning she apparently retained), or marking the end of a sequence of actions or sentences (what I had in mind). Although this coincided with the scheduled time, she could not help but think that I was showing my approval for what she had just said. The patient clearly had had an insight into this fantasy after the session, but had censored it from her consciousness, while all her conscious fantasies were producing the "loving" behavior.

2 Unconscious-Preconscious Repression

The other kind of repression is more difficult to illustrate, because the fantasy content cannot be described precisely with the subject's words. Freud gave us a few examples, such as that of "The Ratman", when he wrote: "At all the more important moments while he was telling his story, his face took on a very strange, composite expression, I could only interpret it as one of horror at pleasure of his own of which he himself was unaware" (Freud 1909, 166–167). There is also the second phase of "A Child is being beaten" (1919): "Profound transformations have taken place between this first phase and the next. It is true that the person beating remains the same (that is, the father); but the child who is beaten has been changed into another one and is now invariably the child producing the fantasy [...] Now, therefore, the wording runs: 'I am being beaten by my father'. It is of an unmistakably masochistic character. This second phase is the most important and the most momentous of all. But we may say of it in a certain sense that it has never had a real existence. It is never remembered, it has never succeeded in becoming conscious. It is a construction of analysis, but it is no less a necessity on that account." (Freud 1919, 185). The end of the session whose first part I reported earlier appears to be a good illustration of the structural unconscious. The patient, after remembering the "conscious" fantasy that had marked the end of the last session, told me she would like me to tell her what I thought of her idea, and how I understood what she wanted to say. She insisted, pressing me, and at the same time felt embarrassed by her own insistence, but could not help it. She just could not "control" herself. I then told her that by pressuring me in such a way, she was behaving just like her sister, who worried her mother by always interrogating her, which in turn made her jealous.

"Oh yes," she says "when I asked you that question, I did not feel that I was myself saying it, I had the feeling of being in a game [...] that I wanted to play."

In terms of clinical accessibility, the differences between the two types of repression are obvious. In the first situation, the patient's awareness or attentional investment enabled her to overcome the second censorship and express the fantasy consciously. In the second situation, only construction work permitted her to reconstruct the scenario from several concrete scenes. In one case the scene was included in the biographic concrete memory, while in the other it was only expressed as a hypothetical construct. In one case the scene could be represented with words, in the other, the words were merely used to describe it.

The preconscious-unconscious, the repressed memory is the "narrative" description of an act, as any representation that may be constructed in the preconscious-conscious system, naming the sources, the actors and the forms of the action represented, in a narrative manner, whereas in the "unconscious proper" the representation is more like a hallucination whereby the action in progress can be represented.

The question is how the unconscious shares this capacity to give rise to such a belief with external perception, and why unconscious fantasy may have the same power as real facts. This is the crucial point in the debate: what is the role played by language in this process, and how does Lacan's point of view respond to the question?

Very controversial, in regard of the concept of psychic reality, is the origin of the unconscious discourse. Who is speaking? From where, from whom do the signifiers as a message come? Paradoxically, the message comes from nobody. According to Lacan's transcendental point of view, the Other represents the locus of the symbolic function, a collective symbolic discourse. The Other, with a capital "O", is the scene of the Word insofar as the scene of the Word is always in a third position between two subjects. So, psychic reality is no longer part of the subject's creativity. It is reduced to an external discourse whose source is in the abstract and symbolic discourse of the Other: a message, without any personal and direct intentionality, coming from outside. Can we still name psychic reality a reality coming from outside? It is another expression of the Real, through its symbolic form. To explain this new property of the Real, Lacan puts together a "linguistic" approach of the concept of "symbolic" and a "anthropological" approach, by linking the "symbolic" and the triangularity of the Œdipus Complex. It is a fundamental link for Lacan and his followers. Dismissing the concept of "Drive" [Trieb] as too closely related to a biological explanation, Lacan introduces the concept of "Desire" [Wunsch], as expressing a basic emptiness of the Human condition. The message comes from nobody but, through its signifiers, expresses to who receives it as the unconscious discourse, the reality of the Symbolic order, a world of rules defining Human nature (desire and interdict, incest prohibition and father law). I am among many others who are not so convinced by what I consider more as a shift than as a link: a shift from a linguistic to an anthropological meaning. The fact that both acceptations of the symbolic are opposed to the concept of the imaginary, imaginary representation in one sense, dual relationship and narcissistic imagery in the other, is not convincing and, furthermore, reduces the unconscious fantasy to the status of an illusory "by-product".

So, it is clear that the Lacanian theory has implications regarding the psychic reality concept that deserve doubt and reservations. On a theoretical level, the role of the unconscious fantasy, its relationship with affects and pleasure experience, its impact on conflicts and defenses, are marginalized, if not erased. Consequences regarding the treatment are far more important. The debate about the length of the sessions, and some other parts of the setting, mask a more important point that is the nature of psychoanalytical listening and the role of interpretation. Consequences on practice needed time and probably are not yet so fully accepted by people who claim the theory. Nevertheless, these points are clearly stated in the Rome report, already as a consequence of the new definition of the Unconscious and, from my point of view, of the shift from an internal process to external symbolic intersubjectivity.

3 The Feeling and Meaning of Psychic Reality

In the paper she presented at the first scientific meeting of the "The Freud-Klein Controversies, 1941–1945" (in King and Steiner 1991) (January 27, 1943), Susan Isaacs wrote: "Of all the fundamental debates which we owe to Freud's genius, none more clearly marks the new epoch of understanding which he initiated than this discovery of *psychical reality*" (p. 269). Ernest Jones felt this statement to be so important that in his introductory paper to the discussion (read by Glover) he wrote: "The stress she lays in her first few pages on the apprehension of psychical reality, and the debate we here owe to Freud, is quite fundamental. I would say that the hall-mark of psychoanalysts is their feeling for unconscious psychical reality [...]" (King and Steiner 1991, 322).

But he adds straight afterwards: "[...] I agree with her remark that even among psychoanalysts this feeling is often not so highly developed as it might be..." (King and Steiner 1991). In what way, as psychoanalysts, do we come to have such a *feeling* of psychical reality? There is no real evidence of this unconscious subjective experience. Only by using the psychoanalytic method of listening we can come to feel it as real. Feeling is not faith nor trust, but just an experience. If we listen to what the other says in an appropriate way (according to the analytic method), we will come to have this experience.

4 The Illusory Nature of Psychic Reality

Now we are faced, however, with a central ambiguity. For while we come to acknowledge the *reality* of the unconscious contents of the mind we also know that a part of the psychic apparatus, the structural "Unconscious", creates in the mind *illusory* belief.

To understand the problem this raises we must better understand the concept of "psychic reality," which was first elaborated by Freud in *Totem and Taboo*. There he writes that it is a basic primitive capacity of the mind to "prefer psychical to factual reality and react just as seriously to thoughts as normal people do to realities" (Freud 1913 [1912–13], 159). Psychic reality is viewed as a second psychic scene. "The fantasies possess psychical as contrasted with material reality, and we gradually learn to understand that, in the world of the neurosis, it is psychical reality which is the decisive kind" (Freud 1913 [1912–13], 368). The term psychic reality is used by most psychoanalysts to mean subjective experience because it is influenced by unconscious processes. Even worse, it is at times equated with subjectivity, the way through which external reality is represented in the mind.

According to the trivial meaning (Good et al. 2005), psychic reality must be considered a simple distortion of perception, an error. From a clinical point of view, this would mean that interpretation only results in the correction of a mental distortion. It would be the task of the analyst's interpretative work to undo or retroactively correct the distortion caused by resistances. Very accurately, however, R. Britton (1995) pointed out that psychic reality is not merely an error but is rather a wrong belief: "[...] belief is to psychic reality what perception is to material reality. Belief gives the force of reality to that which is psychic just as perception does to that which is physical. Belief is not the consequence of an error of judgment, it is an active process influenced by 'desire, fear and expectation'." Britton explains this false judgment as an ego function disorder. Normally, the ego confers the status of psychic reality to "existing mental productions (phantasies), thus creating beliefs." Beliefs require sensory confirmation (reality testing) to become true knowledge. So, contrary to the previous point of view, what is believed is not the result of a false perception but of an inappropriate judgment. When a false belief, an illusion, has to be interpreted it is necessary, not to unveil the perceptive mistake but to disavow a judgment distortion. Britton concludes that conflicts about psychic reality are related to a marked difficulty in relinquishing objects, i.e. accepting the fact of their loss but also accepting all the necessary changes about the world that follow from that loss.

But, are we so convinced that psychic reality is just a result of a compensatory belief, of an illusory capacity to mask the loss of an object? I think that Britton's point of view, while rightly pointing to psychic reality as more than an error, disregards the compulsive power of the unconscious id drive and gives too much place to ego functioning. I suggest that in defining psychic reality the issue is not merely one of belief or disbelief in the reality of fantasy, but the source of the illusory capacity of the fantasy. This capacity is a property of the id and not of the ego. It derives from a hallucinatory activity issued from the id, which imposes itself on the ego as reality. The ego *must* believe in the reality of the unconscious fantasy as it believes in the external world.

5 The Origin of Illusion

If we take into serious consideration the fact that psychical reality is not just a form of belief, but rather has its own structure, "a consistency and resistance" of its own manifested through Id activity, then the question of its origin remains. Indeed were we to consider psychic reality merely as an ego distortion, its origin could have been adequately explained in terms of the role of ego in forming belief. But considering psychic reality as a quality of unconscious thought this is not sufficient. We must ask, what is the source of this illusory, hallucinatory representation issued by the Id?

When Freud, first developed his thinking regarding the concept of psychic reality, in *Totem and Taboo* he explained it as a result of omnipotence of thought: "If children and primitive men find play and imitative representation enough for them, that is not a sign of their being unassuming in our sense or of their resignedly accepting their actual impotence. It is the easily understandable result of the paramount virtue they ascribe to their wishes, of the will that is associated with those wishes and of the methods by which those wishes operate." (Freud 1913 [1912–13], 84). From *Totem and Taboo* through *Moses and Monotheism* Freud develops the thesis that our belief in the content of fantasy as reality is a result of historical sources. An important technical consequence of this view is that if historical truth is the source of belief, the task of psychoanalytical treatment is to reduce illusion, not to do away with fantasy itself but only with mistaken belief. According to a strict historical determination of a symptom "the elucidation of that historical determination is essential to the psychoanalytic process: the aim of the treatment, the goal of interpretation is to recuperate the psychical reality in all its significance and effectiveness." (Avenburg and Guiter 1976). Nevertheless, it is interesting to note that when the unconscious is considered as an id-formation, resulting from drive excitations, the concept of historical truth is no longer referred to and is to appear once again only in *Moses and Monotheism*, albeit in a different perspective.

Here we are confronted with the idea that psychic reality is an individual belief in a memory of an imaginary past, a kind of individual tradition, remembered as a truth with a compulsive character. But this compulsive character that has to be considered as a fundamental quality of psychic reality is not a result of drives, *actual* drives, but is only due to the past misinterpretation of reality. The drives only play a role in the past event but not in the present belief.

The Ego rediscovers the true past, becomes conscious of past illusions, and is thus freed of the distorting effects of the drive. In this context the drives are viewed as that which distorted reality in the past, forming a kind a wrong tradition which is now compulsory; they are not considered in terms of their actual contemporary expression.

What I would like to emphasize is that in this formulation, something is lost from the Freudian view that I described before. After *Totem and Taboo*, and until the end of the twenties, psychic reality is considered as a quality of the unconscious itself, and not as a memory distortion. This view disappears when the unconscious is identified with the Id, as though such a quality could not be considered to be a direct expression of drives whose source is biological.

6 Another Perspective on the Origins of Illusory Nature of Psychic Reality

In my view, instead of being a fixation to an early part of the past, psychic reality must be viewed as a permanent quality of the unconscious thought of the Id. Instead of reducing it to a memory of the past, we should treat psychic reality as another scene which we must play out and in this way the ego is freed of its domination.

If psychic reality is not founded on historical truth but is an expression of the drive itself, we have to explain its compulsive claims of reality. I suggest that this compulsive power of illusion possessed by the unconscious fantasy is an essential property derived from the Id and not a wrong belief coming from the ego nor a simple belief in a historical truth. I now explain this essential Id property by returning to Freud's dream theory.

In the 1909 edition of "The Interpretation of Dreams" Freud adds the following remark regarding the term psychic reality: "If we look at unconscious wishes reduced to their most fundamental and truest shape, we shall have to remember, no doubt, that psychical reality too has more than one form of existence not to be confused with factual (material) reality." Freud here makes room for an ambiguity in his theory about the relationship between dreams and wishes. It is established in *The Interpretation of Dreams* (Freud 1900) that the representations ("scenes") that make up a dream represent the realization of a wish. But the question is whether the act of representing a scene (through all the observed distortions, condensing, and displacement, in particular) means that the wish, once realized in the dream content could come to rest in the illusion of being satisfied. The thesis that it can is extensively developed by Freud, and it corresponds to his views regarding the "hallucinatory satisfaction of our wishes" (Freud 1916–17, 231). But, at a very early stage, Freud had to concede that certain dreams contradicted this theory, and the importance granted to repetition compulsion forced him to revise his perspective.

This theoretical wavering seems linked to Freud's ambiguous use of two different terms: hallucinatory satisfaction of wishes ("halluzinatorische Wunschbefriedigung") and wish fulfillment ("Wunscherfüllung"). The purpose of representing wish realization (or, better still, the representation of a wish in the accomplished mode) through hallucination is not necessarily to make the dreamer consciously aware of the fact that a wish has been satisfied. The ability to represent wish fulfillment (in hallucination) is a mode of configuring in thought, without any aim of ensuring satisfaction (which requires other functions independent of the dream). Dream is not a thing representation. It is an action representation.

The manifest content is best described as a scene within which an action unfolds, or as a succession of scenes. It is always possible to offer an account of the dream by putting the dreamer in the position of an actor who takes an active or passive part in the dream, or as a spectator of an externally unfolding action. The frame of the dream, the objects and persons present, are there to give meaning to the action. There is no very real context all around the scene but only particular concrete signs that are closely related to the content of the dream action.

By the associative method, a network of connections is established, and the links then observed lead to events kept in memory. So a disparate set of events, past or present, long past or recent, constitutes a mosaic of scenes which enter into the composition of the dream. Objects or persons, their names or any symbolic association, are meaningless without the action they contribute. It can be said that the scene signified by the manifest content is the result of a superimposition of scenes imprinted in memory and activated at the time of dream production.

The subject who gives an account of an action in which he is engaged is in a position to describe it with words. The propositional content defines the meaning of the action, the state of the world, and the transformation that reflects it. But the dream follows rules of representation of its own. The manifest content scene always appears without any modality of belief or desire. The event is represented in the accomplished mode; it unfolds in the present (the now) of the dream. One may also think that it is because the activated memory scenes – the scenes of the past – are represented as scenes of the present that their composite expression is also represented in the accomplished mode. The dream therefore contains no belief, no doubt or negation. There are wishful expressions (hope, refusal, will) in the dream's content ("I want to get out of this place") but not in the report of the dream: the scene is there, without any belief or wish mode. The dreamer experiences only that he is performing the action in which he is engaged, whether he is the active agent, the passive subject, or the observer.

The dreamer is the actor of his action. It is a form of existence, in the dream activity opposed to material reality and not a particular belief of the dreamer. The theory of the dream sensitizes us to a property of the unconscious. As the actions described in the account of a dream uncover latent scenes that make up the dream, the scenes that occur in the patient's mind likewise uncover those we usually qualify as derivatives of the unconscious. All the properties of a representation that follows the rules of the primary process are identical to those governing the accomplishment of any action. The intent is implemented by the act: to think is to do, to wish is to accomplish (to achieve).

The absence of a link between unconscious representations may now be better understood insofar as these representations are composed of hallucinatory experiences of action which are guided by a principle whereby any action is independent of others. An action can merely follow another, or it can replace it. The displacement, characteristic of unconscious representations, also results from this property. There cannot be any contradiction between these representations either, for actions cannot be incompatible, they can only cancel each other. In contrast, actions can materialize different intentions simultaneously, thus enabling condensation. Lastly, time cannot be represented in a system whereby each thought is expressed by its materialization into an act.

In short, the functioning rules of the primary process are easily explained if one hypothesizes that the primary process regulates the production of hallucinatory actions. Anything that the unconscious can configure, the primary process implements in that active mode. In this sense, one could say that the unconscious does not wish, it expresses wishes in the mode of accomplishment by simulating their realization.

The scenes, the representations that present themselves to consciousness permit us to discover those scenes that we usually qualify as derivatives of the unconscious, Id derivatives. From this perspective, the unconscious appears less as the bearer of truth than as the agent of an illusory power. The unconscious is less an oracle message to be decoded than a continuous creation of scenes, of stories. Like God, the unconscious creates what it thinks about. Unconscious is illusion.

Working-through results from the analyst's listening: What is at hand is to share the associative work with the patient. It is in order to avoid the ambiguities of the word intersubjectivity that I suggested the term co-thinking to describe the effects of the analysand's representations' associative process on that of the analyst.

The term co-thinking does not refer to some new expedient, but strives to describe a mutual developmental process of the associative activity. Words (the acts of thinking expressed through speech), and what is signified between them, their associations, the words left out, censored, etc., originating in the speech of one penetrate the thought of the other, becoming thus his own objects of thought. The effects of meaning they produce depend on the associative context from which they are extracted and on the associative context they create in the other.

Co-thinking can be considered as the means through which communication from unconscious to unconscious takes place. From the point of view of dynamics, the transference-counter-transference interplay fits into the content and the associative dynamics of co-thinking.

The associative networks produced in the psychoanalyst should be treated as an expression of the analysand's psychic life. This contributes in part to an effect of empathy, but, inasmuch as elements missing in the associative network are at play, the psychic work operating in the analyst enables him to recognize unconscious representations or associations in the analysand and to lift repression. In this way, hypothetical representations, waiting interpretations, are constructed, which, at some given moment, will be able to come to the analyst's mind, as words to communicate to the analysand in order to open new tracks for his associative networks. Co-thinking builds the repertoire of potential interpretations, of "key representations" capable of "unlocking" a preconscious system which is resisting the pressures of the unconscious.

The induction of thinking and the process of co-thinking which results from it are totally different from other modes of expression of the transference-counter-transference relationship. It links patient and analyst through a merging process, a primary identification. Whereas on the contrary, other modes of expression allow the acting out of an interpersonal scene, imagined or materially enacted in the setting of the session.

Here, I would say that not only the work of co-thinking and the associative and interpretative activity it leads to in the analyst should be heard by the patient (accepted, challenged or nuanced), but also, that an associative and interpretative activity should be induced and acknowledged in himself, mirroring that of the analyst. Co-thinking doesn't only go from the analysand to the analyst, but also from the analyst to the analysand.

The illusion is in the past, the belief is in the present. On the contrary, the psychoanalyst, or the analysand, follows another tradition, which is paradoxically to have doubts about any historical truth. They have no conviction about the contents of psychic reality. They know that any product of psychic reality is an illusion and that the unconscious mind is filled with illusions. These illusions have a compulsive power and are perceived as realities. But, and this is the crucial point, the psychoanalyst and/or the analysand perceive them as a reality, but not as truth. This is the underlying paradox which makes sense of the argument previously quoted.

What does it mean to recognize our unconscious illusions and yet not to believe in them? Usually, in the neurotic model, the ego believes in them. When the ego cannot tolerate the pressure of unconscious illusion (a general factor of anxiety and neurotic symptoms), repressive mechanisms are used to mask the compulsory force of the unconscious illusion. Psychoanalysis, by making the ego conscious of its illusions, of its omnipotent wishfulfilment fantasies (or destructive fantasies), makes the ego capable of playing with these realities.

What the child has to develop is a capacity to play with psychic reality in its preconscious formations and to mentalise it, i.e. to represent it as mental states (thought about) in the subject's mind. Playing with is paradoxically recognizing unconscious derivations as true but not real (in terms of material reality).

References

Avenburg, R., and M. Guiter. 1976. The concept of truth in psychoanalysis. *The International Journal of Psychoanalysis* 57: 11–18.

Blass, R. 2003. The puzzle of Freud's puzzle analogy. *The International Journal of Psychoanalysis* 84: 669–682.

Blass, R. 2004. Beyond illusion: Psychoanalysis and the question of religious truth. *The International Journal of Psychoanalysis* 85: 615–634.

Britton, R. 1995. Psychic reality and unconscious belief. *The International Journal of Psychoanalysis* 76: 19–23.

Freud, S. 1900. *The Interpretation of Dreams*. S. E. 4–5.

Freud, S. 1913 [1912–13]. *Totem and Taboo*. S. E. 13.

Freud, S. 1909. *Notes Upon a Case of Obsessional Neurosis*. S. E. 10.

Freud, S. 1913. *On Beginning the Treatment (Further Recommendations on the Technique of Psycho-Analysis I)*. S. E. 12.

Freud, S. 1915. *The Unconscious*. S. E. 14.

Freud, S. 1916. *Introductory Lectures on Psycho-Analysis*. S. E. 15.

Freud, S. 1916–17. *A Metapsychological Supplement to the Theory of Dreams*. S. E. 14.

Freud, S. 1919. *'A Child is Being Beaten'. A Contribution to the Study of the Origin of Sexual Perversions*. S.E. 17.

Freud, S. 1927. *The Future of an Illusion*. S. E. 21.

Freud, S. 1933. *New Introductory Lectures on Psycho-Analysis*. S. E. 22.

Freud, S. 1939. *Moses and Monotheism: Three Essays*. S. E. 23.

Freud, S. 1940. *An Outline of Psycho-Analysis*. S.E. 23.

Good, M., M. Dy, and E. Rowell. 2005. False memories, negative affects, and psychic reality. *The International Journal of Psychoanalysis* 86: 1573–1593.

King, P., and R. Steiner (eds.). 1991. *The Freud-Klein controversies 1941–1945*. London/ New York: Routledge.

Widlöcher, D. 2006. Psychic reality: Belief or illusion? Psychoanalytic tradition as belief in psychic reality. *The American Imago* 63(3): 315–329.

"The Delirious Illusion of Being in the World": Toward a Phenomenology of Schizophrenia

Osborne P. Wiggins and Michael Alan Schwartz

Abstract Our title is an excerpt from a statement by Antonin Artaud, the poet, playwright, and actor, who was almost certainly schizophrenic (Artaud, 1965, 85; Sass, 1992). Born in Marseilles in 1896, Artaud died in Paris in 1948. In 1937 on a boat to Ireland, he had to be placed in a straightjacket after threatening to harm himself. Eight of his fifty-two years he spent in mental institutions in Rouen, Paris, and Rodez (Artaud, 1965, p. 6). Artaud was one of those relatively rare individuals who succeeded in harnessing certain aspects of his schizophrenia to serving a revolutionary creativity. Most people afflicted with schizophrenia remain incapable of creative breakthroughs. As we shall see, however, with the onset of schizophrenia the individual is liberated from the structures and norms that powerfully govern normal human experience. In this condition even the most basic formations of the world-taken-for-granted, the lifeworld, are shaken. In the place of these previously habitual structures, new visions emerge. If the individual can somehow manage to control and shape these novel images, genius – in most cases an initially bewildering genius – may perhaps flourish.
Here we shall not examine the creativity that may – albeit rarely – issue from schizophrenic mental life (Sass, 1992). We shall rather analyze the more common forms of schizophrenia, forms that bring on only severe suffering and hardship without the compensation of greater originality. We shall approach these more common components from the point of view of phenomenological-anthropological psychiatry. We shall first provide a brief introduction to the phenomenological-anthropological perspective. This introduction will paint the background for our

O.P. Wiggins (✉)
Department of Philosophy, University of Louisville,
Louisville, KY 40292, USA
e-mail: opwigg01@louisville.edu

M.A. Schwartz M.D.
Texas A&M Health Science Center, College of Medicine,
1106 Blackacre Trail, Austin, TX, USA
e-mail: michael.schwartz@mas1.cnc.net

D. Lohmar and J. Brudzińska (eds.), *Founding Psychoanalysis Phenomenologically*, Phaenomenologica 199, DOI 10.1007/978-94-007-1848-7_15,

own explication of basic phenomenological concepts, namely, intentionality, synthesis, constitution, automatic and active mental life, and the ego (Husserl, 1973; Husserl, 1982; Gurwitsch, 1964 ; Gurwitsch, 1966). We shall then address schizophrenic mental life as a whole, claiming that the transformation of experience that it entails affects even the most basic *ontological* constituents of the world, namely, space, time, causality, and the nature of objects. This phenomenological discussion will allow us to adapt a set of concepts from philosophical anthropology and apply it to schizophrenia, namely, the concept of "world openness" and the need to reduce that openness. We shall focus on one of the more puzzling aspects of schizophrenia, what psychiatrists call "thought insertion" (Stephens and Graham, *When self-consciousness breaks: Alien voices and inserted thoughts.* The MIT Press, Cambridge, 2000). We shall then all-too-briefly indicate the difference between an early stage of schizophrenia and a later one. '-- End of Abstract'

1 Phenomenological-Anthropological Psychiatry

Our approach to schizophrenia falls within the multifaceted tradition of phenomenological-anthropological psychiatry (Dörr-Zegers 2000; Kraus 2000). The adjectives "phenomenological" and "anthropological" refer to two sources in Continental philosophy of the *methodological* and *conceptual* components of the approach (Blankenburg 1962). Phenomenological-anthropological psychiatry should be seen as having been inspired by different Continental philosophers but as also having been developed much further by a variety of psychiatrists who have themselves been identified as phenomenological, anthropological, or sometimes both (May et al. 1958; Spiegelberg 1972; De Koning and Jenner 1982; Dörr-Zegers 2000; Kraus 2000). "Phenomenological" refers to those components of the approach that were initially derived from Edmund Husserl (1970, 1973, 1982; Dörr-Zegers 2000, 357) although other influences stem from Jean-Paul Sartre (1956), Maurice Merleau-Ponty (2000), and Michel Henry (1975). The *methodological* components of phenomenological psychiatry were initially delineated by Karl Jaspers (1963; Wiggins and Schwartz 1997). "Anthropological" connotes those elements that originated primarily with Martin Heidegger (1996, 2001). All of these philosophers, however, represent only points of origin (Binswanger 1963; Boss 1963). The psychiatrists who were influenced by them developed remarkably original and fruitful concepts and theories of their own (Blankenburg 1971; Boss 1979; De Koning and Jenner 1982; Ey 1978; Kraus 1977; Natanson 1969; Naudin 1997; Straus 1982; Tatossian 1997). Therefore, it is important to understand that "phenomenological-anthropological psychiatry" signifies today an ongoing *research program* rather than an achieved theory and set of categories. At this juncture in its development the research program, we maintain, should incorporate results from empirical neuroscience as well as some concepts from the philosophical anthropologists, Max Scheler (1962), Helmuth Plessner (1981), and Arnold Gehlen (1988), and the philosophical biologists, Hans Jonas (1966), Adolf Portmann (1990a, b), and Marjorie Grene (1974).

A fundamental thesis of phenomenological-anthropological psychiatry is that the patient, in order not to be misconceived, must be comprehended as inseparably related to his or her world (Dörr-Zegers 2000; Kraus 2000). Hence in this psychiatry one is always examining a relationship, *the relationship of an experiencing subject to his or her experienced world.*

In phenomenology this relationship is called "intentionality" (Husserl 1973, 1982; Gurwitsch 1964, 1966; Sartre 2004; Merleau-Ponty 2000). The true fruitfulness of this concept for psychiatry lies in the implications it carries for the phenomenon "world." The world is described *strictly as the subject experiences it.* This phenomenological psychiatry thereby differs from other psychopathologies which tend to confine their analyses to the *minds* of pathological subjects. The phenomenologist asserts that this limitation severs the psychopathologist from the very phenomenon that most reveals the true nature of the pathology. Many pathologies, if not all, become much more intelligible if the *world* that the subject experiences is depicted precisely as he or she experiences it.

From the anthropological point of view the relationship between the human subject and his or her experienced world is called "being-in-the-world" (Heidegger 1996; Binswanger 1963). Hyphens appear in the phrase "being-in-the-world" because it designates a single complex reality, a unified whole. Of course, this whole is composed of constituent parts, but these parts must ultimately be understood in their relations to the other parts of the whole. Hence one may examine the part, mind, the part, brain, or the part, body; but these parts must ultimately be more fully construed in terms of their world-relatedness in order to comprehend them adequately. Mind, brain, body, and world are interrelated parts of the complex whole, "being-in-the-world" (Zaner 1981).

The notion of being-in-the-world plays a further role in anthropological psychiatry. It permits us to conceive of different kinds of pathology outside of a medical context. For example, schizophrenia can be thought of as one mode of human being-in-the-world while the manic-depressive condition is understood as another. The human modes of being that, in medical psychiatry, are fruitfully conceived and treated as "mental disorders" or "mental illnesses" are seen in anthropology as different modes of being-in-the-world. Moreover, any argument over which one of these approaches – medical *or* anthropological– is "the correct" one is foolish. The phenomenological-anthropologist, we think, should endorse Karl Jaspers' important thesis that in order to comprehend human pathology no single theory or standpoint is sufficient; a multiplicity of conceptual perspectives must be utilized (Jaspers 1963, 1971).

2 Some Concepts of Phenomenological-Anthropological Psychology: Intentionality, Synthesis, and Constitution

In order to ensure that the phenomenological vocabulary we shall apply to schizophrenia is clear, we shall sketch its basic terms here.

From Husserlian phenomenology we adopt the concept of intentionality (Husserl 1973, 27–55, 1982, 171–303), and we shall follow Gurwitsch's characterization of it as a noetico-noematic correlation (Gurwitsch 1964, 280–305, 1966, 124–140).

It is important to view intentional processes as never occurring in isolation. Any object intended by mental life is intended by a multiplicity of mental processes (Husserl 1973, 41–44). For example, the same physical thing is intended by a multiplicity of experiences of it. Even the same brief sound can be meant by a multiplicity of intendings of it; once I have actually heard the sound, I can always recall it in memory again and again. In all of these multiple mental processes their object can be experienced as one and the same (Husserl 1973, 41–55; Gurwitsch 1966, 124–140).

When an object is meant as identically same by manifold mental processes, the Husserlian phenomenologist speaks of a "synthesis" (Husserl 1973, 41–44; Gurwitsch 1964, 287–295, 1966, 243–250, 337–338). The mental processes are synthetically joined together by virtue of the intended sameness of their object. It should be noted that syntheses of identification also differentiate objects from one another. Without the synthesis of the multiple mental processes that are intending multiple aspects of the same object, objects would not be experienced as different from one another (Husserl 1982, 283–303).

The phenomenological notion of "constitution" should be understood in terms of synthesis. Objects are "constituted" as the objects they are for mental life by virtue of the syntheses through which those objects are intended as one and the same across time. For instance, throughout the exploration of a physical object the various features of it that come to be experienced are all intended as features of an identical object. Hence we can speak of a "unity" of these features by virtue of the fact that they are experienced as belonging to the same entity. It is in this sense that we speak of an object as "constituted" by mental life (Husserl 1982, 171–181; Gurwitsch 1964, 202–305).

Objects are constituted by consciousness in two basically different ways. Some mental processes arise because they are *actively generated by an agency* within mental life. We depart from Gurwitsch's "non-egological conception of consciousness" by employing the term "ego" to refer to this *agent* who *actively* produces some of the processes in mental life (Gurwitsch 1966, 267–300; Husserl 1973, 65–68, 1982, 190–192). For example, the thoughts that are arising in my consciousness as I formulate these sentences are being actively generated by my ego. These thoughts would not simply come into being "on their own," even if I were wide-awake and seated at my computer. *I* must actively *think* them. It is to be noted that the *theme* of my awareness at any given moment is that to which my ego is attending. The mental acts actively generated by my ego are thematizing, attentive, or focal acts.

There are, by contrast, many processes that occur in my mental life without my ego actively producing them. Husserl described these mental processes as "passive," but we follow Dorion Cairns' preference for the term "automatic" as better expressing the manner in which such processes occur in consciousness (Husserl 1973, 41–46). We might say that automatic mental processes arise "behind the back" of the ego. The ego can, of course, turn to objects already automatically intended and thematize them. But below this level of egoic activity automatic mental life is already at work constituting objects of various kinds as well as relationships among them.

3 Ontological Dimensions of the World

Among the many automatic processes that occur in consciousness some function in syntheses that constitute the basic *ontological dimensions* of what we take to be the world. For example, in some automatic syntheses objects are experienced as having spatial relations to one another; say, one object is intended as "in front of" another. Moreover, other automatic syntheses intend events as occurring at different moments of time; for instance, one event may be experienced as taking place "just before" another event occurred. Furthermore, some mental processes synthesize different events as causally related: one event may be experienced as the result or outcome of another event that preceded it. And finally, different features may be automatically meant by mental life as features of the same object: the hardness of the object I hold in my two hands may be intended as a feature of the hammer which I also watch as I with some effort lift it to hit a spike. Automatic mental life organizes the world as spatial, temporal, causal, and populated with objects.

For our automatic mental lives space, time, causality, and objecthood are not experienced as distinct. They are rather entirely interlaced and mutually implicated in one another. At the higher level of intellectual differentiation and abstraction my ego can actively conceptualize space, time, causality, and objecthood as distinct general categories. But at the stratum of automatic consciousness these ontological aspects of things form the interwoven fabric of one, unified reality, the world.

4 A Phenomenological Anthropology of Schizophrenia in its Beginnings: The Overwhelming Complexity of Reality

From the phenomenological-anthropological point of view much can and has been said about schizophrenic experience (Binswanger 1963; Blankenburg 1971; De Koning and Jenner 1982; Wiggins et al. 1990; Schwartz and Wiggins 1992; Schwartz et al. 2005). The component upon which we wish to focus here pertains to *the weakening of the synthetic power of mental life* in schizophrenia (Wiggins et al. 1990; Schwartz et al. 2005). This weakening affects syntheses at both the automatic and active levels of experience. Schizophrenic consciousness no longer synthetically connects worldly events with one another or unites the features of objects with one another in the ways that normal mental life automatically and reliably does. This accounts for the instability, unforeseeability, and mutability of events and objects in a world disturbed by schizophrenia. Even the most fundamental components of this world fragment, disperse, and restructure themselves.

Because of the weakening of mental syntheses in schizophrenia, some aspects of objects – that "normal" subjects experience as clearly there – may not be synthetically joined with one another. A case reported by James Chapman of a patient in the early stages of schizophrenia illustrates this phenomenon. The patient says,

> Everything I see is split up. It's like a photograph that's torn to bits and put together again. If somebody moves or speaks, everything I see disappears quickly and I have to put it together again (Chapman 1966, 229).

Chapman quotes another patient who provides an example of the same kind of experience:

> I have to put things together in my head. If I look at my watch I see the watch, watchstrap, face, hands and so on, then I have got to put them together to get it into one piece (Chapman 1966, 229).

Notice that for this patient, as for the immediately preceding one, his automatic mental life does not synthetically unite the various features of the object, his watch. Hence this patient's experience shows that one basic ontological component of the world, namely, what we have called "objecthood," has crumbled. Because of this fragmenting of the "objecthood" of the object, the patient's *ego* must then come to his aid and *actively* synthesize the constituents together as all features of one object. The objecthood of things must be *actively* rather than *automatically* constituted.

The failure of mental life in early schizophrenia to automatically constitute the *spatial* dimension of reality can be seen in another of Chapman's cases:

> I see things flat. Whenever there is a sudden change I see it flat. That's why I'm reluctant to go forward. It's as if there were a wall there and I would walk into it. There's no depth, but if I take time to look at things I can pick out the pieces like a jigsaw puzzle, then I know what the wall is made of. Moving is like a motion picture. If you move, the picture in front of you changes. The rate of change in the picture depends on the speed of walking. If you run you receive the signals at a faster rate. The picture I see is literally made up of hundreds of pieces. Until I see into things I don't know what distance they are away (Chapman 1966, 230).

Chapman summarizes the sorts of changes in the experience of lived space that the patient undergoes: "...the phenomena experienced by schizophrenic patients include alterations of the size, distance, and shape of objects (metamorphopsia), loss of stereoscopic vision, defective revisualization, and illusory acceleration of moving objects" (Chapman 1966, 230).

Max Scheler claimed in a pioneering work on philosophical anthropology that human beings are inherently "world-open" (Scheler 1962, 35–55). A later philosophical anthropologist, Arnold Gehlen, adopted and extended Scheler's term (Gehlen 1988, 24–31, 248–255). In Gehlen's words, "Human beings are exposed to an excess of stimulation toward which they remain world-open" (Gehlen 1988, 181). Gehlen specified that these "stimuli" may be either internal or external ones; i.e., they may issue from within the individual's body or mind, for example, in inner urges or thoughts, or they may consist of sensory data coming from the external world. Because of this "barrage of sensation and stimulation to which human beings are exposed" (Gehlen 1988, 181), they must develop means for reducing its complexity. The reduction of the complexity of both internal and external stimuli is, from the phenomenological point of view, the achievement of automatic syntheses. Gehlen maintained that if some such reduction of the complexity of stimuli were not automatically achieved, the ego of the person would be *overburdened* with the unrelenting task of having to reduce this complexity through active thinking and selecting. Fortunately, for the normal person the acquisition of innumerable habits and skills that function automatically suffices to structure the person's world such that an adequate reduction of its complexity is achieved. Thanks to this reduction of complexity through the acquisition of skills and habits, the normal individual is free to devote his or her energies to "higher level" intellectual and cultural accomplishments (Gehlen 1988, 54–64).

With the weakening of its automatic syntheses during the early phases of schizophrenia, mental life loses its normal capacity to structure and stabilize the internal and external stimuli to which it is subjected. Hence the subject becomes too "world-open." Again Chapman furnishes several pertinent examples. These cases illustrate both the weakening of the syntheses and their common result, an overabundance of stimuli. The ego must then assume the daunting task of attempting to actively organize these stimuli. The following case shows clearly the overburdening of mental life that occurs when the data remain unstructured.

The patient reports,

> It's like a temporary blackout – with my brain not working properly – like being in a vacuum. I just get cut off from outside things and go into another world. This happens when the tension starts to mount until it bursts in my brain. It has to do with what is going on around me – taking in too much of my surroundings – vital not to miss anything. I can't shut things out of my mind and everything closes in on me. It stops me thinking and then the mind goes a blank and everything gets switched off. I can't pick things up to memorize because I am absorbing everything around me and take in too much so that I can't retain anything for any length of time – only a few seconds, and I can't do simple habits like walking or cleaning my teeth. I have to use all my mind to do these things and sometimes I find myself moving and doing things without knowing it and I'm not controlling it. When this starts I find myself having to use tremendous control to direct my feet and force myself round a corner as if I'm on a bicycle. I want to move and the message goes from my brain down to my legs and they will not move in the right way. What I'm worried about is that I might get myself so controlled that I will cease to be a person. I find it difficult to cope with these situations that get out of control and I can't differentiate myself from other people when this comes on. I can't control what's coming in and it stops me thinking with the mind a blank (Chapman 1966, 231).

Another patient reports the same sort of experience:

> Nothing settles in my mind – not even for a second. It just comes in and then it's out. My mind goes away – too many things come into my head at once and I lose control. I get afraid of walking when this happens. My feet just walk away from me and I've no control over myself. I feel my body breaking up into bits. I get all mixed up so that I don't know myself. I feel like more than one person when this happens. I'm falling apart into bits. My mind is not right if I walk and speak. It's better to stay still and not say a word. I'm frightened to say

> a word in case everything goes fleeing from me so that there's nothing in my mind. It puts me into a trance that's worse than death. There's a kind of hypnotism going on" (Chapman 1966, 232).

As these examples illustrate, the weakening of the automatic syntheses affects even the ones that constitute the basic ontological components of the world. Space, time, causality, and objecthood undergo vacillation, de-structuration, and reconfiguration. The person's lived body too undergoes destructuration. The automatic syntheses that should coordinate bodily movements and that should coordinate those movements with the appearances of things and other people weaken and threaten to dissolve. This de-structuring of the ontological components of the body and reality we have in another essay called "the unbuilding of the world." And, in a manner that attempts to supplement the insights of R.D. Laing, we sought there to depict the "ontological insecurity" that overcomes the experiencing self during early stages of schizophrenia when this unbuilding of body and world occurs (Wiggins et al. 1990).

5 A Phenomenology of "Thought Insertion"

"Thought insertion" is a name given to one of the symptoms of schizophrenia. Here is how a standard clinical handbook in psychiatry characterizes it:

> Thinking, like all conscious activities, is experienced as an activity which is being carried on by a subject.... There is a quality of "my-ness" connected with thought. In schizophrenia this sense of the possession of one's thoughts may be impaired and the patient may suffer from alienation of thought.... (The patient) is certain that alien thoughts have been inserted in his mind (Fish 1962, 48; Stephens and Graham 2000, 119).

For our phenomenological purposes, however, we prefer to work from examples. Here are the remarks of a 29 year old woman:

> I look out of the window and I think that the garden looks nice and the grass looks cool, but the thoughts of Eamonn Andrews come into my mind. There are no other thoughts, only his.... He treats my mind like a screen and flashes thoughts onto it like you flash a picture (Mellor 1970, 17; Stephens and Graham 2000, 120).

These thoughts "come into" the patient's mind. They are therefore in some sense *her* thoughts. And yet they are also the thoughts of Eamonn Andrews, a delusional figure; accordingly they are also *not* her thoughts, but rather *his.* Indeed there are times when she thinks *only* his thoughts. Hence the phenomenological description must account for how some of the woman's thoughts can be experienced paradoxically as both hers and someone else's.

These experiences can be explicated by first laying down two minimal conditions for a normal subject to experience some mental processes, although not others, as *his or her own* processes. In other words, we shall describe some of the minimal conditions for the experienced difference between my mind and the minds of others. One of the main differences between my awareness of someone else's mental processes and my awareness of my own is that I never experience the other person's mental processes as originarily given to me while I do experience some of my own mental processes as originarily given to my mental life. How does this occur?

In the temporal stream of my mental processes, my consciousness automatically protends some experiences as coming (in the future) and automatically retends others as having occurred (as past) (Husserl 1991). All of this takes place at the level of pure automaticity. We would like to add to this conception of inner time Aron Gurwitsch's notion of the internal and implicit self-awareness that each mental process has of itself. Gurwitsch writes,

> Perceiving a material thing, listening to a musical note, thinking of a mathematical theorem, etc., we are not only conscious of the thing, the note, the theorem, etc., but are also aware of our perceiving, listening, thinking, etc. Thus every act of consciousness is accompanied by an awareness of itself (Gurwitsch 1985, 3).

Among other things this notion stresses the fact that not only is mental life automatically protending its future phases and retending its past phases but it is also automatically aware of its present phase. Its own past, present, and future mental processes are all automatically intended by mental life. Mental life is thus implicitly self-aware of its own past, present, and future phases. Through self-reflection I can become explicitly and thematically aware of my mental life too. But the sort of inner time awareness with which we are concerned here takes place implicitly and in the background – Gurwitsch says "margin" – of my consciousness (Gurwitsch 1985).

What we would like to add to Gurwitsch's account is that (at least) my *present* mental processes are *originarily given* to mental life. Present self-awareness is an originary awareness. On the other hand, the other person's mental processes are *never* originarily given to my mental life. Hence one of the features of my consciousness that accounts for my experience of it as *my* mental life is that its present phase is always originarily aware of itself.

The second minimal condition for the experience of "my-ness" lies in the synthetic unification and identification of mental life. By virtue of the automatic retendings, protendings, and present self-awareness of consciousness, the past, present, and future temporal phases are all *synthetically joined* to one another to constitute them as phases of a *single* mental life (Husserl 1991). My mental life is experienced by me as identical over time because of the *syntheses* that it is constantly effecting automatically of its past, present, and future phases.

Let us now try to apply this phenomenology to thought insertion in schizophrenia. We start with another example:

> Thoughts are put into my mind like "Kill God." It is just like my mind working, but it isn't. They come from this chap, Chris. They are his thoughts (Frith 1992, 66; Stephens and Graham 2000, 120).

The thoughts *in the patient's mind* are experienced as *Chris'* thoughts. This patient strikingly formulates the paradoxical character of thought insertion: "It's just like my mind working, but it isn't." We maintain that the patient's thoughts are experienced as occurring in his own mind because they are originarily given to that mind. The patient's mental life is automatically aware of the processes occurring within it, and this implicit self-awareness is an originary awareness. Hence: "It's just like my mind working."

On the other hand, "it isn't," i.e., these same thoughts are the thoughts of Chris. We submit that this awareness of Chris as the subject of these thoughts occurs because of the weakening of the automatic syntheses that normally occur in inner time consciousness. Through retending, protending, and present self-intending, the normal mental life automatically synthesizes its processes as processes of the *same* subject. The weakened schizophrenic mental life does not perform such syntheses with the same reliability and continuity. Hence in schizophrenia the automatic syntheses of self-identification sometimes operate efficiently, and sometimes they do not. When such syntheses of self-identification fail, the subject's mental life may synthesize "his thoughts" with some other subject. Eamonn Andrews or Chris is synthetically constituted, however weakly, as the subject – the Other -- whose mental processes are now occurring in patient's mind.

6 Schizophrenia as It Continues: The Reduction of Complexity

In the beginning stages of schizophrenia the individual comes to be over-burdened by the complexity of his or her experience. As the disorder continues, however, this complexity must be somehow reduced. With the persistence of the patient's schizophrenia the reduction does occur in several ways. In a way that we think remains ultimately "un-understandable" – to appropriate Jaspers' term – new automatic syntheses do emerge in the patient's mental life and the person's world begins to achieve a novel and idiosyncratic structure. We deem the emergence of these new syntheses "un-understandable" because we believe, like Jaspers, that it is inexplicable why the person's world comes to be re-constituted in the way it does rather than some other. Nevertheless, new syntheses do come to constitute the world in new ways.

The hitherto weak syntheses are not entirely eliminated by the emergence of new ones, however. The world of the person with schizophrenia still remains "unbuilt" to some extent; and consequently space, time, causality, objects, and the body remain relatively unstructured.

Moreover, this novel make-up of reality that begins to take form may only slightly resemble the structure of the world that other people intersubjectively share. In other words, the world that other people take to be the "real world" because it appears to them as the same for all will cohere in only limited respects with the newly constituted world of the person with schizophrenia.

Another way in which the complexity of schizophrenic experience is reduced is through the emergence of hallucinations and delusions. Hallucinations and delusions impart an organization to the patient's mental life that at least minimally stabilize his or her world and self. Hallucinations and delusions thus at least partially diminish the extreme "world-openness" that had strained consciousness in the early stages of schizophrenia. Hallucinations and delusions thereby accord a degree of relief to this mental life, albeit a relief that is purchased at the price of severing the individual even further from the realm of experience shared with others.

7 Conclusion: Did Artaud Know the Answer?

We would like to conclude by returning to the title of our paper and thus to Artaud. The phrase in the title "the delirious illusion of being in the world," of course, reminds us of Heidegger (1996). And it might prove fascinating to consider "the delirious illusion of being in the world" in the light of Heidegger's famous notion. However, the assertion that being in the world is a delirious illusion could conceivably remind us of Husserl. Artaud's phrase is embedded in the following context:

> I struggled in my attempt to exist, in my attempt to consent to the forms (all the forms) with which the delirious illusion of being in the world has clothed reality.
>
> I no longer wish to be a Believer in Illusions (Artaud 1965, 85).

Artaud calls "being in the world" an *illusion,* indeed a "delirious illusion." For readers of Husserl, the idea of the world as illusion should not be entirely new. In Section 7 of the First of his *Cartesian Meditations,* Husserl considers the evidence for the existence of the world. Regarding that evidence he writes,

> Not only can a particular experienced thing suffer devaluation as an illusion of the senses; the whole unitarily surveyable nexus, experienced throughout a period of time, can prove to be an illusion, a coherent dream (Husserl 1973, 17).

The phenomenologist *imagines the possibility* that the world is an illusion, and Artaud declares that it is *in truth.* There are, of course, gigantic differences between Husserl's and Artaud's ideas. One of them is this: Husserl states that, although possibly a dream, the world is still "a coherent dream." Artaud, however, has for years experienced the *incoherence* of that dream. We have indicated how this schizophrenic incoherence occurs in human life. And as for Artaud, we shall let him give his own explanation. He writes, "This is a real Madman talking to you,..." (Artaud 1965, 86).

References

Artaud, Antonin. 1965. *Artaud anthology.* San Francisco: City Lights Books.

Bleuler, Eugen. 1950. *Dementia praecox or the group of schizophrenias.* New York: International Universities Press.

Blankenburg, Wolfgang. 1962. Aus dem phänomenologischen Erfahrungsfeld innerhalb der Psychiatrie (unter Berücksichtigung methodologischer Fragen). *Schweizer Archiv für Neurologie, Neurochirurgie und Psychiatrie* 90(2).

Blankenburg, Wolfgang. 1971. *Der Verlust der natürlichen Selbstverständlichkeit: Ein Beitrag zur Psychopathologie symptomarmer Schizophrenien.* Stuttgart: Ferdinand Enke Verlag.

Binswanger, Ludwig. 1963. *Being-in-the-world*. New York: Harper and Row Publishers.
Boss, Medard. 1963. *Psychoanalysis and Daseinanalysis*. New York: Basic Books, Inc.
Boss, Medard. 1979. *Existential foundations of medicine and psychology*. New York: Jason Aronson.
Chapman, James. 1966. The early symptoms of schizophrenia. *British Journal of Psychiatry* 112: 225–251.
De Koning, A.J.J., and F.A. Jenner (eds.). 1982. *Phenomenology and psychiatry*. New York: Grune and Stratton.
Dörr-Zegers, Otto. 2000. Existential and phenomenological approach to psychiatry. In *New Oxford textbook of psychiatry*, eds. Michael G. Gelder, Juan J. Lopez-Ibo, and Nancy Andreasen. Oxford: Oxford University Press.
Ey, Henri. 1978. *Consciousness: A phenomenological study of being conscious and becoming conscious*. Bloomington: Indiana University Press.
Fish, F.J. 1962. *Fish's schizophrenia*, ed. M. Hamilton. New York: Wright.
Frith, C.D. 1992. *The cognitive neuropsychology of schizophrenia*. Mahwah: Lawrence Erlbaum Associates.
Gehlen, Arnold. 1988. *Man: His nature and place in the world*. New York: Columbia University Press.
Grene, Marjorie. 1974. *The understanding of nature: Essays in the philosophy of biology*. Dordrecht: D. Reidel Publishing Co.
Gurwitsch, Aron. 1964. *Field of consciousness*. Pittsburgh: Duquesne University Press.
Gurwitsch, Aron. 1966. *Studies in phenomenology and psychology*. Evanston: Northwestern University Press.
Gurwitsch, Aron. 1985. *Marginal consciousness*, ed. L. Embree. Athens: Ohio University Press.
Heidegger, Martin. 1996. *Being and time*. Albany: State University of New York Press.
Heidegger, Martin. 2001. *Zollikon seminars*, ed. Boss Medard. Evanston: Northwestern University Press.
Henry, Michel. 1975. *Philosophy and phenomenology of the body*. The Hague: Martinus Nijhoff.
Husserl, Edmund. 1970. *The crisis of European sciences and transcendental phenomenology*. Evanston: Northwestern University Press.
Husserl, Edmund. 1973. *Cartesian meditations: An introduction to phenomenology*. The Hague: Martinus Nijhoff.
Husserl, Edmund. 1982. *Ideas pertaining to a pure phenomenology and to a phenomenological philosophy, first book*. The Hague: Martinus Nijhoff Publishers.
Husserl, Edmund. 1991. *On the phenomenology of the consciousness of internal time (1893–1917)*. Dordrecht: Kluwer Academic Publishers.
Jaspers, Karl. 1963. *General psychopathology*. Chicago: University of Chicago Press.
Jaspers, Karl. 1971. *Psychologie der Weltanschauungen*. Berlin: Springer Verlag.
Jonas, Hans. 1966. *The phenomenon of life: Toward a philosophical biology*. New York: A Delta Book.
Kraus, Alfred. 1977. *Sozialverhalten und Psychose Manisch-Depressiver: Eine existenz- und rollenanalytische Untersuchung*. Stuttgart: Ferdinand Enke Verlag.
Kraus, Alfred. 2000. *Phenomenological-anthropological psychiatry*. In *Contemporary psychiatry, vol. 1, foundations of psychiatry*, eds. F. Henn, N. Sartorius, H. Helmchen, and H. Lauter. New York: Springer.
May, Rollo, E. Angel, and Henri F. Ellenberger. 1958. *Existence: A new direction in psychiatry and psychology*. New York: Simon and Schuster.
Mellor, C.S. 1970. First rank symptoms of schizophrenia. *British Journal of Psychiatry* 117: 15–23.
Merleau-Ponty, M. 2000. *Phenomenology of perception*. New York: Routledge.
Natanson, Maurice (ed.). 1969. *Psychiatry and philosophy*. New York: Springer.
Naudin, Jean. 1997. *Phénoménologie et psychiatrie: Les voix et la chose*. Toulouse: Presses Universitaires du Mirail.
Plessner, Helmuth. 1981. *Die Stufen des Organischen und der Mensch, Gesammelte Schriften IV*. Frankfurt am Main: Suhrkamp Verlag.

Portmann, Adolf. 1990a. *Essays in philosophical zoology: The living form and the seeing eye*. Lewiston: The Edwin Mellen Press.

Portmann, Adolf. 1990b. *A zoologist looks at humankind*. New York: Columbia University Press.

Sartre, Jean-Paul. 1956. *Being and nothingness: An essay in phenomenological ontology*. New York: Philosophical Library.

Sartre, Jean-Paul. 2004. Intentionality: A fundamental idea of Husserl's phenomenology. In *The phenomenology reader*, ed. D. Moran and T. Mooney. London: Routledge.

Sass, Louis. 1992. *Madness and modernism: Insanity in the light of modern art, literature, and thought*. New York: Basic Books.

Scheler, Max. 1962. *Man's place in nature*. New York: The Noonday Press.

Schwartz, M.A., and O.P. Wiggins. 1992. The phenomenology of schizophrenic delusions. In *Phenomenology, language & schizophrenia*, ed. Manfred Spitzer, Friedrich Uehlein, Michael A. Schwartz, and Mundt Christoph. New York: Springer-Verlag.

Schwartz, Michael A., Osborne P. Wiggins, Jean Naudin, and Manfred Spitzer. 2005. Rebuilding reality: A phenomenology of aspects of chronic schizophrenia. *Phenomenology and Cognitive Science* 4: 91–115.

Spiegelberg, Herbert. 1972. *Phenomenology in psychology and psychiatry: A historical introduction*. Evanston: Northwestern University Press.

Stephens, G. Lynn, and George Graham. 2000. *When self-consciousness breaks: Alien voices and inserted thoughts*. Cambridge: The MIT Press.

Straus, Erwin. 1958. Aesthesiology and hallucinations. In *Existence: A new direction in psychiatry and psychology*, ed. R. May, E. Angel, and H.F. Ellenberger, 139–169. New York: Simon and Schuster.

Straus, Erwin. 1980. *Phenomenological psychology*. New York: Garland.

Straus, Erwin. 1982. *Man, time, and world: Two contributions to anthropological psychology*. Pittsburgh: Duquesne University Press.

Tatossian, Arthur. 1997. *La phenomenologie des psychoses*. Paris: L'art du comprendre.

Wiggins, Osborne P., Michael A. Schwartz, and George Northoff. 1990. Toward a Husserlian phenomenology of the initial stages of schizophrenia. In *Philosophy and psychopathology*, ed. Manfred Spitzer and A. Brendan. New York: Springer.

Wiggins, Osborne, and Michael Alan Schwartz. 1997. Edmund Husserl's influence on Karl Jaspers' phenomenology. *Philosophy, Psychiatry, Psychology – PPP* 4(1): 15–36.

Zaner, Richard M. 1981. *The context of self: A phenomenological inquiry using medicine as a clue*. Athens: Ohio University Press.

Subject Index

D. Lohmar and J. Brudzińska (eds.), *Founding Psychoanalysis Phenomenologically*, Phaenomenologica 199, DOI 10.1007/978-94-007-1848-7,